# PACIFIC ASIA

## IN QUEST OF
## DEMOCRACY

# PACIFIC
# ASIA
# IN QUEST OF
# DEMOCRACY

## Roland Rich

LYNNE
RIENNER
PUBLISHERS

BOULDER
LONDON

Published in the United States of America in 2007 by
Lynne Rienner Publishers, Inc.
1800 30th Street, Boulder, Colorado 80301
www.rienner.com

and in the United Kingdom by
Lynne Rienner Publishers, Inc.
3 Henrietta Street, Covent Garden, London WC2E 8LU

**Library of Congress Cataloging-in-Publication Data**
Rich, Roland.
    Pacific Asia in quest of democracy / Roland Rich.
        p. cm.
    Includes bibliographical references and index.
    ISBN 978-1-58826-550-0 (hardcover : alk. paper)
    ISBN 978-1-58826-575-3 (pbk. : alk. paper)
    1. Democracy—Pacific Area. 2. Democracy—East Asia. 3. Pacific
Area—Politics and government. 4. East Asia—Politics and government. I. Title.
    JQ5995.R53 2007
    320.959—dc22
                                                        2007012323

**British Cataloguing in Publication Data**
A Cataloguing in Publication record for this book
is available from the British Library.


Printed and bound in the United States of America

        The paper used in this publication meets the requirements
  ∞    of the American National Standard for Permanence of
        Paper for Printed Library Materials Z39.48-1992.

    5    4    3    2    1

*To my mother, Babette Rich,*
*Auschwitz number A-13741,*
*who survived the worst,*
*to give me and my brother, Georges, the best*

———————————

# Contents

# Figures and Tables

# Foreword

## *Larry Diamond*

It is a pleasure to welcome Roland Rich's timely study of the principal emerging democracies of Pacific Asia. Two decades have now passed since the popular movements that brought transitions to democracy in the Philippines and South Korea. As this book goes to press, South Korea is preparing to elect its fifth democratic president since the 1987 transition, while Taiwan is completing the two-term maximum tenure of its second democratically elected president. Each country has suffered from political scandals and ongoing political polarization, but each is a vigorous, liberal democracy. The Philippines is struggling quite a bit more with the travails of elite-driven money politics, but twenty years later, democracy endures. In Indonesia democratic institutions are beginning to settle in, to a degree that many observers might have found hard to imagine a decade earlier when the East Asian financial crisis brought down Suharto's "New Order" authoritarian regime after three decades in power. Meanwhile, during the period under study, Thailand has twice gone full circle, from a military-dominated semi-democracy to an electoral democracy, to a military coup displacing that turbulent democracy, followed by the restoration of democracy, historic constitutional reform, the apparent progress of democratic institutions, and then their reversal once again—culminating in another military coup in September 2006.

For anyone wanting to understand the political future of Asia, and for anyone wanting to understand the future of democracy globally, this is an important set of cases to chart and comprehend. Among the many reasons for doing so (including the fascinating mix of diversity and commonality among these five cases, which Rich exposes so well), I wish to underscore two. One obvious reason for importance is sheer demographics. Asia contains two-fifths of the world's population, including the biggest and most powerful dictatorship, China, which Rich rightly calls the "core state" of Pacific Asia. Which way China goes politically will have an enormous impact on the future of democracy in the world, and that in turn will be shaped to some extent by the success or failure of democracy on China's periphery, in the cases that Rich examines in this book. This is perhaps particularly true for Taiwan, with which mainland China shares so much in language, culture, and political history, and which most Chinese continue to see as a part of China. But it is true for the other democracies of the region as well, which share with Taiwan the capacity to disprove the argument that Asian values are so distinct from those of the liberal West—for example, in supposedly privileging the community over the individual and order over freedom—that democracy cannot work in this part of the world. The communist leaderships of China and Vietnam would like their peoples to accept that thesis, and the surrender of freedom that it encourages. But in this fine comparative study, Rich gives us cautious but well-reasoned grounds to believe that Pacific Asia is headed in a different, more democratic direction.

A second reason for the importance of these cases—and this book—is that the Pacific Asia region has been, and remains, the most economically dynamic part of the developing world. It may therefore be reasonable to expect that democracy should be functioning better here than in much of the rest of the world touched by the third wave of democratization. In particular, to the extent that democracy is facilitated by economic development, we would expect to find it working quite well in Taiwan and South Korea, which have been two of the most remarkable economic-development success stories of the post–World War II era. That this is not entirely the case—and that the presumably stable democracy in Thailand should have collapsed altogether—cries out for attention and explanation. Rich highlights some of the problems that have retarded democratic development in the region.

Combining as he does scholarship on the region with the practice of diplomacy and democracy promotion in the region, Roland Rich is well placed to write this comparative study (which from time to time extends beyond the above five democracies to Japan, India, and even Papua New Guinea). As an Australian diplomat in Burma, the Philippines, and Laos (the latter, as Australia's ambassador), and then as the first director of Australia's flagship democracy-promotion organization, the Centre for Democratic Institutions, Rich observed firsthand the challenges of political development and democracy building in Asia across several decades. Thus, he brings to this study a feel for the politics of Pacific Asia that is not only scholarly but also personal, intuitive, and nuanced. His experience helps him to transcend the rigid confines of ideologies and academic theories and to see Pacific Asia's democracies as they are—a not always flattering picture. But he also sees them as they are becoming, or struggling to become, higher-quality democracies, and thus gives us a hopeful analysis of democracy in the Pacific Asia region.

There is a certain institutional pride, as well, in welcoming this work, which began during the period Rich spent in Washington in 2005 as a Reagan-Fascell Democracy Fellow at the National Endowment for Democracy (NED). I know that Marc Plattner, my codirector of NED's International Forum for Democratic Studies, which hosts the Reagan-Fascell fellows, joins me in congratulating Roland and thanking him for making such excellent use of his time with us at NED.

# Preface

This book owes as much to compulsion as it does to the fruits of dispassionate research. After thirty years of observing Asia, I felt an urgent need to distill my thoughts and complete my ideas in written form. The recurring theme of those thirty years, which developed into an insistent drumbeat over the past decade, has been democracy, or more specifically: Has democracy become integral to political life in Asia?

*Observing* is a useful all-purpose term. It covers the official requirement of a diplomat to become an expert about the country to which he or she is posted. Ten of those thirty years were spent doing just that in Burma, the Philippines, and Laos. It covers the more scholarly appreciation of Asian society. Seven of the thirty years were spent learning about and promoting democracy in six countries in Southeast Asia—Cambodia, Indonesia, Laos, the Philippines, Thailand, and Vietnam—and learning about democracy in Japan, India, South Korea, and Taiwan. It also covers the insights gained from the hundreds of interpersonal relationships I was lucky enough to have during those thirty years. And it covers the quirky and endearing revelations from spending a decade married into an Asian family.

There are a number of ways of using the written form to talk about democracy. Pramoedya Ananta Toer used the form of a novel to tell his tale about Indonesia's emergence in the modern world. Christopher Patten used a form of memoir to tell us about Hong Kong, China, and democracy. Lacking Pram's talent and Patten's celebrity, I have chosen the academic tome as my means of discussing this issue. The reader may, however, have some justification for suspecting a frustrated novelist and a barely repressed memoirist lurking within the academic cloak and occasionally making their presence felt.

The academic form has certain advantages. As Sir Isaac Newton once observed, we can see a bit further only because we are standing on the shoulders of giants. Accordingly, I am able to contribute to a tradition of thinking and writing that has been particularly strong in the present academic generation and whose standard-bearers the reader will find sprinkled throughout the footnotes. Having come to academia later in life, my curiosity has not been constrained by the inevitable professional requirement of ever narrower specialization. I have perhaps stumbled through too many academic fields, from political science to law and from anthropology to communications, in all likelihood therefore causing disquiet to their academic guardians, who might see this trampling through their domains as a form of trespass. Some country specialists will be distressed by what they may regard as cursory observations directed at their subjects. Some comparativists may be concerned that I have not adopted their approach or methods. My defense is twofold. First, democracy is such a big issue that it can be looked at from many perspectives and through various disciplines and in relation to a number of different countries. Second, I am not offering the definitive answer to the big question I am posing. I am offering my answer based partly on the literature, partly on my experience, and perhaps also partly on gut feeling.

The academic form, insofar as it deals with modern politics, suffers from a particular disadvantage. It is out of date virtually from the moment the final full stop is typed. From the perspective of the author, this is invariably one election short of proving a certain point or one change of leadership shy of demonstrating the wisdom of a certain thesis. Another inevitable occurrence is that as soon as the work is completed, a particularly apposite study will be published that cannot be incorporated or criticized. In other words, a line must be drawn and future events left to pursue their own course, without the benefit of the author's analysis. For me, the line has had to be drawn in September 2006 with the distressing coup in Thailand, and subsequent events will simply have to fall into order by their own volition without any help from me. Accordingly, election results, political developments, and all tables are up to date as of September 2006 and not beyond. I have nevertheless retained Thailand in this study because of its considerable contribution to the development of democracy in the region, even if that process has suffered a serious setback.

At this point, certain disclosures about my approach might be in order. This is not a book intended to demonstrate that democracy is the best, or perhaps least worst, form of governance. Others have done so admirably and I simply have adopted this fact as one of my working assumptions. So this is not a book about why democracy is best, but about the processes through which democracy is practiced and consolidated. Although I am Australian, this book is not about Australia or meant to be biased in favor of the Australian practice of democracy. If there is a bias in the book it flows from my attraction to Asia. I want to see its nations succeed and its people's aspirations fulfilled. I believe democracy holds the key to that fulfillment. While there may be references in the book to history and, in particular, post–World War II history, it is not intended to be a history of democracy in the various countries of Pacific Asia under review. That would be a far more ambitious task, which I leave to those better qualified to accomplish. Were it a history book, it would attempt to delineate how centuries of Western experimentation in crafting democratic institutions, conventions, and practices are being compressed into mere decades in Pacific Asia. What this book does attempt to hint at is the whirlwind of changes being experienced in the countries of Pacific Asia as they grapple with the fundamental questions of how best to govern themselves.

Over the past decade the drum to which I have marched has had several beats. From 1994 to 1997, I was Australia's ambassador to the Lao People's Democratic Republic. The third word of its name always struck me as incongruous, as the country had few of the democratic features it proclaimed to adhere to in its very title. From 1998 to 2004, I had the great privilege to gain selection for appointment as the founding director of Australia's publicly funded democracy promotion body, the Centre for Democratic Institutions (CDI) at the Australian National University (ANU). In policymaking, an idea not only has to be worthwhile, it also has to be timely. The decision of the Australian minister for foreign affairs, Alexander Downer, to establish CDI was neither behind the times nor ahead of its time; it was exactly what was required at that very moment. Freed from the constraints of the Cold War, the countries of Asia were looking to democracy as a means of giving their people legitimate self-expression, and CDI was an instrument designed to add a bit of fuel to that fire.

As director of CDI, I was in the happy position of being a close observer of the building of democracy in Pacific Asia. I was able to discuss issues with Asian policymakers and parliamentarians, judges and journalists, and academics and civil society leaders, sharing both their frustration and elation as the difficult edifice was under construction. It was and remains a time of excitement and ferment, with high public interest and even higher public expectations. Perhaps it is too early to tell this story, as the construction of democracy is still in its early stages in many parts of Pacific Asia, but my compulsion permitted no further delays.

The third beat of my march was drummed by the National Endowment for Democracy (NED), the much-admired democracy promotion foundation in the United States, which granted me a Reagan-Fascell Democracy Fellowship that allowed me to spend 2005 in Washington researching and writing the first draft of this book. Once again the word *privilege* is appropriate, because there is no better way to describe the status of one who is accorded the facility to have no responsibility other than to read, think, and write. The NED fellowship is administered by the International Forum for Democratic Studies, which edits the *Journal of Democracy*, the world's leading publication on the theory and practice of democracy. The resources of NED, the International Forum, and the journal were generously put at the disposal of the fellows.

CDI was established in Australia's leading research university, and it was at the ANU that this project was conceived. My first list of acknowledgments therefore begins at the ANU. The directors of the two humanities research schools situated in the Coombs Building, Ian McAllister and Jim Fox, provided excellent institutional and personal support. There are so many colleagues from Coombs who shared their views with me in seminar rooms, over a cup of tea, or while imbibing other beverages in the University House beer garden, that it is not possible to list all their names. The initial discussions about investigating Asian democracy were held in the context of two conferences in 2002, and I am indebted to Ian Marsh and Ron May for their advice as well as the sage contribution from a visitor at the time, Jean Blondel. Thanks must also go to my colleagues at CDI over the years: Sharon Bessel, Cathy Boyle, Pierre Huetter, Felicity Pascoe, Don Porter, Sally Thompson, and Barbara Trewin.

As noted, NED's support has been critical. I wish to extend my gratitude to its president, Carl Gershman, for his personal support, encouragement, and insights, and to its chairman, Vin Weber, for his interest in my work. NED is a big happy family out of which I received much encouragement from David Lowe, Louisa Coan Greve, Barbara Haig, Art Kaufman, and Tom Skladony. The Reagan-Fascell Democracy Fellowship staff members were terrific, and I extend my sincere gratitude to Sally Blair, Zerxes Spencer, Maria Fleetwood, Joe Tucker, Melissa Aten, and Satoko Okamoto. The library staff, in particular Allen Overland and Tim Myers, was always helpful and efficient. One of the luxuries of the program is the support of an intern, and I thank Max Lipset and Ryan White for their assistance. Another benefit of the program is the ability to bounce ideas off and become friends with other fellows, including Fatimakhon Ahadovna Ahmedova (Tajikistan), Andrew Finkel (United States and Turkey), Raul Gangotena (Ecuador), Young Howard (South Korea), Hoon Juang (South Korea), Guabiao Jiao (China), Robert Britt Mattes (United States and South Africa), Vitali Silitski (Belarus), and Michael McFaul (United States).

I have left two members of the NED crowd for last for particular mention. Larry Diamond and Marc Plattner go by a number of different titles. They are directors of the International Forum for Democratic Studies, editors of the *Journal of Democracy*, and distinguished academic authors. But the title that means most to me is that of mentor, because, but for their encouragement, commentaries, and criticisms, this project would not have progressed. From his attendance at the 2002 conferences at the ANU, to his advice about publication, Larry has been a guide and a friend. Marc has variously been my editor, adviser, and daily office mate. I thank them both wholeheartedly.

I thank Ken Berry for his close reading of the manuscript and for the suggestions he made for its improvement, most of which were taken up.

Wendell Katerenchuk and his colleagues at King Prajadhipok's Institute in Bangkok helped with some important fact checking. I also thank Lynne Rienner for doing all the things a good publisher does and her anonymous reviewers who provided very useful feedback. This book was completed while I was on the staff of the Centre for Defence and Strategic Studies at the Australian Defence College, and I thank my colleagues there for providing such a congenial work environment and for granting me the possibility to complete my research. It is being published while I am on duty as executive director of the United Nations Democracy Fund.

I have dedicated this book to my mother, and I would also like to mention my children, who have sustained me with their love and support. Elliat, Zak, and Julia all helped me in their various ways as graphic designers, sounding boards, and cheerful companions.

I have left until last the person most deserving of my gratitude and love, my partner, Nelly Lahoud. She has found the way to be my muse and mentor, colleague and companion, critic and encourager. I hope this book pleases her.

A number of institutions and many people have been mentioned in this preface. They all played a role in the process of molding my understandings and views on the subject matter of this book, but none is responsible for those understandings or views. The book has been written in the first person and that is the only person who is responsible for those views. It follows that any views expressed in this book are not necessarily shared by the Australian Department of Foreign Affairs and Trade, the Centre for Democratic Institutions, the National Endowment for Democracy, the Australian Defence College, or the United Nations. In submitting to the judgment of the reader, I stand alone.

# 1

# Seeking Universality

"As an old fighter against dictatorship, I belong to a generation
that learned from experience the value of democracy and the importance
of liberty, a generation that knows what it means to be subject to
dictatorship and deprived of basic human rights."
—Mário Soares, "The Democratic Invention"[1]

The year 1975 was a good one for me but a bad one for democracy. I had finished my university studies and completed serving my time as an articled clerk, a quaint remnant of feudalism whereby new lawyers learn the tricks of the trade from their master solicitors. I liked the law, but I was not ready to be shackled to it. When the letter came accepting me for a position in the Australian foreign service, I had no hesitation in packing my bags for Canberra. I left behind my loving family, my old law firm Clayton Utz, my favorite city of Sydney, and my hippy communal household, and reinvented myself as an Australian diplomat. Awaiting me was my new family, the Department of Foreign Affairs. It was small enough in those days for everybody to know everybody else and for the old hands to take an interest in the fresh blood, but big enough to shelter a host of eccentric characters and to provide a world of interesting experiences.

Democracy was not faring as well in 1975. At home, Gough Whitlam's Labor government was in its last year in power. Having won the 1972 elections after decades of conservative rule, Labor set off on an ambitious march to change the nation. It succeeded, but not without stumbling repeatedly, thus emboldening its political enemies. When I arrived in Canberra, the government was already in crisis mode and would remain so for the entire year, during which time the Opposition tightened the screws by refusing to pass the government's budget through the Senate, in which the government did not have a majority. Australia was entering uncharted political waters in which the written rules were unclear and the unwritten parliamentary conventions were unenforceable. On 11 November 1975, the unelected governor-general, who represents the distant monarch and has the powers of a nonexecutive president in a republic, surprised the nation by dismissing the Whitlam government and appointing the leader of the Opposition, Malcolm Fraser, as interim prime minister to prepare for a December election, which Fraser easily won. Was this democracy? Should the populace rise up and revolt? Well, yes and no. After all, the West Indies were touring over the southern summer and they always provided cracking good cricket matches. Australians reserve their passions for sports, not politics.

Our neighbors to the north did not have the luxury of finding solace in sport in 1975, for it seemed the whole of Asia was at war. It was a self-imposed impression because the term that had entered Australia's international relations vocabulary during this period, courtesy of the Pentagon, was "domino theory."[2] The Cold War was at its apogee and our side was not winning. Dealing with each domino was monopolizing virtually all the attention of the foreign ministry, and we spent the year in the unhappy situation of being both breathlessly busy and pathetically powerless. The year had begun with the final push of the North Vietnamese army to reunite their country, and as it progressed, I scrambled to the atlas to learn where each town had fallen. First it was Phouc Binh, not far from Saigon, then Quang Tri on the central coast, then Hue, the old royal capital near the border with North Vietnam. The dominoes were falling. When Danang fell at the end of March, the war was effectively over. This was the biggest US naval base in the country and it fell with hardly a shot fired. Xuan Loc, next door to Saigon, fell some weeks later and Saigon only had a few days left. The Australian Embassy staff had already left Vietnam by then, and the staff in Phnom Penh had to be evacuated as well as the next domino, Cambodia, fell, followed soon after by Laos. It looked like the "theory" we had lampooned as students had been proven.

I was reading Aleksandr Solzhenitsyn's *Gulag Archipelago,* which had just appeared in paperback, and my Cold War blues darkened. The Soviet system looked strong to the outside observer, and the best result we could dare hope for was international parity. The challenge was to hold on to your dominoes as best you could. From the perspective of the newly independent countries of Asia, Africa, and Latin America, it meant having to take sides. The establishment of the Non-Aligned Movement was testimony to these nations' discomfiture with that process. It was a time to count allies, not democracies. Democracy looked like a vulnerable system of government, practiced in only a few parts of the world. The word itself was highly contested because of its appropriation by the "People's Democracies." There seemed no alternative but to view the world as a battle between capitalism and communism, with democracy as a side issue of limited academic interest.

A survey of the practice of democracy in Asia at the time would have returned glum results. Indochina had "fallen." Mao's China was still reeling under the Cultural Revolution. Taiwan was in the iron grip of Generalissimo

Chiang Kai-shek. The Philippines was under martial law. Malaysia and Singapore had embarked on their road to soft authoritarianism. A student uprising was brewing in Thailand and would be brutally repressed by the dominant military the following year. Indonesia was run by General Suharto. Burma was in the hands of General Ne Win. South Korea was ruled by another military figure in Park Chung Hee, while North Korea was marching along its totalitarian path. Indira Gandhi declared her emergency in June 1975, ending twenty-five years of parliamentary democracy in India. Japan was run by the party of big business with no viable opposition to contest its domestic hegemony. So when I first started studying Asia, I was struck with the somber realization that democracy was practiced nowhere on the entire continent. Others reached a similar pessimistic conclusion.[3] To round off a bad year, Indonesia invaded East Timor.

Everyone necessarily looks at the world through their personal lenses, and in my eyes 1975 was not a good year for democracy. That may be why when Samuel Huntington published *The Third Wave*[4] telling us that 1974 was the triumphal year in which began the third wave of global democratization, it struck me intuitively as odd.

## The Third Wave Versus the Clash of Civilizations?

Most great thinkers would be satisfied at having given the world one big idea, an idea that grips the imagination and is widely, if simply, understood and discussed by the common citizen, often without the benefit of having read the book. But Huntington has given us two big ideas, each powerfully encapsulated in a few well-chosen words and each attempting to answer fundamental questions about modern global society. *The Third Wave*, published in 1991, explained the global progress of democracy by looking at broad historical phases. *The Clash of Civilizations*,[5] published in 1996, argued that the civilizational divides mark the friction points of future conflicts. As others have already noted,[6] these may be big ideas, but are they consistent with each other? *The Third Wave* treats the waves of democratization as global phenomena not bounded by civilizational contexts, while *The Clash of Civilizations* casts global politics under the thrall of civilizational divides. Huntington indirectly acknowledged the problem by an attempt at reconciliation of the two ideas in 1997.[7] My initial purpose in this introductory chapter is not to reconcile but to review some of Huntington's findings by using his tools—waves of democratization, historical phases, and civilizational perspectives.

### The First and Second Waves

Huntington notes the difficulty of explaining broad global political developments because the causes may vary, may be multiple, and may be different for various countries. He also makes clear that history is messy and never unilinear. Nevertheless, he convincingly identifies the broad sweeps of history that brought the first two modern waves of democratization. The first wave of democratization was a long process that drew on British political thought and was triggered by the American and French revolutions. It progressed haltingly in the nineteenth century as milestones such as universal suffrage, constitutionalism, and responsible parliamentary government were reached. Different countries reached the key milestones at different times, culminating after World War I in some thirty-two countries adopting some or most of the key aspects of democratic governance.[8] Drawing on Huntington's civilizational divides, a subject to which this chapter will return, and backpedaling to the first phase, thirty-one of the thirty-two first wave democracies were Western countries: twenty-three in Europe; four British settler societies; and four countries in Latin America. Interestingly, the thirty-second country on Huntington's list is Japan, thus referring to the brief period of "Taishō democracy" in the 1910s and 1920s when Western-inspired ideals of constitutional monarchy and people's rights were beginning to be practiced.[9]

The between-wars period brought what Huntington describes as a "reverse wave" in which twenty-one of the first wave democracies would abandon democratic practice.[10] This left eleven democracies in the world, all Western nations: six in Europe (Finland, Iceland, Ireland, Sweden, Switzerland, United Kingdom); four British settler societies (Australia, Canada, New Zealand, United States); and Chile, which would later abandon democracy under General Augusto Pinochet's military rule. The reason for the reverse first wave and the reason for the second wave are tied together in a single historical phase, the struggle against fascism. Fascism arose out of the rubble of war and was given impetus by the Great Depression. It brought hope of orderliness and discipline when democracy seemed to offer little of either. Fascism placed the people's faith in strong leadership, where alternation of power could only be achieved through the hand of the assassin. Based on a facile social Darwinism, it practiced the most brutal form of majoritarianism by excluding, and even eliminating, minorities. Large swathes of Europe and Latin America, as well as Japan, fell under its spell. The struggle against fascism culminated in World War II, and the Allied victory marked the beginning of both the second wave of democratization as well as the process of decolonization. According to Huntington, fifteen reverse first wavers, including Japan, returned to the democracy fold,[11] and twenty-six new countries joined them.[12] Among the twenty-six were ten from Western civilization, including nine from Latin America, eight from Asia, four from Africa, three from the Middle East, and one from the Pacific. These figures bring a more global flavor to the second wave.

At this point, however, it is necessary to look behind the numbers at some of the countries comprising them to gain a better appreciation of the quality of this global diversity of democratization. The first qualification in understanding the second wave is to subtract Huntington's figure of sixteen countries in the subsequent reverse wave,[13] therefore leaving only ten new second wavers that hold the course. When the four Latin Americans and Malta are taken off, there are then only five non-Western countries remaining in the second wave to join Japan. This is a sufficiently small group to warrant some individual analysis. Africa's flag is flown by Botswana and the Gambia, countries each with a population of less than two million people. Admirable in many ways though it may be, the reality of Botswana is that it has been ruled by the same party since independence. The Gambia endured a coup soon after Huntington wrote *The Third Wave* and the coup leader remains in power, though later partially legitimized by an election victory. In any case, one could not conclude on the basis of these examples that the second wave had washed over Africa. The Middle Eastern country on the list is Israel, which should be seen as having largely been established with Western ideals and institutions. This, according to Huntington, leaves two Asian countries to fly the flag of cross-civilizational acceptance of democracy. Sri Lanka has regularly held elections and has seen the alternation of power pass consensually as a result. Sadly, it has been caught in the grip of civil war for over two decades, in which time Freedom House has only been able to classify it as "Partly Free." The final country on Huntington's list is Malaysia, a highly debatable choice to be listed under a heading of democracies.

It is accordingly a most modest conclusion to argue that the first two waves of democratization were Western phenomena. Japan edges its way onto the list of nations that adopted democracy in its first two waves, and it did so as a nation that had unconditionally surrendered and had "embraced" a democratic system imposed on it by the United States. An argument could be made for including Botswana and Sri Lanka only by adopting a rather minimalist conception of democracy.

### When Did the Third Wave Begin?

Huntington would probably have few problems with the civilizational analysis thus far. It is on his interpretation of the next historical phase in global democratization that this analysis adopts a different course. Huntington argues that the third wave of democratization begins in 1974 with the collapse of the Portuguese empire in a military coup that toppled the dictatorship of Marcello Caetano, inheritor of António Salazar's fascist ideology. It was followed by the defeat of the authoritarian military regime in Greece and the holding of elections, thus returning democracy to the country that invented the word. Then in 1975, Europe's last fascist dictator, General Francisco Franco, died, allowing Spain to negotiate its way to democracy. Does this sound like a new wave? It sounds more like the final death throes of fascism, the final victory over an ideology that democratic Europe had struggled with for half a century. The fall of the Iberian dictators and the Greek colonels marked the concluding phase of the second wave of democratization. Iberian fascism had been tolerated though marginalized in Europe for a generation after the war. It had never been accepted as part of the European mainstream or of the European integration community. Europe had simply awaited the passing of the generals and colonels, and when it occurred in the mid-1970s, Europe could finally file away that ugly chapter of its history.

Huntington then sees the new wave of democratization move to Latin America. In the late 1970s Ecuador, Peru, and Bolivia saw the military replaced by civilian leadership in a positive version of the domino theory. Argentina's 1982 defeat in the Falklands War marked the end of the military's legitimacy and of its dictatorship. Following in Portugal's footsteps, Brazil had begun the process of reopening its political system in 1974, leading ten years later to a civilian president. Several Central American countries, Honduras, El Salvador, and Guatemala, also saw the military withdraw from government in the early 1980s. Latin America provides a more promising candidate for the commencement of the third wave. It takes place on a new continent and it has considerable momentum, involving some eight countries including the continent's two largest nations. The problem is that commencing the third wave in the 1970s flies in the face of historical reality. The 1970s marked the darkest days of the Cold War. International relations were virtually frozen into two political camps. There may have been some moments of thaw, such as Nikita Khrushchev's denunciation of Stalin's crimes and Jimmy Carter's championing of human rights, but these were the exceptions to the rule of stasis. It is difficult to accept that such a significant international event could begin in this frozen political period. A better explanation for this period of Latin America's democratization is to see it as part of the struggle against fascism. Iberian fascism had indirectly legitimized Latin American military dictatorship, but Iberian democratization subtly delegitimized it. In a study of the Latin American transition to democracy, Stephen Schwartz opines that the application of the lessons of the Spanish transition to the Western Hemisphere is "easily demonstrated."[14]

So far, the story of democratization has been predominantly a story of Western civilization, but Huntington now switches continents and travels to Asia. India returns to its parliamentary path in 1977, having been one of the second wave democracies that did not stay the course. But the dominoes now start falling in Asia in a more felicitous manner: Philippine People Power in 1986; the commencement of South Korea's transition in 1987; and Taiwan's acceptance of political contestability the following year. This is a far more propitious point to mark the beginning of the third wave. But to do so, it has to be linked with a historical event of global significance analogous to the American and French revolutions and to democracy's victory over fascism. That historical event, the eclipse of Soviet communism, can be summarized in one name—Mikhail Gorbachev. If the first wave of democratization can be described as Jeffersonian and the second wave as Churchillian, then the third wave must carry the name of the then general secretary of the Central Committee of the Communist Party of the Union of Soviet Socialist Republics. Gorbachev's great gift to the world was inaction. Unlike his predecessors who were prepared to use force to punish deviation, Gorbachev understood the futility of maintaining an untenable system and holding together an impossible empire by force. The world could come out of the freezer. The next democratic moment had arrived. The third wave had begun.

History is messy and dividing lines can often look blurred, but beginning the third wave in the Gorbachev period thus has the advantage of tying a major global development to a major global event between which there is strong evidence of causality. It also establishes the third wave as a true global wave of democracy transcending the Western ancestry of the first two waves. Finally, it accords much more closely with the facts of the democratic transitions and the intensity achieved as the Cold War was coming to an end. This is nicely illustrated in a study of democratic transitions by Vani Borooah and Martin Paldam in which they use the Gastil Index, on which the Freedom House measures are based, to plot the transitions to democracy in the period from 1972 to 2003, thus encompassing both Huntington's suggested 1974 start of the third wave and the Gorbachev incumbency.[15] (See Figure 1.1.)

The intensity of the third wave in the Gorbachev period cannot be denied. Those analysts who retain the Huntington periodicity have had to shoehorn the facts to fit in with the erroneous 1974 start of the third wave. Michael McFaul argues that the postcommunist transitions were of such a different character from transitions in the 1970s and 1980s that they should be considered as a fourth wave.[16] Renske Doorenspleet contents herself with mathematics and chronology, and on this score also proposes that it would be more accurate to describe the post–Cold War democratization process as the fourth wave.[17] McFaul accepts Huntington's commencement date for the third wave without discussion, and Doorenspleet simply took off where Huntington left off and did not attempt to fit his waves into a deeper historical perspective. Yet Huntington himself recognizes that there is something amiss with his wave periodicity, and he attempts to correct it by arguing, rather clumsily, that in 1989 the "the third wave entered a second phase."[18] In the preface to *The Third Wave*, Huntington explains that the book was written in 1989 and 1990. This was a momentous period, full of excitement and bewilderment, and Huntington, while witnessing the

**Figure 1.1 The Average Path of Democracy
in 171 Countries, 1972–2003**

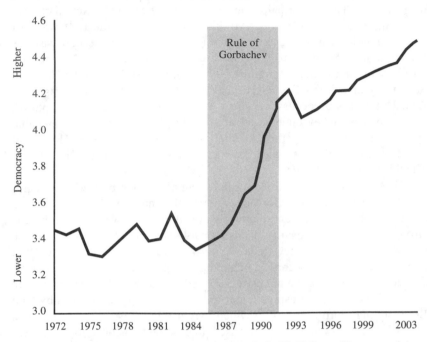

*Source:* Vani Borooah and Martin Paldam, "Why Is the World Short of Democracy? A Cross-Country Analysis of Barriers to Representative Government," paper presented at the European Public Choice Society Annual Conference, University of Durham, 31 March–3 April 2005.

early Gorbachev years, could not have been expected to divine the collapse of the Soviet Union at the end of 1991. Had he written his book a couple of years later, Huntington would have given the end of the Cold War its proper place in the sweep of history and would have acknowledged it as the harbinger of a new wave of democratization.

## The First Global Wave of Democratization

### Choosing Democracy
The Gorbachevian wave and the end of the Cold War had a global impact. As previously argued, the first two waves settled European ideological debates and found their reflection in the practices of Western civilization. The thawing of the Cold War had an early impact in Asia where the US allies, South Korea and Taiwan, though still facing fraternal communist

threats, could no longer rely on the unquestioned domestic military practices sanctioned by the Cold War to bring legitimacy to their authoritarian governance systems. Philippine president Ferdinand Marcos could only rely on the Americans to provide a helicopter to fly him out of the besieged Malacañang presidential palace. Thereafter, the next region that would benefit from the end of the Cold War would be the constituent parts of the former Soviet empire.

I was fortunate to be in a privileged position to witness this event as head of the East Europe section of the Australian Foreign Ministry. I remember one frantic day when I had to write two speeches in the morning: one for Prime Minister Bob Hawke to deliver that afternoon in the House of Representatives, and one for Foreign Minister Gareth Evans to make in the Senate later the same day. Everything was happening in a rush as the fall of the Berlin Wall was coming over the morning news. The guidance I had was that the speeches had to be "important." Evans was my minister, but Hawke was the prime minister. They needed to say different things but nevertheless speak to the main issue. In the event, to respect the requirements of hierarchy, Hawke spoke about the global implications and Evans about the regional implications. I heard later that the prime minister had appreciated the comparison I had written into the speech about great walls in history. The Walls of Jericho, the Great Wall of China, and Hadrian's Wall had all been built to keep the enemy out, but the Berlin Wall was unique in being built to keep the people in.

One of the reasons I enjoyed this assignment was that it allowed me to practice both politics and law. As an international lawyer, I had shared the view of the mainstream of the fraternity that the legal issues concerning the recognition of states were pretty much settled with the closing of the decolonization era. We were wrong, as all of a sudden the international community was faced with a series of difficult recognition decisions as the constituent republics of two federated nations, Yugoslavia and the Soviet Union, clamored for independence and demanded recognition from the international community. Some twenty new states emerged from the rubble. Having been involved in so many complex new recognition decisions in such a short time, I felt I had an obligation to write it all down, and so, after the dust had settled, I published an article on the subject that I was later pleasantly surprised to learn is widely used in law schools to demonstrate the impact of political realities on the development of international law.[19]

In terms of democratization, the end of the Cold War allowed newly established countries to choose their form of governance, and it was democracy they chose. For many of the Central European states, this was a return to parliaments and political parties from previous times. In Hungary, for example, the institutions of democracy and almost the identical political parties sprang back into existence as if half a century of Soviet domination had hardly occurred. It is testimony to the enduring resilience of the national memory of democracy that its practice can be taken up so readily after two generations of desuetude. Many of the other parts of the Soviet empire had no memory of democracy and began the difficult task of building its foundations and governance structures while requiring those very structures to perform their tasks in a difficult new world. Some fifteen European countries emerged from the period with newly minted democratic forms of government.

The end of the Cold War would also bring its democratic dividends beyond Europe. Doorenspleet lists sixteen African countries that made the transition to democracy in the decade after the end of the Cold War, including countries of the former Portuguese empire, countries from francophone West Africa, and, significantly, countries from southern Africa where apartheid finally ground to a halt.[20] In Latin America, a first wave democracy, Chile, returned to the fold and was joined by seven other Latin American countries.[21] In Asia, where the third wave had begun with the Philippines, South Korea, and Taiwan, further transitions occurred in Bangladesh, Indonesia, Mongolia, Nepal, and Thailand. In total, well over fifty countries would seize the democratic moment and turn to democratic forms of governance in the Gorbachev wave.

Freedom House published a document at the close of the twentieth century entitled *Democracy's Century* in which it undertook the count of democracies after the third wave.[22] It pointed out that the number of liberal and electoral democracies "expanded significantly in the Third Wave, which has brought democracy to much of the post-Communist world and to Latin America and parts of Asia and Africa. Electoral democracies now represent 121 of the 192 existing countries and constitute 62.5 percent of the world's population." Of these, 84 were placed in the liberal democracy category of countries that respect human rights and practice the rule of law, or in Freedom House terms are "free." In its 2002 Human Development Report, the UN Development Programme came to a not dissimilar conclusion, listing 140 of the then 188 countries that held multiparty elections, while its list of "fully democratic" countries was 82, leaving 106 countries not fully respecting civil and political rights though 58 of these nevertheless held multiparty elections.[23]

## A Civilizational Breakdown

The third wave thus had an impact well beyond the previous two waves of democratization and generated a certain triumphal commentary. The US State Department sees "the growth of democracy—from 30 countries in 1974 to 117 today—as one of the United States' greatest legacies."[24] While pleasure at the trend to democratization is appropriate, self-congratulation is always more dubious, and triumphalism is simply unsupported by the facts. In deconstructing the third wave in search of the enduring adoption of democratic governance, we need to maintain the distinction between electoral and liberal democracies and divide the countries according to their civilizational categories. This breakdown demonstrates that the trend is in fact far from global and indeed is dominated by the practice of democracy in Western societies. (See Table 1.1.)

Almost 70 percent of liberal democracies are thus Western countries if one includes Latin America. But even this figure is an understatement. The Middle Eastern country is Israel, which, as stated above, was established on the basis of Western ideals. The eleven Pacific island nations have a total population of less than 8 million people, comprised largely of Papua New Guinea's 5.5 million inhabitants. These nations practice a low-quality form of democracy. It is deceptive to allow such a large number of countries, with such small populations, to skew the global figures in the table. Adding Israel to the Western column and subtracting the Pacific islands from the list, the Western countries climb to 80 percent of the seventy-three countries. Seven of Africa's fifty-three states are on the list. Of these, five have populations of fewer than 2 million people, leaving just Benin and South Africa. The seven Asian countries listed as liberal democracies are Japan, South Korea, India, Mongolia, the Philippines, Taiwan, and Thailand.

The survey highlights Western civilization's widespread acceptance of liberal or high-quality democracy. The survey also highlights that, aside from the West, the area of greatest interest in terms of the transition to the practice of liberal democracy is Asia, and Pacific Asia in particular. Thus if we are seeking evidence of the appropriateness of the practice of liberal democracy universally, the study of democracy in Asia is of critical importance.

## Consolidation Is the Key Issue

The study of democracy is an enormous field. What particular aspects should we focus on? The waves of democratization concern the transition paradigm. The third wave is simply a heading for those countries that turned from some form of authoritarian rule to a form of democratic governance

Table 1.1  **Civilizational Breakdown of Democracies in Freedom House's 2000 Survey**

|  | Western[a] | African | Asian | Pacific | Middle Eastern |
|---|---|---|---|---|---|
| Electoral democracies (121 total) | 75 (28) | 21 | 12 | 11 | 2 |
| Liberal democracies (84 total) | 58 (20) | 7 | 7 | 11 | 1 |

*Note:* a. Includes Latin American and Caribbean in parentheses.

since the Cold War began to thaw. Democratic transitions can be spectacular events attracting wide popular attention internationally, and it is understandable that they should be the focus of quantitative research. The key event is the transition election through which an incoming government gains popular legitimacy by winning a free and fair ballot. The day after the winner is declared, however, is the day the hard work of consolidating democracy begins. Ultimately, consolidation is the key issue for qualitative research because democratization depends on whether the transition holds its course.

Consolidation requires democracy to be sustainable. In this respect it is wise not to fall into what Guillermo O'Donnell describes as a teleological trap that assumes the existence of a single path from transition to democratization that some nations "complete," and on which some countries may get stuck or even fall off.[25] There are clearly many paths, and each nation begins on its own democratization journey not knowing exactly where that path may lead. O'Donnell's warning means that each journey will not follow the same path. There may be detours, shortcuts and, sadly, dead ends in the pathways of democratization. The absence of inevitability of completion does not, however, preclude the paths from having milestones along the way. The milestones can be given descriptive titles, and even though various paths may have these milestones in different orders and at varying distances, they may nevertheless resemble milestones on other paths. This allows for a degree of comparability between the various pathways, allowing for the adoption of generalizations and perhaps even the drawing of common lessons.

The milestones may have titles such as transition election; first, second, or third alternation of power; assertion of judicial independence; or overcoming constitutional crisis. One nation may pass all these milestones in a mere decade; others may continue to glimpse them on the distant horizon. O'Donnell's challenge can be formulated in a question: Is it possible ever to name a milestone "consolidation"? I believe it is, as long as that milestone is not considered as the end of the journey, but rather as the point of no return. The journey continues with many more milestones of wide public participation, high-quality deliberation, and peace dividends, but there is no turning back to the authoritarianism of the past. Determining exactly where this milestone is located may not be possible. But a point in the journey comes where a society knows it has passed it. This way of identifying consolidation accords with the idea put forward by Juan Linz and Alfred Stepan of democracy as "the only game in town."[26]

### Three Qualifications and Three Tests

Linz and Stepan elaborate the meaning of this telling phrase by setting down three qualifications and three tests.[27] The first qualification is that the polity in question needs to be generally accepted by the populace as a state. They put this requirement bluntly—no state, no democracy. This might seem a rather basic point, but there are entities where popular allegiance is to a tribe, region, or island rather than to the state itself. Some African states confront this problem within their colonial borders. This is also a particular problem in Melanesia, where some nations are finding it difficult to build the national institutions of democracy. The key reason is that the road to Westminster passes through Westphalia.

The second qualification is that Robert Dahl's indispensable seven conditions for polyarchy must be met:[28]

1. Constitutionally invested elected officials implement government policy.
2. Elected officials are chosen in free, fair, and frequent elections.
3. Elections are run on the basis of universal adult suffrage.
4. Virtually all adults have the right to run for elective office.
5. Citizens have freedom of expression.
6. Citizens have a right to seek alternative sources of information.
7. Citizens have a right to form political parties and nongovernmental organizations (NGOs).

Third, the elected governments need to govern democratically, which in turn requires a commitment to constitutionality, the rule of law, and respect for human rights. This qualification excludes pseudodemocracies in which some democratic institutions such as elected parliaments exist alongside nondemocratic institutions such as judiciaries controlled by the executive branch.

Having passed these threshold conditions, Linz and Stepan posit three tests of a consolidated democracy:

> *Behaviorally,* a democratic regime in a territory is consolidated when no significant national, social, economic, political, or institutional actors spend significant resources attempting to achieve their objectives by creating a nondemocratic regime or by seceding from the state. *Attitudinally,* a democratic regime is consolidated when a strong majority of public opinion, even in the midst of major economic problems and deep dissatisfaction with incumbents, holds the belief that democratic procedures and institutions are the most appropriate way to govern collective life, and when support for antisystem alternatives is quite small or more-or-less isolated from prodemocratic forces. *Constitutionally,* a democratic regime is consolidated when governmental and nongovernmental forces alike become subject to, and habituated to, the resolution of conflict within the bounds of the specific laws, procedures, and institutions sanctioned by the new democratic process.[29]

    Though these may sound like relatively simple propositions to Western
ears accustomed to their central principles, they are in reality difficult tests.
They are difficult to achieve and difficult to measure. Huntington suggests a
far more user-friendly test of consolidation: "A democracy may be viewed
as consolidated if the party or group that takes power in the initial election
at the time of transition loses a subsequent election and turns over power to
those election winners, and if those election winners then peacefully turn
over power to the winners of a later election."[30] The two-turnovers test has
the advantage of being easily measurable. It also makes practical sense to
require the winner of the transition election to hand over power to a subsequent election winner, thus demonstrating that the transitional change was
not simply a change of regime but a change of system. While a useful measurement, the two-turnovers test does not appear sufficiently rigorous to
allow a confident conclusion of consolidation to be reached. A system of
swapping the bounty of office between divisions of the elite according to
elections does not constitute a consolidated democracy but may simply
demonstrate a domestic balance of power between oligopolistic forces of
society. Thailand has held many elections, and in the mid-1970s, the brothers Kukrit and Seni Pramoj alternated in power after putting together various coalitions following elections. However, although technically meeting
the two-turnovers test, nobody is suggesting Thailand was a consolidated
democracy at the time. Neither would the presidential transitions in the
Philippines from Corazon Aquino to Fidel Ramos to Joseph Estrada to the
present elected leader, Gloria Macapagal-Arroyo, necessarily lead to a conclusion of consolidation in that country.
    What we need to look for in consolidation is the extent to which the
political arrangements are, in Philippe Schmitter's formulation, "reliably
known, regularly practiced, and voluntarily accepted by . . . politicians and
citizens" such that democratic processes result.[31] This formulation boils down
to the issues of knowledge, practice, and volition that are at the heart of the
consolidation process. Consolidation requires a certain behavioral consensus
among the elites in their acceptance of democracy's strictures and limitations.
Consolidation requires a certain popular attitudinal consensus that allows the
system to be maintained even when crises and downturns are experienced.
Consolidation requires a national consensus for the constitutional settlement
of those serious crises. In this regard, the consolidation issue dovetails with
another important aspect of democracy studies that concerns itself with the
quality of democracy.[32] Concepts such as consolidation or liberal democracy
can simply be seen as the higher-quality practice of democracy.


## Democracy Is a System

It follows from the foregoing that democracy is more than an election, more
than a government, and more than a set of laws. Democracy is a system of

governance. That system has many aspects to it. Some are essential for its existence, others are important to improve its quality. My aim in this book is to focus on the key aspects of democracy. Accordingly, the shape of the book is thematic, focusing on these key aspects and how strongly developed they may be in the various countries of Pacific Asia. It might be possible to have accomplished this task by adopting a country-by-country approach and devoting a chapter on each country under review, but this method would have downplayed the thematic elements and weakened the comparative analysis.

How to identify these key elements? Dahl's seven points deal with constitutions, elections, politicians, freedom of information and expression, and the right to form political parties and NGOs. Inspired by Dahl's analysis, the themes I have chosen to examine are institutional design encompassing elections and representative bodies; the rule of law guaranteed by a constitution and protecting basic rights; political parties, which translate political thought into action; politicians, as the indispensable vectors of governance; the public conversation through which information and opinion are expressed and received; and political culture in which civil society operates.

Analogies are a useful explanatory device though they cannot be taken beyond their superficial comparative utility. Recurring throughout this project is the analogy of the system of democracy resembling the system of the human body. The comparison is useful because the complexity of each system can be simplified by reference to its key parts. In this analogy, the skeleton provides the structure for the system and it resembles the institutions of democracy—parliaments, executives, elections, courts, auditors, ombudsmen, and so forth. Within this structure are the organs pumping blood and oxygen into the system and they can be compared to political parties as well as politicians and perhaps other policy leaders. The flesh around the skeletal structure can be compared to the people taking the form of deliberators, civil society activists, voters, as well as consumers of the impacts of policy decisions. Accordingly, the public conversation being conducted and the political culture of the populace become key themes. Living systems grow and change. Life forms, even of the same species, are individually different from each other. The analogy between the democratic system and the human body can comfortably extend to include both change and lack of uniformity. The benefit of using this analogy is that it makes clear that various parts of the system must work together to create the whole. Looking only at elections, for instance, is like looking at only one part of the system. It might be the spine of the skeleton, but it remains only one part of the body. The body comprises far more than its skeleton, its organs, and its flesh, just as democracy comprises far more than the key aspects I have highlighted. But these key aspects nevertheless make democracy recognizable and allow for an assessment of the health of the system.

Having touched on the "what" question, it is necessary to provide a brief comment on the "how" question—methodology. Political science allows various approaches. Each approach, whether based on psephology, veto player analysis, rational choice, elite theory, or opinion sampling, has its place in the discipline. The research has been undertaken on the basis of a fairly traditional political science approach. It examines political structure and political culture within a historical framework. It draws on the political science literature on democratic development pioneered by towering figures such as Dahl, Seymour Martin Lipset, and Maurice Duverger, further molded by writers such as Linz, Stepan, and Schmitter, and adapted for comparative purposes by analysts such as O'Donnell, Larry Diamond, and Richard Gunther. The research draws on the comparativist literature as well as the country-specific literature. While the main lines of investigation concern institutional structure, the discussion will be infused with questions of behavior and attitude. It delves into the detail of some of the key practices of democracy in Pacific Asia, attempts to place that practice in a historical process, and seeks to situate this democratic practice in a global context.

### Outline of the Book

The next issue that requires introduction is the "where" question. Before coming to the thematic discussions of democracy, it is necessary to identify the geographic subject matter of this study. Chapter 2 charts the meaning of *Pacific Asia*. It is a spatial concept viewed through various lenses such as history, geography, civilizations, institutional architecture. and the imaginations of its peoples and leaders. Among the nations of Pacific Asia, I have identified Indonesia, the Philippines, South Korea, Taiwan, and Thailand as the key democratizing countries that will be the principal subject matter of this project. (See Figure 1.2.) Accordingly, for those not familiar with these countries, I have provided pen sketches highlighting their political paths to democratization.

The aspect that is most apparent to any student of democratic consolidation is its institutional character. Chapter 3 looks at key governance institutions of democracy through an analysis of the power of parliaments and presidents, the coherence of the electoral systems that elect them, and the integrity of the oversight institutions that monitor them. It examines the crafting of these institutions in Pacific Asia. Two new concepts are introduced: *systematization* and the *dimensions* of electoral expression. The underlying question that haunts the crafters of these new institutions is whether such bodies can indeed be successfully crafted or whether they can only succeed if they have evolved over time and been tested under diverse conditions. In other words, can political evolution be short-cut by clever design?

Chapter 4 tackles democracy's need for law. It is a generally accepted proposition that there can be no democracy without rule of law. The chapter

## Figure 2.1   Map of Asia

*Shaded areas indicate the key democratizing countries discussed in this book.*

also supports the converse proposition, that the effective establishment of the rule of law requires democracy, and so the two concepts are mutually supportive and interdependent. The chapter elaborates three historical and three conceptual challenges to the establishment of rule of law in Pacific Asia. The growing hold of *constitutionalism* in the region is identified and explained. The recurring question in this chapter is whether there are determinative aspects of Pacific Asian civilization that are inimical to the establishment of the rule of law.

Chapter 5 deals with the vexed issue of political parties. The practice of consolidated democracies demonstrates that political parties are an essential ingredient in their governance systems. Accordingly, it is important to reach an understanding of the nature of political parties in Pacific Asia, their longevity and *embeddedness* in society, as well as their ability to play the roles required of political parties in modern democratic states. We know that political parties in the long-established democracies played a crucial role in shaping their nations' democratic systems, but is it reasonable to turn the tables of history and expect the newly crafted political systems of the transition democracies to nurture and sustain political parties? In conclusion, the chapter explains the trend toward elections being fought by two parties or blocs of parties by reference to the growing *meaningfulness* of those elections.

In Chapter 6, I focus on the difficult issue of the region's politicians by analyzing salient characteristics of these Asian leaders and determining the extent to which the rules of the democratic game are voluntarily accepted by them. Being an individual, the politician necessarily defies any "one size fits all" description. Does that mean that politicians cannot be the subject of assessments that attempt to build broad generalizations about their conduct and worth? If such assessments are possible, what methodology is available? This chapter attempts to answer these questions by describing and analyzing politicians in Pacific Asian democracies using a method proposed by Linz, who asks a series of probing questions to test political leaders against an idealized framework. The chapter identifies a number of trends concerning the quality of politicians emerging in Pacific Asia, including the decline in influence of military figures, the growing role of women, the struggle against the gangsterization of politics, and a recent turn toward the "celebritification" of politics.

When the study turns to the more general behavior and attitudes of elites and electorates in relation to the public sphere, we drift away from the refuge of institutional compliance with formal rules and enter a vast space where rules may define its boundaries but are not of much assistance in understanding its substance. Chapter 7 examines the public conversation being conducted in a democracy and the role of the mass media that facilitate this conversation. The question being asked in this chapter concerns the quality of the public conversations taking place in Pacific Asia's democracies. Has it reached the level of deliberation that is a hallmark of consolidated or high-quality democracies? And how should we assess the quality of the mass media, the instrument through which that conversation is shaped and disseminated?

Chapter 8 strays even further away from the institutional methods of analyzing democratic practice by examining the difficult question of political culture, which, in the Asian context, requires a discussion of issues such as political behavior, Confucianism, and Asian Values. The chapter rejects the traditional view of Asians as pliant observers of the public sphere and lists the various popular explosions that have occurred in Pacific Asian societies. But it also looks beyond the volcanic explosions in society to determine the extent of the bubbling lava hidden within. This entails a search for Pacific Asian civil society. The key question being addressed in this chapter is whether the political cultures of the emerging democracies of Pacific Asia lend themselves to the consolidation of democracy. And if some aspects of those cultures are antithetical to democratic practice, can they be changed?

Countries practicing democracy may have similar-looking institutions, yet the most casual of visitors will see the distinctions among them far more readily than their supposed similarity. Is the term *democracy* appropriate to compartmentalize this group of countries in contradistinction to its neighbors? Chapter 9 seeks to explain why democracies do not all look alike. It begins by measuring differences in the structures of governance, but in describing such structures there is a nagging suspicion of simply dealing with a façade. Are we appreciating the infrastructure of governance or glancing lazily at its superstructure? The means of answering this question is to look at the character and quality of the democratic practices of the individual countries of Pacific Asia.

The three waves of democratization have all been premised on the existence of nation-states and the structures of successful democratic governance have been built on national institutions, national practices, and a broad national consensus. Yet the reality of that practice points to the success of democracy beyond individual nations. It is the Western world that has consolidated its national democracy. Is the consolidation of democracy in Western civilization simply a sum of the acceptance of democracy in its various national parts? Or is there a civilizational component contributing to democratic consolidation in the West? In posing this question in the concluding chapter, another question suggests itself: Does consolidation of democracy require a civilizational consensus? And if so, is a civilizational consensus in favor of democracy forming in Pacific Asia?

The following chapters therefore seek to answer the what, how, and why questions. The "when" question concerns the end point of this work, and the answer is September 2006 with the Thai coup. There remains a final

g question—why? In dealing with Pacific Asia's quest for democra-
ɹope to shed a little light beyond the individual polities' practice of
ɔracy. By examining countries not part of Western civilization, I am
hing for a part of the answer to a very large question: Is democracy,
ɹuman rights, of universal application?

tes

1. Mário Soares, "The Democratic Invention," Marc F. Plattner and João
ɪrlos Espada (eds.), *The Democratic Invention* (Baltimore: Johns Hopkins
niversity Press, 2000), p. 34.

2. Patrick O'Sullivan, "Dominoes or Dice: Geography and the Diffusion of
Political Violence," *The Journal of Conflict Studies* 16, no. 2 (Fall 1997): 97.

3. Marc Plattner, "The Democratic Moment," Larry Diamond and Marc
Plattner (eds.), *The Global Resurgence of Democracy,* 2nd ed. (Baltimore: Johns
Hopkins University Press, 1996), p. 37.

4. Samuel P. Huntington, *The Third Wave—Democratization in the Late
Twentieth Century* (Norman and London: Oklahoma University Press, 1991).

5. Samuel P. Huntington, *The Clash of Civilizations and the Remaking of
World Order* (New York: Simon and Schuster, 1996).

6. Carl Gershman, "The Clash Within Civilizations," *Journal of Democracy*
8, no. 4 (1997): 165–170.

7. Samuel P. Huntington, "After Twenty Years: The Future of the Third
Wave," *Journal of Democracy* 8, no. 4 (1997): 3–12.

8. Huntington confusingly includes East Germany in his list, but for plausi-
bility purposes it is excluded from this count: Argentina, Australia, Austria,
Belgium, Canada, Chile, Colombia, Czechoslovakia, Denmark, Estonia, France,
Finland, Germany, Greece, Hungary, Iceland, Ireland, Italy, Japan, Latvia,
Lithuania, Netherlands, New Zealand, Norway, Poland, Portugal, Spain, Sweden,
Switzerland, United Kingdom, United States, Uruguay.

9. John W. Dower, *Embracing Defeat: Japan in the Wake of World War II*
(New York: W. W. Norton and Company, 1999), p. 180.

10. Argentina, Austria, Belgium, Czechoslovakia, Colombia, Denmark,
Estonia, France, Germany, Greece, Hungary, Italy, Japan, Latvia, Lithuania,
Netherlands, Norway, Poland, Portugal, Spain, Uruguay.

11. Argentina, Austria, Belgium, Colombia, Czechoslovakia, Denmark,
France, Germany, Greece, Hungary, Italy, Japan, Netherlands, Norway, Uruguay.

12. Bolivia, Botswana, Brazil, Burma, Costa Rica, Ecuador, Fiji, Gambia,
Ghana, Guyana, India, Indonesia, Israel, Jamaica, South Korea, Lebanon, Malaysia,
Malta, Nigeria, Pakistan, Peru, Philippines, Sri Lanka, Trinidad and Tobago, Turkey,
Venezuela.

13. Bolivia, Brazil, Burma, Ecuador, Fiji, Ghana, Guyana, India, Indonesia,
South Korea, Lebanon, Nigeria, Pakistan, Peru, Philippines, Turkey.

14. Stephen Schwartz, "Introduction," Stephen Schwartz (ed.), *The Transition
from Authoritarianism to Democracy in the Hispanic World* (San Francisco: Institute
for Contemporary Studies, 1986), p. xxi.

15. Vani Borooah and Martin Paldam, "Why Is the World Short of Democracy?
A Cross-Country Analysis of Barriers to Representative Government," paper pre-
sented at the European Public Choice Society Annual Conference, University of
Durham, 31 March–3 April 2005.

16. Michael McFaul, "The Fourth Wave of Democracy and Dictatorship—Noncooperative Transitions in the Postcommunist World," *World Politics* 54, no. 2 (2002): 212–244.

17. Renske Doorenspleet, *Democratic Transitions: Exploring the Structural Source of the Fourth Wave* (Boulder: Lynne Rienner Publishers, 2005), pp. 48–52.

18. Huntington, *The Third Wave,* p. 44.

19. Roland Rich, "Recognition of States: The Collapse of Yugoslavia and the Soviet Union," *European Journal of International Law* 4, no. 1 (1993): 36–65.

20. Benin, Central African Republic, Comoro Islands, Congo-Brazzaville, Guinea-Bissau, Lesotho, Madagascar, Malawi, Mali, Mozambique, Niger, Nigeria, Senegal, South Africa, Sierra Leone, Zambia. Doorenspleet, *Democratic Transitions*, p. 51.

21. Guatemala, Guyana, Haiti, Mexico, Nicaragua, Panama, Paraguay. Ibid.

22. Freedom House, *Democracy's Century—A Survey of Global Political Change in the Twentieth Century*, www.freedomhouse.org/reports/century.html.

23. UN Development Programme, *Human Development Report 2002—Deepening Democracy in a Fragmented World*, http://hdr.undp.org/reports/global/2002/en/.

24. US Department of State, *Democracy*, www.state.gov/g/drl/democ/.

25. Guillermo O'Donnell, "Illusions About Consolidation," Larry Diamond et al. (eds.), *Consolidating the Third Wave Democracies—Themes and Perspectives* (Baltimore: Johns Hopkins University Press, 1997), pp. 40–57.

26. Juan J. Linz and Alfred Stepan, "Toward Consolidated Democracies," *Journal of Democracy* 7, no. 2 (1996): 15.

27. Ibid.

28. Robert A. Dahl, "Polyarchy," *Toward Democracy: A Journey—Reflections: 1940–1997, Volume 1* (Berkeley: Institute of Government Studies Press, 1997), pp. 94–95.

29. Linz and Stepan, "Toward Consolidated Democracies," p. 16.

30. Huntington, *The Third Wave*, pp. 266–267.

31. Philippe C. Schmitter, "Parties Are Not What They Once Were," Larry Diamond and Richard Gunther (eds.), *Political Parties and Democracy* (Baltimore: Johns Hopkins University Press, 2001), p. 68.

32. Larry Diamond and Leonardo Morlino, *Assessing the Quality of Democracy* (Baltimore: Johns Hopkins University Press, 2005).

# 2

# Charting Pacific Asia

"Within this general sphere of the political culture of
Pacific Asia we can note that local theorists are speaking
now of a Pacific Asian model of democracy."
—P. W. Preston, *Pacific Asia in the Global System*[1]

Before embarking on the study of democracy in Pacific Asia, we need to describe the subject countries and place them in a civilizational context. I have chosen what I believe to be the most accurate description for the area I wish to survey: *Pacific Asia,* a term that is being increasingly used in the academic literature.[2] It covers a different, though overlapping, set of countries than does the term *Asia Pacific.* Asia Pacific is a compound of two nouns to describe an area that combines both Asia and the Pacific. This is a vast area that can be interpreted to stretch from the huge Asian landmass, east to both American continents, south to Australia and New Zealand, while encompassing all the Pacific islands along the way. By contrast, in the term *Pacific Asia,* Asia is the noun and Pacific is the adjective. We are talking about a specific part of Asia. What constitutes Pacific Asia and how do we chart it? I suggest six ways to answer that question.

## Six Ways of Looking at Pacific Asia

### Mapping by Cardinal Points
Employing the cardinal points, Pacific Asia comprises those countries that are often described as forming Northeast Asia and Southeast Asia, or sometimes simply East Asia. The problem with these "objective" geographic terms is the underlying subjectivity by which they are formulated. The fact of the equator gives *north* and *south* broad objective meanings but, like *east* and *west,* the specific meanings can only be determined in relation to where the observer is located. The language of social science at our disposal is

predominantly a European discourse, and so the world's geography is Eurocentric. As Edward Said explained, this Eurocentrism leads to far deeper problems than geographic place names.[3] It leads to a process, often implied though unarticulated, of comparison and hierarchy that inevitably creates distortions and misunderstandings.

The problem of geographic descriptors touches not simply regions of the world but also the designation of entire continents. Grant Evans puts the matter clearly when he states that "the idea of Asia or the Orient is an artifact of the European imagination."[4] Asia existed in the European imagination as that vast area east of Europe, that area where European civilization was not practiced. Accordingly, Asia was seen in the negative, for what it was not. But was there an Asia that was seen in the positive, for what it was? In other words did the people living in that area designated as Asia by Europeans see themselves as living in any sort of geographic community broadly coterminous with the European geographic imagination of Asia? The historical answer must be "no." No Asian society prior to contact with Europe recognized Asia as a meaningful geographic entity. Indeed, though gathering the proof of this statement would be onerous, in my discussions with Evans he agreed that no language spoken in the area known to Europeans as Asia had a word for "Asia" in its vocabulary prior to contact with Europeans. Nevertheless, while the terms can be problematized in this way, we are left with a positive geographic description of Pacific Asia as Northeast Asia plus Southeast Asia, or simply East Asia.

## Mapping by Negative Geography

A second way to describe Pacific Asia is to do so by way of negative geography and say what it is not. It is not Russia. It is not the Indian subcontinent. It is not Himalayan Asia. It is not the former Soviet Central Asia. It is not Islamic West Asia. It is not Melanesia. And it is not Australia and New Zealand. Like most categorical pronouncements, even this peremptory negative list requires some elaboration. Timor-Leste is drawn in several directions. Ethnically, its people are probably closer to the Melanesians than to the Malays, but its textile weaving culture draws it toward Indonesia. Historically, it wishes to highlight its Portuguese colonial past rather than the more recent Indonesian occupation. Geographically, it is part of the Indonesian archipelago, though its major economic resource is in the sea shared with Australia. Politically, it remains effectively a ward of the international community rather than a confident participant in Pacific Asia's affairs. West Papua, or Irian Jaya, is politically a part of Indonesia and therefore by definition part of Pacific Asia, but it forms part of this region far more by the definition of political boundaries than by reason of ethnicity, lifestyle, or, most probably, inclination of its native people. Mongolia also defies easy categorization. Its history is intertwined with that of China, but its recent past put it in the Soviet orbit. In many ways it has distinguished itself from the former Soviet republics of Central Asia through its commitment to reform and democratization, but in other ways it lacks the bustling economic dynamism and maritime trading culture that is a hallmark of Pacific Asia. Australia and New Zealand are not in Asia and are therefore not in Pacific Asia. They could only become part of Pacific Asia if that community were imagined to include them. When we put to one side these areas that are not part of Pacific Asia, we are left, once again, with East Asia.

## Pacific Ocean Perspective

The word *Pacific* in my descriptor comes from the ocean, not, alas, from an absence of warfare or bellicosity. A third way to describe Pacific Asia is to think of it as the littoral countries of the Pacific Ocean on the Asian continent. It is Asia's Pacific Rim. A literal reading of this descriptor would, however, provide a skewed list of countries. The littoral list would begin with Russia, though it is not generally seen as part of Pacific Asia despite its mistaken membership in the Asia Pacific Economic Cooperation (APEC) forum. It would then include China, the Koreas, and Vietnam. The list would also include the contiguous archipelagic nations of the Pacific: Japan, the Philippines, Indonesia, and Taiwan, plus Brunei. Also included are the peninsula countries of Singapore, Malaysia, Thailand, and Cambodia. While they are not littoral countries, Pacific Asia is normally understood to include landlocked Laos, because all five of its neighbors form part of Pacific Asia, and Association of South East Asian Nations (ASEAN) member Burma, which has predominantly seen itself as part of the Theravada Buddhist world to its east, rather than the Hindu world to its west in which it was administratively located for no better reason than British colonial convenience. So although littoral can not be taken literally, the western reaches of the Pacific Ocean in Asia provide the frame in which to view Pacific Asia.

## Civilizational Perspective

Instead of describing areas in terms of positive or negative geography, a more fitting way to look at Asian peoples may be in terms of social groups. Beginning with the family and continuing with the village, the tribe, and the nation, the important question to be asked is, at what point in these peoples' self-consciousness does the "we" end and the "other" begin? The answer can be found by returning to Samuel Huntington's civilizational divides. Viewing world history as civilizational continuities may now approach the status of popular intuition, but it is a modern academic construct. The viewing of history in civilizational terms came to fruition only in the twentieth century, flowing from the work of Oswald Spengler and Arnold Toynbee.[5] Huntington consults this literature to arrive at his list of eight contemporary civilizations (the six below plus Japan and Latin America, which he accepts could also be included in Sinic and Western civilizations, respectively).[6] However, I prefer the conclusion that there are six major living civilizations, for which I employ boundaries of nation-states for ease of description, though the civilizational boundaries may be less distinct:

• Western: encompassing Europe, North America, Latin America, Australia, and New Zealand. Latin America is such a recent offspring of European civilization and its indigenous heritage has been so dominated by European settler society that, although the differences between North and South America are considerable, it cannot readily be seen as forming its own civilizational category.

• Orthodox Christian: comprised mainly of Slavic people such as the Russians and drawing on the Byzantine heritage.

• Islamic: originating on the Arabian Peninsula and progressively including North African, Turkic, and Persian cultures as well as strongly influencing aspects of Malay and Indic culture.

• Hindu: sometimes referred to as Indic civilization, including India and Pakistan as well as Bangladesh and Sri Lanka plus parts of Himalayan Asia.

• Sinic: sometimes referred to as Confucian civilization. Chinese civilization was the dominant influence in its region. Japanese civilization is an early offspring of the Chinese and may have grounds for arguing its distinctive character. Vietnam is a later offshoot. The Theravada Buddhist grouping of Burma, Cambodia, Laos, and Thailand may also have grounds to see itself as a separate civilization. Its earliest influences came from or through India, but Chinese influence was nevertheless strong, and in more modern times Chinese influence has waxed as Indian influence waned. Malay ethnicity has absorbed various cultural and religious influences, again originating from or through India, but like the Theravada Buddhist world, in more modern times, peninsula Southeast Asia must be seen as within the Sinic civilizational orbit. The influence of China over the millennia, and particularly in the few centuries before and during colonialism when Chinese diasporas in the region grew more powerful, has created Sinic civilizational bonds in the form of people, language, and culture throughout the region I have described as Pacific Asia.

• African: though this area lacks the broad religious basis and coherence of the others, Fernand Braudel includes Africa, south of the Sahara, in this list.[7]

The civilizational divides are not airtight and the boundaries and exact composition leave room for debate, but in the broad they provide the ultimate layer of the social self-conscious. Beyond these, "we" refers to a species or to the inhabitants of a planet. Even though it is the ultimate layer, many people will stop well short of it in their self-categorization. The Hmong have progressively moved south from China and may be citizens of several different neighboring countries and thus part of Sinic civilization by default, but they generally think of themselves only as members of the Hmong tribe.[8] Japanese, Koreans, Thais, and Vietnamese are understandably proud of their histories and achievements and many may therefore downplay their debt to Chinese heritage. Civilizational boundaries may go beyond political regionalism, and many people of the ten countries of ASEAN may well see this grouping as the limit of their self-categorization. This is an example of self-identification by way of allegiance. It does not deny the reality of the social and cultural heritage through which modern societies were shaped. So another answer to the question of what constitutes Pacific Asia may be seen in the context of Sinic civilization, which perhaps has now outgrown its Chinese ancestry and might better be called Pacific Asian civilization.

### Regional Economic and Political Architecture

A fifth perspective for an understanding of Pacific Asia is through the prism of regional economic and political architecture. Pacific Asia has not expressed the ambition to form an integrated community like the European Union, but it has expressed the goal of close cooperation and dialogue in the political, economic, and security fields. Accordingly, various regional organizations have been formed to bring together these regional political, economic, and security communities. The locus of these communities is ASEAN, which was established on 8 August 1967, by Indonesia, Malaysia, the Philippines, Singapore, and Thailand. Brunei joined in 1984, Vietnam in 1995, Laos and Myanmar (the military regime's official name for Burma) in 1997, and Cambodia in 1999.[9]

ASEAN began life in the shadow of the United States' Indochina War and after Sukarno's confrontation with Malaysia in the period 1962–1966. While the economic cooperation rhetoric has predominated, the security imperative has provided the underlying rationale for the organization. The membership of ASEAN by the three countries with communist leaderships from 1995 marked the formal conclusion of the Cold War in Southeast Asia. (Interestingly, while the symbol for the end of the Cold War in Europe was the destruction of the Berlin Wall, the symbol in Southeast Asia was the construction by Australia of the Friendship Bridge over the Mekong River between Thailand and Laos, thus linking the fraternal erstwhile Cold War enemies.) The various pieces of regional architecture have been constructed using ASEAN as their core. The annual meeting of

ASEAN and its dialogue partners constitutes the region's major political dialogue. The ASEAN Regional Forum (ARF) hosts the region's security dialogue. The APEC forum is the key grouping for economic issues, though it is increasingly also becoming the most important political organization in the region.

Alongside these groupings, the latest piece of regional architecture links the ten ASEAN countries with the other three major countries of Pacific Asia—China, Japan, and South Korea—in a forum described as ASEAN plus Three. The rationale is "strengthening and deepening East Asia cooperation at various levels and in various areas, particularly in economic and social, political, and other fields."[10] So this list of thirteen countries provides another means of appreciating the contours of Pacific Asia. Australia, New Zealand, and India joined this grouping in 2005 to form the East Asian Summit, and, should the regional imagination so develop, may well, in time, be seen as part of Pacific Asia.

The countries making up the various groupings in this regional architecture can be seen from the Venn diagram in Figure 2.1.

### Pacific Asia as an Imagined Community

A sixth and final way to look at Pacific Asia is to do so by adopting the insight offered to us by Benedict Anderson in his *Imagined Communities*.[11] In so doing, we leave the fields of geography and history and embark upon an examination of broad societal understandings. Anderson tracks the roots of nationalism in European culture and history but, surprisingly, finds that the concept took form outside Europe in the imaginations of the settler societies of the Americas. It required a break from the old continent, and its old religious modes of thought, to be able to perceive the world, and one's place in it, in a new spatial and temporal context. The key to this categorization is the group self-image and its boundaries. The countries of Pacific Asia remain strongly nationalistic, all the more so when nationalism is the best available justification of regime legitimacy in a world of discredited ideologies. In the ASEAN plus Three grouping we can perhaps see the embryonic image of a new community. The official rhetoric lends credence to this image: "While growing interdependence among East Asian countries in the age of globalization has been further strengthening regional cooperation, the 1997 Asian financial crisis has awakened the urgent need for institutionalized cooperation and stronger economic integration that transcends the geographical distinction between Northeast Asia and Southeast Asia."[12]

It must nevertheless be conceded that for this image to take hold among the people of the region, it will need to transcend its current top-down perspective, because this imagined community is currently primarily held in the imaginations of leaders and functionaries, not the masses of people. For the imagined community of Pacific Asia to take hold, the people of Pacific

**Figure 2.1  Pacific Asia's Political, Economic,
and Security Architecture, 2006**

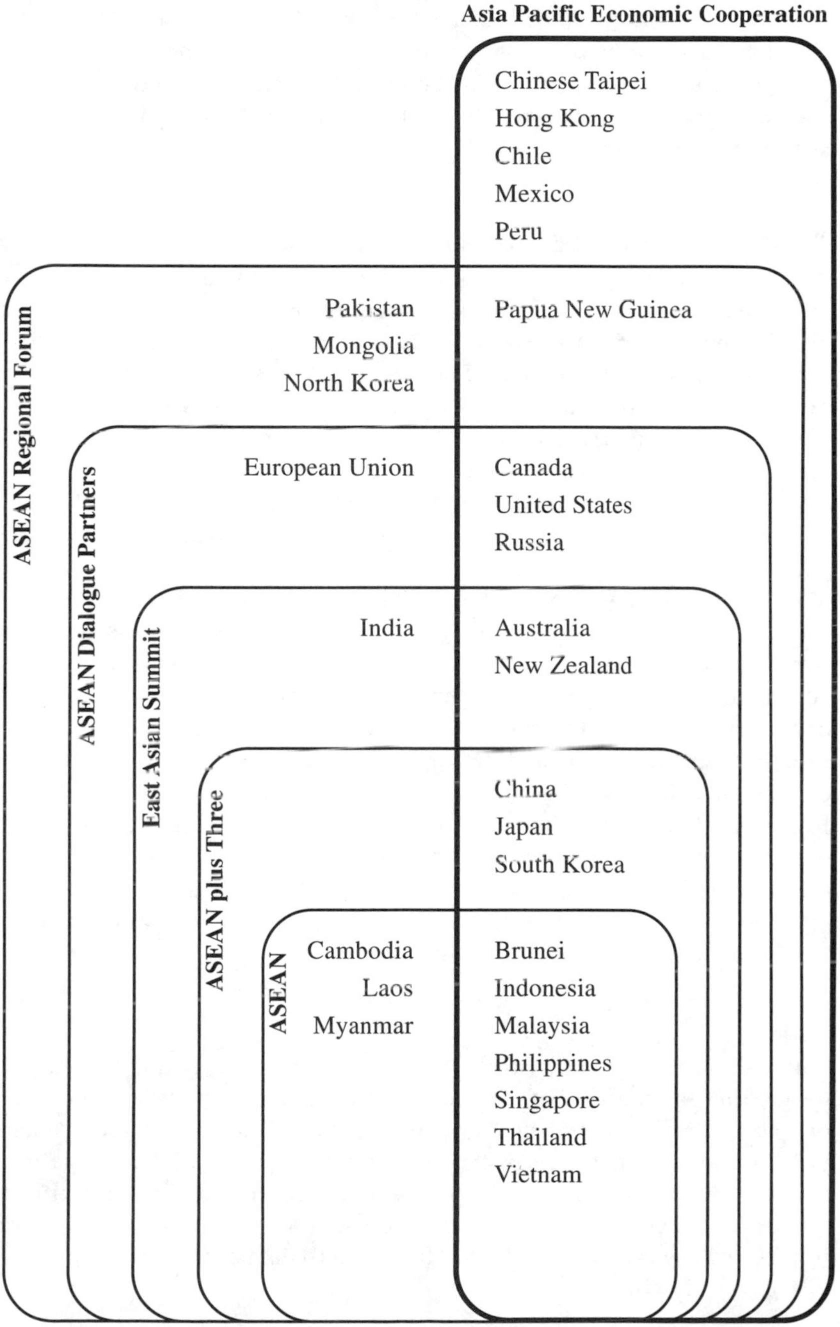

Asia Pacific Economic Cooperation

Chinese Taipei
Hong Kong
Chile
Mexico
Peru

ASEAN Regional Forum

Pakistan
Mongolia
North Korea

Papua New Guinea

ASEAN Dialogue Partners

European Union

Canada
United States
Russia

East Asian Summit

India

Australia
New Zealand

ASEAN plus Three

China
Japan
South Korea

ASEAN

Cambodia
Laos
Myanmar

Brunei
Indonesia
Malaysia
Philippines
Singapore
Thailand
Vietnam

Asia will need to imagine themselves as members of this wider community. It certainly cannot be said to be the case today in the way, for example, Europeans imagine themselves as part of the European family. But it does exist in embryonic form, particularly among the opinion leaders. One of the questions that will be posed throughout this book is whether there exists a Pacific Asian policy community that compares, evaluates, and borrows governance processes. In other words, do the nations of Pacific Asia follow and learn from each other's democratic progress?

## Five Democratizing Countries of Pacific Asia

Aside from the geographic, civilizational, architectural, and imagined ways of looking at Pacific Asia, perhaps it might be prudent simply to provide a list. This book is primarily about the five democratizing countries of Pacific Asia: Indonesia, the Philippines, South Korea, Taiwan, and Thailand. To the extent that it is part of the imagined democratic community of Pacific Asia, Japan is also examined. Because of its towering presence and influence as the world's most populous democracy, another Asian country, India, will also be referred to from time to time. Malaysia and Singapore are electoral democracies, but they cannot be described as liberal democracies on the path to democratic consolidation because of the continuing hold of aspects of soft authoritarianism. Nevertheless, because they are such obvious candidates for full democratization, they are also occasionally discussed in this work. Timor-Leste is the newest democracy in the region and therefore will be mentioned from time to time, but there is as yet little practice on which to base commentary. Insofar as there are other countries in Pacific Asia using some of the forms and part of the rhetoric of democracy, this book occasionally discusses Cambodia, Laos, and Vietnam. Totalitarian North Korea and dictatorial Burma may at times be raised because they provide a necessary (negative) perspective. And because it simply cannot be ignored, some concluding thoughts about China will also enter the debate.

This might be the place to make a few scene-setting comments about the five countries listed as democratizing.

### Indonesia

Indonesia is a colonial construct of the Dutch, who were first attracted to the archipelago in the sixteenth century by the lure of wealth in the form of spices. Dutch colonialism aside, the 17,000 islands of the archipelago had little to unite them given the vast ethnic, cultural, and language disparities. While Dutch colonialism was the key factor in determining Indonesia's boundaries, the archipelago's cultural legacies go far deeper in time, with waves of Buddhist, Hindu, and Islamic influences washing over its various local belief and social systems in the millennium before colonization. Today, one can survey these influences in the nation's architecture: the Buddhist temple of Borobudur, the Hindu temple of Prambanan, the mosques and *pesantran* (Islamic schools) dotting thousands of villages, and the colonial buildings of old Batavia, now Jakarta. Dutch colonialism did not penetrate deeply into the lives of the peasants and workers of the archipelago, but it nevertheless helped forge a national identity. Through the introduction of modern state-building institutions such as bureaucracies staffed by both expatriates and locals, through written laws and regulations, and by mediating access to European ideas and concepts through the Dutch language, the contemporary Indonesian state began to take shape.

Indonesia's declaration of independence, in August 1945 immediately prior to the surrender of the Japanese, who had invaded the archipelago in World War II, was not accepted by the returning colonial power and it would take several more years of fighting and negotiations before the Dutch relinquished all claims. The early years of independence saw the rise to power of the nationalist figure and gifted orator Sukarno, supported by Vice President Mohammed Hatta and Prime Minister Sjahrir. It was an unstable period when competing forces including nationalists, communists, Islamists, and regional champions struggled to influence the character of the new nation. This struggle took the form of contestation by political parties representing the various strands of thinking in what is referred to as the "parliamentary period," which had its high point in the 1955 free elections, a phenomenon that would not be repeated until 1999. Tiring of the fractiousness of parliamentary democracy, Sukarno decreed martial law in 1957 and proclaimed his "Guided Democracy" in 1959 under his authoritarian leadership with major support from the Communist Party of Indonesia (PKI).

The figure that would dominate Indonesia for the next three decades, Suharto, came to power in gradual steps. As a leading army general he opposed PKI influence, and when an abortive and indeed mysterious coup took place in 1965, he challenged Sukarno and assumed the leadership of the efforts to put down the supposed communist perpetrators, a process that would result in as many as half a million deaths. In 1967, Suharto became acting president and formally assumed this office the following year. He inaugurated the New Order, which brought a certain sense of purpose to Indonesia after the chaotic Sukarno years. The army was his enforcement tool and a newly established political party, Golkar, was his political tool. Unlike Sukarno's reliance on rhetoric and oratory, Suharto consciously staked his legitimacy on economic development. This formula produced three decades of growth sufficient to appease popular sentiments that to a certain extent accepted the authoritarianism and corruption of the Suharto

era. The 1997 financial crisis put an end to the New Order's economic success and, within a year, to Suharto's rule.

Suharto would tease visiting Australian prime ministers by noting how
many of them he had met in the course of his time as president. John
Howard was the seventh. These days it is John Howard who can tease his
Indonesian interlocutors, because Susilo Bambang Yudhoyono is the fifth
Indonesian president he has met. After Suharto's resignation, his vice president, B. J. Habibie, took over the reins for eighteen tempestuous months
during which time a raft of reforms and innovations were forced on him,
including the end of censorship, the proclamation of adherence to human
rights, the return to open contestation between political parties, and the
granting of an act of self-determination to Timor-Leste. After the 1999 election that marked Indonesia's return to electoral democracy, Abdurrahman
Wahid (better known as Gus Dur) took over in a period of continuing confusion but far fewer achievements until he was deposed by his vice president,
Megawati Sukarnoputri, daughter of the first president. Megawati dragged
Indonesia back to a period of relative calm by presiding over the affairs of
state rather than trying too much to influence their reform. That task has
now been left to the first directly elected president, Yudhoyono, who began
his five-year term in 2004.

Indonesia is a country of 245 million people, 90 percent of whom are
Muslims. It is the largest Muslim country in the world. Its success in consolidating its democracy would have consequences going well beyond its
immediate region of Southeast Asia. It would have implications for the
entire international community.

### The Philippines

There is a well-known shorthand version of Philippine modern history—
300 years in a Spanish convent, followed by 50 years in Hollywood.
Spanish colonialism began inauspiciously in 1521 when Ferdinand
Magellan landed at Mactan Island near Cebu, where he was killed by the
local chief Lapu-Lapu. The first Spanish settlement under Legaspi was
begun in 1565, and Manila was founded in 1572. Spanish colonialism
would last until 1898, when Spain was defeat by the United States in a war
over the issue of control of Cuba. After this defeat, Spain was forced to sell
Puerto Rico, Guam, and the Philippines to the United States for $20 million.
Unlike Dutch colonialism in Indonesia, Spanish colonialism fundamentally
changed the everyday lives of the local Malay people of the Philippines by
savagely destroying indigenous cultural and social systems and replacing
them with rigorous Spanish Catholicism. By the late nineteenth century,
educated Filipinos began their struggle for independence under the intellectual leadership of Jose Rizal and the military leadership of Emilio
Aguinaldo and his rival Andres Bonifacio. Victory over Spain was to come

indirectly via the 1898 victory of US forces, led by Admiral George Dewey, over the Spanish squadron in Manila, allowing Aguinaldo to declare independence that year. Fearing German claims over the Philippines, the United States took over from Spain as colonial master, triggering an insurrection that would last some fifteen years, ultimately to be repressed by brutal US tactics.

The United States began to prepare the Philippines for independence in the 1920s and 1930s, leading to commonwealth status in 1935. Independence finally came in 1946 after the defeat of the Japanese invaders. After 300 years of Spanish rule, the Philippines was a devoutly Catholic nation, though parts of its southern islands had retained their Islamic identity. US colonialism for 50 years had instilled in Philippine culture a facility with US political rhetoric and had established institutions of democratic government generally modeled on those of the United States. Colonialism did not extinguish the existing linguistic distinctions, and the Philippines remains divided into twelve major regional language groups, one of which, Tagalog, has been standardized as the national language. English is widely spoken, while Spanish remains spoken only by the "old money" elite of Manila.

The Philippines was one of the first colonies to gain independence. The early years were marked by a difficult rebellion inspired by communist ideas that was to last into the 1950s and eventually be succeeded by further communist insurgencies that continue in parts of the country to this day. Electoral politics maintained the dominant role of the elite, though reformist presidents like Ramon Magsaysay and Ferdinand Marcos were able to gain office. The initial achievements of the Marcos administration were compromised by his declaration of martial law in 1972, but he was to remain in power, with the tacit support of the United States, until 1986. By then, the Cold War had begun to thaw and the United States was content to look on as the "people power" revolution swept Corazon Aquino, widow of an assassinated opposition senator, to power. Since the grand hopes of those days, Philippine democracy has struggled and its economy, weighed down by inefficiency, corruption, and population pressure, has been outperformed by virtually all its neighbors. Fidel Ramos succeeded Aquino and seemed to reverse the nation's economic decline, but his accomplishments were compromised in the corrupt populist administration of Joseph "Erap" Estrada, who was chased from office half way through his term by another people power revolt after having lost the support and protection of the armed forces. His vice president, Gloria Macapagal-Arroyo, daughter of a previous president, succeeded him, completed his term, and won a further term in office. Her administration continues to be beset by deep social and structural problems in this complicated country of 90 million people.

## South Korea

To compare South Korea (the Republic of Korea) to Poland may seem whimsical as the two nations are so different in so many ways. But they share one important trait—they are both permanently condemned to be sandwiched between their regions' putative hegemons. Throughout its modern history, Poland could not escape its fate of being a natural battlefield between Germany and Russia. Throughout its history, Korea has had to contend with its position between China and Japan, which at times has enhanced Korea and at other times hobbled it. Given its borrowing of writing, Buddhist religion, and aspects of Confucianism from ancient China, Korea can confidently be said to be part of Sinic civilization. While the early period of Korean history saw enduring warfare with China, by the seventeenth century, it was Japan that posed the most potent threat. Modern Korean history is closely tied to Japan, which annexed Korea in 1910, in part because of its need for Korean natural resources and in part to forestall a possible similar move by Russia. Perhaps this uncomfortable geography best explains why Korea was long known as the "Hermit Kingdom" that tried to shut itself off from the rest of the world.

Given the one and a half millennia of its existence as a unit, Korea can certainly be said to have achieved the status of a unified imagined community. It is ethnically homogeneous with no significant minorities living among the Koreans, though today South Korea plays host to half a million guest workers. Korea is linguistically homogeneous and the writing script, *hangul*, developed in the fifteenth century by King Sejong, came into use throughout Korean lands. In view of this degree of homogeneity, it is an ironic fact of Korea's existence that its main political feature today is marked by a deep division. The end of World War II and the decolonization that accompanied it did not restore Korea as a single nation. The Cold War engineered a division of the country along the 38th parallel that has seen South Korea prosper as a market-driven country with a population today approaching the 50 million mark, and North Korea, with a population of 23 million, fall into a state of penury under an obscure form of autarky and governed under a mystifying cult of personality. Yet even in South Korea, homogeneity did not lead to uniformity of political perspectives as the nation maintained its own deep division into three regions: Kyongsang in the southwest, Cholla in the southeast, and Chungchong in the central areas. One of the most surprising features of South Korean politics has been the enduring hold of regionalism on the body politic.

The Cold War also is the key to understanding the governance system in Seoul over the past several decades. Having fought a bitter civil war to a standstill, a devastated nation and its US and allied supporters asked for little more than a strong government to be in charge both politically and economically. After the civil war, the president of pre–civil war Korea,

Syngman Rhee, returned to lead South Korea and remained an autocratic leader until toppled by the student revolts of 1960. In a reaction to Syngman Rhee's unpopular rule, South Korea turned briefly to a parliamentary form of governance under Prime Minister Chang Myon but he was soon sidelined in a military coup from which General Park Chung Hee eventually emerged as leader in a return to presidential government. First elected president in 1963, he was twice reelected, beating Kim Dae Jung in 1971. Thereafter, he declared martial law and ruled unfettered by any checks or balances until his assassination in 1979. In the course of his long term in office, South Korea's economic development took off under a form of partnership between government and the dozen or so *chaebols*, Korea's giant business conglomerates.

The military retained the reins of government, first through General Chun Doo Hwan and then his colleague, General Roh Tae Woo. While South Korea went from strength to strength economically under the generals' rule, there was growing civil society opposition to military rule, which in 1980 in Gwangju had to be violently suppressed. The end of the Cold War saw the end of tolerance for military rule and insistent demands for democratic governance. When Kim Young Sam was elected president in 1992, he became the first civilian president in thirty years. In 1997, he was followed in office by Kim Dae Jung, the perennial oppositionist, and in 2002, another outsider, Roh Moo Hyun, was elected as president. While developments since the end of the Cold War have no doubt seen the end of military rule in South Korea, some of the key institutions of democracy, such as a party system and a well-oiled legal system, are still under construction.

## Taiwan

Taiwan's politics is dominated by its relationship to the Chinese mainland. Although human settlement in Taiwan dates back several tens of thousands of years, the link with the mainland is far more recent. While there was contact with the mainland and even some Han Chinese settlement in Taiwan, it was the Netherlands who established a settlement and made Taiwan their colony in the seventeenth century. The Dutch were soon defeated by the Ming dynasty's naval power, and from 1662 Taiwan was administered as part of China. This was to last until 1895 when Taiwan was ceded to Japan following China's defeat in war. Taiwan was ruled as a Japanese colony until Japan's defeat in World War II.

Taiwan thus returned as a part of China in 1945 but was administered from the mainland for only a few years because, with the communist victory over the Nationalist Kuomintang (KMT) in the Chinese civil war, General Chiang Kai-shek retreated to Taiwan, and it has been governed from Taipei ever since. Some 1.3 million refugees from mainland China, including Nationalist soldiers, KMT party members, and dispossessed mainlanders, arrived in Taiwan at that time and proceeded to dominate the economy and administration of the island. The KMT saw itself as the continuing government of the whole of China and, until 1971, even represented the whole of China at the UN under its formal title as the Republic of China (ROC).

Chiang Kai-shek's rule was to last until his death in 1975. It could be characterized as autocratic, mainland dominated, and gaining its legitimacy mainly through its relationship with the United States as well as its solid economic performance. The success of this formula was clearly tied to the politics of the Cold War, and as that conflict showed signs of waning, Taiwan would need to search for another formula for legitimacy and domestic support. The general's son, Chiang Ching-kuo, took charge, and in his term of office gradual economic and political liberalization began to take place. Martial law, in place since the arrival of the KMT in 1948, was lifted in 1987, and the opposition Democratic Progressive Party (DPP) was formed from a mixture of opposition groups and allowed to participate openly in politics. After Chiang Ching-kuo died in 1988, Vice President Lee Teng-hui became the first Taiwan-born president and chairman of the KMT. Lee also became the first ROC president elected by popular vote in 1996. While allowing for a continuation of KMT rule, Lee's election was a harbinger of deep changes in Taiwanese politics. The nativist voice, so long muted by mainlander dominance, began to be heard and would soon form a dominant theme of politics.

The DPP was to tap into this nativist revival and profit politically from it, given the preponderance of native born in the voting population. In 2000, Chen Shui-bian won the presidential election, which he described as the first ever peaceful democratic transition of power to an opposition party in Chinese history. It also ended the KMT's monopoly in holding all positions in government service. Chen won a second term as president in 2004, but his means to power became a burden when in office. Unlike the KMT, whose history tied it closely with the mainland and who therefore kept comfortably to the reunification rhetoric, the DPP had a different constituency. Chen stirred hopes among his nativist supporters of a formalization of Taiwan's self-governing status, but China made it clear that it would regard a declaration of independence by its "province" as a cause for war. Chen's incumbency has been like walking a tightrope between these nativist ambitions and global realpolitik where he finds so little support for any independence ambitions.

Taiwan's legitimacy now flows less from economic success and the US link and far more from the democratic transition accomplished by its 23 million people. The irony is that it is the democratic transition and the voice it has given to nativist sentiments that have increased the tensions in the region as the DPP searches for gestures short of independence that will appease its supporters while not triggering a violent reaction in Beijing. Whether it likes it or not, Taiwan's politics remains dominated by the issue of its link with the mainland.

## Thailand

Thai-speaking people have lived in Southeast Asia for a thousand years and formed their first kingdom at Sukhothai in central Thailand in the thirteenth century. While the modern histories of so many developing countries are dominated by their colonial experience, the key feature of Thailand's modern history is that it was never colonized. The balance between the British and French colonial empires was maintained by retaining Thailand as a buffer state. This narrow advantage was cleverly played out by Thailand's nineteenth-century kings, whose tactic it was to modernize like the Europeans and to take on some of their political discourse. Modernization was initiated by King Mongkut, a process depicted in Western cinema in *The King and I,* the story of the British woman Anna Leonowens, who became governess to the king's children. It gained momentum under his successor, King Chulalongkorn. Faced with threatening British and French colonial powers at its borders, Siam, as Thailand was then called, strove to demonstrate that it was a sovereign equal, not a putative vassal. The pressure exerted by colonizing powers was difficult to manage and was described by Mongkut as like having to decide whether "to swim upriver and make friends with the crocodile (the French) or to swim out to sea and hang on to the whale (the British)."[13] As it turned out, Thailand borrowed selectively from various models and managed to play off the colonial superpowers of the day.

The bloodless coup of 1932 is probably the most appropriate starting point for modern Thai politics because this is when the principles of constitutional monarchy were introduced. The next sixty years of Thai politics might be described as the process of learning how to live up to the high ideals of constitutional monarchy, and the last decade can be seen as the struggle to make constitutional democracy work. As of September 2006, Thailand has had seventeen constitutions, most of which were drafted as exercises in how to maintain power rather than limit it. After the 1932 coup, the monarchy lost absolute power, which was thereafter held by a partnership of military and bureaucratic elites and only marginally constrained by courts, parliaments, or civil society. The elites spawned various military and civilian leaders, some of whom, like General Prem Tinsulanonda, prime minister for most of the 1980s, were more competent and honest than others. While elections continued to be held, they were less influential in determining national political leadership than palace coups.

The halting progress toward democracy suffered a serious setback in 1992 when the military killed dozens of civilian demonstrators protesting the assumption of power by General Suchinda Kraprayoon. With the Cold War ended, the tolerance for military strongmen had well and truly ebbed, and the Thai middle class, a growing segment of the 65 million strong population, demanded change. This was to come in the form of the 1997 Constitution, which inaugurated a new period of purpose-designed parliamentary democracy. Ironically, the greatest challenge to parliamentary democracy in Thailand came from its greatest beneficiary, Prime Minister Thaksin Shinawatra, who twice defied the factionalism of Thai party politics to win huge parliamentary majorities for his Thai Rak Thai Party. Thaksin's penchant to behave like a powerful corporate chief executive officer (CEO) rather than a democratic leader posed a challenge to the entire system. Probably with the consent of the king, the Thai military overturned Thaksin's government in September 2006 and decreed an interim constitution. Thailand's return to democracy remains unfulfilled and uncertain.

Another challenge facing Thailand is the succession to King Bhumibol Adulyadej, Thailand's Ninth Rama. Born in 1927 and having ascended the throne in 1946, he is the world's longest reigning monarch and has several times made decisive interventions in Thai politics. The interventions did not require the deployment of any formal reserve powers but simply manifestations of his displeasure with individual politicians. Because of the esteem in which the king is held in Thailand, such displeasure is sufficient to influence political developments and, as shown in 2006, to move the military. It is not clear if King Bhumibol's successor will carry the same weight in domestic politics.

## Conclusion

Before the end of the Cold War, there would have been little point in examining democratic practice in Pacific Asia. As noted in the opening chapter, in 1975, democracy was practiced nowhere on the Asian mainland. The term itself would have had little resonance because the main division of the continent remained that between the communist and capitalist worlds and there would have been very little substance on which to construct a Pacific Asian community or to examine democratic practice. The Cold War no longer has a decisive influence on Pacific Asia even though its echo remains in the form of the various communist regimes in the region and two divided nations.

The most influential development in Pacific Asia since the end of the Cold War has been the burgeoning of the practice of democracy. With that growing practice and as each year passes in which electorates and elites gain greater confidence in its practice, there is today considerable substance for analysis. It can now be said that the countries building their democracies form a certain *critical mass* in Pacific Asia. After all, the five democratizing countries of Pacific Asia have a combined population of almost half a billion, not counting democratic Japan's 130 million people. Since the people power revolution in the Philippines, the five democratizing countries have held many elections, have seen governments come and go peacefully, and have, with the glaring Thai exception, respected constitutional requirements. This amounts to critical mass in practice as well as critical mass in size. Do the democracies of Pacific Asia form a community? Are they capable, as Peter Preston speculates in the quotation opening this chapter, of forming a Pacific Asian model of democracy? These are questions I shall tackle in the final chapter, after exploring the growth of democracy in more detail.

## Notes

1. P. W. Preston, *Pacific Asia in the Global System: An Introduction* (Oxford: Blackwell Publishers, 1998), p. 196.
2. The following recent titles include the term *Pacific Asia*: Mark Borthwick, *Pacific Century: The Emergence of Modern Pacific Asia*, 2nd ed. (Boulder: Westview Press, 1998); David Drakakis-Smith, *Pacific Asia (Routledge Introductions to Development)* (London and New York: Routledge Publishers, 1992); David Goodman and Gerald Segal, *Towards Recovery in Pacific Asia (ESRC Pacific Asia)*, 1st ed. (London and New York: Routledge, 2000); David Martin Jones, *Political Development in Pacific Asia* (Cambridge: Polity Press, 1997); Fu-chen Lo and Yue-man Yeung (eds.), *Emerging World Cities in Pacific Asia* (Tokyo: United Nations University Press, 1993); Duncan McCargo, *Media and Politics in Pacific Asia* (London: Routledge Publishers, 2002); P. W. Preston, *Pacific Asia in the Global System*; Yumei Zhang, *Pacific Asia (The Making of the Contemporary World)*, 1st ed. (London and New York: Routledge, 2002).
3. Edward Said, *Orientalism* (London: Peregrine Books, 1985).
4. Grant Evans, *Asia's Cultural Mosaic—An Anthropological Introduction* (Singapore: Prentice Hall, 1993), p. 1.
5. Explained in Peter Cruttwell, *History Out of Control—Confronting Global Anarchy* (Devon, UK: Resurgence Books, 1995).
6. Samuel Huntington, *The Clash of Civilizations and the Remaking of World Order* (New York: Simon and Schuster, 1996), pp. 45–47.
7. Fernand Braudel, *A History of Civilization* (trans. by Richard Mayne) (New York: Allen Lane, The Penguin Press, 1994).
8. See Nicholas Tapp et al. (eds.), *Hmong/Miao in Asia* (Chiang Mai: Silkworm Press, 2004).
9. ASEAN website, available at www.aseansec.org.
10. Ibid.
11. Benedict Anderson, *Imagined Communities*, 2nd ed. (London: Verso, 1991).
12. ASEAN Secretariat, "Final Report of the East Asia Study Group," 4 November 2002, p. 1, available from www.aseansec.org/viewpdf.asp?file=/pdf/easg.pdf.
13. Quoted from Seni Pramoj and Kukrit Pramoj, *A King of Siam Speaks*, in Paul Kratoska and Ben Batson, "Nationalism and Modernist Reform," Nicholas Tarling (ed.), *The Cambridge History of Southeast Asia—Volume Two: The Nineteenth and Twentieth Centuries* (Cambridge: Cambridge University Press, 1992), p. 292.

# 3

# Crafting
# Democratic Institutions

"Historical legacies do not fully disappear, and socioeconomic
transformation cannot be achieved by fiat, so we are left with
the search for those political institutions that will best suit
the circumstances of this or that particular country."
—Juan J. Linz, "The Virtues of Parliamentarism"[1]

## A Laboratory for Democracy

In a paper I wrote in 2001, I described Asia as a "laboratory for democracy
in the twenty-first century."[2] This reflected the ferment evident within
democratizing Asia in constructing democratic institutions, learning democratic practice, and shaping democratic culture. Unlike the first and second
wave democracies, which have largely settled on their democratic forms
and practices, with electoral systems and the basic structure of government
well established and understood, Asian democracies are drafting constitutions, experimenting with electoral systems, and debating government systems. It is perhaps this ferment in the third wave democracies that is encouraging the established democracies to dust off their design books and look
again at their own institutions of democracy.

Pippa Norris noted that when Arend Lijphart conducted his study of
established democracies, he found that only one[3] had instituted major
changes in its electoral system in the period 1945–1990, yet since that time
five[4] have made major changes and three[5] have undertaken more modest
reforms.[6] Since Giuseppe Di Palma in 1990[7] enjoined the transition democracies to "craft" their democratic systems to meet their particular needs and
circumstances, an industry of craftspeople has arisen to help design and
build the required institutions. Yet for all the energy being put into the
design of democratic institutions, the exercise is not without its dilemmas.
The basic question that haunts the crafters of these new institutions is

whether such bodies can indeed be successfully crafted or whether they can only succeed if they have evolved over considerable time and been tested under diverse conditions. In other words, can political evolution be short-cut by clever design? A corollary dilemma is whether this question can only be answered *after* the event, so that those caught in the midst of designing institutions and implementing those designs simply do not know whether the fruit of their labors will take root and mature.

This chapter will examine the process of institution design in Pacific Asia and attempt to grapple with these dilemmas. It will begin with a discussion of a preliminary problem concerning the degree of *systematization* of the various countries under review. The more systematized, the greater the chance of the intent of the institutional designers being fulfilled. It will then briefly examine three of the key institutional features of democracies: parliaments, electoral systems, and accountability institutions. In so doing, the chapter does not attempt to conduct a comprehensive survey but rather looks for seminal developments, key innovations, and whether there is any evidence of regional coherence in design fashions.

An overarching feature that needs to be highlighted at this point is the considerable scale and strength of the institutional design project in Pacific Asia. The starkest evidence for this is in the energy being invested in constitution drafting. Since the end of the Cold War, and the freedom it has given the region to review governance structures, the democratizing nations of Pacific Asia have been engaged in a strenuous process of drafting, revising, and amending their constitutions. The issue of the impact of constitutionality on democracy is discussed in the following chapter dealing with the rule of law. In relation to the issue of institutional design, it is simply worth noting the national deliberative energies being applied to settling basic questions about governance machinery and processes. Constitution drafting in Pacific Asia entails both adapting existing constructions and crafting new ones. The governance innovations being developed in these instruments are sometimes obscured by the publicity given to the international implications. Amending Taiwan's constitution attracts interest because of its possible implication for the island's independence, which China has consistently described as a casus belli. Japan's constitutional debate is dominated by discussion on Article IX renouncing war and whether the time has come to change the basis of Japan's defense arrangements. Beyond these headline stories has been a less well known story of resourcefulness, originality, and experimentation. Table 3.1 shows ongoing constitutional activity in Pacific Asia in the post–Cold War period.

## Degree of Systematization

In 2004, I conducted research on the issue of political parties in the Pacific islands. It is not a particularly encouraging story, and the weakness of par-

**Table 3.1  Constitution Drafting in Pacific Asia, Post–Cold War Period to 2006**

| Country | Year | Description |
|---|---|---|
| Philippines | 1987 | Fourth constitution |
| South Korea | 1987 | Ninth revision |
| Taiwan | 1991–2000 | Six revisions |
| | 2005 | Seventh revision |
| Thailand | 1991 | Charter of Administration (fourteenth constitution) |
| | 1991 | Fifteenth constitution |
| | 1997 | Sixteenth constitution |
| | 2006 | Seventeenth constitution |
| Indonesia | 1999–2002 | Four major amendments |
| Timor-Leste | 2002 | Independence constitution |
| Japan | 2010 | First amendment possible |

ties and party systems in some of the Pacific island polities has compromised the quality of their democracies. When I posed the question of why the many craftspeople who had worked on these political and electoral systems had not achieved a better result, I came to a disturbing conclusion: "The South Pacific may prove to be so under systematized as to be impervious to institutional redesign."[8] The level of systematization is an underappreciated premise in our understanding of the process of crafting democratic institutions. Where the plan on the drawing board has only a tenuous relationship to the reality on the ground, it is no wonder that the plan does not work well. So, where the government's writ does not run very much further than its own offices, where the rules of the game are so sporadically enforced as to become empty threats, where office bearers consistently manipulate the system to their own benefit, where accountability officials usually turn a blind eye to these manipulations, and where the public has become so inured to the abuses that it takes them as standard procedures, it is little wonder that even the best designs turn out to have little impact. I cannot rid myself of the vision of election day in the highlands of Papua New Guinea (PNG) where a candidate's supporters had confiscated reams of blank ballot papers and were studiously filling them all in. All the engaged debates and careful designs about electoral systems become fairly meaningless in such an environment.

The concept of systematization fits in between notions of "stateness" and "institutionalization," and is linked to both. *Stateness* concerns the relationship between the territorial unit of the state and the perceptions of national belonging of the people who inhabit this territory.[9] *Institutionalization* is more closely linked to public sector organizations and the process whereby those organizations and their procedures "acquire value and stability."[10] Systematization deals with the degree to which reality matches society's rules and rhetoric of governance. It encompasses the behavior of both the population of a state and its organizations. Systematization therefore concerns the proper functioning of the processes influencing a state's public space.[11] The preliminary question that arises before we begin to assess the design work being done in the "laboratory of democracy" is whether the experimentation will remain theoretical or, alternatively, whether the newly crafted designs will in fact be properly tested in the field. I believe the broad answer is that the countries of Pacific Asia are generally sufficiently systematized to allow institutional design to be an effective tool in the consolidation of democracy. The level of systematization varies in the region and in most cases may not be as complete as in many established democracies, but it is nevertheless sufficient to allow the designs to take effect. Two forces that greatly weaken the level of systematization—corruption and violence—will be discussed in this section.

An example of systematization through the interface of institutional changes with their public acceptance might be seen in comparing the introduction of compulsory voting in Australia and Thailand. In Australia, compulsory voting was introduced in 1924 after almost a quarter of a century of debate as to its merits, with a major argument being that it would take the pressure off political parties to "get out the vote" and thus allow them to concentrate on policy issues. The result was that voting jumped from 59 percent of the electorate in the 1922 House of Representatives elections to 91 percent in the 1925 election.[12] Voter turnout continued to rise and now consistently hovers around 95 percent.[13] The design idea proved to be capable of implementation, and the impact has been that Australian political parties spend very little energy on cajoling and transporting people to vote. Thailand's 1997 Constitution also established compulsory voting,[14] in part because of the view that with the higher number of voters, it would become too expensive to try to buy votes and the problem of money politics would diminish in significance. In the 1996 parliamentary elections, voter turnout was already quite high at 65 percent, but with the introduction of compulsory voting it jumped to over 70 percent in 2000.[15] In the 2005 elections, the figure reached 72.3 percent.[16] The increase in voter turnout is perhaps not as dramatic as in Australia, but it is nevertheless significant and it suggests a capacity to implement the designers' plan. That does not mean, however, that the design will necessarily achieve its intent. Vote buying remains a difficult problem to eradicate, but the tool of compulsory voting, together with other institutional designs such as counting the vote in provincial centers so that the tally for individual villages is now unknown (and therefore cannot be rewarded according to a preexisting deal), could over time shrink this problem.[17] On this issue, the degree of systematization in Thailand is sufficient to warrant the attempt at new institutional designs.

Systematization has impacts on the workings of the machinery of governance in terms of enforcement and effectiveness. Its presence is an underlying, though often unstated, assumption of those advocating recrafting institutional designs. Only in sufficiently systematized political processes will institutional designs have an impact allowing electorates to react to them in a rational manner. A PNG highlander seeing a candidate's kinfolk capture the ballot papers will be forgiven for not standing in line to vote, regardless of whether the system is first past the post (FPTP) or single transferable vote. Leaving the extremes of the PNG highlands and returning to Thailand, the penalty of the loss of the right to vote at the next election due to failure to vote is so weak that it detracts from the effectiveness of the rule and thus diminishes the systematization of compulsory voting design. Members of the Thai Constitutional Drafting Assembly for the 1997 Constitution told me that they had considered more severe penalties, like the fine imposed in Australia, but decided that it would not be appropriate in a country with many poor people. Whether a fully implemented compulsory voting rule will have the desired impact on money politics is not clear. What is clear is that the limited degree to which compulsory voting is able to be put into practice in Thailand limits its capacity to make vote buying too expensive. One of the lessons learned may be to postulate that the degree of systematization of the machinery of governance will have a commensurate impact on the achievement of the intended benefits of the institutional design.

## Violence

The countries of Pacific Asia under review are sufficiently systematized to reward the energies required to institute new governance designs. But two important factors militating against systematization—violence and corruption—are problem areas. Violence imposes its own logic on the political process and defeats the plans of the designers and implementers. Violence is endemic in society, but political violence need not be. It is a plausible goal to make violence an insignificant aspect of politics. The first step is to formalize and legitimize the use of violence by the state while spelling out the limits on its use. Authoritarian governments are not greatly constrained in their use of violence against their citizens; democratic states are. An important condition is therefore the establishment of the rule of law. But even within polities where the state does not use violence as a political weapon, other actors may. The question we need to pose is not whether violence exists in politics in Pacific Asia, but whether it is significant in determining political outcomes. The answer is generally encouraging.

In some provinces of the Philippines, violence has traditionally been the way to rid oneself of political enemies and to extort money for electoral campaigns, often from criminal gangs who thereby subsequently gain protection from the successful candidate.[18] The continuing level of violence is unacceptable. In elections over the six years to 2004, the total number of casualties was 962.[19] Some of these victims were candidates, but the majority were the goons (from the famous Philippine political formula of "guns, goons, and gold") fighting against each other. Sheila Coronel notes, however, that generally, "violence is not a requisite for electoral success."[20] It cannot be said that violence is the key to success in Philippine politics, though it may be a contributing factor in certain parts of the country.

Whereas the basic organizer of political violence in the Philippines is the provincial clan, in Indonesia it tends to be associated more with political parties. Under Suharto's New Order, the state had shown a tolerance for civilian groups to be organized in paramilitary fashion acting as proxies for the state.[21] The practice of using militia in places like East Timor and West Papua was significantly extended to the political heartland after the fall of Suharto, with the establishment by General Wiranto of the 30,000 strong Pamswarkasa forces drawn from existing Golkar support groups, as well as martial arts groups and unemployed petty criminals.[22] Pamswarkasa proved unwieldy and failed, but it set an example for other political groups to follow. Political forces like Democratic Party of Indonesia–Struggle (PDI-P) and Nahdatul Ulama, which already had modest paramilitary forces, now expanded these to match Pamswarkasa, setting a pattern that one commentator describes as a "party arms race."[23] The phenomenon of criminals gravitating toward politics is not unknown in transition democracies, and it is disturbingly evident in Indonesia. A case has been argued that violence is becoming an embedded feature of the struggle for power and resources at the local level as a result of Indonesia's radical decentralization process.[24] It is noteworthy, however, that in 2004 more than 100 million people voted three times in national elections in Indonesia with virtually no violence reported, testimony to the effectiveness of the Indonesian Electoral Commission's regulations restricting the use of party forces during the election period.[25]

The occasional violent episode still persists in the other democratizing countries of Pacific Asia, most often associated with feuds between local politicians. Thai thugs may patrol their political paymasters' domains, and occasionally a local canvasser may be killed for failing to deliver promised and paid-for votes.[26] But these types of incidents are not the rule, especially as Thai politics becomes increasingly professionalized. Occasionally, violence can be seen on the national stage. In the 2004 presidential elections in Taiwan, some commentators discussed the possibility that Chen's narrow victory was due to "the strange shooting episode" in which the president and Vice President Annette Lu were slightly injured—a purported assassination attempt—on the eve of the vote.[27] The sympathy thus generated may have been sufficient to secure the victory. Once again, episodes of this type are exceptional in most of the countries under review.

## Corruption

The other major distortion to systematization in Pacific Asia, corruption, is a far more widespread phenomenon. Corruption distorts the intent of institutional design and can nullify the intended benefits. Corruption is inimical to the development of a quality democracy for many reasons, including unfairness, compromised meritocracy, and the skewing of distribution of wealth. It is particularly corrosive to the political process because it devalues decisions taken through deliberative and democratic means in favor of results achieved through secretive and unregulated means. Like violence, it constructs a different logic in the political system. Many of the rules and innovations being developed in modern governance systems are intended to deal with the issue of corruption by establishing effective systems of accountability and the necessary degree of transparency in government processes. Asia is in great need of such systems, as the 1997 financial crisis demonstrated. As one commentator put it,

> Almost everywhere in Asia, countries needed far-reaching economic changes: stronger rule of law, swifter bankruptcy proceedings and accounting standards, better capital and bond markets, and a focus on efficiency and profits . . . the most essential changes in Asia have, in a sense, been the least flashy, the least remarked on: the political restructuring that is changing the way these countries work.[28]

Corruption is a problem in virtually all parts of Asia. Because its extent is hidden, it is difficult to measure, even though citizens routinely come across it in their everyday lives. One imperfect method of gaining an impression of the extent of corruption is by measuring the perceptions held by businesspeople and others who know the local market and deal with officialdom. Transparency International has been conducting its Corruption Perception Index since 1995.[29] Table 3.2 plots the comparative place of the countries of democratizing Asia.

There is clearly a corruption problem in the Asian democracies. Even Japan's current high rating puts it outside the top 10 percent. The regional average position lies somewhere in the middle, with the Philippines and Indonesia being particularly poorly rated in 2006. There might, however, be a suggestion from Table 3.2 that the situation is slowly but steadily improving, as the average rating score has risen and the average position has climbed up the list in each of the surveys undertaken in this period. Dealing with corruption nevertheless remains one of the great issues facing institutional design specialists, and Asian countries have been at the forefront of experimentation in designing and implementing accountability mechanisms for the public sector, some of which will be discussed in the last section of this chapter.

There are other factors that weaken systematization. Illiteracy makes it

**Table 3.2   Corruption Perception Index, Democratizing Asian Countries, 2000–2006**

| Country | Position 2006 | Score 2006 | Position 2004 | Score 2004 | Position 2002 | Score 2002 | Position 2000 | Score 2000 |
|---|---|---|---|---|---|---|---|---|
| Japan | 17th | 7.6 | 24th | 6.9 | 20th | 7.1 | 23rd | 6.4 |
| Taiwan | 34th | 5.9 | 35th | 5.6 | 29th | 5.6 | 28th | 5.5 |
| Korea | 42nd | 5.1 | 47th | 4.5 | 40th | 4.5 | 48th | 4.0 |
| Thailand | 63rd | 3.6 | 64th | 3.6 | 64th | 3.2 | 60th | 3.2 |
| India | 70th | 3.3 | 90th | 2.8 | 71st | 2.7 | 69th | 2.8 |
| Philippines | 121st | 2.5 | 102nd | 2.6 | 77th | 2.6 | 69th | 2.8 |
| Indonesia | 130th | 2.4 | 133rd | 2.0 | 96th | 1.9 | 85th | 1.7 |
| Regional average | 68th of 163 (.417) | 4.3 | 70th of 146 (.479) | 4.0 | 56th of 102 (.549) | 3.9 | 55th of 90 (.611) | 3.8 |

particularly difficult to educate the electorate about institutional processes. Widespread poverty poses a similar problem. Insurgency clearly impacts negatively on systematization. Pacific Asia has to a significant extent dealt successfully with these major problems. Indonesia, Thailand, and the Philippines continue to suffer from each of these problems, but poverty and illiteracy are not widespread and insurgencies tend to be on the peripheries of these countries, with relatively little impact on the heartland. So the designers can have some confidence that their designs for representative bodies, electoral systems, and accountability institutions have the possibility of being effective.

## Making Parliaments Perform

One of my tasks when running Australia's democracy promotion center was to bring together Australian parliamentarians with their counterparts from the region. I steered the subject matter of discussions in these meetings away from bilateral relations and toward parliamentarism. After all, the purpose of Australia's democracy promotion was to strengthen neighboring parliaments, not to work through issues on the bilateral agenda. In visits to Asian capitals our parliamentary delegations would be caught in a strange dichotomy. Although Australia is a geologically old continent peopled for tens of thousands of years by the Aboriginals, its modern history begins quite recently in 1788. Australians traveling to the ancient kingdoms and sultanates of Asia are very conscious of the contrast between the representatives of millennial Asian polities and themselves, brash upstarts down under. We are in awe of Angkor Wat or Ayutthaya or Borobudur, partly because of their architectural splendor, but perhaps even more so because they tell us something about the historical and social depth of the societies we are visiting. But when the discussions on parliamentary practice begin, the roles immediately reverse. The Australian federal parliament has functioned continuously and effectively for over a century, and it is built on the knowledge accumulated in the various Australian state parliaments that predate it by half a century and, of course, on the traditions of Westminster over preceding centuries. Among our interlocutors, on the other hand, were the first freely and fairly elected Indonesian parliamentarians since 1955, the first elected Thai senators, and the first-ever Cambodian senators. The Australians therefore had the "street smarts" when it came to the workings of elected representative legislatures and, hopefully, were able to pass on some useful insights.

## Postcolonial Designs

As noted in the previous chapter, the pattern of politics in postcolonial Pacific Asia was the speedy replacement of hastily erected parliamentary government by authoritarian figures. In Thailand, from the proclamation of the 1932 Constitution right up to the early 1990s, the elected civilian politicians were subservient to the military and bureaucratic cliques that competed and cooperated to govern the kingdom. In Indonesia, a form of parliamentary democracy began upon the departure of the Dutch in 1949, but the assembly elected in 1955 only functioned until Sukarno declared martial law in 1957. The South Korean parliamentary system fared little better. Syngman Rhee battled the parliamentary opposition using "a campaign of terror" and setting the pattern of strongman rule that would be further elaborated by Park Chung Hee.[30] It would not be until the end of the Cold War that the South Korean National Assembly would become a significant decisionmaking institution. The Chinese parliamentary system under the Kuomintang met for a few years and adopted the Nanking Constitution, but with Mao's victory and the retreat to Taiwan, the assembly was effectively anesthetized, only to awake after the Cold War thawed.

The Philippine Congress fared slightly better. Adapting the US system to the needs of the provincial elite, the Philippines of the 1950s and 1960s was able to hold elections on a regular basis, and while they were bedeviled by the "guns, goons, and gold" political mentality, there were examples, such as the 1951 congressional elections and the 1953 presidential elections, that were considered to be "remarkably clean."[31] Marcos declared martial law in 1972 by relying on the ever dependable communist threat of the period. With the fall of Marcos, the Philippines could return to its cacique democracy. India has consolidated its democracy, but it should be recalled that there was a moment of doubt in 1975 when Indira Gandhi, seeing her popularity and control slipping, declared her emergency. By 1977, however, India had found its way back to its democratic path and the houses of parliament have been the effective houses of government ever since. Of the countries under the purview of this study, only Japan's Diet has met regularly and constitutionally since its post–World War II constitution was promulgated, though it should be noted that for much of the time, under the "1955 system" of domination by the Liberal Democratic Party (LDP), most of the power sat in other institutions. Table 3.3 shows how tenuous parliamentary democracy was in the post–World War II period in Asia's democracies.

Perhaps an argument can be made that the initial parliamentary and governance designs were inappropriate to the circumstances of these nations. The basic point needs to be accepted that the various designs all originate from Western practice. Arguments about early democracy in India[32] or the casting of lots thousands of years ago in Asia Minor[33] tell us something important about humankind's disposition for self-government, but they do not explain the governance structures adopted in the modern era. As R. H. Taylor notes, these ancient practices do not arise in anyone's memory, so the institutions had to be adopted from elsewhere and then indigenized.[34] The borrowing process was a mixture of deliberative adaptation, accepting colonial models, or having certain institutions imposed by temporary overlords.

Japan and Thailand provide well-known examples of deliberative borrowing and adaptation, with the motivation for change being the economic and military challenges posed by the European colonial powers. In Thailand, the institutions of the British constitutional monarchy turned out to be more in keeping with Siam's situation than those of republican France, as demonstrated in 1856, when King Mongkut received a letter from Queen Victoria thus having him "admitted unreservedly into the brotherhood of European royalty."[35] When it came to other choices, however, the Thais decided to adopt legal codes on the basis of Napoleonic law.[36] It is instructive that when the time came to draft a new constitution in the mid-1990s,

Table 3.3  **Effective Duration of First Post–World War II Parliaments in Democratizing Asia**

| Country | Years | Event |
|---|---|---|
| India | 1952–1975 | Declaration of emergency |
| Indonesia | 1949–1957 | Declaration of martial law |
| Japan | 1947–present | |
| South Korea | 1948–1960 | Popular revolt |
| Philippines | 1946–1972 | Declaration of martial law |
| Taiwan (Nanking Assembly) | 1928–1948 | Temporary provisions adopted |
| Thailand | 1946–1947 | Military coup d'état |

Thailand again embarked on a detailed study of foreign models before settling on the unique 1997 structure. During the Meiji Restoration in the late
nineteenth century, Japan also studied European models and selected carefully to meet its needs. Thus the constitution was modeled on Prussia's and
it provided for a Diet responsible to the emperor, not the people, while the
civil code was based on the French model.[37]

Japan and Thailand were never colonized and so had greater choice in
their deliberations. India and Indonesia were destined to borrow extensively
from the colonist's model. India was able to hold a deliberative process
through the richly argued debates of its constituent assembly. India's parliament bears a strong resemblance to the Westminster parent, but the offspring has taken its own unique path in how it functions. Indonesia did not
have the luxury of deep deliberation as it was engaged in a guerrilla war
with the returning colonial power after the defeat of Japan. The final political settlement with the Dutch required the establishment of a parliamentary
structure and the inclusion of various representative bodies from around the
archipelago.[38] Perhaps the most faithful to the colonial model, however,
was the system adopted in the Philippines. Presidentialism was embraced,
as was a congressional bicameralism, a deep spoils system of civil service,
and all the dirty electoral tricks perfected in the early twentieth century in
the United States, which then boasted "the most corrupt form of electoral-
ism among all the industrial powers."[39] Benedict Anderson argues that the
Philippines was in a weaker position than some other Asian countries in that
its colonizers had not developed a coherent central bureaucracy, nor had the
liberation struggle or the resistance to Japan created a unified armed force.[40]
Without the balancing advantages in terms of wealth, high levels of education, and a robust media enjoyed by the United States, it is not surprising
that the institutions borrowed from the United States did not serve the
Philippines well.

In various ways, the representative bodies of these countries were indigenized. To a certain extent, therefore, what these institutions lacked in
terms of pedigree, they made up for in terms of innovation to meet local circumstances. Longevity certainly brings with it the positive attributes of
legitimacy and experience, but it can also carry the negative feature of stul-
tification. Australia's constitution is a sensible though uninspiring document
that has served the nation well. It has locked in a certain parliamentary
design and, to protect state rights in the federal system, has an amendment
process that makes it exceedingly difficult to change that design. Only eight
of forty-four referendums to amend the constitution have been passed.[41] Of
the countries of Pacific Asia, only Japan can more than match this history of
constitutional immutability, though important changes to Diet elections
have been promulgated through legislation. The other nations of Pacific
Asia have shown a great capacity for change and innovation.

## Challenging the Executive

Since Linz relaunched the debate on the perils of presidentialism in 1990, there has been a sentiment that parliamentary systems may have advantages to offer in the consolidation phase of democracy building.[42] I must admit to a natural sympathy for this argument, coming as I do from a well-oiled parliamentary democracy in which a political head of state is anathema. But a quick survey of Pacific Asia, while not minimizing the problems posed by presidential systems, does not suggest that parliamentary politics necessarily leads to better results. Malaysia and Singapore maintain parliaments whose members sit on the basis of regular elections and who have the constitutional power to defeat the legislative program of the prime minister. Yet these parliamentary systems did not prevent Mahathir Mohammed or Lee Kuan Yew from exercising authoritarian powers. India's parliament did not prevent Indira Gandhi's declaration of emergency. Nor did a parliamentary structure prevent the LDP hegemony over Japanese politics. Nor did it prevent Thaksin from asserting a similar hegemony over Thai politics. Parliamentary systems avoid the problem of dual legitimacy and thus are better placed to avoid policy paralysis caused by a deadlock between the executive and legislative branches of government. But without other effective checks and balances, like an independent judiciary, a robust opposition, and apolitical oversight institutions, parliamentarism can also serve as a platform for authoritarianism. So the basic requirement is that there are some parliamentary checks and balances for oversight of executive power.

In Pacific Asia there is clearly a historical basis for concern that executives, and presidents in particular, veer toward authoritarian methods and overpower their legislatures. The names Chiang Kai-shek, Park Chung Hee, Suharto, and Ferdinand Marcos, who between them were in power for ninety-three years, provide sufficient proof of this proposition. Throughout most of these ninety-three years, the parliaments of these countries were effectively dormant. In Taiwan, the KMT-dominated "Long Parliament," a rubber stamp assembly that doubled as a retirement home for mainland notables, provided no balance to the president's powers. The Philippine Interim Batasang Pambansa (House of Representatives) in the martial law period was made virtually irrelevant. Article 6 of the 1976 Amendment to the already illiberal Marcos Constitution of 1973, allowed the president to rule by decree if, *in the president's opinion*, the Assembly "is unable to act adequately on any matter for any reason that in his judgment requires immediate action." Adam Schwarz points out that in the Suharto era, the Dewan Perwakilan Rakyat (DPR, People's Representative Assembly) never drafted a bill or rejected one from the executive and accordingly suffered from the Indonesian genius for playing on words when its parliamentarians' role was described as the five D's: "*dating, duduk, dengar, diam, duit,* which roughly translated, means 'show up, sit down, listen up, shut up and collect your paycheck.'"[43] Neither would President Park in South Korea pay any heed to his National Assembly, as his political style remained, in a contemporary description, "that of a general who desires that his orders be carried out."[44]

What we see today is almost the diametric opposite. Assertive parliaments are challenging the former dominance of presidents. Since the turn of the century, we have seen impeachment proceedings undertaken in South Korea and the Philippines, though neither succeeded. In South Korea, President Roh's Uri Party won a resounding victory in the intervening elections, and the Constitutional Court dismissed the charges against the president for lack of gravity. The issue was not primarily one of parliamentary prerogatives, but rather an opportunist and tactical step by the opposition forces to use a slight misstep by the president for partisan advantage. Nevertheless, the tactic adopted turned on the capacity of the National Assembly to institute impeachment proceedings. Exercising this parliamentary prerogative is an important step in demonstrating its applicability. The result also contributed to South Korea's construction of the rule of law. As it turned out, the partisan conflict did not destabilize the institutions of democracy—it left them stronger. The weapon of impeachment has been seen to be available in the South Korean system, but the angry rebuff of the electorate against its users will make future recourse to impeachment more carefully considered.

A similar result may have been achieved in Taiwan, where in 2000, the KMT, which was the largest party in the Legislative Yuan, began impeachment proceedings against President Chen as a reaction to his decision to scrap a fourth nuclear plant. The KMT's underlying reason was to destabilize Chen's presidency and to return to the halcyon days when the KMT was the only possible party of government. The decision by the KMT not to proceed with the impeachment was testimony to the likelihood that the electorate would see through the nuclear policy pretext and recognize the move as one of partisan destabilization. Once again a restive Assembly turned to the impeachment weapon and demonstrated its potential threat, thus underlining the power of the Assembly over the president. And once again, the system came through strengthened, though the gridlock of partisanship hangs heavily over Taiwan.

The Philippines has a less positive experience with the impeachment process. Unlike President Roh's technically inappropriate expression of support for the new Uri Party in a system that requires the president to be above politics, or President Chen's commercially unpopular policy decision implementing a campaign promise, President Estrada had committed impeachable offenses in the eyes of virtually the entire Philippine deliberative community. The Philippine Center for Investigative Journalism (PCIJ) revealed in a 2000 report the enormous disparity between the president's wealth and his declared earnings.[45] PCIJ's reporting on the seventeen properties acquired by the president led to further revelations of kickbacks from gambling funds and misappropriation of tobacco taxes, providing Congress with every reason to institute impeachment proceedings. The House of Representatives took the necessary steps to allow the impeachment trial to be conducted by the full Senate under the guidance of the chief justice. In January 2001, the Senate conducted the trial but it became clear that the president had the numbers to block the introduction of incriminating evidence. Impeachment of a corrupt president would have immeasurably strengthened the Philippine political system. Paralysis in the Senate, no doubt purchased by the desperate president, demonstrated the inability of the political system to tackle the crisis and opened the door to the "people power" method with all its unpredictability and risk of unconstitutionality.

Turning to the fourth presidential system under review, we see once again a radical change in the respective powers of the president and the legislature. The pliant nature of the Indonesian parliament under Suharto is well known. His two successors, however, found it in far feistier form. Section 6 of the Annotations to the 1945 Constitution makes explicit the supremacy of the Majelis Permusyaratan Rakyat (MPR) over the president by explaining: "The President is not in an equal position (*neben*) as, but subordinate to (*untergeordnet*) the Majelis." Suharto switched this relationship around in practice, but the MPR turned the tables on his successor, Habibie, by rejecting his accountability speech in 1999 and thus signaling the end of his presidency. The MPR was able to do so because many opposition candidates had been elected earlier that year to the 500-member DPR, thus overcoming the resistance inherent in having many Suharto appointees joining the elected members of the DPR in the 700-member MPR. The vote to reject the Habibie accountability speech was close: 355 to 322 with 9 abstentions and 4 spoiled ballots among those casting a vote.[46] His successor, Abdurrahman Wahid ("Gus Dur"), outmaneuvered Megawati Sukarnoputri in the 1999 MPR election of the president but was to hold that position for less than two years. Gus Dur's talent for antagonizing his supporters finally turned the politicians against him and set off a process akin to impeachment. While the Indonesian process did not entail a trial by a chamber of parliament, it followed a procedure initiated in the DPR and finalized by the MPR in which a number of steps needed to be taken, all of which could take some six months to complete.[47] Gus Dur's unpredictability, his demeaning comments about the elected parliamentarians, and his attempt to declare a state of emergency managed to unite the MPR against him, with the result that the final formal vote ending his presidency taken in July 2001 was 591 in favor and none against, with members of his Partai Kebangkitan Bangsa (PKB) party, seeing the writing on the wall, boycotting the vote.[48]

The Habibie and Gus Dur episodes suggest an almost unfettered power of the MPR to remove a president at will for whatever reason. This clearly had swung the pendulum too far in the direction of the legislative branch. In the course of a five-year term, any president is bound to traverse difficult and unpopular periods. With the MPR precedents as they stood in 2001, an unpopular president may well have received his or her marching orders to placate an angry electorate. The Third Amendment to the 1945 Constitution adopted by the MPR at its November 2001 sitting, a few months after it had so decisively dismissed Gus Dur, significantly redressed the balance by requiring the involvement of the Constitutional Court and setting out the reasons for which impeachment may be undertaken, as well as setting a high qualified majority for the removal of the president.[49] Thus, it would now take 467 of the 700 MPR votes to remove a president, but a possible loophole may be that 176 members boycotting the MPR session would deny it the necessary quorum and thus be sufficient to block the president's removal.[50]

The perils of presidentialism may persist in Pacific Asia, but there is now clearly a far more even balance between presidents and legislatures. In the authoritarian period of these four nations, the presidents' domination of their legislatures was achieved either through constitutional revision or by ignoring the constitution and stacking the legislature with cronies, intimidating opposition politicians and keeping the locus of decisionmaking in the presidents' offices. In the post–Cold War period, the manipulation of the constitution is no longer an available option as Pacific Asia begins to embrace the rule of law. The stacking of parliaments is not possible, as elections are sufficiently free and fair to allow the electorate's choice to prevail. Intimidating the opposition has become a far more problematic tactic. The result is legislatures that insist on having a substantive role in their nations' affairs.

Assessing the legislative work of the parliaments of the region is more difficult than reviewing the higher-profile balance of power issues. A simple *quantitative* method adopted in the study by Jürgen Rüland and his team, is to count the legislative output of the parliaments of Pacific Asia.[51] The findings of this study, however, cannot easily be translated into a comparative scorecard, as issues such as the number of bills introduced, the length of time for legislative deliberation, and the distinctions between legislation with local or national implications all need to be factored into the equation. The study tentatively showed that the Korean legislature was the most productive and that of the Philippines the least.[52] It also showed how balance of power struggles inevitably detract from a parliament's legislative productivity. To judge the *quality* of a parliament's work is a far more difficult proposition, as this would require highly contextualized understandings as well as assessments about the impact of legislation, which in turn would require long-term analyses. To fall back on subjective judgment, I would have to generalize that the quality of these parliaments' legislative output has not matched their newfound assertiveness, leaving us with the realistic conclusion that quality will only improve with further democratic consolidation, greater acculturation to the ways of representative democracy, and increased parliamentary experience in the workings of these now independent and adversarial legislative chambers.

## Innovation, Idealism, and Idiosyncrasy

As noted at the outset of this chapter, transition democracies are not sustained by the legitimacy inherent in the longevity of their democratic institutions, but neither are they constrained by the inertia often accompanying that longevity. So when it comes to crafting their institutions of democracy, they can "think outside the box" and experiment with designs to suit their needs. The identification of those needs is one of the most important requirements of deliberative processes. It requires a public conversation leading to an honest appreciation of what is going right and what is going wrong in society, and an understanding of which institutional structures and what aspects of political culture are contributing to the problem. Having identified the symptoms and their underlying causes, institutional designers are able to look for solutions.

### Nonpartisan Chambers

*Thailand.* The most far-reaching exercise in institutional analysis and design in Pacific Asia has been undertaken by Thailand resulting in the 1997 Constitution.[53] The analysis was informed by a history of military rule abetted by bureaucratic support and justified because of the ineffectual nature of party politics. The mass demonstrations against General Suchinda's assumption of power in 1992 were very much on the minds of the drafters, and the 1997 financial crisis encouraged the electorate to accept strong medicine. The underlying analysis was that Thailand was beset with a corrupt political system in which authoritarian generals alternated with self-serving politicians for the right to profit at the public's expense. The solution was to strengthen the institutions of democracy in this constitutional monarchy in several ways. A major innovation was the creation of a fourth branch of government to assure proper oversight, to be discussed later in this chapter. A second important change was the crafting of a set of rules designed to strengthen the role of political parties, which will be discussed in Chapter 5. Underpinning the integrity of the constitution is another major innovation, a nonpartisan Senate.

Prior to 1997, the Thai Senate was an appointed chamber with many privileges and few responsibilities. The 1997 Constitution created a new creature, an apparent oxymoron in the form of an apolitical chamber of parliament. Unlike many counterparts, the Senate was not the senior house in the Thai National Assembly as most of the legislative duties and the formation of governments were the responsibility of the House of Representatives.[54] The attempt to place the Senate above partisan politics was constructed by two means. A candidate for the Senate could not be a member of a political party (Sect. 126[1]), nor could a candidate for the Senate campaign for this position beyond the "equal introductions" to be provided through state funding (Sect. 129). It was confirmed by a third important provision—senators could not stand for election at the subsequent elections (Sect. 126[3]). And it was reinforced by a fourth provision— senators could not be appointed to the Ministry (Sect. 127). This suggested that the ideal senator the Constitutional Drafting Assembly had in mind was a person already well and favorably known to his or her local community, who was not interested in being a professional politician and who was willing to give six years of his or her life to public service. The result was intended to be 200 men and women of noted integrity. The engineering of a chamber of parliament where integrity was seen as the main requirement was necessary because of the specific role of the Senate. In terms of government formation, the Senate had no role. In relation to legislation, the Senate had only a right of consultation and the power of delay. Regarding deliberation, the Senate had the undoubted capacity to participate in the public conversation but, given its weak position on its other parliamentary roles, it was likely to be outmatched by the 500-member House. The key role played by the Senate was in the appointment process of officials to the fourth branch of government, assuring oversight. The integrity of the appointing process was intended to assure the integrity of the oversight process, and the consequent enforcement of the rules of the game was intended to bring greater integrity and systematization to Thai politics.

There was a great coherence in the analysis and design processes leading up to the 1997 Constitution. The drafters understood the problem and were sufficiently honest not to bow to the etiquette of Thai society that frowns on open criticism of others. They designed a system to tackle the corruption they saw in politics, as it had been practiced for most of Thailand's modern history. The Senate was at the heart of that system. Accompanied by Australian senators, I had several occasions to conduct workshops and hold discussions with various members of the first elected Thai Senate. Nobody could fault the innovation in the design or the idealism inspiring it. But the hard-nosed Australian senators, after noting these aspects, went straight to the core issue: Will it work? They identified a number of problems. The absence of political parties was designed to keep the abuses of party politics out of the Senate, but it created a system of 200 individuals working alone without the benefit of an organized caucus of like-minded peers. Working as individuals does not allow for the division of labor within a group that facilitates specialization. Working alone makes it particularly difficult to champion policy outcomes. The prohibition against seeking reelection was intended to militate against the professionalization of the Senate, but it would also have precluded the building of institutional memory. The next 200 senators who, but for the coup, were to have sat in 2006 would have needed to reinvent virtually every wheel on which the Senate runs. The normal process of mentoring and advice from old hands would have been unavailable to the new group of senators. Some of the Thai senators conceded these problems. They were frustrated by their inability to come to grips with such a broad and technical legislative agenda. They felt the lack of resources to assist them in their tasks. The decisions on vetting candidates for official positions very often had to be taken on the basis of incomplete knowledge. They understood the spirit of the 1997 Constitution was to have them work as individuals, but informal groups naturally sprang up. The senators who came from the NGO community tended to work together best. The senators who had a career in the civil service at times grouped together as well. Regional groupings were discouraged but inevitably arose from the logic of constituency contact and responsibility. The informal and shifting nature of these groups did not seem to bring much more than moral support. The result was an institution finding it difficult to live up to the high ideals that informed its design.

The Thai Senate ultimately failed in that the parliament was dissolved after the 2006 coup. An argument could be constructed that if the Senate had been more forthright and competent in appointing judges to the Constitutional Court, that court would not have found in favor of Prime Minister Thaksin under charges of lodging an incorrect assets declaration. A guilty verdict would have disqualified Thaksin from politics for five years. Perhaps the design put in place under the 1997 Constitution, if properly and systematically applied, would have averted the reasons for the 2006 coup.

*Indonesia.* Were the Third Amendments to the Indonesian Constitution establishing another nonpartisan chamber of parliament influenced by the Thai precedent? I would like to believe that CDI was a vector between two of Australia's neighbors struggling with constitutional change, but I doubt that this was the case. Indonesian deliberative political processes tend to be sophisticated but not worldly. Indonesian thinkers like to go back to first principles and plot a path from there. They tend to discount other nations' experiences because they see Indonesia as so different from the rest of the world.

I found this out the hard way. I had accompanied a group of leaders of Indonesian NGOs dedicated to election monitoring to join the NAMFREL

(National Citizens Movement for Free Elections) teams observing the 2001 Philippine congressional elections. As tends to be the way in the Philippines, the election process was part fiesta and part chaos, somehow kept coherent by the teachers, predominantly women, staffing the electoral centers, and the nuns leading the observer teams. At the end of an exhausting week, I sat down with the Indonesians to discuss our conclusions. The Indonesians were pretty much of a mind that the exercise had been interesting but not very useful "because Indonesia is so different from the Philippines." I confess to succumbing to sarcasm when I responded by asking them whether there was another overpopulated archipelago in Southeast Asia holding free and fair elections that they would like me to take them to. In 2000, when I had hosted a group of Indonesian parliamentarians on a visit to Bangkok to study the Thai process of constitutional deliberation and amendment, I sought feedback at the conclusion of the workshop. This time it was the admiral, who was one of the thirty-eight appointed military members of the DPR at that time, who responded on behalf of the group. He politely noted how interesting the study of the Thai constitutional process had been, but that it was not really applicable to Indonesia "because they have a king and we do not." In the light of the 2006 coup, his simple distinction turned out to be fairly significant. I therefore don't believe the Thai Senate served as any sort of a model for the Dewan Perwakilan Daerah (DPD, Representative Assembly of the Regions). Yet the Indonesian deliberative process also arrived at the concept of a nonpartisan chamber of politics.

The key to the partisanship distinction between the various representative chambers in the Indonesian political system is in new Article 22E of the 1945 Constitution adopted in 2001 as part of the Third Amendments. It concerns the DPR, the DPD, and the Dewan Perwakilan Rakyat Daerah (DPRD, Regional Representative Assemblies in each of Indonesia's 440 districts and municipalities).[55] Participants in elections to the DPR and the DPRD are political parties, while participants in elections to the DPD are individuals. Of course the great majority of members of the MPR who drafted this design are parliamentarians sitting in the DPR, and they make it clear in several critical ways which is the senior chamber. They increased the number of DPR members to 550, while establishing a nexus limiting the size of the DPD to one-third of the number of DPR members (Art. 22C[2]). At the same time, the responsibilities of the DPD were circumscribed to proposing bills or participating in discussions of bills relating only to regional autonomy and other regional governance issues. In 2004, I sat down with a small group of newly elected DPD members to discuss their role. They were already lamenting the lack of powers of the new chamber and the dominance of the established chamber, the DPR. They said they had individually been elected in their provinces as local "champions" with high popular expectations, which they feared they would not be able to live up to. Their strategy was to attempt to renegotiate the division of responsibilities between the two chambers. But this strikes me as fairly futile, as the DPR is likely to jealously safeguard its powers, and its members have the decisive voice in the rule-making MPR.

The DPR is even disputing whether the Indonesian parliament is in fact bicameral. The information provided by the DPR to the Inter-Parliamentary Union (IPU) and available on that website has all the updated information from the elections in 2004, but it has no information about the DPD, which was elected at the same time.[56] Instead, the Indonesian system is described as unicameral. So although the DPD resembles a house of the provinces with each province having four representatives, there is reluctance to call it an upper house, because that would give the impression that Indonesia has adopted a federal system, an idea that has been proscribed from Indonesian politics since Sukarno's time. Federalism is feared because of its possible divisiveness and because the federal idea had been futilely championed by the departing Dutch colonizers.[57] This tends to place Indonesia's parliament in a rather idiosyncratic light. It calls itself unicameral though there is a second chamber representing the provinces. Indeed, when the DPR and DPD are put together to form the MPR, a third chamber is established with the power to dismiss the president and amend the constitution. This might justify a description of Indonesia as a tricameral parliament. Responding to my questions on this point, some DPR members conceded that maybe the Indonesian parliament has one-and-a-half chambers. So the choice is between one, one and half, two, and three!

### Apolitical Politicians?

Taiwan is another Pacific Asian country prepared to make significant changes in the structure of its parliament. In August 2004 the Legislative Yuan passed the Constitution Amendment Bill, and in June 2005, the National Assembly ratified these amendments thus drastically reforming the legislature and the voting process.[58] The most radical step is to halve the number of parliamentarians from 225 to 113, of which 73 will be constituency representatives, 6 will represent aboriginal people, and 34 will be "legislators-at-large" decided by party list. Continuing the reform process, at least half of the names on the party list must be women and half of the candidates presented to constituencies must be women. While a simple mechanism of placing names by alternate gender on a closed party list will ensure that at least 17 women are elected to the seats for legislators-at-large, having women elected to constituency seats will depend on whether they are candidates in winnable seats. Taiwan's sixth legislature has already achieved a figure of 20 percent for women members, so it is highly likely that in voting for the seventh legislature, when the gender quotas kick in, this figure will increase. The National Assembly elected in May 2005 ratified these changes in June 2005 and, in so doing, proceeded to follow a handful of other chambers in parliamentary history that have voted themselves out of existence.[59] Henceforth, constitutional amendment processes will be in the hands of the Legislative Yuan subject to adoption at national referendums.

Two new apolitical elected chambers and a political chamber cut in half—is there a common reason for these changes? I believe an answer can be discerned in a naive form of idealism that wishes to see governance placed above politics. Politicians are a necessary evil, according to this line of thinking, but they should be kept in check. In Taiwan, the popular frustration over gridlock politics led to calls, which enjoyed 70 percent popular support in the polls,[60] for the halving of the number of parliamentarians, and party leaders eventually had to respond. Yet compared to other nations, the Taiwanese electorate is hardly overrepresented. The Legislative Yuan is, after all, a unicameral system in a country of 23 million people. Australia has a slightly smaller population that is represented by 226 federal parliamentarians, not to count the 620 members of state parliaments. In view of the complexity of modern governance in the age of globalization, one wonders whether there will be sufficient members of the Legislative Yuan to allow for specialization in the work of committees.

The decision to make the Thai Senate a body in which political parties are not allowed to operate is saying that mainstream politicians cannot be trusted to make appointments to important public offices. Thailand is not the only polity to come to that conclusion as, increasingly, best practice in such issues as judicial appointments is to rely on ostensibly impartial judicial commissions. Of course, many of these commissions are appointed by governments. But Thailand has attempted to find a circuit breaker to keep appointments completely out of the hands of politicians. It is difficult to see how this can work in practice. Already in relation to the first elected Senate, there were complaints that the appointment process was not working as anticipated.[61] The Indonesian decision to ban parties from DPD elections also flows from a general sentiment to create "clean" politics. Clearly the DPD needs to be given time to demonstrate its worth, but I doubt that "atomizing" the members, who must work under the difficult formula of high public expectations together with highly constrained responsibilities, will contribute to the coherence of the chamber.

Another innovation from this region intended to keep politicians above politics is the South Korean Law on the Election of Public Officials and the Prevention of Election Fraud as amended in 2000, Article 9 of which prohibits public officials from exercising any influence over election matters. This makes every sense in terms of keeping the civil service out of politics, but it certainly seems odd when the concept of "public official" includes the directly elected executive president. The president needs to work with parliament, and it is normal practice in presidential systems for the president to support his or her party in mid-term elections. President Roh succumbed to that temptation and commented favorably on the Uri Party. This was the cause of the impeachment that, though it eventually proved to be unsuccessful, caused the Constitutional Court to scold the president for his lack of neutrality. Perhaps another example from South Korea of institutional reforms with an anti-politician flavor was the reduction in 2000 in the number of seats in the National Assembly, with single-member districts down from 254 to 227 seats in a chamber of 273. The given motive was to try to reduce campaign expenditure.[62] However, in 2004, the decision was taken to return to a chamber of 299 seats, 243 of which are single-member districts.[63]

The motivation for all these innovations seems to be a widespread desire to place politicians above politics. This strikes me as quite problematic. It is doubtful that creating nonpartisan chambers of parliament, or halving the number of parliamentarians, or making a directly elected executive president act as a neutral, will achieve the integrity being sought simply through the power of innovative design. Surely it is better to accept the political nature of democratic government and design systems that make it as responsive as possible to the electorate. At the same time, the electorate must be able to assess and influence the work of parliaments. So a better solution, though necessarily a longer-term one, is to change the political culture to one of engagement and deliberation. An engaged electorate will probably make even poorly designed systems work, while an apathetic electorate will not make the most ingenious design achieve its intended results. India's FPTP electoral system would not be seen today as best practice, but the engagement of the Indian electorate has made it work. On the other hand, the Thai electorate, and especially its elite, was prepared to stand by and accept the 2006 coup that swept away the carefully designed institutions of the 1997 Constitution.

## Engineering Electoral Systems

The design of electoral systems has occupied much of the energies of the institutional crafters. From the time Duverger pondered the impact of electoral designs on party systems, this aspect of psephology has attracted a great deal of attention.[64] Diamond encapsulates the debates in the literature in this field by posing four normative trade-offs that need to be tackled in electoral design.[65]

1. *Governability vs. representativeness.* Governability calls for greater certainty and continuity often achieved by majoritarian systems such as FPTP, which tend to benefit disproportionately the two largest parties.

Representativeness requires representation more in proportion to voting, achieved by proportional representation (PR) systems though they can thus produce many small parties.

2. *Representativeness vs. constituency accessibility.* PR systems work on the basis of party lists, often on a nationwide scale, resulting in no necessary connection between a locality and a representative. Smaller, multi-member districts go some way to resolving this problem. Single-member districts, on the other hand, allow voters to know by whom they are represented, thus increasing that representative's accountability.

3. *Party coherence vs. voter choice.* A PR system based on a closed list, where the voter simply votes for a single party, will maximize the influence of the party over the representative and thus tend to work toward more party coherence. Open lists, where the voter can select favorites from within the party list, increase voter choice. Single-member districts, especially if associated with primary selection systems, give the voter more choice, but they can detract from party coherence to the benefit of "favorite sons."

4. *Simplicity vs. appropriateness.* Simplicity is useful in both the balloting and counting processes, so an electoral system requiring the voter to place a single tick on a ballot paper is ideal. But simplicity may not accommodate more appropriate systems, including relatively sophisticated devices such as open list systems, or transferable votes where voters cascade their preferences.

### Balancing the Trade-offs

Asian democracies have worked their way through each of these trade-offs, seeking a system in consonance with their individual political requirements and political cultures. India adopted the British FPTP system after debating the issue long and hard at the Constituent Assembly. PR had its supporters, given India's extremely diverse society, but FPTP was chosen for the Lok Sabha, or Lower House, mainly to avoid fragmented legislatures and to help the formation of stable governments—so stability was seen as the major requirement.[66] The Rajya Sabha, or Council of States, is the Upper House elected by state legislatures. India has stuck to this formula ever since, and longevity has brought with it a high level of acceptability among India's 600 million voters. While innovations such as computerized electoral rolls and electronic voting have successfully been introduced by the Indian Electoral Commission, the electoral system looks set in stone.

India is, however, the exception. All the other countries under review have made or are about to make significant changes to their electoral systems. The most interesting aspect of this process of reform is that a clear trend in terms of "best practice" electoral systems has emerged in five of the six Pacific Asian democracies. The odd nation out is Indonesia. Indonesia has held many elections on the basis of PR within provincial boundaries. Even though these elections were not competitive in the Suharto era, they were nevertheless orderly and well understood.[67] So from the point of view of simplicity in this vast archipelago, there was a clear bias in favor of retaining the system as understood by the electorate. This was particularly so in 1999, when the first post-Suharto election, and therefore the first competitive one since 1955, was held. The electoral commission had only four months to prepare for the ballot, virtually precluding structural changes to the electoral system. The main complaint from the public after the 1999 elections was that elected representatives seemed to be disconnected from the people.[68] In the most populous province, West Java, eighty-two parliamentarians were elected by PR, so a voter in Bandung could be forgiven for not knowing who his or her representative was. The resolution of this problem was found through downsizing the multimember districts, which now have a maximum of twelve and a minimum of three representatives.[69] Notionally, the party list is open and voters can select an individual candidate from it, but because the threshold for election of an individual was set at a full quota, no candidate was elected solely through this method in 2004. So Indonesia chose a balance leaning toward representativeness, some constituency accessibility, greater party coherence than voter choice, and simplicity through basic continuity. Another form of innovation was the adoption of the French two-round method for election of the president. This meant that in 2004, more than 100 million Indonesians voted three times in an orderly and effective manner in the space of six months.

Japan, South Korea, the Philippines, Taiwan, and, subject to possible post-coup changes, Thailand have all opted for a mixed system of constituency representatives alongside a smaller number of party-list representatives. The ideas behind the introduction of mixed systems are, of course, particular to each country. Electoral systems cannot be bought off the shelf. In the Philippines, the problem is one of domination of politics by cacique elites and the need to find ways of having disadvantaged groups represented in the House of Representatives. So traditional parties are banned from contesting the party-list seats, while a 2 percent threshold means that a party needs to attract half a million votes nationwide to qualify for a seat and another design rule ensures that individual parties cannot hold more than three seats. In the 2004 elections, only 24 of 52 available party-list seats were filled, so party-list representatives make up only 10 percent of the House. In Thailand under the 1997 Constitution, the idea behind the 100 party-list seats in a chamber of 500 was to allow high-quality candidates, who may not be suited to the cut and thrust of electoral campaigning, to be elected and to form a pool from which the prime minister could select the ministry. In Japan, the motive was to lower the value of the traditional and heavily weighted rural seats that unduly encouraged pork barrel politics, by limiting the number of such seats in favor of party-list seats, thus requiring parties to aggregate voters through broader policy proposals. The fact that only 180 of the 480 seats are decided through proportional representation means that there remains a greater emphasis on traditional politics. The reasoning in South Korea and Taiwan was similar to Japan's, with one important difference. Regionalism is a problem in both countries and is particularly acute in South Korea, and so the party list is elected on a nationwide basis, encouraging parties to pitch their policy messages to a national audience rather than concentrate on a regional one. In South Korea, this reform particularly favored the incumbent party, which had both a regional following and a national profile.[70] In both countries, however, the list members of Parliament (MPs) form only around one-third of each parliament. A common majoritarian bias exists toward constituency MPs in these mixed systems (Table 3.4).

Another interesting innovation in electoral system design common to three of the countries under review is the quota for disadvantaged or underrepresented groups. In India, 120 (79 for scheduled castes and 41 for scheduled tribes) of the 543 seats are set aside where only members of those castes and tribes can be candidates.[71] In the Philippines, "indigenous cultural communities" are listed among the groups eligible to run party-list candidates.[72] And in Taiwan, 6 seats will be reserved for aboriginal people, 3 for plains aborigines, and 3 for mountain aborigines under the reformed system.[73] A major topic currently on the agenda is quotas for women, on which only Taiwan has taken decisive steps. Indonesia and South Korea have recommendatory provisions in favor of women representatives, and India continues to debate the issue.

While there are variations in the rules and balances of the mixed system, and different motivations for reform, this convergence in design speaks elo-

**Table 3.4  Mixed Electoral Systems in Lower Houses in Pacific Asia, 2006**

| Country | Constituency Seats | Party-List Seats | Quota Seats | Total |
|---------|-------------------|------------------|-------------|-------|
| Japan | 300 | 180 | — | 480 |
| South Korea | 243 | 56 | — | 299 |
| Philippines | 212 | 24[a] | — | 236 |
| Taiwan[b] | 73 | 34 | 6[c] | 113 |
| Thailand | 400 | 100 | — | 500 |

*Source:* Roland Rich, "Designing Democracy Along the Pacific Rim," *Democracy at Large* 2, no. 1 (December 2005): 11.

*Notes:* a. Only twenty-four of a possible fifty-two party-list seats were filled in the 13th Congress.

b. Electoral system to come into force at the December 2007 elections.

c. Split between highland and lowland aboriginal people.

quently of the nascent imagined community of democracies emerging in Pacific Asia. These countries study each other's systems and follow best practice precedents. The Philippines, South Korea, and Japan led the way in this design process, and the other community members are following suit. The logic of the design process is to maximize the benefits in each of the necessary trade-offs. While the introduction of the PR aspect may have sacrificed some element of stability, it has done so to enhance representativeness. Yet the majority of elected officials remain constituency representatives, and the voter has two votes to deploy, thus enhancing choice. The level of sophistication of these societies allows for a compromise of simplicity in favor of what has been considered to be the most appropriate system.

Table 3.5 summarizes the electoral systems employed in the democratic countries of Pacific Asia and in India.

### Dimensions of Representativeness

The first four information columns in Table 3.5 are descriptive. The fifth column is headed dimensions. This refers to an element of electoral design that receives too little attention. Returning for a moment to the Pacific islands, we see a number of polities with electoral systems with a single form of vote that elects a unicameral chamber from which the unitary state's government emerges.[74] This strikes me as a one-dimensional system—one vote, for one chamber, leading to a single government. A one-dimensional system is understandable in countries with very small populations, but it carries with it a low quality of representativeness. The clue to the need for more than one dimension in the election of representatives comes from the well-understood political maxim that in bicameral parliaments, the two chambers should be elected by different means, to ensure that representation is not fully overlapping and thus enhance bicameral contestability and effectiveness.[75] A single-member district election for the lower house and a proportional representation election for the upper house will produce differences in the two results that allow for a higher quality of representativeness.

The need for this more expansive means of representing the electorate is demonstrated by the trend toward mixed electoral systems for individual chambers. With no upper house, South Korea and Taiwan need mixed electoral systems in the unicameral chamber to achieve the requisite quality. Both South Korea and Taiwan also directly elect the executive president, and this thus gives their electorates a third dimension of representation. Taiwan's quota for certain disadvantaged communities can be seen as a fourth dimension. Japan has mixed electoral systems for each of its chambers, thus establishing four dimensions of representation. India elects its chambers by different means, and though the upper house is indirectly elected, the state houses that form the voting bodies are themselves directly

**Table 3.5 Electoral Systems of Asian Democracies, 2006**

| Country | Lower House | Upper House | Presidential | Federal | Dimensions |
|---|---|---|---|---|---|
| India | SMD by FPTP +Q | Indirect by State Assemblies | No | Yes | 4 |
| Indonesia | MMD by PL(O) | MMD by SNTV | Two rounds | Partial | 3–4 |
| Japan | M:SMD/PR by PL | M:SMD&MMD/PR(N) by PL | No | No | 4 |
| Korea | M:SMD/PR(N) by PL | No | FPTP | No | 3 |
| Philippines | M:SMD/PR(N) by PL(O) | Block Vote (Nationwide) | FPTP | Partial | 4–5 |
| Taiwan | SMD&MMD by SNTV +Q | No | FPTP | No | 3 |
| Taiwan 2007 | M:SMD/PR(N) by PL +Q | No | FPTP | No | 4 |
| Thailand[a] | M:SMD/PR by PL | SMD&MMD by SNTV | No | No | 3 |

*Notes:* Block vote: elector has as many votes as there are positions to be filled; FPTP: first past the post; M: mixed; MMD: multimember district; PL: party list; PL(O): party list (open); PR: proportional representation; PR(N): proportional representation (nationwide district); Q: quota for identified groups; SMD: single-member district; SNTV: single nontransferable vote.

a. Subject to possible redesign post–2006 coup.

elected, though by the same system as used for elections to the Lok Sabha. There is also a system of positive discrimination toward castes and tribes, thus arguably leading to three dimensions of representation. Importantly, India practices a vibrant form of federalism, with elected state parliaments that can be seen as a fourth dimension in representation.

Continuing the survey of dimensionality, under the recent constitutional amendments, Indonesia elects two chambers by different means. The third chamber, the MPR, if one chooses to so describe it, comprises representatives of the other two chambers, so it does not add to the electoral dimensionality. But the move to directly elect the president, and indeed to do so by the two-rounds method, certainly adds a dimension to the quality of representativeness. As noted above, Indonesia does not practice a system under the heading of federalism. But it has 440 directly elected local parliaments with considerable powers in what has been seen as a radical decentralization process.[76] So I would argue that one could probably call this the fourth dimension of its electoral system.

A similar conclusion is available when reviewing the Philippine system. It has a mixed electoral system for the lower house. Because the party-list system is limited to providing disadvantaged groups with a certain quota of seats, this leads to two dimensions of lower house representation, not three. The Senate is elected by a nationwide constituency through a block vote. The presidency is also an elected office, bringing the tally to four dimensions. Again, the Philippines is not a federal country, but it has 81 provinces and some 120 cities each directly electing governors and mayors who have considerable power over local issues and can at times achieve national significance, thus justifying its description as a fifth dimension.

The exact counting of dimensionality requires further fine-tuning and more attention to definitional aspects. For example, elections for the mayor of Taipei are clearly significant, and indeed were the means by which Chen Shui-bian and his DPP were able to stake their claims to national office. It may also be the path to the presidency of the present mayor, Ma Ying-jeou, who is also chairman of the KMT. This election has not been counted for the purpose of measuring the dimensions of representativeness in Taiwan, but perhaps it should be. Similar arguments could be made for elections for the governor of Bangkok and the mayor of Tokyo. The threshold needs to be that the subnational election is of considerable significance nationally before it can be seen as a dimension of national representative quality.

An important qualification needs to be added to the discussion of electoral dimensionality. As with other aspects of electoral systems, trade-offs are necessary. In particular, designers need to be careful not to sacrifice governability for representativeness. The requirement is for checks and balances, not gridlock. As emerges from the survey of democratic Asia, the number of dimensions varies from three to perhaps five. It is difficult to conceive an institutional design where more national dimensions of representativeness could be accommodated without seriously jeopardizing governability. One method of accommodating dimensionality is to do so for election to the one chamber of parliament because the rules and politics of that chamber will act to contain the danger of incoherence caused by the competing interests of the two or three dimensions of representation. For example, under Taiwan's new electoral system, the unicameral chamber will have several cleavages. It will be divided along two or more party lines. It will be divided between government and opposition coalitions. It will be divided among constituency, list, and quota MPs. An argument could be mounted that it will also be divided along gender lines. While these cleavages contribute to the diversity of the chamber and no doubt to the complexity of managing this diversity, they need not lead to its ungovernability.

In 2004, I had occasion to study a parliament with similar cleavages when I accompanied a group of Pacific parliamentarians to Wellington to observe New Zealand's unicameral parliament in action. New Zealand abolished its upper house decades ago and recently abandoned its Westminster majoritarian system under public pressure for higher-quality representativeness. It adopted a mixed system for its 120-member parliament, which at the 2002 elections resulted in 62 general constituency seats, 51 party-list seats, and 7 Maori constituency seats (the indigenous Maori have the choice of registering to vote in either general or Maori constituencies, the number of which therefore may vary depending on registration patterns).[77] Seven parties were represented in parliament. There was a minority government formed by the plurality party and a disunited opposition. One might have considered this a recipe for instability. Yet the minority government was able to enact legislation on the highly sensitive issues of indigenous rights, environmental protection, and economic reform by seeking different coalition partners from among the opposition parties for different issues. The mathematics turned out to be felicitous for Prime Minister Helen Clark, who had a choice of four different parties with which to build a parliamentary majority in support of various pieces of legislation. Managing the cleavages in New Zealand society had led to a higher quality of deliberation and representativeness, with a plurality party able to govern effectively though in minority, and four opposition parties able to achieve some parts of their policy platform. New Zealand's three dimensions of representation within one chamber have, thus far, provided a good balance between governability and representativeness. After the 2005 election, the Labour Party remained the largest party but did not have a majority of seats. It reached coalition and cooperation agreements with four smaller parties to form a government allowing those parties to have aspects of their policy platforms supported by the government as a whole.

Taiwan has adopted a similar system, but it has an additional dimension of representation in the form of a directly elected president. Its parliamentary chamber is unlikely to be as politically diverse as New Zealand's, but Taiwan will need to deal with four dimensions of representation spread over two governing institutions. South Korea's three dimensions also entail an institutional division between parliament and president. India's institutional division arises from its federal character. Thailand's and Japan's institutional divisions are between their two chambers of parliament. The Philippines' five dimensions have three institutional divisions—between the two houses, between the congress and the president, and between the national and local levels of government. Governability problems arise, to adapt Linz's formulation, when systems produce dual or triple legitimacies. Managing these competing legitimacies is one of the critical issues faced by democracies. They need to be resolved through various combinations of constitutionality, party systems, and political culture. It has proven to be a difficult task and may pose particular difficulties for several Asian democracies. The ideal system in theory is to find the best balance between high-quality representativeness through several dimensions of electoral representation, and effective governance through minimizing the institutional divisions.

## Fighting Corruption

Having crafted electoral systems and representative assemblies, an equally important body of work awaits the institutional designers—putting in place accountability systems. Corruption is a threat to each of Asia's existing and emerging democracies. The problem was already encountered in relation to systematization, and it is so well recognized that it requires little elaboration.[78]

In response, the institutional designers have put together an imposing panoply of accountability institutions beginning with edifices to enhance the rule of law and constitutionality, continuing with designs attempting to limit vote buying and fraudulent vote counting, as well as establishing various accountability offices. Much of this accountability superstructure follows standard practice in modern democracies, and some of it leads the world in best practice.

### Taiwan's Control Yuan

Taiwan and Thailand have pioneered systems with accountability institutions as a fourth branch of government. In Taiwan, the Control Yuan is one of five branches of government (the Examinations Yuan, of critical importance in classic Confucian systems, being the fifth). It combines the functions of auditor, ombudsman, and prosecutor in impeachment proceedings. Its 29 members are appointed by the president upon consultation with the National Assembly and are supported by an expert staff. An examination of the Control Yuan's statistics over the period 2000–2004 shows that it handled approximately 15,000 petitions each year, of which some 500 were investigated; it instigated 103 impeachment cases involving 271 persons, including 7 elected officials and 35 officers of the Judicial Yuan, all of whom were referred for some form of punishment; and it reviewed 2,716 asset declarations of which it found 227 to be intentionally false.[79]

The concept of a Control Yuan is 2,000 years old and has therefore had time to develop its methods and styles in keeping with the political culture of the society it serves. So although modern practice is to keep ombudsman, audit, and prosecution functions separated to encourage deep specialization, institutional loyalty, and a certain degree of contestability between accountability institutions, the Control Yuan has to draw on its considerable experience to manage these responsibilities within the one organization. Favoring the efficiency of a single organization over the contestability between several independent oversight agencies is unusual in the liberal democracies. The work of the Control Yuan will therefore be closely watched, especially in small states in transition to democracy that have difficulty meeting the burden of funding overlapping oversight bodies.

### Thailand's Fourth Branch of Government

Thailand does not have two thousand years of experience to fall back on in the construction of its fourth branch of government, but nor is it caught in the grip of unchanging tradition. Thailand's accountability system under the 1997 Constitution comprised seven separate institutions: the National Counter Corruption Commission, the Election Commission, the National Human Rights Commission, the Ombudsmen, the State Audit Commission, the Constitutional Court, and the Administrative Courts, each with its powers and responsibilities spelled out in the constitution. Duncan McCargo criticizes the system as "overengineered" and in danger of causing gridlock and having unintended effects.[80] In support of this view, he cites the powers of the electoral commission to ban or suspend candidates and order reruns of elections. In the 2001 elections, 300 of the 400 constituency elections were subject to formal complaints, leading to 70 reruns of which a further 14 had to be rerun for a second time, while in the Senate elections the commission suspended 70 of the original 200 winners.[81]

As noted earlier, the integrity of the accountability institutions is predicated upon the integrity of the Senate, which is based on its nonpartisan stature. Yet the Senate process for the appointment of the new batch of electoral commissioners in 2001 was described as "highly politicized," leading to "greatly reduced public faith" in the commission.[82] A recent study cites the example of the appointment of the second batch of electoral commissioners, among whom "no woman, no academic and no member of civil society was considered worthy of trying to secure clean elections," as evidence of the means by which the Thaksin administration attempted "to reverse or at least dilute the reforms of the 1997 Constitution."[83] Clearly, Thailand's accountability institutions needed time to develop their practice and to gain the trust of the people. The 2006 coup cut short this process, and it is not clear if the next system will attempt to build on the key concept elaborated in the 1997 Constitution of a fourth branch of government.

## Specialist Agencies

The Philippines boasts some of the oldest and most elaborate accountability institutions in Asia. The Unexplained Wealth Act (Republic Act No. 1379) and the Anti-Graft and Corrupt Practices Act (Republic Act No. 3019) date back to 1955 and 1960, respectively. A special court, the Sandiganbayan, composed of a presiding justice and eight associate justices, has exclusive jurisdiction over crimes or felonies committed by public officials and civil servants in relation to their office. The Ombudsman Office is one of the most powerful in the region, with responsibility to initiate prosecutions. Yet one cannot escape the view that but for exposés in the media, little effective anticorruption action would take place in the Philippines. Even with a vigorous free press, corruption is far outstripping the effectiveness of the accountability mechanisms. In 1997, the Philippine Ombudsman Office estimated that the government had lost $48 billion to corruption in the previous twenty years.[84]

India has stuck to more traditional anticorruption mechanisms, with few positive results to show for them. One estimate claims that ordinary Indians pay $6 billion in bribes each year.[85] The main anticorruption agency, the Central Bureau of Investigations, "is known to be notoriously subservient to its political masters,"[86] and the autonomous Central Vigilance Commission has been described as "toothless."[87] As in the Philippines, it has been the media that has raised the alarm and civil society that has called for action, but the political class has been adept at ensuring the accountability system is weak and porous.

## High-Profile Prosecutions

In Japan and South Korea, the main tactical weapon appears to be high-profile prosecutions responding to public indignation following media exposés. In Japan, the Lockheed scandal in 1976, the Recruit scandal in 1989, and the financial scandals involving LDP vice president Kanemaru Shin in 1993, all led to prosecutions and considerable reform efforts.[88]

In South Korea, it was the prosecutions of two former presidents under

President Kim Young Sam that were the most noteworthy. The arrests of Chun Doo Hwan and Roh Tae Woo for corruption, mutiny, and treason in connection with the 1979 assassination of President Park Chung Hee, and the subsequent violent suppression in May 1980 of the Kwangju demonstrations, led to controversy over the retrospective legislation required to overturn the fifteen-year prosecution cut-off set down in the statute of limitations.[89] But from the perspective of money politics, the most interesting aspect of the court's findings against the former presidents was the fines it imposed— equal to the amounts found to have been received illegally from business corporations while in office: $276 million against Chun and $350 million against Roh.[90] Kim Young Sam was not able to retain his "Mr. Clean" reputation, however, as questions arose over how Roh's illegally acquired money had been spent, with suspicions that it had, in part, funded Kim's subsequent presidential campaign on behalf of Roh's party.[91] Indeed, both the presiden cies of Kim Young Sam and Kim Dae Jung ended surrounded by corruption controversies involving family members and associates.

In relation to Indonesia, we cannot yet point to any groundbreaking innovation in accountability institutions. The prosecution of former president Suharto did not go far, though the prosecution of his son Tommy did succeed, at the tragic subsequent cost of the presiding judge's life. The "Bulog" and "Bruneigate" scandals hurt Gus Dur, but these were not the decisive reasons for his ouster. Important steps have been taken in reorganizing the judiciary, setting up an anticorruption court, establishing an ombudsman institution, and rationalizing the state audit function, but given Indonesia's deplorable record of corruption, it is difficult to be optimistic over the future effectiveness of these bodies.

## Design Options for Accountability Agencies

Designing the oversight agencies is an important element in the accountability package. Another equally important set of rules is required to deal directly with the money required to fund politics.[92] Three broad categories of provisions come into play: (1) rules about contributions to politics and spending by political parties; (2) rules about public funding for campaigns and other aspects of politics; and (3) rules about public disclosure of contributions and spending.

As in the case of electoral systems, it is necessary in designing accountability agencies to find the right balances between regulation and intrusiveness, rhetoric and enforceability, and openness and constraint in public participation. Variations in the design process concern timing (whether the process is iterative or "big bang") and designers (whether the main participants are politicians, experts, or the public). Some systems will deal rigorously with all three aspects, while others will only deal with the issue of contributions. All seven of the countries under review have tackled these issues along a spectrum starting with India, which has contented itself with contribution limits, and ending with South Korea, which has progressively tightened its rules on all three aspects and is showing determination in their implementation.

All seven polities have established rules on contribution limits in an attempt to limit the influence of big business and increase the influence of individuals. The rules are telling political parties to recruit more members and encourage more individual contributors, while denying access to foreign funds. Various formulas are used to determine the calibration and the relationship with the disclosure rules. South Korea, the Philippines, and Taiwan have introduced spending limits on campaigns thus following best practice in this field, given the greater likelihood of being able to enforce such rules. But even so, the Philippine rules remain largely unenforced. All have considered public funding of political parties, and Japan, South Korea, Taiwan, and Thailand have implemented such schemes. The various formulas tie funding to the size of the vote, the size of the electorate, and the success of the party. By various means such as thresholds and weightings, the burden of these funding formulas is generally to favor parties over candidates and to favor big parties over smaller parties. One result of these rules is to encourage movement toward an effective two-party format in politics. The public disclosure rules also vary among the various countries. In Japan it is difficult to access the documentation, while in Thailand the documents are published. Clearly the media need access to this information if the rules are to be effectively monitored.

## Taking Advantage of Crises

A number of observations can be posited in relation to Pacific Asia's experience of crafting accountability institutions. The first observation may well apply to all polities, but it is starkly illustrated in Pacific Asia—significant reforms tend to be generated in response to major crises. The crises often take the form of political scandals involving money politics, but they can also be generated by abrupt regime change and by global or regional economic setbacks. In the case of Japan, the money politics crises of the 1970s, 1980s, and 1990s each led to reforms, the most recent being the most far reaching. In Thailand, it was the 1992 military brutality against demonstrators that started the process, and the 1997 East Asian financial crisis that galvanized the forces of reform to overcome the opposition of traditional politics. The 2006 coup is the latest crisis facing Thailand. Indonesia's ongoing reinvention of its society was triggered by the 1997 financial crisis, which stripped bare Suharto's legitimacy based on economic development and growth. In South Korea, it was the end of military rule that allowed the possibility of reform, and the series of financial scandals that triggered their enactment. A similar process has occurred in Taiwan, while in the Philippines the fall of Marcos allowed important reforms to be instituted.

These crises have the effect of opening a window of opportunity for change. They do so by focusing public attention on the problems and thus providing an incentive for politicians to gain popularity by championing the cause. Societies buffeted by crises and scandals are more willing to take corrective measures than societies basking in success. After all, as the saying goes, "if it ain't broke, don't fix it." Reform may be crisis driven, but this should not be interpreted as a dismissal of the importance of the ongoing process of deliberation about reform of society. Deliberation reaches a peak when the focus is sharpened by crises, but to be able to find solutions, societies need to draw from the continuing debates and proposals on reform options. This is when the academic and think tank studies, as well as the media and NGO ideas, come into their own. So the process of criticism, comparison, and suggestion needs to be a permanent feature of deliberative democracy, even though some of the ideas can only be taken up when a crisis prepares the way.

### The Role of Agency

Reform is rarely a win-win proposition. The curtailment of vote-buying will benefit some politicians and jeopardize the means to power of others. The end of crony preferences may have negative cascading impacts on crony businesses and their employees, investors, and suppliers. The public funding of election campaigns may, if designed by the major parties, lead to the extinction of small parties. In the normal course of events, the potential losers will likely be able to achieve a result of inertia through obfuscation, opposition, and delay. Crisis situations open the window for reform, but it will then require groups and individuals to take advantage of that opened window. This can sometimes take the form of agency whereby a leading actor becomes the critical agent for reform.

Kim Young Sam took the critical decision to prosecute his predecessors even though he may have suspected that it could rebound against him. King Bhumipol of Thailand accepted the prime ministership of General Suchinda after the 1992 elections even though the latter had assured the public he would not seek that post, but after the violent suppression of demonstrations in support of the arrested opposition leader General Srimuang Chamlong, the king stepped back into the political fray and summoned the protagonists. He had few constitutional weapons at his disposal, he had the history of military domination of government to contend with, and his entry into the political battle may have been costly to the institution of the monarchy, but by having the public witness on television his stern admonition to the two former generals, as they knelt before him in abasement as required by royal protocol, he left the clear impression in the public mind that he was displeased with the way developments had been handled. Suchinda had to resign and the reform process was initiated. The role of the king in the 2006 coup remains unclear.

In the Philippines, the agent of change was Benigno Aquino whose assassination upon his return to the Philippines, obviously at the hands of the Marcos administration, was the point of no return to Marcos's authoritarianism. Agency is, however, a difficult subject on which to theorize or generalize. We do not have for study the counterfactual histories of these countries had Kim Young Sam decided to allow the statute of limitations to stay the prosecutions, or had King Bhumipol decided to adopt the normal course and stay out of the political fray, or had Aquino not flown back to Manila. All we can postulate is that individuals will have pivotal roles to play in causing the initiation of a reform process. We can further conclude that those individuals need not necessarily be the political leaders of the day, as the above examples of a constitutional monarch and an opposition figure demonstrate.

## Conclusion

Our first concluding observation is that despite all the reforms, innovations, and prosecutions, corruption persists. Even in its narrow sense of the unlawful taking of public goods for personal gain, corruption is endemic to society. The most that one can expect of systems of accountability is that corruption be kept to tolerable levels. That means making it the exception rather than the rule. It means ensuring that it is not a normal part of the systems of governance. It means public decisions are usually taken on their merits, not purchased by the highest bidder. But when applying the tests of tolerability, I am not sure that the democracies of Pacific Asia have achieved the probity sought in their accountability rhetoric. The comforting response is that the accountability mechanisms will increase in effectiveness over time. The trend of improvement in the corruption perception index (Table 3.2) might provide some support for that view. But there is the more disturbing possibility that the forces of inertia continue to dominate, and that the steps taken so far are little more than token gestures to appease passing public interest. Lax implementation, loopholes in legislation, and ambiguity in obligations are all signs of ambivalence on the part of political leaders. Ultimately, the solution to the problem of systematic political corruption cannot rely on the next crisis or the future possible agent of change; it must come with intense public interest using responsive democratic institutions to achieve sustained reform. Reliance on the public in this way is yet another example of the hold of political culture on the workings of the systems of governance.

This chapter began with the question, Can political evolution be short-cut by clever design? In searching for an answer, we have paid tribute to the cleverness of the various designs being tried in Pacific Asia's democracies in relation to such institutions as representative bodies, electoral systems, and accountability processes. But we are left with a conclusion that clever design alone will not achieve the desired results. Clever design is only ever one element in any successful system. Other elements include systematization, public engagement, integrity of the oversight systems, and the intervention of pivotally placed individuals. Two broad conclusions may be open to us at this stage:

- The degree of systematization of the machinery of governance will have a commensurate impact on the achievement of the intended benefits of the institutional design.
- An engaged electorate will probably make even poorly designed systems work, while an apathetic electorate will not make the most ingenious design achieve its intended results.

We have seen how poor design may yet be made to work by factors such as popular engagement, longevity, and the legitimacy these bring. In relation to electoral systems, the following have been postulated:

- The ideal system is one that finds the best balance between high-quality representativeness through several dimensions of electoral representation, and effective governance through minimizing institutional divisions.
- Significant reforms tend to be generated in response to major crises, but reforms rarely result in win-win outcomes and thus require the mediation of agents of change to make them happen.

More generally, we are left with the rather negative conclusion that well-crafted designs will not solve the problems of lack of public engagement or weak systematization. Poor designs on the other hand will most likely exacerbate these problems. Perhaps the most positive conclusion open to us is that the more appropriate the design, the more chance it has, in combination with other factors, to achieve the acceptability, workability, and effectiveness required in the democratic consolidation process.

## Notes

1. Juan J. Linz, "The Virtues of Parliamentarism," Larry Diamond and Marc F. Plattner (eds.), *The Global Resurgence of Democracy*, 2nd ed. (Baltimore and London: Johns Hopkins University Press, 1996), pp. 160–161.

2. Roland Rich, "Democracy in the Balance," Julian Weiss (ed.), *Tigers' Roar: Asia's Recovery and Its Impact* (New York: M. E. Sharpe, 2001), p. 149.

3. France.

4. Israel, Italy, Japan, New Zealand, United Kingdom.

5. Austria, Portugal, Switzerland.

6. Pippa Norris, *Electoral Engineering—Voting Rules and Political Behavior* (Cambridge: Cambridge University Press, 2004), p. 249.

7. Giuseppe Di Palma, *To Craft Democracies—An Essay on Democratic Transitions* (Berkeley: University of California Press, 1990).

8. Roland Rich, "Analysing and Categorising Political Parties in the Pacific Islands," Roland Rich with Luke Hambly and Michael Morgan (eds.), *Political Parties in the Pacific Islands* (Canberra: Pandanus Books, 2006), p. 21.

9. Juan Linz and Alfred Stepan, *Problems of Democratic Transition and Consolidation: Southern Europe, South America, and Post-communist Europe* (Baltimore: Johns Hopkins University Press, 1996), p. 16.

10. Samuel P. Huntington, *Political Order in Changing Societies* (New Haven and London: Yale University Press, 1968), p. 12.

11. Inchoate stateness will certainly impact negatively on the level of systematization, but states that have satisfactorily resolved their issues of nationality and borders may continue to have deep problems of systematization. Cambodia provides an example. Weak institutionalization will also impact negatively on the level of systematization, but even where key organizations of the state have acquired value and stability, the state may continue to suffer from problems of systematization. The Philippines provides an example. In these examples, the state may be imagined as having substance and legitimacy by its citizens, and its official organizations may even function adequately, but the decisions taken in the public space are more influenced by forces outside the system than they are by the formal workings of the state's institutions.

12. Australian Electoral Commission, *Voter Turnout 1901–Present (National Summary)*, available from www.aec.gov.au/_content/what/voting/turnout.htm.

13. Ibid.

14. Section 68 states in part: "Every person shall have a duty to exercise his or her right to vote at an election. The person who fails to attend an election for voting without notifying the appropriate cause of such failure shall lose his or her right to vote as provided by law. Every person shall have a duty to exercise his or her right to vote at an election."

15. International Institute for Democracy and Electoral Assistance, "Voter Turnout Thailand," available from www.idea.int/vt/country_view.cfm? CountryCode=TH.

16. "Unprecedented 72% Turnout for Latest Poll," *The Nation*, 10 February 2005.

17. Michael Nelson, however, doubts that this measure will be effective. Michael H. Nelson, "Thai Politics Monitor," Michael H. Nelson (ed.), *Thailand's New Politics—KPI Yearbook 2001* (Bangkok: King Prajadhipok's Institute and White Lotus, 2002), p. 344.

18. Sheila S. Coronel, "Guns and Goons," Sheila S. Coronel et al., *The Rulemakers: How the Wealthy and Well-Born Dominate Congress* (Manila: Philippine Center for Investigative Journalism, 2004), p. 80.

19. Ibid., p. 84.

20. Ibid., p. 83.

21. Robert Lowry, *The Armed Forces of Indonesia* (Sydney: Allen and Unwin, 1996), p. 88.

22. Ian Douglas Wilson, "The Changing Contours of Organised Violence in Post New Order Indonesia," Asia Research Centre Working Paper No. 118, April 2005, p. 3.

23. Phil King, "Putting the (Para)Military Back into Politics—The Taskforces of the Political Parties," *Inside Indonesia*, January–March 2003, available from www.insideindonesia.org/edit73/king%20satgas.htm.

24. Vedi Hadiz, "Indonesian Local Party Politics: A Site of Resistance to Neo-Liberal Reform," City University of Hong Kong Working Paper Series No. 61, March 2004.

25. Ian Wilson, "Changing Contours of Organized Violence," p. 8.

26. Duncan McCargo and Ukrist Pathmanand, *The Thaksinization of Thailand* (Copenhagen: Nordic Institute of Asian Studies, 2005), p. 72.

27. Yun-han Chu, "Taiwan's Year of Stress," *Journal of Democracy* 16, no. 2 (April 2005): 51.

28. Sheryl WuDunn, "Reinventing Lives," Nicholas D. Kristof and Sheryl WuDunn, *Thunder from the East—Portrait of a Rising Asia* (New York: Alfred A. Knopf, 2000), p. 150.

29. Transparency International, *Corruption Surveys and Indices,* available from www.transparency.org/surveys/index.html#cpi.

30. Jeong-ho Roh, "Crafting and Consolidating Constitutional Democracy in Korea," Samuel S. King (ed.), *Korea's Democratization* (Cambridge: Cambridge University Press, 2003), p. 189.

31. Benedict J. Tria Kerkvliet, "Contested Meanings of Elections in the Philippines," R. H. Taylor (ed.), *The Politics of Elections in Southeast Asia* (Washington, DC: Woodrow Wilson Center Press and Cambridge: Cambridge University Press, 1996), p. 144.

32. Steve Muhlberger, "Democracy in Ancient India," available from www.nipissingu.ca/department/history/muhlberger/histdem/indiadem.htm.

33. R. H. Taylor, "Introduction," Taylor (ed.), *The Politics of Elections in Southeast Asia*, p. 10.

34. Ibid.

35. Nicholas Tarling, *Nations and States in Southeast Asia* (Cambridge: Cambridge University Press, 1998), p. 113.

36. Paul Kratoska and Ben Batson, "Nationalism and Modernist Reform," Nicholas Tarling, *The Cambridge History of Southeast Asia,* Vol. 2, p. 296.

37. Alan T. Wood, *Asian Democracy in World History* (New York: Routledge, 2004), p. 40.

38. Benedict R. Anderson, "Elections and Participation," Taylor (ed.), *The Politics of Elections in Southeast Asia,* p. 28.

39. Ibid., p. 21.

40. Ibid., p. 23.

41. Australian Parliamentary Handbook, "Referendums and Plebiscites," available from www.aph.gov.au/library/handbook/referendums/index.htm. Of the successful referendums, two affected the structure of parliament: minor alterations concerning Senate elections and terms of senators in 1906 and an amendment in 1977 aimed at ensuring that a replacement senator should be from the same political party as the senator departing in mid-term. Nine referendums to change the design of parliament or elections for parliament have been defeated, including eminently sensible provisions supported by all major parties on issues such as extending the term of parliament from three to four years (defeated in 1988) and holding simultaneous elections for both houses (defeated in 1977 and again in 1984).

42. Juan J. Linz, "The Perils of Presidentialism," *Journal of Democracy* 1, no. 1 (Winter 1990): 51–69.

43. Adam Schwarz, *A Nation in Waiting: Indonesia in the 1990s* (Boulder: Westview Press, 1994), p. 272.

44. Don Oberdorfer, *The Two Koreas: A Contemporary History* (New York: Basic Books 1997), p. 33.

45. Sheila S. Coronel, "Investigating the President," Philippine Center for Investigative Journalism, 2000, available from www.pcij.org/investigate.html.

46. Embassy of the United States of America, Jakarta, "Wrap-up of MPR Legislative Actions, 1999," available from www.usembassyjakarta.org/econ/wrapup-mpr.html.

47. National Democratic Institute for International Affairs, "Indonesia's Change of President and Prospects for Constitutional Reform," October 2001, p. 12, available from www.accessdemocracy.org/library/1319_id_presconstref102001.pdf.

48. Ibid., p. 17.

49. National Democratic Institute for International Affairs, "The Fundamental Change That Nobody Noticed—The MPR Annual Session, November 2001," January 2002, p. 6, available from www.accessdemocracy.org/library/1378_id_gov_112002.pdf.

50. Paragraphs (1) and (7) of Article 7B of the 1945 Constitution now read:

(1) Any proposal for the dismissal of the President and/or the Vice-President may be submitted by the DPR to the MPR only by first submitting a request to the Constitutional Court to investigate, bring to trial, and issue a decision on the opinion of the DPR either that the President and/or Vice-President has violated the law through an act of treason, corruption, bribery, or other act of a grave criminal nature, or through moral turpitude, and/or that the President and/or Vice-President no longer meets the qualifications to serve as President and/or Vice-President.

(7) The decision of the MPR over the proposal to impeach the President and/or Vice-President shall be taken during a plenary session of the MPR which is attended by at least 3/4 of the total membership and shall require the approval of at least 2/3 of the total of members who are present, after the President and/or Vice-President have been given the opportunity to present his/her explanation to the plenary session of the MPR.

51. Jürgen Rüland et al., *Parliaments and Political Change in Asia* (Singapore: Institute of Southeast Asian Studies, 2005), pp. 226–242.

52. Ibid., p. 232.

53. Bowronsak Uwanno and Wayne D. Burns, "The Thai Constitution of 1997: Sources and Process," *University of British Columbia Law Review* 32, no. 2 (1998): 227–247.

54. The status hierarchy can be seen in formal terms in that a joint sitting of the two houses is presided over by the president of the House of Representatives (Sect. 91), all legislative bills must originate in the House of Representatives (Sect. 169), and bills can eventually be adopted even if rejected by the Senate (Sects. 174–176).

55. As at September 2004, Statoids, "Regencies of Indonesia," available from www.statoids.com/yid.html.

56. Inter-Parliamentary Union, "Indonesia—General Information About the

Parliamentary Chamber or Unicameral Parliament," PARLINE database, available from www.ipu.org/parline-e/reports/2147_A.htm.

57. Yong Mun Cheong, "The Political Structures of the Independent States," Nicholas Tarling (ed.), *The Cambridge History of Southeast Asia—Volume Two: The Nineteenth and Twentieth Centuries* (Cambridge: Cambridge University Press, 1992), p. 422.

58. Government Information Office (Taiwan), *The Significance of Taiwan's Constitutional Reforms*, 10 June 2005, www.gio.gov.tw/taiwan-website/4-oa/20050610/2005061001.html.

59. Ibid.

60. See http://en.wikipedia.org/wiki/Legislative_Yuan.

61. Pasuk Phongpaichit and Chris Baker, "'Business Populism' in Thailand," *Journal of Democracy* 16, no. 2 (April 2005): 64.

62. Aurel Croissant, "Electoral Politics in South Korea," Aurel Croissant (ed.), *Electoral Politics in Southeast & East Asia* (Singapore: Friedrich-Ebert Stiftung, Office for Regional Co-operation in Southeast Asia, 2002), p. 259.

63. South Korean National Assembly, website, available from http://korea.assembly.go.kr/index.jsp.

64. Maurice Duverger, *Political Parties: Their Organisation and Activity in the Modern State* (London: Methuen, 1954).

65. Larry Diamond, *Developing Democracy: Toward Consolidation* (Baltimore: Johns Hopkins University Press, 1999), pp. 100–103.

66. Mahesh Rangarajan and Vijay Patidar, *India—First Past the Post on a Grand Scale*, Administration and Cost of Elections Project, available from www.aceproject.org/main/english/es/esy_in.htm.

67. R. William Liddle, "A Useful Fiction: Democratic Legitimation in New Order Indonesia," Taylor (ed.), *Politics of Elections in Southeast Asia*, p. 45.

68. National Democratic Institute for International Affairs, "Advancing Democracy in Indonesia: The Second Democratic Legislative Elections Since the Transition," June 2004, p. 4, available from www.accessdemocracy.org/library/1728_id_legelections_063004.pdf.

69. Ibid.

70. Aurel Croissant, "Electoral Politics in South Korea," p. 257.

71. Indian elections website, available from www.indian-elections.com/electionfaqs/delimitation-of-constituencies.html.

72. Philippines Constitution of 1987, Article VI, Section 5(2).

73. Government Information Office (Taiwan), *Taiwan 2004 Legislative Yuan Election,* available from www.gio.gov.tw/taiwan-website/5-gp/election2004/ele_10.html.

74. Samoa and Vanuatu are examples. With an unelected upper house and a unitary system, the UK would also have been in this one-dimensional category, but devolution and European integration have brought additional dimensions of representation to the UK electorate.

75. Andrew Reynolds, Ben Reilly, and Andrew Ellis, *Electoral System Design: The New International IDEA Handbook* (Stockholm: International Institute for Democracy and Electoral Assistance, 2005), pp. 138–139.

76. Mark Turner and Owen Podger, "Decentralization in Indonesia—Lessons for Policy Makers and Practitioners," Asian Development Bank, available from www.decentralization.ws/icd2/papers/decent_indonesia.htm.

77. Elections New Zealand, "General Elections 1996–2005—Seats Won by Party," available from www.elections.org.nz/elections/article_126.html.

78. It therefore suffices to encapsulate the existence of this threat to democratic consolidation in the following quotes covering each of the countries under review:

• In India "the centrality of elections, and the desperate value staked on winning them, made for engrained political corruption in the public arena: the scandals that tumbled over one another in the 1980s and 1990s were evidence of this." Sunil Khilnani, *The Idea of India* (New York: Farrar, Straus and Giroux, 2001), p. 54.

• "The average Korean believes that seven out of ten elected officials are corrupt and that about five out of ten civil servants are corrupt." Doh Chull Shin, "Mass Politics, Public Opinion, and Democracy in Korea," Samuel S. King (ed.), *Korea's Democratization* (Cambridge: Cambridge University Press, 2003), p. 62.

• In the Philippines and Thailand, "extensive corruption by politicians, judges, and military and police officials has been a major factor in undermining the quality of democracy and the rule of law." Larry Diamond, *Developing Democracy*, p. 52.

• "Even though elections became a process in which voters selected their political leadership, they were marred by corrupt electoral behaviour and manipulation by influential local leaders: vote buying, cheating, the partisan conduct of government officers and violence. Thailand had turned to money politics." Orathai Kokpol, "Electoral Politics in Thailand," Croissant (ed.), *Electoral Politics in Southeast & East Asia,* p. 281.

• "During 1992–93, Japanese media exposed to the public a series of seriously corrupt political practices involving some of the country's largest business corporations as well as some of its most powerful conservative political figures." Akira Kubota, "Big Business and Politics in Japan—1993–95," Takashi Inoguchi and Purnendra C. Jain (eds.), *Japanese Politics Today: Beyond Karaoke Democracy?* (Melbourne: MacMillan, 1997), pp. 124–125.

• "Corruption in Taiwan is an impediment to economic recovery and is one of the public's most serious concerns." David Kovick, "Taiwan," Peter M. Manikas and Laura L. Thornton (eds.), *Political Parties in Asia—Promoting Reform and Combating Corruption in Eight Countries* (Washington, DC: National Democratic Institute for International Affairs, 2003), p. 323.

• "Allegations of corruption (in Indonesia) could potentially derail the democratization process. Such allegations have already played a role in the political demise of the past three presidents." Peter M. Manikas and Dawn Emling, "Indonesia," Peter M. Manikas and Laura L. Thornton, *Political Parties in Asia*, p. 83.

79. Control Yuan of Taiwan website, www.cy.gov.tw/English/Statistics.asp.

80. Duncan McCargo, "Democracy Under Stress in Thaksin's Thailand," *Journal of Democracy* 13, no. 4 (October 2002): 114–115.

81. Ibid., p. 117.

82. Ibid., p. 119.

83. Jürgen Rüland et al., *Parliaments and Political Change*, p. 124.

84. Sheila Coronel, "The Philippines: Robin Hood Politics," *The Corruption Notebooks* (Washington, DC: The Center for Public Integrity, Public Integrity Books, 2004), p. 252.

85. Rakesh Kalshian, "India: Scam Plagued," *The Corruption Notebooks,* p. 92.

86. Ibid., p. 90.

87. Ibid., p. 95.

88. Steven R. Reed, "A Story of Three Booms: From the New Liberal Club to

the Hosokawa Coalition Government," Inoguchi and Jain (eds.), *Japanese Politics Today: Beyond Karaoke Democracy?* pp. 108–109.

89. Jeong-ho Roh, "Crafting and Consolidating Constitutional Democracy," pp. 185–188.

90. Doh C. Shin, *Mass Politics and Culture in Democratizing Korea* (Cambridge: Cambridge University Press, 1999), p. 8.

91. C. S. Eliot Kang, "The Development State and Democratic Consolidation in South Korea," Samuel S. King (ed.), *Korea's Democratization*, p. 232.

92. Drawn from several sources: Reginald Austin and Maja Tjernström (eds.), *Funding of Political Parties and Election Campaigns* (Stockholm: International Institute for Democracy and Electoral Assistance, 2003); papers presented at "Political Finance and Democracy in East Asia: The Use and Abuse of Money in Campaigns and Elections," Democracy Forum for East Asia, Seoul, Korea, 28–30 June 2001, available from www.ned.org/forum/asia/june01/introduction.html; National Democratic Institute for International Affairs, "Political Party Strategies to Combat Corruption, A Joint Project of NDI and the Council of Asian Liberals and Democrats (CALD),www.ndi.org/worldwide/asia/combatcorruption/executivesummary.asp; and Peter M. Manikas and Laura L. Thornton, *Political Parties in Asia.*

# 4

# Establishing
# the Rule of Law

"People want change, freedom, democracy
and most of all rule of law in China."
—Wu Qing, "The Rule of Law in Service to the People"[1]

What is rule of law? Is there another concept on which so many can agree
but so few are able to put into practice? In many ways, the concept of the
rule of law resembles the concept of democracy in its elusiveness. It is difficult to define and even more difficult to disaggregate. To attempt to lay
down the underlying premises on which the rule of law is built is to open a
Pandora's box of fundamental requirements, each of which presents its own
deep problems. One immediately thinks of courts and judges, police and
prisons, prosecutors and defense attorneys. But going slightly deeper than
institutions and office holders, one is confronted with the concepts of
respect for the law, enforcement of law, and equality before the law. And
having grappled with these conundrums, one arrives at the more philosophical question of the relationship of the law to justice, equity, and rights.

It is a generally accepted proposition that there can be no democracy
without rule of law.[2] The converse proposition is, I believe, also true, and so
the two concepts are mutually supportive and interdependent. The question
we must grapple with in this chapter is whether there are determinative
aspects of Pacific Asian civilization that are inimical to the establishment of
the rule of law. Are there deep-rooted aspects of Asian society antithetical to
the construction of a nation of laws? Is the term *rule of law* and its
European language synonyms, *rechtsstaat* and *état de droit*, so tied to
Western institutions and thought as to be incapable of proper application in
a non-Western culture? If so, democracy may be beyond Pacific Asia's
reach.

Drawing from the literature analyzing the meaning of the rule of law, it seems prudent to define the term by reference to its component parts.[3] This method necessarily has a bias favoring a functional definition rather than a more philosophical or jurisprudential definition. The functionalist bias is in keeping with the tone and purpose of this project. There are six key components of the rule of law:

1. Judicial independence protected in a basic instrument such as the constitution and acted upon by the judiciary.
2. An executive arm of government accepting that it is subject to laws, including, increasingly in the era of globalization, international law.
3. Procedural fairness in the making of laws, delivery of justice, and enforcement of laws, including such concepts as equality before the law and application of natural justice.
4. A significant degree of effectiveness of the law, an expectation of its enforcement, and a reliance on its provisions.
5. A significant level of predictability of the law, and a public that understands the likely predictable consequences of unlawful acts.
6. Public acceptance of the legitimacy of the legal processes, often achieved through longevity.

Returning to the question posed in this chapter, we need to examine the structure and implementation of the rule of law in the Asian countries under review. In our examination of the issues, it is imperative that we look beyond the titles and institutional structures of local legal institutions. To chisel the words *supreme court* on the impressive stone façade of a portentous building is not the same as having an independent body that skillfully and effectively reviews the legality of official, corporate, and individual public conduct. Pacific Asia has a number of imposing courthouses and many judges to sit on their benches, but even the most cursory study of contemporary Asia suggests that it does not yet have many particularly admirable systems of rule of law. So what is wrong? And what is going right?

## Three Historical Challenges
## to the Rule of Law in Pacific Asia

### Not Indigenous
The first and most obvious challenge to the applicability of the rule of law in Asia is that the modern legal systems under construction are not indigenous. Indigenous concepts of law in Pacific Asia were by and large oral and had difficulty withstanding the impact of written forms.[4] They did not take modern legal form but rather were imbedded in the ethical and behavioral

messages built into custom, folk tales, Indonesian *wayang* puppetry, and time-honored local practices. Their influence may well persist in various forms and in certain isolated communities, but the only example of their survival as a significant and influential body of law in Asia is the Adat system of Java, which the Dutch allowed to be used in legal relations not involving colonial interests and which were, in any case, largely reduced to writing in colonial times.[5]

As the reader will come to realize, while respectful of and interested in the origins of concepts, I reject the notion that only indigenous concepts can properly take root in any community. To accept this notion is to see the world in a profoundly ahistorical manner and to dismiss the borrowing of ideas and techniques by peoples from each other over millennia. An idea must be tested on its utility, not its origins. So in relation to the modern construction of the rule of law, it is true that it does not have the solidity of an institution traced back to "time immemorial," but very few institutions in very few countries can make such a claim.

### Different Sources

The next challenge that history posed was the various borrowings of legal institutions from different sources. The three major early legal influences on the region came from Indian law, Chinese law, and Islamic law, roughly in the following geographic pattern:

- Indian law including Buddhist law in Burma, Cambodia, Java, Bali, and Thailand.
- Chinese law in Japan, Korea, and Vietnam.
- Islamic law in parts of the Malay Peninsula and island Southeast Asia.[6]

This is not the place for a comprehensive description or comparison of these vastly different systems of law, but some points on their impact on societies with oral traditions of law require emphasis. What characterized the new systems in comparison with existing village law was their relative complexity, being carefully written, dealing with a growing range of utilitarian subjects, and, critically, requiring some administrative architecture. Rules covered a broader scope of issues. Recent scholarship on early Buddhist law lists issues such as natural justice, determining market value, definitions of theft, rules concerning treatment of slaves, as well as the duties of marriage partners.[7] The written form of the law in an age before printing required the difficult skills of copying and, often, translating. Words were derived from Sanskrit, which is to South and Southeast Asia as Latin is to Europe. Errors in translation and transcription continue to bedevil Asian scholars of legal history, suggesting that it was also an inexact science among its earlier practitioners. Islamic law dealt extensively with subjects concerning maritime transport and trade. Finally, and of critical importance for the development of law in Pacific Asia, the elaborate new forms required new administrative architecture in the form of courts, judges, and officials.

Another broadly common aspect of these systems of law, whether drawn from Buddhist *dhamma*, Koranic strictures, or Imperial Chinese rules, is the revealed nature of the respective laws. Whether set down by the deity or the emperor as deity incarnate, the rules had a divine provenance that elevated and sanctified them. Having been revealed meant that revision or amendment became a difficult and contorted process. The revealed law was by definition perfect, and changing its impact would have to be achieved by methods of interpretation and application, both of which are subject to human imperfection. Here lies a considerable challenge to modern conceptions of the rule of law. Today, we see law as being in service to humanity, adapted to the circumstances of society and subject to regular reform and renewal. We might speak of the majesty of the law but we reject any notion of its divinity. The tension between revealed law and living law is one of the historical challenges facing some Asian communities.

### Colonial Heritage

Finally, there is a challenge cast by the diversity of colonial and postcolonial influences on Asia. We can gain an impression of these legal influences from the following list:

* British law in Burma, Borneo, Hong Kong, the Malay Peninsula, South Asia, and the Straits settlements.
* French law in Vietnam, Cambodia, Laos, and, to a certain extent, borrowed by Japan and Thailand.
* German law, in part borrowed by Japan and, indirectly, by Korea.
* Dutch law in Indonesia.
* Spanish law in the Philippines.
* Portuguese law in East Timor, Goa, and Macau.
* Soviet concepts of law in China, Vietnam, Cambodia, Laos, and North Korea.
* US practice of law in the Philippines and Japan as well as influencing others such as South Korea.

While these occidental forms of law have many variations, subject to the exception of the recognition of class origins in Soviet law, they share a concept of the individual whose status is theoretically unseen by the process of law and who is subject to abstract normative obligations that may have been originally derived from a religious base, but that have since become secular.

They see law in the broad sense as in service to society, and not a reflection of a cosmic or religious order. Accordingly, law is far from fixed and can be amended to the requirements of society, or at least its ruling interests.

Each of these various influences continues to have an impact, perhaps slight in some cases and significant in others. The inclusion of judgment tales and anecdotes in Buddhist law texts may owe its origins to the Southeast Asian penchant for folk tales.[8] On the weightier part of the ledger, the almost unchecked power of procuracies in China and Vietnam is based on a Soviet view of the role of law serving primarily the interests of the party and, by virtue of the party's leading role, indirectly serving those of the state. As the diversity of influences demonstrates, Asian countries have had to deal with a legal mosaic requiring them to piece together systems that respond to political and popular needs. This applies to both voluntarily borrowed and imposed systems and ideas. Some countries have been better able than others to assimilate these systems and operate them to the benefit of their people. But the mere fact alone that the systems have come in various waves of influences does not preclude a positive outcome in their adoption and adaptation.

## Three Conceptual Challenges
## to the Rule of Law in Pacific Asia

It may be helpful to focus on three arguments that have been hazarded from time to time suggesting that Asia has difficulty in adopting the rigors of the rule of law. The first concerns a mooted cultural aversion to reliance on formally written and administered rules as opposed to a reliance on moral virtue based on Confucian precepts.[9] This cultural distinction, if valid, would have a deep impact on the most basic process of administering a system of rule of law. The second possible difficulty has to do with enduring Asian perceptions of the individual that militate against achieving any notion of equality before the law.[10] Individuals come in categories and, according to this view, they never escape these categories. Resultant public systems continue to pigeonhole individuals into their categories and thus impose a set logic on their relationship with the law. The third problem turns on the Asian concept of what is the public realm.[11] The argument made in this regard is that in the view of the Asian villager, the public realm is divorced from ordinary individuals who observe the goings on there as if in a theater.

### Written Law

Let me begin this discussion with an exchange that occurred in the 1980s, the early days of global environmental consciousness, when an earnest Japanese diplomat called on me in the Department of Foreign Affairs to explain Japan's position on extending its "scientific" whaling. After he had gone down the list of his talking points, I thanked him but politely explained that none of these arguments would alter Australia's position of seeking to protect all cetaceans from commercial exploitation. Slightly exasperated, my Japanese visitor said that Australia's position was not scientific but cultural, and that we were simply pursuing a bias originating from the biblical inclusion of whales in the story of Jonah. Why should the rest of the world be bound by Western myths? he pouted. Reflecting on this argument in the following weeks, I decided that it was wrong about whales, the Australian government was simply responding to legitimate democratic pressure from a very secular electorate that found the slaughter of intelligent aquatic mammals unacceptable, but that there may well be an element of truth to the argument that some of the West's conceptions of universal truths are culturally inspired. In relation to the rule of law, the argument flowing from cultural relativism would link the West's respect for written laws to its Judeo-Christian origins in Moses coming down Mount Sinai with those two stone tablets containing ten written rules.

Cultural relativists would point to the Confucian tradition as the key influence in Pacific Asia, under which the dominant themes are virtue, morality, and leadership by example.[12] Confucianism seeks out the virtuous man, not the virtuous law, under the belief that such a person is in a better position than a written law to deal with the breadth and complexity of issues coming before humankind. Surely, however, a better interpretation of Chinese history is that there has been a constant debate between morality and legalism, with the inevitable Hegelian result of a synthesis emerging. The Legalist and Dynastic schools of law had significant influence in Chinese history and left their mark alongside Confucianism.[13] That is why even countries with deep Confucian influence are comfortably able to work with Western-style constitutions.[14]

A debate on the most effective means of influencing social behavior between morality and self-restraint on the one hand, and law and enforcement on the other, strikes me as both universal and eternal. It reflects the human personality. In Western societies, moral education has accompanied legal strictures, and enforcement is only effective because the vast majority of the people practice self-restraint. Asian societies have wrestled with the same problem over time. If there is a difference, it will be in the exact proportions of the mix employed in any one polity at any one time. So an argument that Confucius somehow cancels out Moses or Hammurabi is unconvincing. All societies approaching a certain size and complexity need written rules to govern themselves, and once written rules take the character of laws, they need dissemination, adjudication, and enforcement processes that compose the basic skeleton of a legal system.

Curiously, there was an Asian country that for fifteen years tried to live without written law. When communist forces triumphed in Indochina in 1975, the Lao People's Revolutionary Party took power in Vientiane. Unlike their Vietnamese neighbors who maintained the existing structure of law going back to colonial times and simply amended those they disliked, the Lao communists decided to abolish all previous law and thus created a national legal vacuum that was to last until 1991, when a new constitution was adopted and the slow process of drafting basic laws began. Of course, for the great majority of Lao peasants, the absence of laws had little impact.[15] They live by requirements imposed by the seasons and focus on subsistence. But urban dwellers found themselves in the curious position of having to intuit whether behavior was right or wrong, or more to the point, whether it was punishable or not. Party decrees would provide some guide to those who had access to them. The rest of the population would have to follow the official media for reports on who had been arrested and draw their own conclusions. Conduct regarded as felonious in a nation of laws was also punishable in tabula rasa Laos, but when it came to victimless conduct, things became murky. For example, it was not clear what sort of speech might be punishable, and the safest conduct was simply not to engage in any type of public comment except for lavish praise for the country's leadership. Fifteen years after the decision to return to the concept of law, the Lao are struggling to build their legal infrastructure and are finding that building a legal system from the ground up is far more difficult than amending an existing system.

### Status-Based Law

Precolonial Asian systems of law generally saw the individual in terms of his or her race, gender, caste, family, and religion. For that reason these "oriental" legal forms have been described as status-based law designed to maintain a certain social order where a person's status is known and fixed.[16] These systems tend to be based on a relatively fixed and static view of rights and obligations and thus have limited mechanisms for amendment or interpretation of the revealed or derived rules of law. The rules were designed to keep individuals within their caste, race, religious, or gender status, which may nevertheless have allowed for a system of justice perceived as fair to be delivered in disputes within each group, but were far more problematic in disputes across the groups where hierarchy would become the dominant focus. Colonial processes often grafted on to such systems a new caste of colonial masters who invariably had the law on their side, thus unintentionally reinforcing the concept of status-based law. Today, one can find a curious reverse echo in the common practice in many Asian countries of simply assuming that in any traffic accident, the foreigner is in the wrong! Status-based law is antithetical to any concept of democracy wherein the right to vote is analogous to other rights in being enjoyed simply because of reasons of citizenship or membership of the polity, regardless of other distinguishing factors.

An example of status-based law coming into confrontation with more modern notions of law occurred in a recent case decided by the Constitutional Court in Thailand, which had before it the traditional requirement that married women take on their husband's family name. This seemed in conflict with Section 30 of Thailand's 1997 Constitution, which makes clear that "men and women shall enjoy equal rights." The court held that Thai women have the right to retain their maiden names if they so choose.[17] Yet the same court turned down an appeal from two disabled persons whose applications for judicial office were refused because they limped. In this case, the court pandered to an old-fashioned idea that the physical disability made the persons less admirable in public perceptions and thus unsuited to be judges.[18]

The Greek goddess of Justice, Themis, is represented as having a set of scales to weigh evidence and a sword to enforce her judgments. Asian systems of status-based law have both these concepts. But Themis has a third feature that is missing from status-based systems—a blindfold. She does not see the parties before her and thus is impartial, whereas status-based systems examine the petitioners carefully to determine their social pedigree and usually make their decisions based on this status.

### Public Law

The final conceptual hurdle raised in this section concerns the perception of law by ordinary people in many Asian countries. It is seen by many villagers as part of a public sphere divorced from the everyday lives of ordinary people. In this regard, the perception of law is not dissimilar from perceptions of the workings of parliament or the observation of the comings and goings of foreign leaders. According to Niels Mulder with reference to Southeast Asia, "the public world has never existed. . . . What existed, at best, was the theatre state, visible to all but monopolized by the political centre."[19]

Again we have come to a concept deeply antithetical to the notion in a democracy that power is in the hands of the people. In a "theatre state," ordinary people are necessarily reduced to the role of spectators and cannot conceive of themselves as actors. The disconnection between their lives and the machinations going on in the public space is deep. Yet every now and then, an actor will leap from the stage and impose the political center's will on the hapless beholder. The instrument through which this is primarily achieved is the law.

I had a firsthand account of this perspective when I served in the

Australian embassy in Rangoon in the early 1980s. There was a well-trodden tourist trail in Burma, but the rest of the country was basically off-limits. Australia and Burma were friends at a time when issues of human rights, corruption, and bad governance were not discussed in polite company. Australia had some large development assistance projects that allowed its diplomats to visit parts of the country that would otherwise have been out of bounds. And so, one day I found myself crossing to the west bank of the Irrawaddy River, over the bridge at Ava in Mandalay, and traveling deep into Sagaing province along dusty dirt roads. Modernity was receding in the rearview mirror as we traveled into a timeless land. The landscape was bland, fallow fields with an occasional buffalo seeking shade, except when we came across any hill, on top of which would be a bright stupa, either whitewashed or with a golden point, in honor of the Buddha. We drove endlessly, past Monywa, before we reached our destination, a small village where the crew was to begin work drilling a well to the aquifer believed to be in the area. Although the equipment for this task, and the type of tube well to be installed, were simple pieces of mechanical technology with no complex electronics, they were still millennia ahead of anything the villagers had seen. And as it turns out, anybody younger than thirteen would also have their first view of a foreigner, me. Thirteen years before, the villagers recalled, a Swedish man from the United Nations Children's Fund (UNICEF) wandered around here, and I was to be their next exhibit. The children's curiosity had them mobbing me, with a particular interest in the hair on my exposed arms, which they would touch, stroke, and occasionally pluck, until an adult would shoo them away and give me a few minutes respite, in which time the kids would build the courage to regroup for another assault.

That night, after a village feast, where I had the dubious but delicious pleasure of tasting "barking deer," which I feared might have been an endangered species, and with the children banished from the inner circles, we sat around talking to the village leaders. It looked like a type of gerontocracy, but the leaders had titles that went with their age. There was the village headman, the representative of the cooperatives movement, and the representative of the Burma Socialist Programme Party (BSPP). The conversation was conducted through translation, and we advanced along a steady and safe path talking about the weather, the trip to the village, and all the benefits the new well would bring. At this point, I thought I would ask a more political question. "What sort of policies are you looking for from your government in Rangoon?" The translation did not seem to hit the mark. I tried various formulations until I was down to, "What do you want from your government?" Having finally understood such a silly question, the headman had no hesitation and no need for consultation in replying, "We want the people in Rangoon to leave us alone."

To these villagers, as with a billion other Asian villagers, law is an instrument of taxation, conscription, and exploitation. Local disputes are settled locally or fester locally. Intervention by soldiers or police is invariably deleterious to the interests of the villagers. To be left alone is the greatest governance blessing to which they can aspire. These are the views of subjects, not citizens. Appealing to the law to resolve a problem is totally foreign to these villagers, as it is for the great majority of poor urbanites as well. Unless law has the qualities of a protector, a fair means to resolve disputes, and a guarantor of rights, it will be seen by people subject to its rules as either irrelevant or, even more concerning, as part of an outside system of unjust political control.

## Rule by Law

It may sound like faint praise, but at least some Asian countries are moving toward systems of rule by law. There is a world of difference between the two prepositions *of* and *by*. The distinction has been helpful in understanding Pacific Asian law, and I find it more useful than the "thick" and "thin" conceptions of law preferred by some scholars.[20] One definition for rule by law is "a rule which is simply in accordance with law, but generally not embodying the legal guarantees to safeguard against abuse of state power and provide for independent remedies which are implied in the rule of law."[21] Returning to the six points at the commencement of this chapter encompassing the rule *of* law, a system of rule *by* law lacks the first three: judicial independence, submission of the executive to the rule of law, and consequentially, procedural fairness. But it may well achieve the next two points: effectiveness of the law and a certain degree of predictability, which may even lead to some public acceptance of its legitimacy. It might be difficult for people living in nations governed by the rule of law to accept the value of a lesser system, but for those living in societies governed through rule by whim, rule by law is a progressive step. At least rule by law provides the citizenry with some basis for understanding the relationship with officialdom. At least it provides for a written set of rules that is published before it comes into effect. And it may even provide some basis for exoneration from accusations of having committed a crime, though not if the executive is determined on conviction.

### The Conviction of Anwar Ibrahim

Executive determination to convict cannot be averted in a system of rule by law. A good example is the sodomy conviction against Malaysian former deputy prime minister Anwar Ibrahim. The sodomy charge was a particularly devastating indictment in a country where homosexuality is not generally accepted. It portrayed Anwar as unfit to lead in the eyes of the population, whether Malay, Chinese, or Indian. I recall sharing a table in 1999 with Anwar's leading defense attorney Christopher Fernando. He was deeply disappointed that the Malaysian court system had simply ignored clear exculpatory evidence. A sodomy charge cannot be leveled in general; it must be specified in terms of persons, time, and place where the act is alleged to have been committed. This the prosecution did, but on examining the allegation, the defense team found that the building in which the act was alleged to have taken place was not ready for occupation at the alleged date. Fernando admitted to me that he and his partner, Karpal Singh, made a critical tactical error in their handling of this key fact. Instead of allowing the prosecution to conclude its case based on the impossible date, the defense immediately advised the court of this exculpatory fact in the expectation that the court would dismiss the charge. Instead, the court simply allowed the prosecution to change the date, twice![22]

Fernando and Singh were behaving as officers of the court in immediately bringing the key discrepancy to the court's attention. An independent judiciary would have acted logically in dismissing the charges. But in former prime minister Mahathir Mohammed's Malaysia, the judiciary's independence had been emasculated, and the bench cowed into accepting the executive's wishes regardless of their lawfulness. In 1988, Mahathir sacked the chief justice and two of his brethren and amended the constitution to divest the courts of their "judicial power," thus making it clear that judicial independence did not in practice include a right to reject government wishes.[23] The Anwar case has served as a barometer of the credibility of the Malaysian judiciary, and it was therefore a positive sign that in September 2004, after Mahathir's resignation and under the far less pugnacious leadership of Abdullah Badawi, Anwar's appeal against his conviction was successful, in part because, the majority held, Anwar should have been given the benefit of the doubt arising from the uncertain date of the alleged offense.[24]

### Rule by Whim

Anyone who has lived under rule by whim will crave rule by law. Authoritarian systems tend to develop greater scope for whim the longer the autocrat is in power. Marcos began as a popularly elected reformer in the Philippines but overstayed his welcome after declaring martial law. The well-known excesses, particularly by his partner in crime, Imelda, date from the autocratic period. Suharto seized power in a difficult time, and the early period of his presidency was marked by sensible policy settings and generally productive public expenditure. A quarter of a century later, Indonesia had become a kleptocracy for the benefit of the Suharto clan and cronies.

At least in these cases, executive decisions could be understood in terms of presidential greed and grandstanding. Burma's General Ne Win was an autocrat who ran the country by idiosyncratic whim fueled by cunning, ignorance, and superstition. His decisions often baffled the entire country and took it from poverty to penury. In 1987, he had been in power for some twenty-five years when even those used to his excesses were stunned by his decision to declare war on the decimal system! His lucky number was nine, and so he declared the existing currency worthless and in its place introduced bank notes in denominations of 15, 45, and 90 kyats.[25] Those few trusting enough to keep their money in the bank were saved. Everybody else was ruined. This included some of the black marketeers, the ostensible targets of the demonetization, though many of the smarter ones would have had their holdings in Thai baht or US dollars anyway. The real losers were the members of the small urban middle classes who had kept their savings under the mattress. Although he resigned on 8 August 1988, a propitious day according to his soothsayers, Ne Win continued to be puppet master, and it was not for another six years until the military junta felt sufficiently emboldened to bring back decimal currency.

Rule by whim means the decisionmaker's superstitions and prejudices have the force of law. On another occasion, Ne Win decided to change Burma's system of driving on the left to driving on the right side of the road, with only the most perfunctory consultations or preparations. In his dotage, he began a massive pagoda construction venture at public expense to build merit for the next life. As for his political enemies or rivals, they could all eventually expect to meet each other in Insein prison on the outskirts of Rangoon, where they would be serving lengthy sentences. The pattern of rule by whim was maintained by Ne Win's successors in the military. In observing the Tatmadaw, the Burmese military, I could never dispel the image of Ne Win as Napoleon in George Orwell's *Animal Farm,* taking away the newborn puppies only to release them later as savage dogs. This is an apt description of the current leadership of Burma, since renamed Myanmar, an even less inclusive name than the one it replaced.[26] They wield the law as a weapon. I have previously written on how the military uses the law to control every aspect of the media.[27] A court sentenced journalist San San Nweh to seven years in prison for "spreading information prejudicial to the State." But she was luckier than Win Tin, editor of *Hanthawadi,* who was given a ten-year sentence. One who did not survive his sentence was Leo Nichol, an Anglo-Burmese acting honorary consul for several European countries. Not enjoying the privilege of diplomatic immunity, he was sentenced to three years in prison for the heinous crime of owning an unregistered fax machine. In his sixties when he entered prison, he died a few months into his sentence.

I followed an interesting manifestation of rule by whim when the rules of international law were insufficient to meet the wishes of Ne Win. I was not an eyewitness to the bombing of the Aung San mausoleum in Rangoon on 9 October 1983, but I heard the explosion from my house a couple of kilometers away. Aung San is considered to be the father of the modern nation of Burma. He was the leader of the army and became the leader of the antifascist movement, and he would have become prime minister but for his assassination by a political rival a few months before independence. It is one of those terrible ironies of history that the next generation of army leaders should keep his daughter Suu Kyi under house arrest for decades on end. But in 1983, no ironies presented themselves when the visiting South Korean president Chun Doo Hwan and party were scheduled to lay a wreath at the mausoleum, as this was standard practice for visitors to Rangoon. What followed was clearly not standard. A massive explosion killed twenty-one people and wounded forty-six others. Among the dead were several Korean cabinet ministers, including Foreign Minister Lee Bum Suk, though President Chun was spared.

The next few weeks saw high political drama. The Burmese had to deal with body identification, hospital admissions, medical evacuations, and repatriation of remains—a grisly and difficult business not made much easier by a furious South Korean public demanding to know what had happened. Initial suspicion fell on the old ethnic enemy of the Burmans, the Karen, but only a day or two passed before the three North Korean saboteurs were cornered trying to make their getaway. One was killed and two were wounded and arrested. It was left for the Burmese to mop up the political and legal mess.

One of Ne Win's cunning ideas was not to take sides overtly in the Cold War. This was a difficult balancing act, and Burmese foreign policy was one of cool but correct relations with the two superpowers of the day; wariness of neighbors; testiness with the United Kingdom, the former colonial master; commercial flirtatiousness with economic powerhouses Japan and South Korea; cordiality with distant aid donors such as Australia or Germany; and friendship with . . . North Korea. Ne Win considered the ("Great") leader of the Democratic People's Republic of Korea (DPRK), Kim Il Sung, a friend. Ne Win's BSPP declined to have party-to-party relations with any of the Soviet-bloc parties or with the Chinese Communist Party, which continued to have fraternal relations with the outlawed Burmese Communist Party, then conducting a vicious war against the Burmese army near the Chinese border. The only party with which the BSPP consented to have fraternal relations was Kim Il Sung's Korean Workers' Party. So when the saboteurs were arrested and, under interrogation, it became clear they were from Pyongyang and under the control of Kim Il Sung's son, Kim Jong Il, North Korea's current ("Dear") leader, Ne Win felt angry and betrayed: friends do not assassinate their friend's guests.

The next part of this story came to me through a friend in the Protocol Department at the Foreign Ministry, an intelligent fellow with a permanent expression of bemused irony on his handsome face. Ne Win wanted retaliation against North Korea and, having no military options, called for a recommendation from the Foreign Ministry. The Foreign Ministry recommended the expulsion of the North Korean ambassador in Rangoon and the withdrawal of the Burmese ambassador in Pyongyang. Ne Win rejected this as too weak. The ministry upped the ante and recommended the closure of the diplomatic missions in both countries. Again this was rejected as insufficient. The staff in the Protocol Department were scratching their heads by now, looking for a more severe form of protest, and came up with the closure of diplomatic missions, the withdrawal of all official contact, and the breaking of diplomatic relations. This would require a future agreement on the reestablishment of diplomatic relations before any formal contacts could be held. They submitted their recommendations with the calmness of a team having completed a difficult mission. To their shock, Ne Win rejected the recommendation once again, demanding an even tougher response. By this stage, the Protocol Department had come to the last page of the diplomatic manual and had still not found the answer to satisfy "the old man." Ne Win had a volcanic temper, and there were now fears that the advisers would be swallowed up in the lava flow.

They eventually came up with an idea that pleased their boss but left international lawyers scratching their heads. Each recommendation had been accepted insofar as it went; Ne Win had wanted them toughened up each time. So all the steps recommended to date were to be taken with one additional step—Burma formally de-recognized the existence of the DPRK, a state of affairs that continues at the time of writing, though an informal strategic alliance between the two pariah states may be blossoming.[28] De-recognition does not change the map of the world; there is still a northern part of the Korean peninsula above the thirty-eighth parallel. But as far as Burma is concerned, it may as well be blank, because it does not recognize the existence of a nation in that territory.

The final part of this sad tale tells us something else about the rule of law in Burma, because, with the assassins in hand, Ne Win decided to put them on trial. Trials in Burma are usually quite dull affairs with perfunctory recitations of crimes committed, followed by pleas for mercy falling invariably on deaf ears. As the outcome is clear beforehand, there is no tension or suspense. So the members of the diplomatic community were surprised to be invited to a show trial for the two North Koreans. Unlike the theatrics Stalin was able to display, Ne Win had very little material to work with. The defendants had been shot and shrapnelled in the course of their capture and were a sorry sight, covered in bandages and one sitting in a wheelchair. They spoke only Korean and so could make no stunning confessions to shock the gallery. In fact, they both looked bewildered and lost, hardly justifying the expansive show the Burmese were putting on. What was important was the form, the façade, the show, not the outcome, for they would surely be found guilty. Interestingly, they were not both executed, and one of the saboteurs has survived and remains in prison in Burma.

### Rule by Law in Communist Pacific Asia

People ruled by whim in places like Burma and North Korea thus aspire to be ruled by some notion of law. This is what China and Vietnam are attempting to achieve. It is a particularly creditable venture in view of the fact that a mere generation ago, upon emerging from the colonial era, Vietnam had to endure decades of war to achieve national unification, and China suffered through a long period of Maoist nihilism. It is also a vast undertaking requiring the drafting of legislation, its enactment, the establishment of legal infrastructure, and the training and upskilling of thousands of lawyers. The driving force for this change of course is largely a top-down process, but this is not to discount the popular resentments that inspired it. The authorities came to understand that they need the rigor and clarity that law can bring to government. Delivering economic reforms, regulating an increasingly market-based economy, and complying with mutually beneficial international obligations all require a mechanism for disseminating and enforcing government decisions. Tackling corruption is another reason to strengthen the legal system, as the internal party mechanisms were clearly failing in this task. The construction of legal institutions thus responds to popular resentment over corruption and the inequalities of who may benefit from it with impunity. Developing the legal system was seen as a practical necessity and also as a means of enhancing regime legitimacy.

But as others have made clear, adopting legal structures falls short of establishing the rule of law.[29] Indeed, there is a divergence at the very core of the two systems. The rhetoric and the genuine intention of the Chinese and Vietnamese authorities are to safeguard the people from maladministration. This is not dissimilar from notions inspiring the rule of law. But the means of achieving these two concepts are quite distinct. The Chinese and Vietnamese idea is to set rules, make them known, and establish state institutions to enforce them. There is a paternalistic premise at the core of the system. The authorities are building the system, running it, and reviewing its effectiveness. Rule by law becomes a gift from the authorities to the people they are governing. Gifts are usually well received, but they carry inherent problems. They are at the discretion of the giver. They may not correspond to the aspirations of the receiver. There is an expectation of gratitude and a corollary contempt for ingrates. The underlying premise of a rule-of-law system, on the other hand, is to empower individuals to pursue their rights and to provide legal institutions in which they can do so. Rights are not gifts, they are inherent and inalienable. There may also be an expectation of gratitude, but it is expressed in votes and is thus famously fickle.

One of the great disadvantages the Chinese and Vietnamese systems carry is their communist heritage. Both systems are built on the rhetoric of continuity to draw legitimacy from their modern nation-building phases. The current economic policies are portrayed as reforms and renovations, even though they have eroded the central logic of systems based on central planning. So, there is a need for some continuity in the Chinese and Vietnamese institutions of government. Regardless of constitutional blandishments, the court systems in communist countries are basically at the service of the ruling party and the executive branch. The clearest expression of this fact is the status of the procuracy, which by virtue of its power to oversee the courts, is at the apex of the legal system.[30]

The procuracy is both the prosecutor and the guarantor of the proper functioning of the legal system. In such a system, it is not possible to speak of the independence of the judiciary because judges, though they may enjoy high social status, are ultimately mere employees of the state, subject to oversight by a part of the executive. In addition to the problem of the status of courts, the systems of both countries are based on the ultimate supremacy of the Leninist party at the helm. In theory, the party provides broad policy direction to the institutions of state, but all policy needs implementation and the devil is invariably in the details. It is difficult to trace exactly how far party decisions reach in the day-to-day work of the courts, but it is undeniable that the party retains a crucial role, perhaps stronger in Vietnam than in China. In Vietnam, judges are expected to abide by the party's policies, and there are supervisory party groups operating inside the court.[31] In China, the sheer scale of the country and the increasing complexity of decisions make it impractical for the party to attempt to supervise every decision, and it therefore seems to have adopted the tactic to govern less in order to govern more effectively.[32] The bottom line is that courts in both countries will not make a decision contrary to party wishes, which will be made clear to the judge if the party considers the issue to be of sufficient importance to make its view known.

My own experience in this regard derives from working with Lao and Vietnamese judiciaries and procuracies as a trainer and adviser at various intervals in the course of a decade or so. The most striking impression is how different Lao and Vietnamese judges are from Australian judges. The latter are an opinionated and rather pompous lot, devoted to the law and jealously protecting their central place in the system. The former are very much in the gray public service mold, focused on administering processes and staying out of trouble. They may both sit on benches in buildings called courts, but few other similarities are discernible. An Australian judge will be assisted by learned counsel for each party who will guide the judge to the legal issues that need to be decided. The decision will be based on precedent drawing on centuries of legal scholarship and will be taken in the full knowledge that it may be subject to appeal before senior judges. As has been repeatedly demonstrated, upsetting the Australian government will be the least of the judge's concerns, because the judge knows that tenure is secure and that any discipline issues are largely in the hands of other judges. A Vietnamese judge does not enjoy these luxuries. There is a shallow legal tradition to fall back on, most recently including discredited and exploitative colonial law, social-ist legality in service to the party, and the current experiment with rule by law. There is not much by way of a legal profession to guide the judge or support judicial independence. Finally, the judge's conduct is subject to supervision by the procuracy, and the judge's future is ultimately in the hands of the party, of which the judge will invariably be a member.

While these basic distinctions are well known, what came as a shock to me was the lack of effectiveness of some courts. A senior Lao judge once confided in me that he and his colleagues were reluctant to make decisions in civil cases because of fear of loss of face should that decision simply be ignored. In a society based on the rule of law, there is a presumption of effectiveness of the law, in that court decisions will be carried out. But to implement certain decisions requires bailiffs and police to respect and enforce court orders. If one can simply bribe the police not to take action, then there is no rule of law and not even rule by law. Bribery is one way to circumvent the system, but there are formal ways as well. The procuracy in China, Vietnam, and Laos may petition to have court cases reconsidered even where judicial appeals have been exhausted.[33] The underlying reason is concerns about judicial corruption. But the message it sends is the absence of separation of powers and the subsidiary role of the judiciary. A remarkable example elsewhere in Pacific Asia of the effective superiority of the executive branch is the Indonesian legal institution known as the *surat sakti* (magic memos). This is a mechanism whereby a superior judge can countermand a decision of an inferior court, even, in the case of the chief justice, a final decision of the highest court, by issuing the *surat sakti*. It tended to be issued upon the behest of the executive branch, often in the form of President Suharto summoning the chief justice to explain the inter-ests of the state in having an unfavorable decision reversed.[34]

In my dealings with Vietnamese procuracy officials, a number of odd aspects stood out. They are in dread of making errors, as if making errors would be tantamount to an indictment of the entire system. An error means that someone, the police investigator, the judge, or the procurator oversee-ing the system, did not do their job properly. This flows in part from some of the civil law origins of the system, which see the judicial process as able to achieve scientific truths where the right result can always be obtained.

But mostly it flows from the law's lack of popular legitimacy and concerns that admission of error will pull down the whole edifice. The result is a criminal conviction rate approaching 100 percent. In effect, this means the decision to prosecute is the decision to convict. Another perverse effect of the high conviction rate is that it effectively reverses the onus of proof. My Vietnamese colleagues agreed that an accused person had no option but to provide information that demonstrated innocence. They were interested in the jury system but preferred their system of civilian assessors, two of whom sit with the judge and can thus theoretically outvote the judge. No one could recall if this had ever happened. The civilian assessors are not simply drawn randomly from the public. They are selected because of their good character, trained by the state, and then sit on the bench for five years. The problem with the jury system, according to my Vietnamese interlocutors, is that decisions are being made by untrained people. My explanations that the judge directed the jury on points of law and that the jurors' very ordinariness and disconnection from officialdom was their most valuable qualification cut no ice.

The Japanese criminal justice system also has a conviction rate of over 99 percent. Is this due to forced confessions or government pressure on judges? While these explanations are open, one study concluded that the probable cause was low prosecution budgets forcing decisions only to proceed with the strongest possible cases.[35] Yet even with this bureaucratic explanation, the fact of such a high conviction rate nevertheless has the practical effect of reversing the onus of proof. Japan is currently in the process of deliberating on deep reforms of its criminal justice system, including the use of juries, and South Korea and Taiwan are watching closely.

Ultimately, the problem with systems of rule by law is that while they may provide some certainty and they may facilitate governance, they do not readily offer individuals the possibility of using the law to redress wrongs by the government. Law becomes an instrumental tool, not a defender of rights. People in countries ruled by law do not see the legal system as available to them to solve problems. It is also true that ordinary people in Western countries may have limited access to the law because of its costs and complexities. But a democratic system attempts to mitigate these handicaps by processes such as legal aid, class actions, and freedom of information.

### Rule of Law Compromised

The last section dealt with countries that do not profess to be multiparty democracies and that use law in the service of the state. How have the region's multiparty electoral democracies progressed in building the rule of law? Indonesia, Japan, South Korea, the Philippines, Taiwan, and even Thailand all profess to function on the basis of the rule of law.

The process of applying the rule of law is neither simple nor speedy. It is a frustrating process with built-in uncertainties and delays. Speedy justice is an oxymoron. To build and sustain a system of rule of law requires patience and determination by society as a whole. It requires opinion leaders and ordinary people to accept that the whole is far greater than the sum of its parts; that things are at times going to go wrong in a system where most things need to go right; and that the usual prescription for fixing the system is to leave it alone. These are difficult, self-denying requirements that need to withstand the inevitable attacks from politicians and journalists looking for an easy target. As the rule of law can only exist in a democratic setting, it must deal with a situation where people are free to make their own choices, good and bad.

Authoritarian systems may appear to be in a better position to control criminality. Their police forces are under fewer restraints and society as a whole is more regimented. Suharto's Indonesia practiced a form of soft authoritarianism mainly targeted at what were considered troublemakers for the regime. When criminality came to be perceived as a particular problem, Suharto authorized extrajudicial methods to deal with it. In 1983–1985, some five thousand suspects were executed in the streets of various Indonesian cities and their bodies left there for others to contemplate.[36] In his 1991 autobiography, Suharto admitted responsibility and explained that "this was meant as shock therapy so that people would realize that loathsome acts would meet with strong action."[37]

This sort of conduct has come to be associated with authoritarian regimes in the Colonels' Greece or military rule in Latin America, but must be seen as abhorrent to any democracy basing itself on the rule of law. Extrajudicial conduct by officials of the state remains a problem in Indonesia under electoral democracy. It does not appear to be directed as a campaign against criminals, but it continues to be wielded by the armed forces against political opponents. The events after the 1999 act of self-determination in East Timor and the involvement of the Indonesian armed forces and their militias are now well known.[38] Extrajudicial executions also blight the Philippines and Thailand. In Thailand, the National Human Rights Commission found that the Thaksin government's campaign against drug pushers had led to thousands of deaths.[39] Human Rights Watch put the number of deaths between February and June 2003 at 2,275.[40] In the Philippines, extrajudicial executions have become a mundane fact of life, no longer tied to short-term campaigns but an enduring feature of political and criminal life.[41] One report claimed that in Davao City alone, over 70 criminals were executed with the blessing of the mayor in the first three months of 2005.[42] That leaders should lose patience with the criminal justice system and turn to drastic extrajudicial processes is regrettable, but my greater concern is with the passivity of the general population in the face of these tactics. Human rights NGOs complain alongside some public intellectuals, but there has been very little echo in Indonesian, Philippine, or Thai society at large. The people seem prepared to share this dark secret. Those that blow the whistle, like the National Human Rights Commission in Thailand, are seen by many as traitorous for washing dirty national linen in the international spotlight. Can a democratic culture grow in societies where the rule of law is so compromised?

## Rule of Law Constructed

The rhetoric of the democratizing countries of Pacific Asia accepts the need to construct systems of rule of law. It is a long and difficult undertaking, and we need to be patient in formulating our observations. It may be too soon to expect to see a finished edifice. At this stage we should be content to ensure that good progress is being made in its construction. After all, even in countries that have long practiced a system of rule of law, problems continue to be identified, reforms continue to be called for, and striving for greater justice continues to be a requirement. Several positive directions can be identified in the construction of rule of law systems in Pacific Asia.

### Globalization

One factor militating strongly toward greater coherence and convergence in law is globalization. Trade and, particularly, investment bring with them the necessity for agreed-upon rules and agreed-upon processes of dispute settlement. Increasingly, the world is converging toward a broadly accepted set of legal principles to cover trade and investment, which are progressively being translated into national practice. Whether achieved through codification in world bodies such as the World Trade Organization, decisions of supranational arbitration bodies such as the International Centre for the Settlement of Investment Disputes, or simply through the pressures of global competition, we are moving toward something approaching a global commercial legal system. Aspects of the system include a generally accepted prohibition on nationalization without due process and compensation based on market value; a generally agreed-upon acceptance of the enforcement of international arbitral awards; increasingly sophisticated rules against bribery; and strengthening of rules on nondiscrimination in investment and trade regimes. That the system at times sees breaches of its rules does not invalidate the trend. The media will often focus on the breaches—the foreign businessman arrested as negotiating leverage, the international arbitral award reinterpreted by a local court in favor of local interests, and the egregious corrupt practice. But my contention remains that globalization could not have achieved its current level of intensity without the gradual emergence of a global system of commercial rule of law.

The profit motive is a powerful device in favor of commercial rules, but the construction of commercial rule of law will have a significant cascading effect on other legal processes. Similar global systems of rules of conduct exist for human rights, environment protection, and health management, and, though they may sometimes be respected in the breach, this reflects upon the enforcement regime more than the value of the normative regimes. As environmental consciousness grows, as the fear of pandemics spread, and as the universal value of human rights is recognized, these drivers will become incentives as powerful as the profit motive in shaping international rule of law. It is for this reason that I have always found it curious that the people excoriating globalization are the same people calling for ever more vigilant observation of global rules of conduct in human rights and environmental protection. Globalization is a force that will contribute to that very end.

## Constitutionalism

In the life of a nation, constitutionalism is the highest expression of the rule of law. It is the articulation of the will of the polity to be governed according to its rules. It is often written with an aspirational preamble, usually followed by explicit rules conferring powers on institutions and rights on individuals, and from this constitutional fountainhead flow all the laws and regulations of the nation. In Pacific Asia, constitutionalism was far more than simply a basis for law. It was an expression of nationhood, independence, and modernity. Japan's rush to modernity under the Meiji Restoration was inchoate without the adoption of a constitution, and this was handed down by the emperor in 1889 in grudging response to liberal demands.[43] The Philippines' expression of nationhood, articulated in the small window of opportunity that briefly opened between Spanish and US colonialism, was the Malolos Constitution of 1899, a remarkably progressive document in which 26 of the 101 articles were devoted to guaranteeing individual rights.[44] In Thailand, it was the modern idea of putting an end to 700 years of absolute monarchy that led to the bloodless coup in 1932, after which the first constitution was promulgated.[45] In other countries of the region, the end of colonialism was the trigger for constitution drafting. The defeat of the Dutch by the Japanese allowed a form of Javanese constituent assembly to debate the future shape of the nation, in the course of which Sukarno made his case for the five principles (which became known as Pancasila—nationalism, humanitarianism, democracy, social justice, belief in one God) that would henceforth be the basis of the state ideology.[46] Upon the proclamation of independence in August 1945, the Indonesian Constitution, which had been speedily debated and drafted, could be formally adopted.

In spite of these heroic origins, constitutionalism in Pacific Asia has had a checkered history. Clearly, once a constitution is in force, it needs to have sufficient authority to shape political developments in the country. It provides the template through which political actors must navigate. It needs to constrain behavior that the constitutional drafters considered to be, or at least thought should be, outside society's accepted norms and rules. This is asking a lot of a *bout de papier*. For a constitution to be able to play this role, it needs to have teeth and those teeth occasionally need to bite. Many of the region's constitutions have turned out to be toothless: evaded, amended, or ignored by political leaders, unenforced by courts, and disrespected by the people. In the two Asian countries that can arguably be considered as consolidated democracies, however, constitutionalism has taken a firm hold. So a question arises as to why Japan and India have succeeded while others have yet to do so. The more encouraging supplementary question is whether there has been a move toward constitutionalism in the region as a whole.

Two elements that would seem to be necessary for constitutionalism to take hold are local ownership and unbending authority. The ideal situation could be characterized as founding fathers embarking on a deliberative process to set down the principles by which the nation should live, followed by popular acceptance, and supported through the constitution's longevity and unwavering authority. Curiously, neither Japan nor India can be said to follow this ideal. Japan's Meiji Constitution was handed down by the emperor and was subject to very little by way of negotiations involving popular participation. Japan's next constitution was adopted after its defeat at the hands of the United States, leading to the popular belief that it was imposed on a reluctant Japanese nation by General Douglas MacArthur.[47] There is clearly much truth to the popular belief about the provenance of the 1946 Constitution, described by one commentator at the time of its adoption as "somewhat ill fitted, like a borrowed suit of clothes."[48] The draft originated in MacArthur's headquarters, and as John Dower puts it, "had foreign fingerprints all over it, not only in its broad principles but also in its awkward style."[49] Yet Dower also argues that the draft nevertheless went through a process of "Japanizing" through both translation and discussions in the House of Representatives.[50] Japan has certainly had many opportunities to amend its constitution but has passed these up. It remains unchanged after sixty years. The key issue in all the debates on amendment has been the peace provision in Article IX, which follows the concept laid down in the contemporaneous Charter of the United Nations to end the threat or use of force in international relations, by forever renouncing that threat or use of force. Sixty years of authority without amendment is a strong basis for constitutionalism. Japan is now embarked on a process of updating its constitution with committees in both houses of parliament having put forward suggestions for revision and the press appearing to be favoring change.[51] Accordingly, Japan may soon achieve demonstrated local ownership at the cost of belated revision, further strengthening the hold of constitutionalism.

India appears to present the diametric opposite picture—a constitution locally owned and drafted but over the years subject to constant change, with nearly 100 amendments. India's Constituent Assembly met between 1946 and 1949 to debate the character of the new state and draft the constitution, promulgated on 26 January 1950. Sunil Khilnani describes the key debate as a confrontation between Vallabhbhai Patel, supporting the status quo of traditional India, and Jawarhalal Nehru, proposing a vision of a reformist and democratic nation.[52] On closer inspection, however, the concept of local ownership looks more dubious unless one understands *local* to refer simply to the elite. The Constituent Assembly was elected on a restricted franchise with its 300 men overwhelmingly drawn from the upper and Brahminic castes.[53] The drafting was left to "two dozen lawyers" who produced "a baroque legal promissory note" of inordinate length with 400 articles.[54] Against all odds, the Indian Constitution has had "a commanding influence over India's subsequent history" and the Supreme Court has "become a central institution of the nation's public life."[55] It is a living document, constantly being debated and amended to stay in tune with the nation's needs.

*Constituent assemblies.* Local ownership is an important condition, but as the example of Japan demonstrates, it is not a necessary condition to establish the authority of constitutionalism. Clearly it is not a sufficient condition, as many nations of the region have conducted their constitution drafting through representative assemblies without ultimately succeeding in planting the seeds of constitutionalism. Table 4.1 lists the constituent assemblies held in Asian countries.

Of the countries on this list, only India can be said to have a modern history of constitutionalism. While holding a constitutional assembly is therefore not a sufficient condition for the subsequent establishment of constitutionalism, it is nevertheless seen as best practice in the drafting of constitutions. The more open, deliberative, and publicized the debates, the more opportunity for the public to inform itself and, if possible, involve itself in the deliberations. Perhaps the most extensive process of public consultation conducted recently in an Asian country was in Thailand when its Constitutional Drafting Assembly held hearings in 1996–1997 throughout the country, followed by a national referendum on the adoption of the constitution.[56] I was living next door in Vientiane at the time, and I faithfully read Thailand's English-language press. The constitution-drafting process was thoroughly covered and generated considerable interest. The press did its job in looking behind the technical aspects of the drafting to deal with the objectives that were being dealt with. It was the equivalent of an entire nation taking its own temperature, diagnosing the symptoms, and prescribing the cure. Thailand is now embarking on this process yet again, but I do

**Table 4.1   Constituent Assemblies Held in Asian Countries, to 2006**

| Country | Year(s) |
| --- | --- |
| Bangladesh | 1970–1971 |
| Burma | 1947, 1971, 1993–1997 |
| Cambodia | 1993 |
| China/Taiwan | 1946 |
| India | 1947–1948 |
| Indonesia | 1945, 1955–1959 |
| Pakistan | 1953, 1956, 1970 |
| Philippines | 1898, 1934, 1971–1972, 1986 |
| Thailand | 1948, 1959, 1996–1997, 2006– |
| Timor-Leste | 2001–2002 |

*Source:* Elaborated from Graham Hassall and Cheryl Saunders, *Asia-Pacific Constitutional Systems* (Cambridge: Cambridge University Press, 2002), p. 65.

not sense the same level of national enthusiasm. I also happened to be serving in Manila in the early post-Marcos period, where there was similar public interest in the work of the Philippine Constitutional Commission in 1986, and the result was an inspirational document guarding against the perils of authoritarianism and attempting to engineer greater social justice, but many of whose provisions will remain dead letters. In Timor-Leste, the process also encouraged public participation but was more akin to a process of civic education in the workings of government.[57]

*Constitutional amendment.*   In Japan, the constitution has been seen as verging on the sacrosanct, while India's constitution has been amended often. What they have in common is their hold over the public processes of their nations. In the other Asian countries under review, the tendency has been in the other direction: constitutions have been instruments in the hands of the authorities. A brief survey on this point discloses a disquieting pattern of authoritarian leaders abrogating, amending, or suspending the constitution to meet their political needs, often followed by the drafting of more accommodating instruments. While Thailand's 1997 Constitution was much admired for its innovation and idealism, it has now followed its fifteen predecessors since 1932 in being abrogated. So we cannot be certain that the previous pattern of constitutions as "instruments drafted by the current regime, be it military or civilian, to ensure that they retain power"[58] will not be repeated in the future. The 2006 Interim Constitution reverted to a pattern of several of its predecessors in giving the executive branch a dominant position in the nation's governance.

The pattern of toying with the constitution for the benefit of the incumbent is repeated in other Pacific Asian countries. The Nanking Constitution of 1947 was suspended in 1948 under the Temporary Provisions effective during the period of communist rebellion.[59] This was the constitutional structure brought to Taiwan in 1950 by Generalissimo Chiang Kai-shek and the Kuomintang. Among the effects of the Temporary Provisions was the granting of the power to the president over administrative and personnel matters and virtually all other aspects of public administration, the prohibition on new political parties, and the control of the media.[60] Very conveniently, Article 47 of the constitution restricting the president to two terms no longer applied under the Temporary Provisions. Accordingly, there was very little incentive for the ruling party to bring the emergency to an end, and the "Long Parliament" thus lasted forty-one years. Since 1991, there have been six revisions of the constitution to bring it into line with modern practices and, in some cases such as quarantining the budget of the judiciary from the legislative branch, to be at the forefront of governance reform ideas.[61]

Marcos also faced a two-term limit under the 1935 Constitution, and rather than hand power over to his opponents, he declared martial law and suspended the constitution, warning of a communist takeover plot. He then put in place a constitution that was far more amenable to his governance style, which had deteriorated from that of a committed reformer to a classic authoritarian complete with kleptocratic family and cronies. Needless to say, the 1973 Constitution placed few limits on Marcos, and certainly did not require him ever to abandon his presidency—it would take "people power" to do that.

Among the reactions to the Marcos period has been the 1986 Constitution's one-term limit on the president, though this is partially balanced by its being a six-year term. I recall that when Cory Aquino was nearing the end of her term, arguments were developed that the one-term limit did not apply to her because her incumbency began before the 1986 Constitution came into force. It is to her credit that she never entertained the idea of staying on. Indeed her greatest contribution to her country was her acceptance of her transitional role and the cementing of the constitution that resulted. When her successor Ramos was nearing the end of his term, his supporters began a move to amend the constitution to allow him a second term in office. Ramos did not discourage these attempts, but they foundered when his predecessor led a move strongly in favor of maintaining the one-term limit. In Ramos's place came Estrada, who would be hounded out of office less than half way through his term by yet another people power movement. His successor, Gloria Macapagal-Arroyo, is able to serve a nine-year term because her first three years were completing Estrada's failed presidency, and she was therefore only subject to the one-term limit upon subsequently being elected to office. Her success at winning the 2004 presidential election was partly due to her announcement the previous year that she would not be a candidate, thus blunting the criticisms of her administration. She abandoned this position when it looked like she could win a race against an opposition split between two strong candidates. Through all these maneuvers, the authority of the constitution was somehow kept intact.

Cavalier treatment of the constitution is clearly discernible in authoritarian South Korea before the 1987 reforms. As Samuel Kim puts it: "A review of constitutional amendments in Korea is testimony not only to political instability but also clearly demonstrates how those in power attempted to extend their terms of office by revising the constitution in response to challenges to political legitimacy."[62] That is why, following French practice of numbering the Republics in parallel with significant changes to the national governance structures under the constitution, South Korea is in its Sixth Republic, with the changes coming over a period of only forty years. This puts a premium on giving the current constitutional structure as much authority as possible, in part through longevity. The encouraging feature is that since the proclamation of the Sixth Republic in 1988, there have been four presidents who have governed according to constitutional requirements and have not tried to alter the rules to suit themselves.

Indonesia has had the least experience of constitutionalism among the democratizing countries of Pacific Asia. The 1945 Constitution is a spare document of less than 1,800 words that prides itself on its conciseness. Annotation IV makes a virtue of the fact that the constitution only has thirty-seven articles and, oddly, even compares itself to another constitution, noting that "this draft constitution is very brief if compared, for example, with the constitution of the Philippines." The 1935 Philippine Constitution is comparatively prolix at 8,500 words. The brevity of the 1945 Indonesian Constitution can be explained partly by the haste in which it was drafted, as well as uncertainties at the end of the war and, subsequently, in the struggle against the death throes of colonialism. The constitution lacked specificity and left many powers in the hands of the executive, on the basis that they were subject to elaboration in subsequent laws. Its brevity is thus symptomatic of a weak belief in constitutionality, which, in the Sukarno and Suharto periods, led to a limited role for the judicial branch. This has been described as "quietism," as opposed to judicial "activism," and was exemplified by the Indonesian courts' meek acceptance of presidential dictate.[63]

In the post-Suharto era, there has been a far greater emphasis on constitutionalism as Indonesia strives to establish the rule of law. The People's Consultative Assembly (MPR) is the body charged with amending the constitution. After a strenuous debate over whether to draft a new document or amend the existing one, the MPR opted for stability and longevity to enhance legitimacy in spite of the 1945 document's limitations. The result has been four sets of amendments to the constitution that have transformed the document and almost quadrupled its length.[64] Among the innovations has been the move to a popularly elected president and vice president, the establishment of a new chamber of the parliament, and the inclusion of a new bill of rights based almost fully on the Universal Declaration of Human Rights. Indonesia has thus embarked along the road to constitutionalism, but as all established democracies know, this is a difficult path that will inevitably be severely tested in the future.

Brevity and prolixity are weak tests of constitutional quality. They reflect legal traditions and historical circumstances. Japan's 1946 Constitution is quite short while Thailand's 1997 Constitution is particularly long. As noted, Thailand and South Korea have had a history of drafting new constitutions to meet new circumstances, so the key test is not the length of the document but how long it will remain in force. Indonesia and Taiwan have both opted largely for reasons of history and legitimacy to retain their original constitutions. In the last few years, both constitutions have been the subject of significant amendment processes. In both these cases, the amendments have in effect changed the nature of the constitutions, transforming governance structures and adding critical accountability and human rights provisions. Indonesia's amendments dwarf the original document, while Taiwan's amendments drafted in 2000 add considerably to the length of the original. India's constitution is subject to steady revision in light of circumstances, though as we will note in the next section, they are undertaken under the close supervision of the judiciary. So for reasons of scholarly curiosity more than any specific analytical conclusion, Table 4.2 provides the number of words in the constitutions, or their English translations, of the countries of democratizing Pacific Asia.

### Constitutional Courts

Constitutionality depends in large measure on judicial interpretation and enforcement. Ultimately, a constitutional system requires the rigor of a court deciding which laws are constitutional and which are not. So if we are to conclude that there is a growing trend toward constitutionalism in Pacific Asia, we ought to be able to discern a corollary trend in the stature and activism of courts charged with deciding questions of constitutionality. I believe the beginning of this trend can be seen in developments over the past few years.

Until the Third Amendment to the 1945 Constitution in 2001, Indonesian courts did not have a power of judicial review of the constitutionality of legislation.[65] This seems almost a contradiction in terms, for surely the most vital role of a supreme court is to determine the constitutionality of legislation and government actions. But Indonesian judges were held in low esteem by the nation's leaders and the public alike, and the judiciary was subservient to the executive branch in theory and practice. The judiciary of this period was known for its corruption. One of its most dis-

Table 4.2    **Word Lengths of Constitutions of Democratizing Asian Countries, to 2006**

| Country and Year | Number of Words | Amendments (Words) | Total Words |
|---|---|---|---|
| Japan 1946 | 5,344 | | 5,344 |
| Indonesia 1945 | 1,789 | 1999–2002: 4,153 | 5,942 |
| South Korea 1988 | 9,160 | | 9,160 |
| Taiwan 1946 | 7,832 | 2000: 3,431 | 11,263 |
| Timor-Leste 2002 | 15,513 | | 15,513 |
| Philippines 1987 | 21,661 | | 21,661 |
| India 1950 as amended | 22,134 | Up to 78th amendment | 22,134 |
| Thailand 1997 | 40,968 | | 40,968 |
| Thailand 2006 (interim) | 4,563 | | 4,563 |

*Source:* Drawn from texts from University of Richmond website, available from http://confinder.richmond.edu; and website of the Senate of Thailand, 1 October 2006, available from http://www.senate.go.th/pdf/const.pdf.

turbing aspects was related to me by Adi Andoyo Sutjipto, a former justice of the Supreme Court known for his probity, who at the time had been chased off the bench and had become dean of the law faculty at Trisakti University. He said his former judicial colleagues would discuss among themselves, without embarrassment or qualms, what the going rate should be for a favorable ruling. Adi's refusal to behave in this way led to his falling foul of his colleagues on the bench. When, in 1999, I discussed with officials of the Justice Ministry the need to end the ministry's supervision over issues such as the budget of the court system, the appointment of judges, and their assignments and promotions, in accordance with accepted practice throughout the world of having the judiciary independent from the executive, their response was one of immediate alarm, protesting that if the judiciary was unsupervised, there would be no limit to judicial corruption.

It is against this background that Indonesia's daunting challenge in building the rule of law should be seen. The Justice Ministry's supervision has now ended, and new personnel are being appointed and supervised by a judicial commission whose members are appointed by the president in consultation with the DPR.[66] Critically, a Constitutional Court has been established with the power to review laws concerning the constitution.[67] In one of its first cases, the court had the courage to make a most unpopular decision in finding that one of the Bali bombers had been wrongfully convicted under an antiterrorism law that did not exist at the time of bombing. The newly incorporated Bill of Rights in Article 28 of the constitution has a strict prohibition on retrospective application of "a law," whereas the Universal Declaration of Human Rights, on which it is modeled, allows for prosecution if the act was an offense under domestic *or* international law at the time of its commission.[68] This divergence may have been intended to protect former military figures from prosecution in Indonesia under international law.[69] While the Constitutional Court's decision demonstrated its independence, subsequent conduct of its chief justice led to some confusion. The uproar over the decision caused Chief Justice Jimly Asshiddique to appear before a press conference with Justice Minister Yusril Ihza Mahendra to explain that the Constitutional Court's decision will only apply to future cases and has no impact on the applicant's appeal.[70] Making judicial pronouncements at joint press conferences with the justice minister is a problem in itself. Another problem arose when the chief justice of the Supreme Court Bagir Manan suggested that in any case, Constitutional Court decisions are not necessarily enforceable by the Supreme Court.[71] While progress toward establishing the rule of law is being made in Indonesia, the court system's current contortions demonstrate how difficult a process this is.

During South Korea's authoritarian period, the Supreme Court had the power to review the constitutionality of legislation and administrative actions, but chose to remain "cautiously silent" as, over a period of forty years, only four cases held laws to be unconstitutional, and the judges that so decided were then forced to leave the bench.[72] Since the 1987 reforms, however, the Constitutional Court has been particularly assertive, and by 2005, some 12 percent of the five thousand cases it subsequently decided have found constitutional infirmities with a statute or a government action.[73] In 2003 and 2004, the court found itself in the middle of the nation's political crises, which pitted President Roh Moo Hyun against his political foes, including the then opposition-led National Assembly. On both occasions the court chastised the president but ultimately found in his favor.[74] It should be noted, however, that in the 2004 impeachment case against the president, the court had the benefit of knowing that the intervening national elections had delivered a solid victory to the president's political party, making a decision against impeachment that much more logical.

Thailand's Constitutional Court under the 1997 Constitution has also held the fate of the nation's leaders in its hands. According to one close observer, in its first few years, the court has taken a rather narrow and cautious view of its role but has nevertheless decided a number of cases against the government.[75] Its toughest tests have come when hearing appeals from decisions of the national Counter Corruption Commission to expel officials from office for having filed false declarations of assets as required under the constitution. In the first high-profile case, the court found against the incumbent deputy prime minister, Major General Sanan Kachornprasart, who had falsely portrayed a payment from a company as a loan. The court found unanimously against him, and he was thus forced from office.[76] The next major case was even more difficult because the appellant before the court was the prime minister himself. The case was complicated by the fact that the statement complained of had been lodged when Thaksin Shinawatra had been deputy prime minister in a previous administration; because as the nation's wealthiest person, his declaration was necessarily complex; and because, in the intervening period, he had won a landslide victory in the general elections. James Klein finds much to criticize in the court's 8 to 7 decision in favor of Thaksin as the majority was constituted by judges holding conflicting opinions.[77] The confused reasoning in the case and the suspicion that the decision was more political than legal have damaged the court's reputation.

The Constitutional Court of Thailand took an equally significant step in May 2006 to declare null and void the legislative elections held the previous month.[78] Thaksin had brought on these elections as a form of plebiscite in support of his rule, and the opposition Democrat Party decided to boycott the poll. So the resulting 60 percent vote in favor of the Thai Rak Thai Party did not look quite as convincing as Thaksin might have hoped, and in some seats the unopposed Thai Rak Thai candidate did not even surpass the required 20 percent threshold. Rather than confirming Thaksin's hold on the political system, the election complicated it. At this point, the king stepped in and lectured the judiciary to get involved and sort out the mess. The Constitutional Court acted within days of the king's admonition, relying on what would appear to be two relatively minor technical factors (the positioning of the voting booths was held to violate privacy, and thirty-seven days was held in practice to be an insufficient time since dissolution to conduct the election), and they voted 8 to 6 for nullification. So, at first sight, this would seem to be another example of judicial assertiveness vis-à-vis the executive, but on reflection, doubts arise. While this episode shows a trend toward the greater justiciability of political issues, it cannot be interpreted as strengthening the rule of law in Thailand. If anything, it demonstrates the continuing power of the aging king.

Taiwan has taken steps to make impeachment a justiciable process. A constitutional amendment bill passed on 23 August 2004 requires a vote of two-thirds of the Legislative Yuan to adopt a resolution of impeachment, which is then passed to the Council of Grand Justices for review. If the judges agree with the resolution, the impeachment process is complete and the office holder is relieved of that office.[79]

Continuing the pattern of increasing justiciability of political outcomes has been the action of the Supreme Court of the Philippines in upholding the assumption of the presidency by Gloria Macapagal-Arroyo against the complaints of her predecessor that he remained in office. President Estrada's corrupt conduct was clearly demonstrated by the media, but the Senate, whose job it was to rule on his impeachment, was blocked by Estrada supporters. People power took over, the military abandoned the incumbent, and the chief justice, Hilarion Davide, swore in the vice president as president. The Supreme Court, on which the chief justice recused himself for the case, had to disentangle the facts and law in the full knowledge that certain seemingly unalterable political facts had come to pass. Its decision against Estrada's claim was based on the argument that Estrada had resigned from office by his actions in leaving Malacañang Palace.[80] The evidence for this constructive resignation was based on the diary of his executive secretary, which had been serialized in the local press.[81] The decision was clearly politically astute and allowed the nation to move forward, but by stretching the law to encompass the ouster of a president through extraconstitutional means, it may have laid down a dangerous precedent for the future.[82]

At least the senior Philippine appellate courts have a well-earned reputation for competence and probity in contrast to courts lower in the hierarchy. The Malaysian judiciary is now trying to rebuild its reputation after Mahathir's suspension of the chief justice and a number of his colleagues in 1988 and their replacement with more pliant judges.[83] The decision to release Anwar Ibrahim is a step in the rehabilitation of the judiciary's reputation. The Indian judiciary emerged from the confrontation with Indira Gandhi in the mid-1970s with its stature intact, and perhaps as a reaction has become ever more vigilant of its independence and authority. This culminated in 1993 in the landmark decision that the appointment of senior judges lay with the chief justice and not with the government.[84]

Seeing constitutional courts around Pacific Asia asserting their authority and imposing the rule of law on political actors is one of the most decisive indicators on the path to democratic consolidation. This assertiveness and independence is a relatively recent development. The judges are very aware of what their counterparts are doing in other countries of Pacific Asia. They meet at various regional and international conferences and they compare notes. They look up to the senior judiciaries of the region and carefully read the judgments of the leading regional jurists. CDI played a modest part in this process of cross-fertilization by bringing judges together and distributing leading judgments and journal articles written by them. The cross-fertilization of the region's judicial brethren is another aspect of the emergence of a regional policy community.

## Conclusion

Returning to the question posed at the commencement of this chapter—Are there deep-rooted aspects of Asian society antithetical to the construction of a nation of laws?—I believe we can confidently answer it in the negative. There may be historical and conceptual challenges and these may influence the shape of the eventual pattern, but they do not preclude Asian nations from adopting the rule of law. There are a number of drivers pushing in that direction. Globalization is one and it is likely to become more rather than less influential a force in coming years. The growing trend toward constitutionalism is another driver helping to consolidate the rule of law in the region. This is not a uniform trend, nor is it linear, but a normative model is increasingly being accepted that governance should follow constitutional requirements. Courts are playing their role to bring about that result, and one manifestation of this phenomenon is the apparent growing justiciability of political questions. Of course, even in a long-established democracy such as that of the United States, the Supreme Court needed to decide who won the 2000 presidential election. So court decisions having significant political outcomes are not new nor are they necessarily evidence of political pathology, but they do demonstrate the importance of the judiciary.

This chapter began with the assertion that democracy and rule of law are mutually supportive and interdependent. Modern democracy is unimaginable without rules directing conduct. Rule by law may be possible in an authoritarian system, but rule of law needs the freedom and contestability that democracy brings to be able to thrive.

## Notes

1. Wu Qing, "The Rule of Law in Service to the People," *Enhancing Democratic Governance in East Asia—Empowering People and Institutions for Building Sustainable Society*, Report of the international workshop on Asian democratic governance held on 26–27 March 2004, United Nations University, Tokyo, p. 96, available from www4.ocn.ne.jp/~adp/ADG.pdf.

2. Juan J. Linz and Alfred Stepan, "Towards Consolidated Democracies," *Journal of Democracy* 7, no. 2 (April 1996): 14–33.

3. I am particularly indebted to the guidance provided by Martin Krygier, some of which was drawn from his "Transitional Questions About the Rule of Law: Why, What, and How?" *East Central Europe–L'Europe du Centre Est. Eine wissenschaftliche Zeitschrift*, 1 (2001): 28.

4. M. B. Hooker, *A Concise Legal History of South East Asia* (Oxford: Clarendon Press, 1978).

5. M. B. Hooker, *Adat Law in Modern Indonesia* (Kuala Lumpur: Oxford University Press, 1978).

6. Hooker, *A Concise Legal History.*

7. Andrew Huxley, "Introduction," Andrew Huxley (ed.), *Thai Law: Buddhist Law—Essays on the Legal History of Thailand, Laos, and Burma* (Bangkok: White Orchid Press, 1996), p. 19.

8. Andrew Huxley, "Thai, Mon, and Burmese Dhammathats—Who Influenced Whom?" Huxley (ed.), *Thai Law: Buddhist Law*, p. 109.

9. Randall Peerenboom, *China's March Toward Rule of Law* (Cambridge: Cambridge University Press, 2002), pp. 28–33.

10. Hooker, *A Concise Legal History.*

11. Niels Mulder, *Inside Southeast Asia—Religion, Everyday Life, Cultural Change* (Amsterdam: The Pepein Press, 1996).

12. Randall Peerenboom, "Competing Conceptions of Rule of Law in China," Randall Peerenboom (ed.), *Asian Discourses of Rule of Law* (London: Routledge Curzon, 2004), p. 114.

13. Wm. Theodore de Bary, "Confucianism and Human Rights in China," Larry Diamond and Marc F. Plattner, *Democracy in East Asia* (Baltimore: Johns Hopkins University Press, 1998), pp. 42–54.

14. Ibid.

15. Grant Evans, *Lao Peasants Under Socialism* (New Haven: Yale University Press, 1990).

16. Hooker, *A Concise Legal History*, p. 10.

17. Vitit Muntarbhorn, "Rule of Law and Aspects of Human Rights in Thailand: From Conceptualization to Implementation?" Peerenboom (ed.), *Asian Discourses of Rule of Law*, p. 370.

18. Ibid., p. 363.

19. Mulder, *Inside Southeast Asia*, p. 215.

20. For example, Peerenboom, *China's March Toward Rule of Law*.

21. Karin Buhmann, *Implementing Human Rights Through Administrative Law Reforms—The Potential in China and Vietnam* (Copenhagen: Djøf Publishing, 2001), p. 134.

22. For an account of the defense case, see Christopher Fernando, *Skeletal Submission*, at www.freeanwar.net/news/SkeletalSubmission.html.

23. H. P. Lee, "Competing Conceptions of Rule of Law in Malaysia," Peerenboom (ed.), *Asian Discourses of Rule of Law*, p. 243.

24. "Judgment of 2 September 2004," Dalam Mahkamah Persekutuan Malaysia (bidang kuasa rayuan) rayuan jenayah no: 05-6-2003 (w), published in *Malaysia Today,* available from www.malaysia-today.net/english/Judgement_DSAI_1.htm.

25. Stan Sesser, *The Lands of Charm and Cruelty—Travels in Southeast Asia* (London: Picador, 1994), pp. 205–207.

26. Burma is a multiethnic country where the Burmans live in the central plains while minority peoples live on the country's mountainous periphery. Myanmar is the name of an ancient kingdom around Mandalay and is thus an even less inclusive name geographically and ethnically than is the name Burma.

27. Roland Rich, "Brunei, Burma, Cambodia, Laos, Mongolia—A Few Rays of Light," Louise Williams and Roland Rich (eds.), *Losing Control—Freedom of the Press in Asia* (Canberra: Asia-Pacific Press, 2000), pp. 16–36.

28. Bertil Lintner, "Myanmar and North Korea Share a Tunnel Vision," *Asia Times*, 19 July 2006.

29. John Gillespie, "Concept of Law in Vietnam: Transforming Statist Socialism," Peerenboom (ed.), *Asian Discourses of Rule of Law,* pp. 113–145.

30. Peerenboom, *China's March Toward Rule of Law*, pp. 312–313.

31. Gillespie, "Concept of Law in Vietnam," p. 167.

32. Peerenboom, *China's March Toward Rule of Law*, pp. 188–190.

33. Ibid., pp. 313–314.

34. David Bourchier, "Politics of Law in Contemporary Indonesia," Kanishka Jayasuriya (ed.), *Law, Capitalism, and Power—The Rule of Law and Legal Institutions* (London: Routledge, 1999), p. 246.

35. J. Mark Ramseyer and Eric Rasmusen, "Why Is the Japanese Conviction Rate So High?" *Journal of Legal Studies* 30, no. 1 (2001): 53–88.

36. Adam Schwarz, *A Nation in Waiting—Indonesia in the 1990s* (Boulder: Westview Press, 1994), p. 249.

37. Ibid.

38. UN, *Report of the International Commission of Inquiry on East Timor to the Secretary-General*, A/54/726, S/2000/59, 31 January 2000.

39. National Human Rights Commission of Thailand, "The Government's War

on Drugs in Right(s) Perspective," *Right Angle* 2, no. 2 (April–June 2003): 1–3, available from www.nhrc.or.th/en/publications/Eng%20Right%20Angle%20V2N2. pdf.

40. Human Rights Watch, "Thailand: Anti-Drug Campaign Reaches New Low," *Human Rights News,* 6 October 2004, available from http://hrw.org/english/docs/2004/10/05/thaila9445.htm.

41. US Department of State, *Philippines—Country Reports on Human Rights Practices 2004,* available from www.state.gov/g/drl/rls/hrrpt/2004/41657.htm.

42. Carlos H. Conde, "Philippine Death Squads Extend Their Reach," *International Herald Tribune,* 23 March 2005.

43. Ian Neary, *The State and Politics in Japan* (Cambridge: Polity Press, 2002), p. 17.

44. Paul Kratoska and Ben Batson, "Nationalism and Modernist Reform," Nicholas Tarling (ed.), *The Cambridge History of Southeast Asia—Volume Two: The Nineteenth and Twentieth Centuries* (Cambridge: Cambridge University Press, 1992), p. 260.

45. Bowronsak Uwanno and Wayne D. Burns, "The Thai Constitution of 1997: Sources and Process," *University of British Columbia Law Review* 32, no. 2 (1998): 229.

46. Leo Suryadinatra, *Elections and Politics in Indonesia* (Singapore: Institute of Southeast Asian Studies, 2002), p. 10.

47. Neary, *The State and Politics in Japan,* p. 42.

48. *Asahi* editorial quoted in John W. Dower, *Embracing Defeat: Japan in the Wake of World War II* (New York: W. W. Norton and Company, 1999), p. 386.

49. Ibid.

50. Ibid., pp. 374–404.

51. David Jacobson, "Media Change Tone on Constitutional Revision," *Japan Media Review,* 9 May 2005, available from www.japanmediareview.com/japan/blog/Events/519/index.cfm.

52. Sunil Khilnani, *The Idea of India* (New York: Farrar, Straus and Giroux, 2001), p. 33.

53. Ibid., p. 34.

54. Ibid., pp. 34–35.

55. Ibid., p. 35.

56. Uwanno and Burns, "The Thai Constitution of 1997," p. 240.

57. Tanja Hohe, "Delivering Feudal Democracy in East Timor," Edward Newman and Roland Rich (eds.), *The UN Role in Promoting Democracy: Between Ideals and Reality* (Tokyo: United Nations University Press, 2004), p. 312.

58. Uwanno and Burns, "The Thai Constitution of 1997," p. 229.

59. Government Information Office (Taiwan), *History of Constitutional Revisions in the Republic of China,* available from www.taiwandocuments.org/constitution07.htm.

60. Tun-Jen Cheng, "Democratizing the Quasi-Leninist Regime in Taiwan," *World Politics* 41, no. 4 (July 1989), p. 471.

61. Government Information Office (Taiwan), *History of Constitutional Revisions.* The Fifth Revision was, however, struck down by the Council of Grand Justices.

62. Jeong-ho Roh, "Crafting and Consolidating Constitutional Democracy in Korea," Samuel S. King (ed.), *Korea's Democratization* (Cambridge: Cambridge University Press, 2003), p. 189.

63. Graham Hassall and Cheryl Saunders, *Asia-Pacific Constitutional Systems* (Cambridge: Cambridge University Press, 2002), p. 170.

64. National Democratic Institute for International Affairs, "Indonesia's Road to Constitutional Reform: The 2000 MPR Annual Session," October 2000, available from www.accessdemocracy.org/library/1077_id_constireform.pdf; National Democratic Institute for International Affairs, "The Fundamental Changes that Nobody Noticed: The MPR Annual Session, November 2001," January 2002, available from www.accessdemocracy.org/library/1378_id_gov_112002.pdf.

65. Hassall and Saunders, *Asia-Pacific Constitutional Systems,* pp. 177–178.

66. Indonesian Constitution, Article 24B, available from http://confinder.richmond.edu/Indonesia_third_amend.html.

67. Indonesian Constitution, Article 24C, available from http://confinder.richmond.edu/Indonesia_third_amend.html.

68. Indonesian Constitution, Article 28I(1) states, "The rights to life, freedom from torture, freedom of thought and conscience, freedom of religion, freedom from enslavement, recognition as a person before the law, and the right not to be tried under a law with retrospective effect are all human rights that cannot be limited under any circumstances" (available from http://confinder.richmond.edu/Indonesia2d.htm). Article 11(2) of UDHR states in part: "No one shall be held guilty of any penal offence on account of any act or omission which did not constitute a penal offence, under national or international law, at the time when it was committed" (available from http://www.unhchr.ch/udhr/lang/eng.htm).

69. In any case, it is most unlikely that international law would be considered a sufficient source of law on which to base a prosecution given that MPR Decree III/2000, on The Sources of Law and the Hierarchy of Laws and Regulations, makes no mention of international law.

70. Tim Lindsey and Simon Butt, "Indonesian Judiciary in Constitutional Crisis," *Jakarta Post,* 6–7 August 2004, reproduced in www.law.unimelb.edu.au/alc/wip/.

71. Ibid.

72. Hassall and Saunders, *Asia-Pacific Constitutional Systems,* pp. 170–171.

73. Hahm Chaihark and Sung Ho Kim, "Constitutionalism on Trial in South Korea," *Journal of Democracy* 16, no. 2 (April 2005): 32.

74. Ibid., pp. 35–36.

75. James R. Klein, *The Battle for Rule of Law in Thailand: The Constitutional Court of Thailand,* Centre for Democratic Institutions, available from www.cdi.anu.edu.au/CDIwebsite_1998-2004/thailand/ThaiUpdate2003_Klien.htm.

76. Ibid., pp. 39–41.

77. Ibid., pp. 42–47.

78. This account is drawn primarily from Michael H. Nelson, "Political Turmoil in Thailand: Thaksin, Protests, Elections, and the King," *eastasia.at* 5, no. 1 (September 2006).

79. Debby Wu, "Constitutional Amendment Bill Passes," *Taipei Times,* 24 August 2004.

80. *Estrada v Desierto et al.,* 3 April 2001, available from www.supremecourt.gov.ph/jurisprudence/2001/apr2001/146710_15_r.htm.

81. *Philippine Daily Inquirer,* 4–6 February 2001.

82. Francis Fukuyama, Björn Dressel, and Boo-Seung Chang, "Facing the Perils of Presidentialism?" *Journal of Democracy* 16, no. 2 (April 2005): 103–106.

83. Hassall and Saunders, *Asia-Pacific Constitutional Systems,* p. 189.

84. Ibid., pp. 183–184.

# 5

# Anchoring Political Parties

"The crisis of representation and intermediation through partisan channels
seems to be generic, not specific to those countries that have recently
changed their mode of political domination."
—Philippe C. Schmitter, "Parties Are Not What They Once Were"[1]

Political parties in the long-established democracies are showing their age.
They are losing the bonds that once tied them to their support bases, they
are not developing new attachments among the young, and they are struggling to find new strategies to mobilize support.[2] Is this a problem of
Western democratic gerontology or is it a sign of global times? Perhaps
both. Political parties in democratizing Pacific Asia need to cope with the
generic problems being faced by parties worldwide while also having to
come to terms with the consolidation of their democracies. They are faced
with an ever more discerning electorate, tougher disciplines in relation to
oversight, and a mass media waiting expectantly for the next political misstep. Some parties are finding it difficult to change with the times, while
others have found ways of reaching the voters. The mixed result in Pacific
Asia is as true of party systems as of parties.

In the long-established democracies, political parties grew up with the
system of electoral politics. Like any creature that evolves in consonance
with its environment, a surviving political party in the long-established
democracies has both fitted into the political environment and helped shape
it to suit its needs. Political parties in transition democracies do not have the
luxury of evolution. Where the longevity of these electoral systems is measured in years or perhaps a decade or two as opposed to centuries, the actors
still need to fit in with, adapt to, and shape the system, but they do so with
limited knowledge of the reactions of the system, limited experience of how
to fit into it, and often, limited loyalty on the part of supporters. In Britain,
franchise politics emerged with the industrial revolution and allowed for the
development of dichotomous programmatic parties based on an "us and
them" class cleavage. This classic form of party development is the product

of a specific history. It is generally shared with some neighboring countries that lived through similar historical periods of nation building and class formation, but it cannot be expected to be replicated in a different social and historical context. Parties in Pacific Asia are products of their national and regional histories, and it follows that they will be as different from European parties as are the variations in the histories and social developments of the two regions. Whereas the European parties grew through the associational energy of committed individuals sharing various social visions, this occurred at a time when civil society had not strongly taken the modern form of participation in NGOs. In the transitional democracies, the expression of voluntarism and idealism finds a home less in a political party than it does in an NGO. This is a significant handicap facing Asian political parties when compared with the situation in the formative period of their European counterparts.

These introductory comments lead us to the underlying question being posed in this chapter. We know that political parties in the long-established democracies played a crucial role in shaping their nations' democratic systems, but is it reasonable to turn the tables on history and expect the newly crafted political systems of the transition democracies to nurture and sustain political parties?

## Reviewing the Roles of Asian Parties

Similarities and comparabilities arise between long-established democracies and newly developing democracies in that political parties, wherever they operate, must still do the basic things expected of parties in democracies, but they may not do them to the same degree, in the same way, or with the same success. Diamond and Gunther summarize the tasks of political parties as follows:[3]

1. Recruit and nominate candidates for elective office.
2. Mobilize electoral support for these candidates.
3. Structure the issue choices between different groups of candidates.
4. Represent different social groups or specific interests.
5. Aggregate specific interests into broader electoral coalitions.
6. Form and sustain governments.
7. Integrate citizens into the nation's political processes.

These seven tasks are not of equal importance, nor are they ranked in any hierarchy other than broad chronology. Fundamentally, parties are required to form governments. This is the prize that fuels the engines of politics. To do so in presidential systems, they must be able to have the champion wearing their colors win an election, or, in parliamentary systems, they need to muster sufficient elected representatives to form that government in whole or in part. In some countries, this is the limit of the role of the political party with, among the countries under review, the Philippines coming closest to this minimalist mode. Philippine parties are little more than vehicles for various individuals' presidential ambitions as well as convenient though impermanent collections of local notables who had themselves elected to Congress. Elsewhere, political parties take more robust shape and are not content to simply muster parliamentarians but insist on having loyal party members in their putative government team, and thus take pains to recruit, select, and nominate candidates. They do so from a base of party members. They then generate electoral support for those candidates. Accordingly, a party that seeks success in having its candidates elected will organize itself in the most effective way to achieve it, thus requiring attributes such as leadership, strategy, and discipline. The tasks to be achieved by a political party accordingly have an important impact on its organization. Given the similarity in tasks of most modern political parties in democracies in Asia and elsewhere, it is understandable that they should resemble each other in structural ways, thus allowing for a degree of comparability.

Generating votes is the name of the game, and the means of doing so opens up certain options. I have elsewhere argued that in Africa and the Pacific, the most important attribute for electoral success is for a party to have evolved from a triumphant national liberation movement.[4] There is some echo of this in Asia, with several parties that existed in the colonial period forming governments in the immediate postindependence period and able to carry forward nationwide support from the anticolonial struggle. The Congress Party in India is the best example. If a party cannot gain legitimacy from having defeated, or at least outlasted, colonialism, then it may be possible to replicate a similar level of popularity by being seen to have struggled against authoritarianism. Taiwan's DPP can fit into this category.[5] Indonesia's PDI-P was able to claim this mantle after Suharto clumsily had Megawati thrown out as its leader.[6] Thailand's Phalang Dharma Party and Democrat Party both gained electorally from having opposed General Suchinda's coup in 1991.[7] This means of support, however, may only sustain a party as long as memories of authoritarianism remain raw. PDI-P's momentum from the 1999 elections did not continue into the 2004 elections. The Democrats are in opposition in Thailand, but at least they have survived, unlike the Phalang Dharma Party. DPP has stayed in power, but it must rely on other policies and cleavages to do so.

But if a party does not have this initial wellspring of legitimacy, it must go out into the community and mobilize support as best it can. Parties formed well after the industrial revolution may not be able to emerge and evolve on the basis of class cleavage but may nevertheless attempt to draw on such cleavages for support. Aside from class, other classic cleavages, described by Lipset and Stein Rokkan, providing options for gathering party support are the urban-rural, center-periphery, and interreligious cleavages.[8] In Asia, one can add ethnicity, language, and caste to this list. All available options have been taken up by Asian political parties. India's cleavages of religion, caste, and ethnicity all find expression in political parties. Malaysia's political parties are engineered along ethnic and religious lines. Indonesian parties have a certain regional focus, a certain religious leaning, and a certain historical basis. Even in a society where class, ethnicity, and religion do not form significant divides, geographic differences may be pronounced, as they are in South Korea where regionalism retains a surprising hold. Social cleavage has been the basic building block of political parties in Asia as elsewhere, though the cleavages drawn on vary from the classic models.

Where parties in Asia's democracies stray farthest away from the major tasks is in the role of structuring policy choices for voters. Articulation of policy options has not been the traditional means of winning elections in Asia, where money politics, pork barrel promises, and appealing to ascriptive loyalties have predominated. If the emergence of programmatic parties is an indication of the consolidation of democracy, then there are clearly problems in Pacific Asia on this point. Where the programmatic content of parties is shallow, then the aggregative effect of building popular support for policy outcomes will necessarily be weak. The search for policy positions that excite the electorate's support is proving difficult for virtually all parties in multiparty democracies in the postindustrial and post–Cold War period. Asian political parties, nevertheless, must still perform the key aggregating role in mediating the interests of different communities within the one party or in a coalition of parties.

In terms of being the link between the community and the political process, the story in Pacific Asia is varied. There are examples of parties in authoritarian Asia that insist on monopolizing this role. The single-party states are clearly in this category by having the party involved in all aspects of social organization while instinctively disallowing other means of community expression. This is why the decision to allow independent civil society organizations to operate in China is so significant. Equally, though negatively, telling is Vietnam's decision to preclude the operations of NGOs that are not tied to the party. There are also a few examples of parties in democratic Asia being the most effective means of expression by segments of the community. While the Indian National Congress Party was able to claim to speak for all cleavages in its early years, today there are many parties in India that play the role of speaking out for various disadvantaged or dissatisfied communities. Taiwan's DPP was the principal means of bringing many native Taiwanese into the political game dominated for decades by mainlanders. Aside from these examples of catering to acute cleavage-based politics, however, mainstream Asian parties in the transition democracies have had to find other means of integrating themselves into the life of democratic polities.

## Situating Asian Parties

Different parties therefore perform the necessary tasks in different ways and with different degrees of success. Classifications of political parties tend to flow less from their success in performing these tasks than from their memberships, methods, and organization. But before even arriving at the issue of classifications of political parties in Pacific Asia, an important question is their motivation. All parties want access to power, but is that access to power intended for the party or for its leader? Prior to the arrival on the scene of Silvio Berlusconi, this would not have been a particularly relevant question in democratic Europe. In Pacific Asia, on the other hand, a political party is often the possession of a politician, giving rise to the labels *personalistic* or *charismatic* parties. A prime example is Thaksin's Thai Rak Thai Party, which will be discussed below. The personalistic nature of many parties in the region highlights one of the difficulties of situating the Asian scene within the classic political party literature that emerged from the study of European political parties. In their admirable 1998 two-volume study of Asian political parties, Wolfgang Sachsenröder and Ulrike Frings considered the European literature inappropriate for the study of Asian parties, noting that these typologies "appear rather difficult to apply."[9] While I do not disagree, I believe we can overcome the difficulty.

### Evolution of Political Party Taxonomies

Duverger was content in 1954 to begin the discipline of classification of parties and party systems by simply counting the number of parties.[10] Jean Blondel in 1968 looked beyond mere numbers of parties and asked questions about their relative size.[11] By 1971, Dahl had added the important consideration of the competitiveness of the opposition.[12] Rokkan in 1970 also sought a level of analysis beyond mere numbers and included criteria concerning the likelihood of single-party majorities and the distribution of minority-party strengths.[13] In 1976, Giovani Sartori added an important new criterion concerning the degree of polarization of the party system through an examination of ideological distance between parties.[14] Measurements can thus be devised to calculate the numbers of parties, their size and strength, their potential to enter into or block government formation, and the choices they offer the electorate. Sartori drew from the numbers of parties to ask questions about whether the party system was one of monopoly, hierarchy, unimodal concentration, bipolar concentration, low fragmentation, or high fragmentation.[15] Sartori also introduced another measurement spectrum, the ideology-to-pragmatism continuum.[16] Are political parties motivated by policy outcomes in the interests of their supporters, or are they vehicles for politicians to pursue the accumulation of wealth and power? All these concepts can be drawn on in our discussion of political parties in Pacific Asia, but the Western, and to a large degree, European basis of the classic taxonomies tends to detract from their utility when applied to other systems. There is a need for a broader and more universal taxonomy.

Gunther and Diamond have taken the taxonomy to its most sophisticated and least Eurocentric point in their elaboration of a matrix with fifteen segments that measures the degree of organization of the party along a thin-thick axis, as well as a historical description of party development along an axis from 1850 to 2000 (see Figure 5.1).[17] The chart therefore situates parties in terms of their chronology, their organizational depth, and their primary distinguishing characteristics. As completed by Figure 5.1, the literature provides us with a vocabulary with which to attempt comparisons of political parties in Pacific Asia, both among themselves and in relation to parties elsewhere. The fifteen typologies should not be seen as static or fully compartmentalized. Parties can change and grow from an earlier and simpler form to one of more complex organization. Parties may also straddle the distinctions. Clientelistic parties may retain parts of their original identity while finding a niche within the broad church of a congress party; mass movements may ally themselves to electoralist parties; and even some parties linked to a religious denomination may behave like electoralist parties. The fifteen typologies are therefore particularly useful in examining Asian parties.

### Applying the Taxonomies to Pacific Asia

Examples of each of these fifteen types of political parties can be found in Asia and placed at each end of the two measures. At the thin end of the organizational spectrum, parties sprang up—and disappeared just as quickly—in the run-up to the first post-Suharto elections in Indonesia in 1999. A total of 148 parties, including the Taxi Drivers Party, nominated for the elections, but only 48 were eventually found to be eligible to run candidates under party formation rules that required parties to prove their archipelago-wide support.[18] Of the 48 competing parties, only 5 significant parties emerged, each with over 30 seats.[19] At the thick end of the axis are the world's two largest Leninist parties in China and Vietnam. Along the timeline we also have a broad range of examples. The Congress Party currently in power in India was established in 1885. The Uri Party that holds power in South Korea was established in 2004. As noted, personalistic parties are common. Basic clientelistic parties are also common. In terms of ideology,

**Figure 5.1 Species of Political Parties**

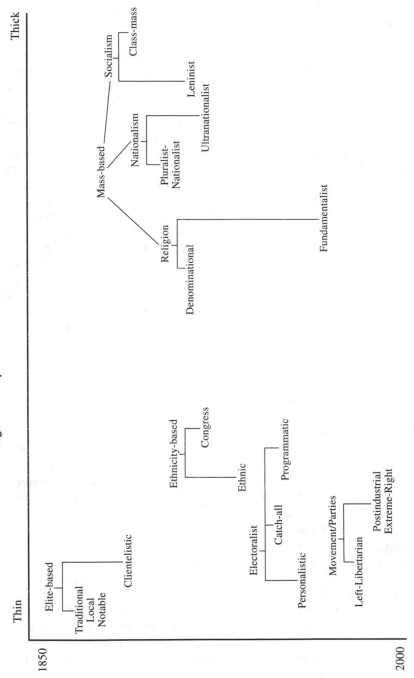

*Source:* Gunther and Diamond, "Species of Political Parties—A New Typology," p. 173.

examples can be found of ethnic, religious, nationalist, and socialist parties. As foreshadowed, however, the area of weakness, the limited number of significant programmatic parties, is the area most important for consolidating democracies.

Given the vast field of political parties in political systems so varying, generalizations are bound to be difficult. The classic taxonomies are useful, especially if complemented by the fifteen-segment typology. Yet even when utilizing these tools, the result assists in interregional comparisons but lacks the parsimony to make it completely satisfying. To attempt a broad generalization in the analytical categorization of Asian political parties, it is necessary to go beyond the classical typologies and the various species and examine a far more elementary aspect of basic interest for the study of democratic consolidation. The proposed categorization might be termed the "Goldilocks typology." It provides a useful distinction, though it suffers from inevitable subjectivity, by dividing parties into three broad groups, the first two of which describe them as either too strong or too weak. Those that are too strong overwhelm the systems in which they operate and thus stifle democracy. Those that are too weak do not effectively perform the basic tasks required of political parties and thus do not contribute significantly to building democracy. It is the middle ground—robust programmatic parties with viable structure and community roots, able to govern competently but prepared to step aside upon defeat in elections—where the numbers are thin, though even here there are some hopeful signs.

## The Goldilocks Typology

### Too Strong

As the Uri Party's astounding victory in the 2004 South Korean legislative elections demonstrated, the absence of pedigree is no bar to success. The right person, the right message, and the right circumstance can conspire to propel a party to electoral success. The shifting sands of South Korean party politics allow for new actors to burst onto the scene, though at some point one would expect to see greater stability in political parties as South Korean democracy consolidates. The remarkable victories of the Thai Rak Thai Party in the 2001 and 2005 elections, having only been established in 1999, also demonstrate the possibility of new parties gaining immediate success in the early stages of democratic consolidation.

Yet these successes should be seen as exceptional. Generally, longevity is an important political attribute generating legitimacy, visibility, and loyalty, which in turn are the keys to electoral success. This is broadly true in Asia as it is in Europe. While a common first impression of Asian political parties is their personalistic character and therefore their consequent short lifespan tied to the popularity of the politician for whom they have been established, as Table 5.1 shows, Asia has over twenty active political parties that are at least fifty years old.

*Leninist parties.* Of the twenty-two parties listed, nine are currently in power and indeed seven have never been out of power upon gaining incumbency. The number of parties never out of power would be eight but for a few months in 1993–1994 when Japan's LDP was briefly shunted aside. Three of the incumbents, in China, Laos, and Vietnam, are communist parties that fit squarely within the Leninist category. They reject the notion of multiparty competition and believe that intraparty contestability provides sufficient space for debate and deliberation. The decision to allow individuals outside the party to run for office in local elections in China and Vietnam does not preclude their being placed in Sartori's monopoly category, as those non–Communist Party candidates are independents who cannot openly belong to a competing political party. Nor does the fact that these

**Table 5.1  Currently Active Asian Political Parties over Fifty Years Old, 2006**

| Political Party | Country | Established |
|---|---|---|
| Congress | India | 1885 |
| Communist Party of China | China | 1921 |
| Communist Party of Japan | Japan | 1922 |
| Communist Party of India | India | 1925 |
| Kuomintang (KMT) | China/Taiwan | 1919 |
| PNI/PDI/PDI-P Democratic Party of Struggle | Indonesia | 1927 |
| Communist Party of Vietnam | Indochina/Vietnam | 1930 |
| Jamaat-e-Islami | India/Pakistan | 1941 |
| Japan Socialist Party/Social Democratic Party | Japan | 1945 |
| Liberal Party | Philippines | 1946 |
| Democrats | Thailand | 1946 |
| United Malays National Organisation (UMNO) | Malaysia | 1946 |
| Malaysian Indian Congress (MIC) | Malaysia | 1946 |
| United National Party (UNP) | Sri Lanka | 1946 |
| Malaysian Chinese Association (MCA) | Malaysia | 1949 |
| Nepali Congress Party (NPC) | Nepal | 1950 |
| Bharatiya Jana Sangh (RSS)/Bharatiya Janata Party (BJP) | India | 1951 |
| Sri Lankan Freedom Party (SLFP) | Sri Lanka | 1951 |
| Islamic Party of Malaysia (PAS) | Malaysia | 1951 |
| People's Action Party (PAP) | Singapore | 1954 |
| Liberal Democratic Party (LDP) | Japan | 1955 |
| Lao People's Party (LPP)/Lao People's Revolutionary Party (LPRP) | Indochina/Laos | 1955 |

*Note:* Names may have changed and continuity may have been interrupted by oppressive governments.

Leninist parties have turned to limited market policies to rescue their stulti-
fied centrally planned economies, in and of itself, change the Leninist
nature of the party, though it puts doubt on the Marxist part of the label. The
Leninist character flows from the parties' insistence on maintaining a parallel structure for supervision over state bodies. The state and its institutions
are seen as functionally important, but control over policy remains in the
hands of the party. Even the delegation of some policy functions to state
bodies does not alter this equation. Any policy issue of importance to the
party will remain in party hands or within its reach. The political systems of
these countries are dominated by the ruling party, but their economic and
social systems, decreasingly so. One of the questions to be grappled with in
the concluding chapter is whether this governance method can be sustained.

Oddly, another party on the list, the KMT, has often been regarded as a
Leninist or quasi-Leninist party.[20] For almost a half century it also maintained a system of organizational parallelism extending even to the commis-
sar system operating within the military forces.[21] A Leninist party must
remain in government to be able to practice its Leninist methods of governance. Out of government, its resources will dissipate, the organs it previously controlled will begin to follow a different logic of power, and the people who once relied on it for advancement will drift away in search of new
patrons. Experience in Europe following the collapse of the Soviet Union is
that those communist parties that lost power and then later regained it by
electoral means were not able to return to Leninist processes of governance
and had no choice but to adapt to the new rules of the game.[22] A major test
for Taiwanese democracy will be the eventual return to power of the KMT
and the way it will then behave. If the European precedents are followed,
there will be no choice but to accept the rules of electoral democracy. The
danger of a return to authoritarianism may be at its highest if the KMT wins
power as a result of a national crisis seen by the electorate as precipitated by
policies of the incumbent DPP and leading to a sharp decline in that party's
strength and influence. The rules of the game in Taiwan may be in jeopardy
if there is no viable opposition, alongside other checks and balances, to
ensure that they are respected. The KMT was "too strong" for a long period
while in government, and the consolidation of democracy in Taiwan will
suffer if it is once again too strong upon returning to power.

A party not on the list because it emerged only in the Khmer Rouge
period and came to power in 1979 upon the fall of the Khmer Rouge should
also be seen as Leninist in origin and placed in the "too strong" category:
Hun Sen's Cambodian People's Party (CPP). The CPP began life as
Cambodia's single ruling party under Vietnamese tutelage upon the fall of
the Khmer Rouge. The UN's involvement in the reconciliation of
Cambodia's fractious political groups forced the CPP to moderate its rhetoric and aspects of its style, but a strong argument can be made that the party

retains a Leninist disposition. Ultimately, one can only say that the UN's influence on Cambodia's politics was modest at best.[23] Hun Sen refused to accept the CPP's loss in the UN-supervised 1993 elections and insisted on being part of a coalition government with Prince Ranariddh's FUNCINPEC Party, which he ousted in a 1997 coup, allowing him to organize subsequent elections in 1998 and 2003 in which the CPP used all the advantages of incumbency, fair and otherwise, to assure its victory.[24] Opposition parties operate in Cambodia, as do NGOs, but there is a persistent sentiment that the CPP will remain in government for as long as it continues to organize elections. There being no international conflict situation, the UN will not ride in a second time to act as the circuit breaker.

*Success of UMNO and PAP explained.* The CPP could therefore join four parties on the longevity list that can be placed in Sartori's hierarchy category where alternation in holding power is unthinkable though the rules and rhetoric theoretically allow for open competition between parties. Three— UMNO, MIC, and MCA—form part of Malaysia's ruling Barisan Nasional, or National Front, now entering its sixth decade of rule, and the other is the PAP, which is embarking on its fifth decade of running Singapore. At times, these parties behave like Leninist parties, monopolizing the key positions of state for their members and ensuring business interests and party interests form a symbiotic relationship. But they have not adopted the structures of parallelism that are the hallmarks of Leninist parties. In the Gunther-Diamond typology, UMNO would be considered a mass-based party, combining elements of nationalism and ethnoreligious affiliation. UMNO's Indian and Chinese partner parties are ethnically based parties that have demonstrated their coalition value by providing the evidence of apparent consociationalism. But it is an induced and rather artificial form of consociationalism, and it is doubtful that these parties have very much by way of veto power. The MCA and MIC represent the favored elites of these communities who have no obvious place to go other than their partnership with UMNO. Seen through their eyes, the business bounty flowing from their association with UMNO, combined with its relatively moderate Islamism, is far preferable to the more uncertain options under the Islamic Party (PAS), also on the longevity list. Until a more plausible alternative government presents itself with which the MCA and MIC might be able to negotiate coalition status, they remain trapped in the UMNO-dominated Barisan Nasional.

The success of UMNO and PAP is noteworthy and requires explanation. Soft authoritarianism provides an important part of the explanation. Both parties have maximized their use of government power to hound their political opponents, while at the same time allowing a considerable level of freedom, both economic and social, for society at large. Yet soft authoritarian governments have fallen elsewhere, so why have these two parties succeeded, with almost a century of incumbency between them? One theory has put emphasis on the degree of unity within the parties.[25] There is considerable merit in this argument about the need for elite cohesion, but it strikes me as insufficient. We have seen the PAP survive the early splitting away of its left wing and, more recently, shrug off a spat between Lee Kuan Yew and Goh Chok Tong. UMNO has, to all appearances, overcome the purging of Anwar Ibrahim. I believe the balance of the explanation can be found in the following theory—UMNO and PAP have demonstrated the ability to sell themselves to the electorates as competent managers of what is perceived as a permanent crisis situation. As able managers of the insoluble crisis, each party has portrayed itself as the natural party of government. This formula, however, requires several conditions to be in place. First, the crisis has to be seen as structural rather than transient, and it has to be accepted as a dangerous part of the landscape. Second, the parties have to display a certain degree of competence, most readily demonstrated in terms of economic growth leading to broadly shared benefits, but also shown through issues of security and international status. Third, the political parties need to control the media through which the messages of crisis and competence are delivered. As will be explained in Chapter 7, both UMNO and PAP have been assiduous in owning, controlling, or intimidating the various forms of mass media, allowing the parties to shape the public conversation in a way that is forever flattering to them.

But what are the crises these nations are facing? The quest for economic development is insufficient in this regard. It lacks the required drama, and the problem of poverty has been shown to be soluble in Pacific Asia. The crisis must give the impression of being permanently threatening to national life and thus requiring proven competent management. In Malaysia, that crisis has been constructed out of the interactions between the three major ethnic communities. The May 1969 race riots are portrayed as the ever-present alternative to competent UMNO management of the race issue. But for UMNO, the official subtext runs, Malaysia would soon be in flames. Being in permanent crisis management, heroically dealing with a crisis foisted on Malays by the colonial masters, allows the crisis managers a fairly free hand in putting in place policies to handle this tricky problem. *Bumiputera* (sons of the soil) preference for ethnic Malays is thus seen as a means to counter Chinese and Indian success in business and in the professions. A balance also needs to be found by the crisis managers between championing the rhetoric and the symbols of Islam to please segments of the Malay community, while allaying the concerns of the non-Islamic minority communities. The crisis is presented as insoluble, and so UMNO's management is needed indefinitely. To break this cycle requires a change in the way intercommunal relations are seen by the electorate, and this in turn requires the majority Malay community to place more confidence in its own strengths and abilities, thus precluding the need for a permanent UMNO protector.

Singapore's permanent crisis is also carefully constructed. The construction is made to look particularly solid because the building materials are geography and history. Singapore faces a crisis of vulnerability. A tiny island with its industrious Chinese community is surrounded by vast masses of Malay Muslims. To the south is the unpredictable giant of Indonesia, to the north is its difficult ex-spouse Malaysia. Instability in Indonesia can spill over to Singapore as easily as the smoke haze from Sumatran fires can drift over the island. Malaysia holds Singapore's lifeline to the Asian mainland and can, literally, turn off the tap of the water pipeline it controls if it so pleases. Singapore has to constantly maneuver its way between its neighbors, and this is a job for proven crisis managers. Perhaps it will take the consolidation of democracy in the region, and the peace dividend this would bring, before Singaporeans will have the confidence and courage to look beyond PAP for leadership.

Robust democracies need strong political parties, but Asia's largest and most successful political parties are either antidemocratic in theory and practice, or simply antidemocratic in practice. These parties cannot be expected to vacate the political stage of their own volition. Ruling communist parties have only ever been overthrown, never voted out of office. UMNO and PAP are in a different category. I don't believe either party would use force to remain in power if voted out of office. UMNO has lost state elections under its federal system and given up the reins, while using federal power to undermine the PAS state governments and to punish the recalcitrant electorates. PAP has accepted the occasional defeat in one or two seats, and has also then meted out economic punishment to those constituencies who perversely elect opposition candidates. So, if the electorates of Malaysia and Singapore ever summon the courage to vote their ruling parties out of office, it is likely that these countries will move beyond the rhetoric and toward the practice of democracy. Until that time, the problem remains that these parties are simply too strong.

*Are Japan's LDP and India's Congress too strong?* A party that stays in power for thirty-eight years should be considered strong. A party that so dominates the political stage for thirty-eight years that there is no viable political alternative should be seen as too strong. The LDP of the Japanese political system that crystallized in 1955 and lasted till 1993 clearly overpowered that system. The LDP was formed by the merger of two rival conservative parties in 1955 in a shotgun marriage engineered by the business community alarmed at the emergence of a united Socialist Party.[26] A combination of Cold War politics; a winning electoral alliance of big business, rural voters, and urban salarymen; and the weak condition of the opposition would keep it in power for decades. In this period, it fitted neatly into Sartori's category of unimodal concentration. The party has been described as a "department store" party with something to offer for many shoppers,[27] and so it came under Gunther-Diamond's electoralist catch-all category. In this period of LDP domination, Japan continued rigorously to pursue the requirements of electoral democracy and to maintain a system of rule of law in which basic freedoms were respected. However, while the description of Japan as a democracy remained valid, it was certainly not a robust or high-quality democracy. Contestability of policy options was conducted within the bureaucracy and between the LDP factions, with very little public or parliamentary involvement in the process. The media was free but ham-strung by a culture of conformity and complacency. The difference is evident in comparison with the current fluid period of Japanese party politics where the electorate is being asked to make important choices in terms of policy, personnel, and system design. While many continuities of traditional politics persist, Japan has sufficiently grown in confidence as a society that it is learning to live with the "instability" implied in the possibility of democratic alternations in power.[28]

This survey of parties too strong for their political systems will conclude with a glimpse at that other Asian pole of democratic practice, India. For decades after independence, Congress was the natural party of government until 1977, when the electorate punished Indira Gandhi for suspending parliament under her proclamation of an emergency. The party system in that period has been described as "a party of consensus surrounded by parties of pressure."[29] Congress had successfully parlayed its credentials in the struggle for independence to transform itself from a small group of well-educated notables in the nineteenth century to the natural party of government in the postindependence period. It mastered the almost impossible feat of surmounting India's caste, class, and ethnic cleavages to establish a nationwide organizational base and was able to present itself to the electorate as both a party of the masses and a party of the minorities, as the party committed to democracy as well as to secularism, and as the party protective of federalism.[30] Gunther and Diamond think of it as the archetype congress party in their typology.[31] It would take other Indian parties decades before they were in a position effectively to contest Congress's grand coalition of interests. With its mass base and its enormous popular support over several decades, it is difficult to portray Congress as a personalistic party. Yet the dominance of the Gandhi clan at its helm certainly opens questions as to whether Congress would slip from its "too strong" category to a "too weak" classification should there not be a holder of the Gandhi name to lead the party. Sonia Gandhi's insistence that Manmohan Singh become prime minister after Congress's surprise victory in the 2004 election may well be an important step in taking Congress out of this personalistic paradox.

LDP and Congress may have been considered overpoweringly strong for their political systems at their peak; however, even though both are now back in power, they have lost their aura of invulnerability. Congress is now in a tight battle with the BJP. LDP is looking over its shoulder at a newly established party, the Democratic Party of Japan (DPJ), inheritor of support from the predecessor parties from which it emerged, now offering a viable alternative. The question mark about the consolidation of democracy posed by the former dominance of these parties has largely been answered. One of the most important attributes of a democratic political party is its ability to lose an election and live to fight another day. Learning to lose is not an easy process. It requires a party to have a representational and policy logic beyond the rewards of incumbency. We can confidently say that Congress has learned to lose and to draw strength from the experience. It is not yet completely clear that LDP has learned this lesson, and we need to await evidence of KMT having assimilated the lessons of losing. Should effective political contestability come to Malaysia and Singapore, UMNO and PAP will also one day need to learn the bitter lessons of losing office.

## Too Weak

*The Philippine party system.* In July 2003, I had the great pleasure of hosting a discussion with Philippine senator Francis Pangilinan at the Australian National University. In introducing him, I noted that in the Philippines it would be sufficient to say that the senator is the husband of TV megastar Sharon Cuneta, but that for an Australian audience deprived of access to Sharon's many talents, we needed to know more about the man himself. Pangilinan has a most distinguished background in the law and in public service. He is a person of learning, reflection, and moderation. These are not usually the qualities that win election to the Senate, so it helps to have Sharon Cuneta campaigning for him. Pangilinan's analysis of the major structural problem facing Philippine democracy was the continuing weakness of its political parties in performing the key tasks expected of political parties in democratic polities. His recommended solution begins with public funding of political campaigns.[32]

A brief survey of post-Marcos politics provides ample evidence to illustrate the senator's point.[33] Marcos put an end to the two-party system that had developed since independence in which the Nacionalista Party (NP) and the Liberal Party (LP) competed for power, when he established the Kilusang Bagong Lipunan (KBL, New Society Party) in 1978 and drew in many NP and LP congressmen. This set a pattern for Philippine politics that has been followed in the post-Marcos period. The pattern is for an aspirant presidential candidate with access to funds to form his or her own political party, which, upon that candidate's election, becomes the dominant political party, attracting support across what there is of a political spectrum. Upon the election of the next president, the party can survive if it aligns with the new administration or has sufficiently deep pockets to wait it out. This is clearly not a formula for sustaining strong political parties. The boom and bust pattern can be seen in Table 5.2, which shows political parties that served as vehicles for presidential ambitions.

These vehicles for presidential campaigns can be described as political parties only by stretching the meaning of that term. In our typological vocabulary, they might be described as examples of a system with some fragmentation and as electoralist and personalistic parties. But because they are basically temporary aggregations of tactical interests, the term *political party* may not even be appropriate. They have grand electioneering meetings in hotel ballrooms, and they have huge rallies largely populated by people paid to attend or hoping to be given a free T-shirt, but the parties tend to disappear from the public stage right after the election. Philippine political parties do not have full-time secretariats to manage party affairs or research units to provide policy options.[34] The main clue that they continue to exist between elections comes from the party acronym attached to the description of the sitting congresspersons in official documents. There is not much of a concept of party loyalty, though there is some loyalty to a paymaster, and accordingly there is very little party discipline among the congresspersons. Incumbency is the main motivating factor for politicians, who thus like to switch to the winning side as this provides the greatest prospects for pork barrel rewards. It follows that ideology, vision, and policy positions can be annoying encumbrances in such a system, though they can be useful to fill up campaign speeches.

Table 5.2   **Personalistic Philippine Political Parties, 1978–2004**

| Party Name | Year | Vehicle For | Survival |
|---|---|---|---|
| Kilusang Bagong Lipunan (KBL) | 1978 | Ferdinand Marcos | No[a] |
| Laban ng Demokratikong Pilipina (LDP) | 1988 | Corazon Aquino | Yes |
| Lakas-Christian Muslim Democrats | 1992 | Fidel Ramos | Yes |
| Nationalist People's Coalition (NPC) | 1992 | Danding Cojuangco | Yes |
| Aksyon Demokratikong | 1997 | Raul Roco | No[a] |
| Laban ng Makabayang Masang Pilipino (LAMMP) | 1998 | Joseph Estrada | No[b] |
| Lakas, major party in K4 coalition | 2004 | Gloria Macapagal-Arroyo | Yes |

*Notes:* a. KBL and Aksyon each have only one member in the 13th House of Representatives. The KBL representative is Marcos's daughter Imee.

b. A rump of LAMMP, Partido ng Masang Pilipino (PMP), continues to have several representatives in the Senate built around Estrada's wife and son, and two representatives in the House of Representatives.

*Thailand's personalistic parties.* Thailand's political parties also have a strong personalistic flavor. The party leader is invariably the dominant figure, with both the political and financial clout to enforce his (they have all been men) will. Thaksin's Thai Rak Thai Party (TRTP) is a glaring example. The Thai parties are largely electoralist parties.[35] But they tend to have more substance and cohesion than their Philippine counterparts. The personalistic nature of Thai parties can be glimpsed from the comparison of three political parties that served the interests of three retired generals.

As events would show, the Phalang Dharma Party (PDP) would not survive the political retirement of its founder, Major-General Chamlong Srimuang, who created it as a vehicle for his election as Bangkok governor in 1985. Chamlong's emphasis on "clean" government based on Buddhist ethics won it considerable support in Bangkok. In the second 1992 national election, it won forty-seven seats and led to thoughts that Thai politics may be evolving to a more issues-based level. But its popularity never extended far beyond the capital and in any case plummeted with Chamlong's retirement. He handed over the leadership to a political novice, Thaksin Shinawatra, under whose leadership party representation in the parliament elected in 1996 collapsed to a single seat. The party died, and it is a remarkable testament to Thaksin's ambition that he was able to reinvent himself politically so soon after such a debacle.

General Chatichai Choonhavan's entry into national politics, leading eventually to his ascension to the prime ministership from 1988 to 1991, was with the Chart Thai Party. In 1992, however, he fell out with his party colleagues and formed a new party, the Chart Pattana Party (CP). CP continued to win a significant slice of seats in the 1990s, relying heavily on Chatichai's leadership qualities. Its fortunes declined in the 2001 elections, after which it became a junior partner in Thaksin's TRTP-dominated coalition, and under Suwat Liptapanlop's leadership, it decided to merge with TRTP. The logic of incumbency and the magnetism of Thaksin's success thus proved irresistible.

A similar story can be told about the New Aspiration Party (NAP) formed in 1990 as a vehicle for General Chavalit Yongchaiyudh, who rode it to the prime ministership from 1996 to 1997. NAP was also eventually swallowed up by TRTP after Chavalit's political eclipse in the wake of the 1997 financial crisis.

The story in each of the three cases is similar, though the policies of the three parties were distinct. While PDP presented itself as the party of Buddhist ethics, CP was seen as a party to consolidate Thailand's return to civilian government and NAP tended to project itself as a law-and-order party. Yet beyond the differences in party platforms there is a distinct similarity: three retired generals, three new parties, and three deceased parties soon after the founder's passing from the political scene. In other words, these are examples of weak parties. But this is not the full story of Thailand's political parties, and TRTP, the Democrats, Chart Thai, and the Mahachon Party—the four remaining political parties—will be discussed in the next section.

*Parties too weak to seek government.* Philippine presidentialism and Thai personalism have tended to mean that the candidate comes first and the party a distant last. Parties thus come and go, are formed or reformed, joined or split, depending on the needs of the candidate for which it is a passing political vehicle. But at least these parties operate in a competitive system, allowing some prospect of electoral success and the possible rewards of incumbency. Where the party system has a dominant political party, as in Malaysia, Singapore, or Japan from 1955 to 1993, opposition parties are put in a chronic dilemma of how to respond to the dominant party.

PAS, the Islamic Party in federal Malaysia, has been able to turn to state elections in search of success and relevance, but this response is not open to opposition parties in unitary systems. One response has been to accept the impossibility of winning government, and the startling manifestation of that philosophy is only to stand in a limited number of seats and thus advertise to the electorate that a vote for the party is "safe" because it cannot be a vote to place that party in government. And thus the Singapore Workers' Party in the six elections since 1980 presented only eight, fifteen, thirty-two, thirteen, fourteen, and fourteen candidates.[36]

The same tactic was used by the Japan Socialist Party (JSP) from the 1950s to the 1990s, running fewer candidates than required to form a parliamentary majority.[37] Stockwin describes the JSP of this period as a party that "often gave the impression that it did not really want to take office, and would not know what to do with government."[38] The party's hesitation to seek government proved well founded, because when it entered into coalition with the LDP in 1994, it lost its identity and much of its support and had to go back to the drawing board.[39] Clearly, it is an impossible proposition for a democracy to have the major opposition party unwilling to seek office or intimidated by the dominant governing party from doing so. These parties are simply too weak.

*Is Golkar strong or weak?* A decade ago Indonesia's ruling party, Golkar (an Indonesian-language abbreviation for Golongan Karya, Joint Secretariat of Functional Groups), gave the impression of being in the "too strong" category. The party appeared to have great solidity, with party branches throughout the country, enormous party rallies at election time, and unquestioned electoral success. In reality, Golkar was simply Suharto's electoral machine, a personalistic entity masquerading as a party of national unity. Indeed, even the term *political party* may not be appropriate; Golkar was never politically tested, because there was never a chance that it would lose any of the stage-managed elections it contested in Suharto's era. Neither was it a policymaking instrument overseeing government instrumentalities, as this role was reserved for Suharto and his inner circle. Golkar was therefore less of a political party and more of a huge cheer squad. Today, however, attempting to build up substance from the large pool of party officials left behind after Suharto, Golkar looks the strongest of the Indonesian political parties and won the highest plurality of votes in the 2004 legislative elections.[40] This tells us something about Golkar, but it also points to problems with its competitors.[41] Three of Indonesia's big five parties from the 1999 elections and big seven parties from the 2004 elections are long-established: PDI-P (Indonesian Democratic Party–Struggle) traces its ancestry back to the anticolonial struggle; Golkar was formed in 1964; and PPP (Development Unity Party) was established in 1973 by forcibly fusing together four Islamic parties. But it would be wrong to judge them by reference to their longevity, because it was only in 1999 that they had to begin to act like political parties rather than mere performers in Suharto's quinquennial theatrical production he liked to describe as the "festival of democracy."

If we look at the Indonesian political party scene from the perspective of a transitional democracy with basically new parties learning the ropes, the picture is not all bleak. No party has emerged as dominant or even powerful. Megawati Sukarnoputri has squandered the popular advantage she enjoyed from projecting herself as an antiauthoritarian figure because of her ouster by Suharto from the (then called) PDI leadership in 1996. Though PDI-P won 33 percent of the vote in 1999, she allowed Gus Dur to outmaneuver her for the presidency by adopting the dubious tactic of simply awaiting serenely to be crowned, while Gus Dur actively lobbied the Islamic parties for support. When the presidency finally came to her in 2001, she was unsure what to do with the position, and the voters expressed their displeasure by cutting PDI-P's 2004 vote down to 18.5 percent. Golkar became the most popular party in Indonesia and began to use its muscle to behave like an opposition party, though curiously, the "opposition" alliance had a majority of seats in the DPR. But in December 2004, Vice President Jusuf Kalla pulled off the coup of replacing Akbar Tanjug in the Golkar leadership. This suggests that divisions remain within Golkar. It also demonstrates the continuing desire of Golkar party members to benefit from the bounty of incumbency. On the more positive side of the ledger, the major political parties have adopted the organizational systems of large parties. They hold regular congresses, appoint leadership hierarchies, adopt rules, and draft policy platforms. With time and practice, the parties may consolidate their electoral bases and strengthen their performances. Indonesian politics may evolve into a system in which a small group of parties represent both policies and cleavages that will shape the political conversation and provide a certain coherence and continuity in the political process.

## Just Right?

To have the temerity to lay down a heading of "Just Right" is to make a host of assumptions about what is in fact right from the perspective of a viable democratic polity. In drawing together these assumptions, we come across an immediate problem of Eurocentric modeling. The word *party* first came to be used in politics in seventeenth-century Europe[42] and remained a contested concept during and beyond the French revolution.[43] Thus, parties only became accepted as positive parts of the political landscape of Europe and the United States in the course of the nineteenth century and influenced the shape of all future parties. They came to represent cleavages in society flowing from nationalist revolutions and the industrial revolution. Needless to say, the national and industrial revolutions of Europe were not repeated in the same way on other continents, and it stands to reason that the cleavage basis of political parties elsewhere will represent those countries' particular histories and circumstances. The danger we need to avoid in assumptions about what makes a party just right is the idealizing of the results of European history in terms of the major parties that emerged there as a universal model of how all parties should look everywhere. So the search for "just right" is not a search for conservative or social democratic parties or, obviously, for Christian Democrat or Gaullist parties.

Flowing from the preceding sections, we also know other features that negate what a political party that is just right may be—it is not so monolithic as to dominate the political scene without the possibility of genuine contestation for governance, and it is not so weak as to represent little more than the ambitions of a single individual. But it is easier to say what just right is not than to be confident exactly what it is. Hence the question mark in the subheading. Going back to first principles, "political parties remain an indispensable institutional framework for representation and governance in a democracy."[44] They need to be representative in terms of representing major groups in society. These may be economic groups, ascriptive groups, regional groups, or groups sharing a broad vision or opinion. From the perspective of governance, they need to have a certain institutional strength and coherence in terms of organization, membership, and loyalty. Different parties will have different mixes of these qualities, but it is these qualities that we need to search for in our brief survey of what is just right.

*Catering to Indonesia's cleavages.* Leaving our gaze on Indonesia, we have the advantage of three national elections over a period of fifty years from which to draw conclusions. The surprising conclusion of a recent study comparing the 1955 election with the 1999 election is that there are important continuities that neither Sukarnoism nor Suhartoism managed to reengineer.[45] Accordingly, one can identify three major cleavages based on nationalist sentiments, *abangan* or nominal Muslim views, and *santri* or pious Muslim views reflected in political party preferences spanning elections forty-four years apart and continuing to form the basis of political party support in the 2004 elections as well. A study of the political ideology of the forty-eight parties contesting the 1999 elections divided the parties into the twenty-nine that supported Pancasila, the five principles upon which Indonesian society was based at independence; sixteen that supported the Islamic *ummah* concept; two that supported both; and one social democratic party.[46] Another study shows important regional continuities in party support between the 1999 and the 2004 elections.[47] While these divisions may not follow the classic European working-class cleavage that tends to define the political dividing line, they point to a basis on which parties can build enduring support.

The next positive conclusion we can reach about Indonesian political parties appears inconsistent with the first conclusion. While there is a cleavage basis in party support, it is not frozen for all time. Indonesian voters will respond to issues and personalities just like voters anywhere else in the world. There is room for the public conversation to have an impact on voting behavior, on party strengths, and on policy outcomes. While Megawati inherited large swathes of support from Christian, secular, and nationalist supporters who had also supported these policies in 1955 in voting for the nationalists and the communists, she squandered a large part of this inheritance through her inaction and her husband's reputation for corruption.

The fluidity in Indonesian politics can also be seen in the success of two new parties. The Democrat Party became the fifth most successful party with 7.5 percent of the vote within a few months of being established as a vehicle to support the presidential ambitions of Susilo Bambang Yudhyono (SBY). The success of the Democrats is thus intrinsically linked to the electorate's perception of the success of the SBY administration. In that sense it has begun life as a personalistic party and will need to gain its own traction if it is to survive SBY's inevitable passing from the political scene. The other important newcomer is the Prosperous Justice Party (PKS), which began life at the 1999 elections as the Justice Party. Its vote jumped from 1.4 percent to 7.3 percent. While it can be described as a Muslim party, and thus one of several parties competing for the *santri* vote, it was able to project itself as the party most committed to fighting corruption, and it developed a successful strategy of using its committed membership to campaign door-to-door.[48] Another party that benefited from the same message and method was the small Christian-based Prosperous Peace Party (PDS), which won twelve seats on 2.1 percent of the vote.[49]

*Philippine Liberal Party and Thai Democrat Party—programmatic parties?* Thus far we have had very little to say about programmatic parties in the Gunther-Diamond typology. The Indonesian parties have a broad but identifiable ideology centered on the degree to which the state should embrace Islam. Individual party policy platforms, however, do not go much beyond opposition to corruption in their degree of specificity. Under SBY, the Democrat Party may develop a more programmatic approach. It would appear that this level of sophistication in party politics only comes about over time. That may be part of the reason why two parties on the "longevity list," the Democrat Party of Thailand and the Liberal Party of the Philippines, are making advances in developing into programmatic parties. The Democrats can point to a history of opposing military rule, supporting gradual reform in social policies, demonstrating fiscal responsibility, and encouraging foreign investment.[50] Senator Pangilinan's Liberal Party in the Philippines shares the Democrats' antiauthoritarian credentials and is also conscious of the need for a programmatic basis in politics and describes itself as follows:

> The Liberal Party is unique in the Philippines for its clear platform and principled stance on essential issues. First and foremost is a zealous regard for human rights and individual freedoms; democratic government and citizen involvement. This is the foundation for the LP's goal of a free, just, democratic and progressive society. The LP's economic platform also reflects this goal. LP favors vigorous land reform, dismantling monopolies towards a freer market, building a sound industrial base, and promotion of local industries. The Party is also committed to fair and adequate wages and conditions for workers, and to the right to collective bargaining.[51]

Both parties have spent a considerable period of their countries' postauthoritarian histories sitting on the government benches, but it is noteworthy that neither party is currently enjoying a high point. In the Philippine House of Representatives, the Liberal Party has only 34 of 235 members, and in the Senate only 4 out of 24 members, but it is a member of Arroyo's government coalition. The Democrats were in opposition in Thailand following the TRTP landslide in 2005, having managed to win 96 of the 500 seats with its vote down to 18 percent compared to TRTP's 60 percent. In the wake of the 2006 coup, the Democrats will need to hang on and fit in with whatever party system is to be devised in the next constitution. Merely having a program does not guarantee electoral success. And it must also be said that neither party is innocent of the sins of traditional politics. Among the Liberal Party's leading families are the Singsons of Ilocos Sur, though the governor of that province, Luis Singson, who triggered Estrada's downfall when he admitted to paying the then president over $8 million in payoffs from illegal gambling and $2.7 million from tobacco taxes, now runs in Lakas colors.[52]

The Democrats have also had their share of corruption scandals, but Pasuk Phongpaichit and Sungsidh Piriyarangsan concede that they are "the least *jao pho* (local godfathers) influenced of all the major parties."[53]

*Is the Thai Rak Thai Party just right?* Should Thaksin's TRTP be placed in the "just right" category? Can TRTP survive Thaksin's eclipse? It is certainly a dilemma given the obvious personalistic nature of the party. It is also a dilemma because TRTP combines the necessary brash freshness needed in Thai politics with a troubling maintenance of enduring problematic features. To dominate two elections in succession is quite a feat in what had been seen as a fragmented party system. To win the 2005 elections with 60 percent of the vote and a massive majority in the National Assembly is, of course, unprecedented. The 2006 election, where TRTP again won over 60 percent of the vote, is less relevant because it was boycotted by the opposition. To begin a political party in 1998 and within a few years to be able to claim eleven million members would make TRTP unique in the democratic world.[54] Success is a virtue in politics, and by this criterion alone, achieved through electoral results, TRTP belongs in the model category. There may be a few other admirable aspects of Thaksin's party. The professionalism of the political campaign, the molding of deliverable populist policies, the ability to appeal to an electorate jaded by decades of broken promises, and the bringing of business savvy to government are all positive qualities. Until the 2006 coup, it looked as if Thaksin's political tactics had been at least as significant in changing Thai politics as the institutional engineering in the 1997 Constitution.

But there were always grave doubts about the Thaksin style of politics. Many of the worst aspects of traditional politics were employed. Thaksin did not simply begin with a blank page; he gathered around him some of the major forces of traditional Thai money politics epitomized by the luring of Sanoh Thiengthong and his faction of sixty to seventy parliamentarians from the New Aspiration Party into the TRTP. This leaves open the question of whether Thaksin had reinvented Thai politics or simply found a way to play the system more effectively. According to the latter interpretation, Thaksin simply represents big business, which has traditionally seen government patronage as a key to success.[55] He also happens to be the major player in big business. The other key element in traditional Thai governance structures has been the military, and Thaksin attempted to co-opt the military into his camp. He recruited dozens of serving generals to oversee the civilian bureaucracy's responsiveness to government policies.[56] Further, there were always grave doubts over Thaksin's commitment to human rights in view of his extraconstitutional war against drugs, his controls over the media, and his disingenuous initial response to explain the many deaths of Muslim demonstrators in the south of the country in the military round-up in October 2004—that they died because they were weak from Ramadan fasting. The most-obvious aspect of traditional Thai politics has been the personalistic nature of TRTP. With Thaksin seemingly banished from Thai political life, the precedents point to the disintegration of TRTP in tandem with the eclipse of its leader and funder. It seems that TRTP can only survive if Thaksin's wallet remains open, thus placing TRTP along with so many other Thai parties in the "too weak" category.

*Taiwan's Democratic Progressive Party.*   There are other viable parties in democratizing Asia. The Democratic Progressive Party (DPP) began life as a collection of oppositionists to KMT authoritarianism and was only launched in 1986, when the prohibition on political parties other than the KMT was no longer enforced. It brought together the various groups, called *Tangwai*, that had opposed the KMT over many years and at considerable cost.[57] Apart from its antiauthoritarian past, the DPP has a vast constituency in Taiwanese natives who bridle against the domination of the mainlanders who dominate the KMT. While it has a stronghold in the southern city of Tainan, its breakthrough electoral success came in Taipei in 1994 when Chen Shui-bian won the mayoral contest. This was followed by Chen's victory in the three-cornered presidential race in 2000, a feat Chen duplicated and indeed exceeded in his defeat of the KMT candidate in the head-to-head contest against a unified opposition in 2004. In the 2005 National Assembly elections, Chen's DPP again came out as the strongest party with 42.5 percent of the vote in a low turnout.[58]

   With 400,000 members,[59] incumbency, and a natural constituency, the DPP's future looks bright. Yet there are shadows over this success. Corruption allegations are dogging the president and his family and should they be proven or even widely believed, the DPP could lose the legitimacy it built up so painfully in the difficult years of opposing KMT authoritarianism. The other dilemma facing the DPP is that it came to power hinting at delivering the impossible—independence. Authoritarian China is probably not bluffing when it says it will never allow that result, and it has the power to enforce its will. Inaction by China upon a Taiwanese declaration of independence may well be a regime-threatening position, as the Communist Party would lose credibility in the eyes of a public brought up on a saturation diet of threats against Taiwan's independence. A democratic China, on the other hand, would largely take away the rationale for Taiwanese independence. As things stand, there may come a point when the DPP will pay the electoral cost for nurturing aspirations it cannot hope to fulfill.

*Has Korea's Uri Party trumped regionalism?*  The South Korean party system is difficult to categorize given its immaturity, its recent volatility, and the continuing hold of regionalism. Parties only emerged in the wake of the

1987 reforms, which ended the authoritarian system. They have tended to be personalistic as well as regional.[60] The southwest, or Kyongsang, has voted for conservative parties, currently taking the form of the Grand National Party (GNP). The southeast, or Cholla, has voted for opposition candidates, culminating in its success in having a favorite son, Kim Dae Jung, elected as president as head of the Millennium Democratic Party (MDP). Supporters of the People First Party, which absorbed the United Liberal Democratic Party (ULD) of Kim Jong Pil, tend to come from the central provinces, or Chungchong. In the 2004 presidential race, the ultimate outsider, Roh Moo Hyun, won, reflecting public exasperation at what were perceived as a series of failed presidencies: failed generals; followed by Kim Young Sam, who had the bad luck to be in power when the 1997 financial crisis hit; succeeded by the perennial oppositionist Kim Dae Jung, who could not control his sons' influence peddling.

With the end of Kim Dae Jung's term and his fall from political grace followed by the impeachment of his successor came the implosion of his MDP, and from its ashes arose the Uri Party (Our Open Party). The Uri Party won a stunning and unexpected victory in the 2004 legislative elections, attracting almost 49 percent of the vote and taking 146 out of 299 seats.[61] The turnout for the elections was high and the age demographics appeared for the first time to trump regionalism with younger voters favoring the Uri Party throughout the country.[62] But it may be too soon to claim an enduring change in South Korean politics. The Uri Party's victory was also due to a colossal miscalculation on the part of the GNP and its allies. Having been shut out of office for two terms, it showed too much desperation for power in its tactic of impeaching President Roh on what looked to the electorate as a mere technicality. The other problem in analyzing South Korean politics is the distortion caused by the reunification prism through which all parties, politicians, and policies are viewed.

*Will Japan's DPJ take the fight up to the LDP?* The Japanese party system is also in a state of flux. The 1955 unimodal system looks to be over, but we cannot yet be quite sure what party system has replaced it. Electoral reforms and greater media vibrancy, together with a more assertive electorate, are changing the system, though the impact of the changes has to a certain extent been counterbalanced by the personal popularity of the prime minister between 2001 and 2006, Junichiro Koizumi, a situation that may not be sustained by his successor, Shinzo Abe. While the Japan Communist Party may be willing to continue life in splendid isolation in the secure knowledge that it will never have to deal with issues of government, those parties interested in winning power realize that they will need to either grow in popularity or merge with coalition partners. There seems to be a race for the political center going on, with the LDP facing a powerful new force in the

Democratic Party of Japan (DPJ) formed in 1998 with the aim of uniting opposition forces to offer the electorate a viable alternative government.

LDP and DPJ dwarf the three other parties represented in the House of Representatives, with 250 and 176 members respectively in a 480-seat chamber in the outgoing parliament in 2005, and 296 and 112 in the incoming parliament.[63] Though badly beaten in 2005, the DPJ can nevertheless take heart from its performance at the House of Councilors election in 2004, where it edged out the LDP, winning 51 seats to the ruling party's 49 and gaining 4 million more proportional representation votes.[64] The new balance in Japanese politics suggests that perhaps the 1955 system was exceptional and grew out of the necessities of Cold War politics. Perhaps the natural state in Japan, as in other consolidated democracies, is for the electorate to have a realistic choice of governments. Similar processes seem to be under way in the other consolidated democracy in Asia, India.

### Conclusion: Toward Two-Party Formats?

The underlying question being posed in this chapter is whether the relatively young political systems of the transition democracies are able to nurture and sustain viable and democratic political parties. In a previous chapter, the point was made that some aspects of the political system are open to engineering. The choice of electoral systems will have a very direct impact on the shape and strength of political parties.

### *Engineering Party Systems*

The electoral system is the most direct means of influencing the shape of a nation's political party system. As previously noted, majoritarian systems will tend to favor the larger parties, and indeed the more rigorously it is applied, the more it will favor the two largest parties. Proportional representation systems will enhance representativeness but possibly at the expense of party coherence and even governability. Closed party lists will strengthen party discipline and coherence while open lists may create competition within a party. FPTP presidential elections strongly favor the two largest parties. Drawing on Tables 3.4 and 3.5, one can discern a trend toward the design of electoral systems that attempt to strengthen political parties. The clearest trend is toward a mixed electoral system, though with a distinct bias toward the constituency electoral system with its majoritarian impact. Systems used for presidential elections are having a similar effect. There is also a trend toward closed lists, and even, as in Indonesia, where the list is open, the quota for gaining a seat is so high that virtually all successful candidates must be high on the party's official list. So, electoral systems are being designed to favor large parties.

Beyond the electoral system, designers have other tools to influence the shape of the party system. One blunt instrument is to disallow parties that do not meet threshold membership requirements, such as the requirement in Thailand for at least 5,000 members within six months of being registered.[65] Another device is to adopt a rule making the attainment of a certain voting threshold in the previous election the qualification for participation in the next election, as is the case in Indonesia.[66] Indonesia has taken the process of engineering parties the furthest. In order to ensure parties had a national rather than a regional character in this sprawling, multiethnic archipelago, parties could only gain registration if they could demonstrate that they had branches in two-thirds of all provinces and sub-branches in two-thirds of the districts within those provinces, while each local party unit was required to have 1,000 members.[67] The Indonesian rules had the required effect of eliminating many small parties. A consequence of these rules is that groups such as the Acehnese or the Papuans cannot have their own political parties but must find a place within the mainstream national parties.

The rules are therefore pushing the party system toward greater concentration. In many of Pacific Asia's democracies this concentration of parties is establishing a clear trend toward the emergence of two-party formats.

### A Brief Survey of Where Things Stood in 2006

The success of Congress and the BJP in India has established them as the only parties able to win government. Yet there are thirty-nine parties represented in the Lok Sabha elected in 2004. Some of these parties may have strong regional and cleavage support bases, but they do not appear to have the potential to become major national parties like Congress and the BJP that have so dominated Indian politics. What seems to be happening, though, is that two major parties have consolidated their hold on national politics, and the others must adopt the subsidiary logic of the coalition partner, the veto player, or the gadfly.

It seemed for a while that Thaksin was able to achieve a result that was thought impossible and thus was not even attempted to be engineered by the constitutional drafting committee[68]—creating a two-party system. Between them, four parties won nearly 99 percent of the vote in the 2005 elections.[69] The Mahachon Party, which broke away from the Democrats before the elections, won 8.28 percent, but this translated into only two seats, leading to the resignation of its leader and doubts about its future. The Chart Thai Party won 11.39 percent of the vote and twenty-five seats, but its base has shrunk down to the fiefdom of its leader, Banharn Silpa-archa, in and around Suphan Buri Province. Already in his seventies at the time of the 2005 election, one wonders how many more he will contest and whether his daughter, Kanchana, will be able to hold together his regional political power base. The Democratic Party's vote has also shrunk down to 18.34 percent, translating to ninety-six seats. It did not do well in Bangkok and it is now dominant only in the south of the country.[70] The other large parties like the NAP and CPP had been folded into the TRTP. McCargo and Ukrist Pathmanand argue that a two-party system was traditionally seen as an ideal in Thailand, and that the "Thaksinization" of Thai politics has forced the Democrats to copy the TRTP example of turning itself into the only other "electoral professional party."[71] The logic of Thaksin's electoral success is that the opposition must strengthen its forces and that future elections could become contests between the two major parties, TRTP and the Democrats. The 2006 coup may yet change this dynamic.

Even where there are three major parties, as in Taiwan, where the DPP and the KMT are joined by James Soong's People First Party (PFP), the logic of FPTP presidential elections is to avoid the three-cornered contest as occurred in 2000. Parliamentary systems at least allow for the option of a third-party balance of power situation to develop, but presidential systems tend to accentuate the marginal position of the third party. There will accordingly be considerable pressure on Soong's party either to return to its roots in the KMT or be wooed by the DPP's entreaties. It is difficult to see the PFP surviving indefinitely as a third party. If the 2005 Taiwan National Assembly elections are an indication of future voting trends, then the demise of the PFP appears to have begun because the two major parties scored 81.5 percent of the vote, pointing to a likely two-party future.

### Are Two-Party Systems Consolidating?

Can we now conclude that democratic Asia's party systems are moving to two-party formats? Conventional wisdom has been to emphasize the multi-party nature of these party systems, a conclusion reached in the study by Rüland et al. that looked at elections in the region up to 2001.[72] But when one examines the next round of election results, a different conclusion appears to present itself. The adversarial equations seem to suggest movement toward two-party systems: Congress vs. BJP; LDP vs. DPJ; Uri vs. GNP; TRTP vs. DP; DPP vs. KMT. These parties have emerged from fragmented party systems or systems of unimodal domination. Having emerged as one of only two parties considered by the electorate as capable of winning power, these parties have it within their capacities to reinforce their preeminent positions and in effect freeze others out of contention. A two-party system developed in the past in the Philippines but was not able to be reengineered after Marcos attempted to establish a dominant party. So, once having arisen, it is not certain that a two-party system will implant itself indefinitely. But aside from coups, authoritarian interventions, or a more-possible catastrophic error committed by one of the two big parties affecting its popularity, the two dominant parties are in a strong position to cement their advantageous situation. They form a type of duopoly that influences the rules of the game, and they thus work together, openly or implicitly, to keep competitors out.

The development of the two-party formats in these five countries is of great significance to democratic consolidation. Two strong parties will be in a better position to achieve the classic tasks required of political parties. Table 5.3, providing the combined vote and seats of the two leading parties, and/or coalitions of parties, in lower house elections between 2003 and 2005, therefore points to a two-party future. The exceptions remain Indonesia and the Philippines. In Indonesia, the House of Representatives has organized itself along the lines of opposing coalitions with the People's Coalition supporting the president and the National Coalition setting itself as the opposition.[73] The Philippine Congress has adopted the US forms of majority and minority groups. But the reality remains that such bifurcations in Indonesia and the Philippines have little by way of programmatic meaning.

Sartori recently returned to the question of engineering two-party formats through electoral systems.[74] In relation to India's FPTP or plurality electoral system, Sartori's rules can be seen as partially explaining the seeming emergence of two major parties in that both are nationwide parties. But the parties representing "incoercible minorities" are also represented in parliament, though not in significant numbers. E. Sridharan and Ashutosh Varshney argue that the impact of federalism together with India's complex cleavages militate against the plurality electoral system generating two-party formats.[75] Perhaps the resolution of this question can be seen in the

**Table 5.3  Performance of Two Leading Parties in Legislative Elections in Six Asian Polities, 2003–2005**

| Country | Year | Two Leading Parties (% Vote) | Percentage for Combined Vote | Seats/ Total | Percentage for Combined Seats |
|---|---|---|---|---|---|
| India | 2004 | Congress (26.8) vs. BJP (22.2) | 49 | 283/545 | 51.9 |
|  |  | +allies (34.6) vs. +allies (35.3) | 69.9 | 402/545 | 73.7 |
| Japan | 2003 | LDP (34.9) vs. DPJ (37.4)[a] | 72.3 | 414/480 | 86.2 |
| South Korea | 2004 | Uri (38.3) vs. GNP (35.8) | 74.1 | 272/300 | 90.7 |
| Taiwan | 2004 | DPP (38) vs. KMT (34.9) | 72.9 | 168/225 | 74.6 |
| Thailand | 2005 | TRT (60.7) vs. Democrats (18.3) | 79 | 471/500 | 94.2 |
| Japan | 2005 | LDP (38.18) vs. DPJ (31.02)[a] | 69.2 | 408/480 | 85.0 |

*Source:* Data obtained from www.electionworld.org and parliamentary websites.
*Note:* a. Percentage of proportional vote.

way India is moving toward a fragmented party system where only two major nationwide parties are *capable* of forming the basis of government and others have little option but to align themselves with one or other of the two parties of government.

### Elections Are Becoming More Meaningful

Why are two-party systems emerging in Japan, South Korea, Thailand, and Taiwan? These countries operate mixed electoral systems, though with an emphasis on the majoritarian part of the mixture. None of these countries has an "incoercible minority" issue. It is too soon to draw conclusions from the few recent elections held under the mixed electoral systems, and Sartori argues that the effects he postulates need time. The tendency toward elections becoming contests between two major contenders for office may also in part flow from circumstances other than the electoral system. In the case of these four countries, an argument can be made that a combination of the rules of the game and the increasing *meaningfulness* of elections are forcing parties to demonstrate to the electorate the capacity to form a government in order to gain votes. Voters begin to see a vote for a small party that cannot win government as a futile gesture and they therefore vote far more strategically for a party that can win. This forces parties to seek to grow in size and reputation until they look like government party material. Taken to its conclusion, the logic of demonstrating and maintaining the perception of strength should squeeze out all but two major contender parties from the political scene. Small parties may survive, depending on various issues such as the applicable thresholds, but will only be able to entertain limited ambitions if they do not have the prospect of becoming the major party in a coalition government.

I am not, however, arguing that the two-party format is the best or most-mature system. Many democracies enjoy stable and competent governance under a multiparty system engineered through proportional representation and designed to represent the interests of various cleavages in heterogeneous societies, or various political views in open societies. But it does seem to me that a core of countries in Pacific Asia is moving toward a process of giving the electorate a simple choice between two coherent parties as an important step in democratic maturation from either fragmented party politics or single-party dominance. Japan, South Korea, Thailand, and Taiwan have cleavages in their societies, but these cleavages are sufficiently shallow to be able to find solace in catch-all parties. At this point, the ever-useful tautology "time will tell" might be employed, but I prefer to conclude with the belief that democratic Asia is moving resolutely in the direction of two-party politics and that this is an important sign of the consolidation of their democratic systems.

## Notes

1. Philippe C. Schmitter, "Parties Are Not What They Once Were," Larry Diamond and Richard Gunther (eds.), *Political Parties and Democracy* (Baltimore: Johns Hopkins University Press, 2001), p. 84.
2. Russell J. Dalton, "Decline of Party Identification," Russell J. Dalton and Martin P. Wattenberg, *Parties Without Partisans* (Oxford: Oxford University Press, 2000), p. 36.
3. Larry Diamond and Richard Gunther, "Introduction," Diamond and Gunther (eds.), *Political Parties and Democracy*, p. xiv.
4. Roland Rich, "Analysing and Categorising Political Parties in the Pacific Islands," Roland Rich with Luke Hambly and Michael Morgan (eds.), *Political Parties in the Pacific Islands* (Canberra: Pandanus Books, 2006), pp. 9–12.
5. Yun-han Chu, "The Legacy of One-Party Hegemony in Taiwan," Diamond and Gunther (eds.), *Political Parties and Democracy*, p. 270.
6. Leo Suryadinata, *Elections and Politics in Indonesia* (Singapore: Institute of Southeast Asian Studies, 2002), p. 33.
7. Anusorn Limmanee, "Thailand," Wolfgang Sachsenröder and Ulrike Frings (eds.), *Political Party Systems and Democratic Development in East and Southeast Asia—Volume I: Southeast Asia* (Aldershot: Ashgate Publishing, 1998), p. 415.
8. Seymour Martin Lipset and Stein Rokkan, "Cleavage Structure, Party Systems, and Voter Alignments: An Introduction," Seymour Martin Lipset and Stein Rokkan (eds.), *Party Systems and Voter Alignments: Cross National Perspectives* (New York: Free Press, 1967), pp. 1–64.
9. Wolfgang Sachsenröder, "Party Politics and Democratic Development in East and Southeast Asia—A Comparative View," Sachsenröder and Frings (eds.), *Political Party Systems and Democratic Development*, p. 12.
10. Maurice Duverger, *Political Parties: Their Organisation and Activity in the Modern State* (London: Methuen, 1954).
11. Jean Blondel, "Party Systems and Patterns of Government in Western Democracies," *Canadian Journal of Political Science* 1, no. 2 (1968): 180–203.
12. Robert Dahl, *Polyarchy: Participation and Opposition* (New Haven: Yale University Press, 1971), pp. 20–21.
13. Stein Rokkan, *Citizen, Elections, Parties. Approaches to the Comparative Study of the Process of Development* (Oslo: Universitetsforlaget), 1970.
14. Giovanni Sartori, *Parties and Party Systems—A Framework for Analysis,* Vol. 1 (Cambridge: Cambridge University Press, 1976), pp. 248–254.
15. Ibid., p. 128.
16. Ibid., p. 78.
17. Richard Gunther and Larry Diamond, "Species of Political Parties—A New Typology," *Party Politics* 9, no. 2 (2003), p. 173.
18. Edward Masters, *Indonesia's 1999 Elections: A Second Chance for Democracy* (New York: Asia Society, 1999), available from www.asiasociety.org/publications/indonesia/#The%20Party%20System.
19. Stephen Sherlock, *Consolidation and Change: The Indonesian Parliament After the 2004 Elections,* Centre for Democratic Institutions, available from www.cdi.anu.edu.au/CDIwebsite_1998-2004/research_publications/research_Consolidation&Change_Indoelections_2004.htm.
20. Tun-Jen Cheng, "Democratizing the Quasi-Leninist Regime in Taiwan," *World Politics* 41, no. 4 (July 1989): 471–499.
21. Ibid., p. 477.

22. Anna Grzymala Busse, *Redeeming the Communist Past: The Regeneration of Communist Successor Parties in East Central Europe* (Cambridge: Cambridge University Press, 2002).

23. Sorpong Peou, "The UN's Modest Impact on Cambodian Democracy," Edward Newman and Roland Rich (eds.), *The UN Role in Promoting Democracy: Between Ideals and Reality* (Tokyo: United Nations University Press, 2004), pp. 258–281.

24. David Kovick and Laura L. Thornton, "Cambodia," Peter M. Manikas and Laura L. Thornton (eds.), *Political Parties in Asia—Promoting Reform and Combating Corruption in Eight Countries* (Washington, DC: National Democratic Institute for International Affairs, 2003), pp. 41–74.

25. James Jesudason, "The Resilience of the Dominant Parties of Malaysia and Singapore," H. Giliomee and C. Simkins (eds.), *The Awkward Embrace: The Dominant Party and Democracy in Mexico, South Africa, Malaysia, and Taiwan* (Amsterdam: Harwood Academic Publishers, 1999), pp. 127–172.

26. Tomohito Shinoda, "Japan," Sachsenröder and Frings (eds.), *Political Party Systems and Democratic Development,* p. 100.

27. Purnendra C. Jain, "Party Politics at the Crossroads," Takashi Inoguchi and Purnendra C. Jain (eds.), *Japanese Politics Today: Beyond Karaoke Democracy?* (Melbourne: MacMillan, 1997), p. 17.

28. Margaret McKean and Ethan Scheiner, "Japan's New Electoral System: la plus ca change . . . ," *Electoral Studies* 19, no. 4 (2000): 447–477.

29. Rajni Kothari quoted in E. Sridharan and Ashutosh Varshney, "Toward Moderate Pluralism: Political Parties in India," Larry Diamond and Richard Gunther (eds.), *Political Parties and Democracy,* p. 219.

30. Ibid.

31. Richard Gunther and Larry Diamond, "Types and Functions of Parties," Diamond and Gunther (eds.), *Political Parties and Democracy,* p. 25.

32. Francis Pangilinan, "Philippine Politics Post Estrada," available from www.cdi.anu.edu.au/CDIwebsite_1998-2004/philippines/Pangilianan_Address_Jul03.htm.

33. Drawn from Sheila S. Coronel, "Born to Rule," Sheila S. Coronel et al., *The Rulemakers—How the Wealthy and Well-Born Dominate Congress* (Manila: Philippine Center for Investigative Journalism, 2004), pp. 56–69.

34. Errol B. Leones and Miel Loraleda, "Philippines," Sachsenröder and Frings (eds.), *Political Party Systems and Democratic Development,* p. 336.

35. Drawn from Limmanee, "Thailand."

36. Hussin Mutalid, *Parties and Politics: A Study of Opposition Parties and the PAP in Singapore* (Singapore: Times Media Private Limited, 2003), p. 153.

37. J. A. A. Stockwin, "Reforming Japanese Politics: Highway to Change or Road to Nowhere?" Inoguchi and C. Jain (eds.), *Japanese Politics Today: Beyond Karaoke Democracy?* footnote 11, p. 90.

38. Ibid., p. 81.

39. Jain, "Party Politics at the Crossroads," p. 24.

40. Sherlock, *Consolidation and Change.*

41. Drawn from Peter M. Manikas and Laura L. Thornton, "Indonesia," Manikas and Thornton (eds.), *Political Parties in Asia,* pp. 75–138.

42. Sartori, *Parties and Party Systems,* p. 4.

43. Ibid., p. 11.

44. Larry Diamond, *Developing Democracy: Toward Consolidation* (Baltimore: Johns Hopkins University Press, 1999), p. 96.

45. Dwight Y. King, *Half-Hearted Reform: Electoral Institutions and the Struggle for Reform in Indonesia* (Westport: Praeger, 2003).

46. Suryadinata, *Elections and Politics in Indonesia*, pp. 78–84.

47. Sherlock, *Consolidation and Change*, pp. 7–10.

48. National Democratic Institute for International Affairs, "Advancing Democracy in Indonesia: The Second Democratic Legislative Elections Since the Transition," June 2004, p. 11, available from www.accessdemocracy.org/library/1728_id_legelections_063004.pdf.

49. Ibid.

50. Laura L. Thornton, "Thailand," Manikas and Thornton (eds.), *Political Parties in Asia*, p. 403.

51. Philippines Liberal Party, *Platform and Policies*, available from www.cald.org/website/lpp.htm.

52. Adam Brown, *Estrada Arrested on Corruption*, Associated Press, 25 April 2001, available from www.globalpolicy.org/nations/corrupt/2001/0425estr.htm.

53. Pasuk Phongpaichit and Singsidh Piriyarangsan, *Corruption and Democracy in Thailand* (Bangkok: Chulalongkorn University, 1994), p. 103.

54. Michael H. Nelson, "Thai Politics Monitor," Michael H. Nelson (ed.), *Thailand's New Politics—KPI Yearbook 2001* (Bangkok: King Prajadhipok's Institute and White Lotus, 2002), p. 291.

55. Pasuk Phongpaichit and Chris Baker, "'Business Populism' in Thailand," *Journal of Democracy* 16, no. 2 (April 2005): 61–64.

56. Nelson, "Thai Politics Monitor," p. 391.

57. David Kovick, "Taiwan," Manikas and Thornton (eds.), *Political Parties in Asia*, p. 350.

58. Keith Bradsher, "Taiwan Vote Hard to Read, Analysts Say," *New York Times*, 16 May 2005.

59. Kovick, "Taiwan," p. 353.

60. Laura L. Thornton and David Kovick, "South Korea," Manikas and Thornton (eds.), *Political Parties in Asia*, p. 292.

61. National Assembly website, http://korea.assembly.go.kr/mem/mem_04.jsp.

62. Balbina Y. Hwang, "The Elections in South Korea: A Victory for the Electoral Process," The Heritage Foundation, 19 April 2004, available from www.heritage.org/Research/AsiaandthePacific/wm484.cfm.

63. Japan parliament website, www.shugiin.go.jp/index.nsf/html/index_e_strength.htm.

64. Japan Democratic Party website, www.dpj.or.jp/english/about_us/dpj_profile.html.

65. Benjamin Reilly, *Democracy and Diversity: Political Engineering in the Asia-Pacific* (Oxford: Oxford University Press, 2006), p. 136.

66. Ibid.

67. Ibid., p. 133.

68. Comment to the author by secretary of the committee, Dr. Bowornsak Uwanno

69. IFES Election Guide, www.electionguide.org/resultsum/thai_parl05.htm.

70. Chang Noi, "The Numbers of the 2005 Election," *The Nation*, 28 February 2005.

71. Duncan McCargo and Ukrist Pathmanand, *The Thaksinization of Thailand* (Copenhagen: Nordic Institute of Asian Studies, 2005), pp. 77–79.

72. Jürgen Rüland et al., *Parliaments and Political Change in Asia* (Singapore: Institute of Southeast Asian Studies, 2005), p. 138.

73. The Habibie Centre, "The House Divided: The Conflict Between the National and the People's Coalition in the Parliament," *Postscript* 1, no. 7 (November 2004), available from www.habibiecenter.or.id/download/postscript_edisi7.pdf.

74. Giovanni Sartori, "The Party Effects of Electoral Systems," Diamond and Gunther (eds.), *Political Parties and Democracy,* pp. 90–105.

75. Sridharan and Varshney, "Toward Moderate Pluralism," pp. 212–213.

# 6

# Assessing Politicians

"The theory of democracy does not treat leaders kindly. Suspicion of rulers, concern over their propensity to abuse power in their own self-interest, the need to hold them accountable, and the belief that legitimate power is lodged originally in the people and granted to leaders only with severe contingencies, all are fixed stars in the democratic galaxy."
—Kenneth P. Ruscio, *The Leadership Dilemma in Modern Democracy*[1]

The focus on institutions, constitutions, and the rule of law takes the study of politics to the systemic and thus above the level of the individual. Looking at deliberation, the public conversation, and political culture involves an understanding of group behavior in which the whole is greater than the sum of its individual parts. Yet, we cannot escape the reality that the basic unit in all these processes is the individual, ranging from the voter to those for whom they vote. In politics, the key individual is the politician. Being an individual, the politician necessarily defies any "one size fits all" description. Does that mean that politicians cannot be the subject of assessments that attempt to build broad generalizations about their conduct and worth? If such assessments are possible, what methodology is available? Does this methodology allow us to focus on politicians in Pacific Asia? This chapter will attempt to answer these questions by describing and analyzing politicians in Pacific Asian democracies using a method proposed by Linz, who asks a series of probing questions to test political leaders against an idealized framework.

## Political Styles
Before turning to Linz, it is important at the outset to separate style from substance. It is often style that attracts attention, yet it is substance that must provide the subject matter of our inquiry. In terms of their work methods, politicians resemble each other the world over. They are simultaneously campaigning, projecting, impressing, deciding, often scheming, and

occasionally, learning. Yet they take on different appearances in different countries. This reflects the different styles required to respond to the cultures and trends in each country. To impress the Japanese electorate, a politician needs to project dignity and imperturbability. To impress the Thai electorate requires the ability to show compassion and sincerity. Filipino voters are dazzled by a bright smile, quick talk, and the ability to belt out a song. These public postures are not unfamiliar to countries where elections are meaningful, because they are directed at the electorate that will actually decide who will govern. If the public decides the result of an election, then the politician must find ways to reach the public and gain approval.

## The Key Audience

Oddly enough, politicians give a not dissimilar appearance in countries where elections do not matter all that much. They are still campaigning, projecting, and impressing, but their audiences are different. In Malaysia, the key audience for a leading politician is the UMNO Assembly. UMNO controls the Barisan Nasional (BN; National Front), which has the ambition of governing the country in perpetuity. The arena for Malaysian politics is thus not the floor of parliament, nor the electoral campaign, but the annual UMNO assemblies. Campaigning for advancement takes place here, and it is the UMNO delegates one must impress and for whom one needs to project one's skills or power in various ways. Malaysian politicians still need to interface with the public, and indeed one of the qualities that their UMNO colleagues will be looking for is a good style of dealing with the public, but the main game is played out in the party room.

It might even be possible to generalize that the less democratic a country is, the smaller the decisionmaking audience that needs to be won over, bought, or cowed. Malaysian politicians have to think about hundreds of UMNO delegates representing four million UMNO members who expect to win large majorities in every national election. A Vietnamese politician has to make calculations within a field of about a dozen politburo members and a few hundred members and aspiring members of the central committee. The critical advancement is to the central committee and is gained by impressing the party leaders. Being elected to the National Assembly in Vietnam is mainly a reward for diligence and enthusiastic acquiescence. Once we come to Burma, the audience has shrunk to the inner circle of generals who run the country. Nobody else's opinion matters very much. It is hard to know who the audience might be in Pyongyang. Perhaps it is Kim Jong Il and his family plus some military confidants, or perhaps it is simply Dear Leader himself.

The style a politician will adopt thus reflects the decisionmaking environment of that country's politics. And it is often the style that dominates the impression one takes away of the politician in question. I recall being swept away from my hotel room by the governor of Antique province on the island of Iloilo in the Philippines, to a beach party at a local holiday resort. Antique is a poor province, but upon arriving at the party, one could but be impressed with the sound system and the banks of speakers and amplifiers that lined one wall. Within a few minutes of the first drinks being served, the crowd requested the governor to sing his successful campaign song. The governor feigned a moment's reticence before grasping the microphone and launching with gusto, a touch of tremolo, and lots of decibels, into his rendition of "The Impossible Dream." At various key lyrics, "to fight the unbeatable foe" or "the world will be better for this," the crowd would burst into enthusiastic applause. It was quite a performance. As the governor took his bows, his acolytes demanded an encore and the governor happily obliged, once again generating the same audience reaction. By the time the governor was in his seventh consecutive rendition I had sunk into a state of deep self-pity and was in no doubt about who was bearing the unbearable sorrow.

It was a small group of Burmese ministers who in an instant of scripted behavior made me understand what the Kremlinologists had been looking for during those Cold War years when poring over pictures of the leadership at May Day parades. In the 1980s, Australia and Burma had cordial relations, and I was at the airport awaiting the visit of an Australian minister. The Burmese understood the language of protocol and demonstrated their satisfaction at hosting this important visit by having four senior ministers at the airport to welcome the visitor. I was chatting amiably with one of them when he broke off in mid-sentence and strode off with the other ministers onto the tarmac. It was only the next day when I saw the photo in the newspaper of the ministers walking along the tarmac that I realized the reason for my interlocutor's haste. They walked in a casual staggered line that, on inspection, corresponded exactly to the ministers' pecking order in the government hierarchy. Had my interlocutor waited to finish his sentence he might have missed his spot and thus triggered speculation about his demotion. He was playing to the rules of a closed and constrained political system.

### Parliamentary Styles

The style of Australian politicians during Question Time, the daily interpellation session in parliament, was considered shocking but fascinating by the Asian parliamentarians I would take along to view the spectacle. Finger-pointing, personal abuse, mockery, and even mimicry are acceptable methods of disparaging opponents in Australian politics but are far more tricky techniques in an Asian parliament where there is usually a stronger emphasis on decorum and politeness. In the essentially two-party tribal politics of Australia, the parliamentary chamber is a place to rally the troops on your side and belittle your opponents. To be made the butt of a successful joke is to sustain a political injury from which some politicians may not recover. Andrew Peacock served Australia honorably and successfully for many years, including as foreign minister, but his political career was compromised by a vicious, but funny, joke by Labor Party prime minister Paul Keating. After a failed attempt by Peacock to win back the leadership of the Liberal Party, Keating had one of his colleagues ask him whether there was any chance of Peacock again leading the Liberal Party. "None, Mr. Speaker," Keating replied, "because it is a well-known fact that a soufflé cannot rise twice." A soufflé is of course an attractive but insubstantial dish filled mainly with hot air. Keating delivered the line with impunity to the laughter of his colleagues and the stony glares of his opponents.

In the parliamentary chambers of Bangkok or Tokyo or Seoul, a joke such as this could just as easily rebound against the deliverer. The Indonesian public has a keen sense of humor, as demonstrated in the popular description of the three presidential candidates in 1999. They were described as the three monkeys who, respectively, do not see, hear, or speak. Gus Dur is almost blind, Habibie is famous for talking at length and never listening to anybody else, and Megawati is equally well known for looking regal but never saying anything. While the public may engage in this type of humor, it is a more problematic weapon for their leaders. Gus Dur used a form of belittling humor against his then vice president and political adversary Megawati when asked whether the vice president was involved in an important Cabinet meeting. "No," he replied "she had to go home and take a shower." Unlike Peacock, Megawati was soon to exact her revenge.

While Asian parliaments are not usually as rowdy and robust as Australia's, there have been a number of times when they have slipped from their normal set-piece decorum and degenerated into brawls and fistfights, at times to gain control of the microphone or the Speaker's gavel, and at other times to settle personal or partisan feuds. This unbecoming conduct has occurred in Indonesia, South Korea, and Taiwan.[2] Perhaps the rowdiness of the Australian parliament acts as a pressure valve, whereas in some Asian parliaments the pressure builds until there is an explosion.

## Political Substance

Because there is so much public focus on style, it is possible to mistake it for substance. When it comes to assessing the worth of politicians, we need a more universal template. Success may be an end in itself, and ultimately

perhaps the only realistic measurement is longevity in office. But this measure, though important, will not distinguish democratic politicians from
authoritarian politicians. A recent study has categorized parliamentarians
from five Asian countries by looking at issues such as occupation, wealth,
education, gender, age, and religion.[3] The data for such an exercise is, however, often spotty, and the insights gained are helpful but limited. So it is
necessary to find a different, perhaps nonquantitative, means of measuring
the worth and quality of politicians in the democratic polities of Asia. Linz
provides five questions that are particularly helpful to test the quality of
political leaders:[4]

1. For what proportion is politics "a vocation" rather than just a way of
   making a living?
2. Is there a commitment to some values or goals relevant to the col-
   lectivity?
3. How much political corruption is there?
4. Is there a use or tolerance of illegal violence, often pandering to a
   majority of citizens who are ready to condone it?
5. Is there a willingness to use extremist elements against other democratic forces?

These are tough tests to apply to Asian politicians. Linz asks these questions
in relation to the "political class" as a whole, and so simply pointing to individual infractions of the quality tests is interesting but insufficient. The
questions need to be posed about the generality of the politicians, and this
of course poses difficult methodological challenges. First, evidence needs to
be collected. Anecdotes provide clues and several anecdotes may amount to
data. Studying individual leaders may provide useful information. Statistics
can at times be of assistance. Comparative data can assist in showing trends
and highlighting issues, particularly when intracivilizational comparisons
are made.

Second, some theoretical constructs are necessary to achieve coherence
in the analysis. Two concepts are particularly useful in this regard: political
structure and political culture. By political structure, I mean the rules and
institutional designs of the political system, both formal and informal.
Certain systems will facilitate the coming to power of certain types of people. The structure will certainly incorporate the ostensible rules of the game,
but must also discount them when they are not enforced. The structure will
be based on the political economy of the system. A particularly useful
method is to examine institutional reform measures to determine what they
may tell us about the problems identified as in need of rectification.

Political culture is a more amorphous concept to come to grips with.

Diamond defines the term broadly as "a people's predominant beliefs, attitudes, values, ideals, sentiments, and evaluations about the political system
of their country and the role of the self in that system."[5] Some aspects of
political culture were alluded to in opening this discussion with a comment
on different styles politicians adopt to respond to public ideals of political
conduct. The problem with political culture is the difficulty in describing it
in relation to any particular polity or even a distinctive group within that
polity. It is a problem that will be tackled in greater detail in Chapter 8 but
referred to at times in this chapter.

A third method of reaching conclusions about politicians is to draw on
opinion and analysis from both scholarly and practitioner sources. This is
where the specialized scholarly literature on individual countries becomes
indispensable to the comparativist.

So the idea is to investigate Linz's issues by reference to political structure and political culture. In so doing, the word *elites* will be employed.
This word forms the basis of a school of political science that analyzes politics through the prism of elite theory. William Case's insightful analysis of
Southeast Asian elites postulates a democratic elite theory.[6] While I find the
method of looking at societies partly through the prism of elites and their
interests useful, the concept strikes me as intrinsically circular as an
explanatory device. It is true that elites in any society have a disproportionate influence on developments, all the more so when the elites remain cohe-
sive. In Asian societies, the elites may include the military top brass, the
business leaders including powerful ethnic Chinese families, and the leading politicians and their families. Clearly, and especially when united, this
is a more influential group than an equal number of taxi drivers or construction workers. It stands to reason that in the general aspects of government
decisionmaking, it is the elites who exert the most influence. But there will
be times when the transformative role in society is played by others.
Students, the working class, and even the lumpen proletariat may at times
be the triggers for change in society. At other times it might be the younger
and better-educated members of the middle class, bridling at the elite's privileges and influence that plays the transformative role. In these cases, elite
theorists tend to explain the situation as a lapse in elite control. But to
explain change in terms of either elite domination or a lapse therein tends to
leave the question open. In the normal course of electoral politics in a liberal democracy, it will once again be the elites who play a critical role in setting the agenda and shaping public opinion. But elite domination can simply
be defeated by the electorate, as was shown by the surly rural vote against
the BJP in the 2004 Indian elections. Elites should therefore be seen as only
one significant part of a far larger equation. Perhaps elite cohesion goes
some way to explain continuities in politics but is a less useful tool in
explaining change.

### Politics as Vocation

When Linz talks about a vocation, he is focusing on the origins of the word, from the Latin *vocare* meaning "to call." He is looking for politicians with a calling who are driven to seek office largely for altruistic rather than materialistic reasons. Linz's alternative to politics as vocation, "just a way of making a living," has a quaint quality when applied to Asia. It suggests politicians might enter their profession because of the attractive salary and allowances. In Asia, the alternative to vocation as a motive is not simply "making a living," but rather entering politics to protect or amass a fortune. As Coronel puts it, "a politician who is elected to Congress has got it made."[7] The major motivation for entry into politics in Asia has traditionally been self-enrichment and self-aggrandizement.

*Politicians in authoritarian parliaments.* Beginning the story at its simplest point among the Asian parliaments claiming the legitimacy of being elected, the Dewan Perwakilan Rakyat (DPR; People's Representative Assembly) in Suharto's New Order Indonesia was said to be like a child; expected to be seen but not heard.[8] It never drafted its own legislation, nor did it ever reject any legislation put forward by the executive.[9] Needless to say, the people who took their seats in this institution needed few skills beyond unquestioned loyalty to the president. Elections were held for the DPR, but the real decisionmaking process was, first, in compiling the list of candidates by the institutions who actually ran the country, the Army, the bureaucracy, and the leaders of Suharto's political party vehicle, Golkar, and, second, by Suharto himself, who vetted the list and crossed out the names of any critics or vacillators.[10] Some of the parliamentarians were certainly intelligent and well educated, but these were not the qualities that gained them selection. Selection to office was a matter of reward and acknowledgment of status in the pecking order. The Suharto-era DPR member was thus the antithesis of the vocational politician. My own impression of dealing with Indonesian politicians of this era was that they focused exclusively on form, not substance. Everything had to look right, protocol had to be respected, and exchanges were of the most banal and scripted variety. One of the problems of the 1999–2004 post-Suharto DPR was that, although quite a few oppositionists were elected in 1999, many of the incumbents remained holdovers from the Suharto era.

We can confidently place the Suharto DPR under the category of rubber-stamp parliament and list this feature as the most-telling aspect of the political structure influencing the character and quality of its politicians. To a greater or lesser extent, the same analysis can apply to other parliaments in the region in varying periods. Parliaments that simply do the executive's bidding will attract very few candidates who can fit under Linz's vocational politician category. They will mainly attract people who see the path of loyalty to a leader as a good way to obtain wealth and privilege. While they may attract some ambitious, talented, and even well-meaning people amongst their number, those demonstrating "vocational" qualities are more than likely to be purged in a rubber-stamp parliament.

Asian politics provides many examples of this phenomenon, the most-celebrated in recent times being the prosecution of Anwar Ibrahim in Malaysia. Multiparty parliaments in such systems may be placed along a spectrum ranging between constrained to controlled. In this category, we can place the Japanese Diet in the period when the LDP was effectively unchallenged, the South Korean National Assembly prior to the 1987 reforms, the Legislative Yuan in Taiwan under KMT domination, the Malaysian parliament under Mahathir and perhaps even beyond, and the Singapore parliament. Parliamentarians sitting in these chambers tended to be former officials tied for career advancement to a powerful patron, family members and business cronies of those powerful patrons, and the occasional academic or expert providing useful advice to the patron.

*Structural problems for vocational politicians.* Today, however, there are a number of parliaments in the region that cannot be said to be controlled and that can be described as having the capacity and the occasional willingness to act in a relatively unconstrained manner. Are there then other aspects of the political structure that militate against the rise of the vocational politician in these parliaments? Two structural problems come to mind; both are well known and will be dealt with in greater detail later in this chapter.

The first, money politics, has been a noted feature of the political systems in all the democratizing countries in Asia. One result of the system is that it makes wealth, or at least access to it, an informal qualification for public office. Not only is wealth required to win election campaigns, but once in office, politicians are informally required to pay a "social tax" in the form of wedding gifts, funeral expenses, and donations to charities and to other worthy requests. Clearly one does not aspire to enter these parliaments simply for the salary.

The other structural problem is the paucity of programmatic political parties. Vocational politicians do not have readily available options of joining powerful parties in which the members share an ideological viewpoint that they can advance by means of intellect, energy, and talent alone. The opening of the avenue of political advancement through membership of a party is one of the most important processes for the encouragement of vocational politicians. The issue of the limited though perhaps growing place of programmatic parties in Asian political systems is the subject of the previous chapter.

Perhaps the best indication of the impact of structural problems in getting the right sort of politicians in office can be seen from the frenetic reform activity that has been a feature of democratizing Asia. One of the most-striking examples of attempting to reengineer the political system to produce the right sort of politicians was contained in the 1997 Constitution of Thailand, which set as a qualification for new parliamentarians "having graduated with not lower than a Bachelor's degree or its equivalent."[11] As has been pointed out, this has the remarkable effect of eliminating 99 percent of rural Thai people as candidates.[12]

I had the opportunity to discuss this rather elitist provision with members of the Constitutional Drafting Commission (CDC), and two explanations emerged. One centered on the Thai people's respect for scholarship and the enhanced status of politicians that this provision would bring. A more down-to-earth explanation was that it was incorporated as a means of keeping provincial gangsters out of parliament. The gangsterization of parliament has been a nagging concern in Thailand and in some other Asian democracies, including India. In the 1998 Lok Sabha elections, some 10 percent of the candidates had criminal records.[13] After all, election to parliament brings considerable rewards in terms of status, access to government contracts, and, importantly, criminal law immunities. If a seat in parliament can in effect be purchased through vote buying, it becomes attractive to local gangsters or their nominees. Thai gangsters generally do not hold university degrees and the rule thus precluded them from running for parliament.

Another innovative provision of the Thai constitution was the requirement that a candidate for the Senate not be a member of a political party.[14] The result under the first vote held for the Senate, it having been an appointed body before 2000, was that the Senate largely comprised three types of people: former bureaucrats or military officers, former politicians, and people from NGOs.[15] This process thus allowed political activists not from the establishment a means of gaining election to the Senate. The senators with NGO backgrounds tended to work together in the Senate and, though not able to muster a majority among themselves, formed a vocal minority. The constitution precluded a senator from seeking a second consecutive term.[16] The CDC members told me that they did not want senators to see their role as a profession, but rather as giving six years to community service. So those Thai senators who had vocational ambitions would not have been able to turn their vocation into a profession.

The Philippine Congress has long been the domain of the establishment, and recognizing this, a provision was engineered in the 1987 Constitution that allows for representation in the House of Representatives for disadvantaged groups:

> For three consecutive terms after the ratification of this Constitution, one-half of the seats allocated to party-list representatives shall be filled, as provided by law, by selection or election from the labor, peasant, urban poor, indigenous cultural communities, women, youth, and such other sectors as may be provided by law, except the religious sector.[17]

This provision has allowed representatives of the Left to enter the political scene. Loretta Ann Rosales from Akbayan, or Citizens' Action Group, is now in her third term of challenging vested interests in the House. Even more remarkable is Satur Ocampo, once a wanted man as leader of the outlawed National Democratic Front, who is now serving his second term in Congress and at one stage had to remain holed up in the parliament building to avoid arrest.

While some of the means of shaping the representatives are formal, and indeed constitutional, other means are more informal. The Japanese government crisis of the mid-1990s was in part triggered by younger members of parliament refusing to accept the rigid system of seniority within the LDP.[18] In South Korea, formal rule changes on the distribution of political funds made it possible for outsiders to run for office, and for a political dissident to successfully run for the highest office. This led to the informal result that a candidate's performance in television debates, rather than his connections to *chaebols* (business conglomerates), is becoming the key factor in gaining electoral popularity, thus marking an important evolution in Korean political culture.[19] These formal and informal changes are allowing new types of politicians to enter the political domain. But while noting this important development, we should nevertheless concede that for the most part, parliaments in democratizing Pacific Asia remain the domain of the privileged, the wealthy, and the well-connected.

*Women in politics.*  The problem of dynastic control of the legislature in the Philippines is so pronounced that the 1987 Constitution states as one of its guiding principles: "The State shall guarantee equal access to public service and prohibit political dynasty as may be defined by law."[20] Legislation to give force to this principle, however, continues to elude the Philippine Congress, though half a dozen bills have been filed. The result is that two-thirds of the legislators elected in the post-Marcos era are members of political families and that over 60 percent have relatives in elective office.[21] The roots of the problem lie in the feudal nature of Philippine society at the time of independence with the provincial *cacique* (chief) or *hacendero* (rural landlord) naturally taking ownership of political representation of the province dominated by his or her family. While the provincial landlord remains well represented, the dynastic feature of Philippine politics also extends to the newer arrivals on the scene, those with wealth from urban industry and those who entered politics upon the fall of Marcos. So it is not unusual to have certain seats in the House held by the same family for the third or fourth generation. It is quite common for the same family to occupy all the senior posts in a province: representative, governor, and mayor of the main town. On several occasions, spouses have replaced each other in these posts. Even the three-term limit has failed to have its intended effect, as in the 2001 congressional elections, 29 percent of "first-termers" were former three-termers who had to sit out one term before again becoming eligible for election.[22] In this dynastic context, the 24 seats currently filled by sectoral representatives of marginalized groups, in a House with a total of 235 members for the 13th Congress, do not appear quite sufficient.

Having relatives in politics is not unusual in democracies the world over. Some families are obsessed by politics, most are not. If one looks simply at the leaders of the democratizing Asian countries, one will find a number of family connections. Thailand has had one brother succeed another as prime minister when, in 1975, Kukrit Pramoj succeeded Seni Pramoj. Not to be outdone, Seni then succeeded Kukrit in 1976. Japan can boast a number of leading political families. It has also had brothers assume the prime ministership, Nobusuke Kishi from 1957 to 1960 and Sato Eisaku from 1964 to 1972. Prime Minister Hatoyama Ichiro's two sons, Kunio and Yukio, both became members of the Diet. Prime Minister Tanaka Kakuei's daughter Makiko was foreign minister in the first Koizumi government. The inheritance of a Diet seat is an accepted practice in Japan, particularly among LDP politicians, and one study showed that in 1990, 31 percent of the Lower House seats and 46 percent of the LDP seats were held by second-generation politicians.[23] In the 2005 election, 158 candidates, or 14 percent of those running, were offspring of present or former Diet members.[24] In India, three generations of the Nehru-Gandhi family have held the prime ministership. North Korea is of course dynastic in the worst sense, but South Korea has not had any presidents whose fathers were also leaders. This may change, however, if Park Geun Hye, daughter of President Park Chung Hee and leader of the Grand National Party, fulfills her ambition to win the presidency in 2007. Politics as a family business is therefore common in Asia and seems to be generally accepted. Intolerance of dynastic politics has only come to a head in the Philippines, where the situation is seen to be so critical that new design measures are required, but, as is so often the case in the Philippines, they remain on the drawing board.

An interesting aspect of the political family trees is the Asian disposition to accept relatives of either gender as representatives of the family tradition. Wives, though usually widows when assuming public office, and daughters have often carried the family's colors onto the political battlefield, at times assuming the highest office. Family ties appear to be stronger than gender biases. The result is a disposition in Asia to accept women leaders. Table 6.1 lists all the women who have either held the leadership, or in

**Table 6.1   Asian Women Leaders, 1953–2006**

| Leader | Office | Country | Date | Relationship |
|---|---|---|---|---|
| Sühbaataryn Yanjmaa | President | Mongolia | 1953–1954 | Widow of national hero Sühbaatar |
| Sirimavo Bandaranaike | Prime minister | Sri Lanka | 1960–1965 1970–1977 1994–2000 | Widow of Prime Minister Solomon Bandaranaike |
| Song Qingling | Acting president | China | 1968–1972 | Widow of national hero Sun Yat-Sen |
| Indira Gandhi | Prime minister | India | 1966 1977 1980–1984 | Daughter of Prime Minister Jawaharlal Nehru |
| Corazon Aquino | President | Philippines | 1986–1992 | Widow of Senator Benigno Aquino |
| Benazir Bhutto | Prime minister | Pakistan | 1988–1990 1993–1996 | Daughter of Prime Minister Zulfikar Ali Bhutto |
| Aung San Suu Kyi | Elected leader | Burma | 1990 | Daughter of national hero Aung San |
| Khaleda Zia | Prime minister | Bangladesh | 1991–1996 2001–2006 | Widow of ruler Ziaur Rahman |
| Chandrika Kumaratunga | Prime minister President | Sri Lanka | 1994 1994–2005 | Daughter of Prime Minister Sirimavo Bandaranaike |
| Sheikh Hasina Wajed | Prime minister | Bangladesh | 1996–2001 | Daughter of Prime Minister Sheikh Mujibur Rahman |
| Maria Gloria Macapagal-Arroyo | President | Philippines | 2001– | Daughter of President Diosdado Macapagal |
| Megawati Sukarnoputri | President | Indonesia | 2001–2004 | Daughter of President Sukarno |

the case of Aung San Suu Kyi, won the electoral contest for leadership, of their countries in Asia.

It is a telling feature of Asian democracies that women are accepted as leaders of nations. After the 1999 elections in Indonesia, Gus Dur blocked Megawati's ascension to the presidency partly by suggesting that a country where 90 percent of the population is Muslim could not accept a woman as a leader. Two years later, in a parliamentary coup, Megawati was to prove him wrong. Women on the list have displayed the qualities one looks for in leadership: strength, resolution, courage, competence, and, indeed, vocational qualities. There is no reason why we will not see more women rise to the highest offices of Asia nations, perhaps as soon as 2007 in the form of Park Geun Hye in South Korea. Yet the final column of the table discloses an important feature of Asia's women leaders. They are *all* widows or daughters of former leaders or leading political figures. It is rare, even in a short list of a dozen, to find a 100 percent result. The problem with this list does not arise because of who is on it, but because of the women not on it. There are no Golda Meirs or Maggie Thatchers or Gro Harlem Brundtlands who came from relatively modest nonpolitical backgrounds and made it to the top through their abilities. These Asian women rode to leadership on the shoulders of their fathers or husbands. One of the tests of the quality of any democracy is its ability to represent women effectively, and this surely requires significant membership by women in elected bodies. From such representation the next batch of women leaders of Asia will arise, and they will not necessarily be family relatives of their political predecessors.

If we examine the ratio of women in the Asian parliaments under review, we find that there is a significant number, though, as common everywhere, not commensurate with demographics (see Table 6.2). It is now generally accepted that certain electoral systems will favor women's participation in parliament over others.[25] Most Asian electoral systems continue to have the largest number of MPs elected through variations on majoritarian systems, and this makes the election of women that much more difficult. The idea of quotas for women has not yet taken root, except in Taiwan, which has changed its electoral system for future elections, starting in December 2007, to incorporate party-list representatives of whom half must be women. There are straws in the wind blowing in that direction elsewhere. India is debating the question. The Philippine Constitution's sectoral representation provision specifically mentions women as a class requiring representation, and women's parties have had some success, including Abanse!Pinay in the 11th Congress, and the militant women's group GABRIELA in the 13th Congress. Taiwan is already leading the league in women members, even before its quota provision comes into effect.

Table 6.2  Women in Democratic Asian Parliaments, 2005

| Country | Year Elected | MPs[a] | Women MPs | Women MPs (%) | Senators | Women Senators | Women Senators (%) | Percentage of Total |
|---|---|---|---|---|---|---|---|---|
| Taiwan | 2004 | 225 | 47 | 20.9 | | | | 20.9 |
| Philippines | 2004 | 236 | 36 | 15.3 | 24 | 4 | 16.7 | 16.0 |
| Indonesia | 2004 | 550 | 62 | 11.2 | 128[b] | 27 | 21.1 | 13.1 |
| South Korea | 2004 | 300 | 39 | 13.0 | | | | 13.0 |
| Thailand | 2005 | 500 | 53 | 10.6 | 200(2000) | 21 | 10.5 | 10.6 |
| Japan | 2005 | 480 | 43 | 9.0 | 242(2003) | 33 | 13.6 | 10.5 |
| India | 2004 | 543 | 45 | 8.3 | 242 | 28 | 11.6 | 9.3 |
| Total | | 2,834 | 325 | 11.5 | 836 | 113 | 13.5 | 11.9 |

*Source:* Table devised from IPU statistics, parliamentary websites, and correspondence with various parliamentary secretariats.
*Notes:* a. MPs of the Lower House.
b. Represents the DPD.

*Military politicians.*  If we look at the background of the leaders more generally, we find that the membership in a political family is an important factor, but the dominant feature of the post–World War II leadership of Asia's five democratizing polities is its military character. Those countries that may be regarded as consolidated democracies, Japan and India, do not share this trait. None of India's fourteen prime ministers have emerged from a military career. The same statement could be made for Japan's twenty-eight postwar prime ministers if we discount the fifty-four days between 17 August and 9 October 1945, when Prince Higashikuni Naruhiko, an admiral, was Japan's thirtieth prime minister. For Indonesia, South Korea, the Philippines, Taiwan, and Thailand, collectively, the reality is that they have been governed by a leader with a military background for a majority of the period since the end of World War II (see Table 6.3).

The preponderance of military figures at the helm over the last half a century is largely due to the international and domestic toleration of authoritarian leadership in the Cold War years. Military figures of this era often came to power by extraconstitutional means and stayed in power for far longer periods than politicians who regularly need to face the electorate. But there is also an echo of the Eisenhower phenomenon where military figures transform themselves into civilian politicians and gain power through constitutional means. General Fidel Ramos in the Philippines; General Susilo Bambang Yudhoyono in Indonesia; and Generals Prem Tinsulananda, Chatichai Choonhavan, and Chavalit Yongchaiyudh in Thailand are examples. Prior to General Prem's prime ministership, elections and constitutions in Thailand were malleable institutions and the coming to power of military figures owed far more to their membership in the military fraternity than to any constitutional authority. Though his military career was fairly short, the connections he made while in uniform were decisive in launching his business career, which was the basis for his political career, and so one would

**Table 6.3    Military Leaders in Five Asian Polities, 1945–2005**

| Country | Leaders | Military Leaders (ML)[a] | ML as Percentage of Total | Percentage of ML Time in Office |
|---------|---------|--------------------------|---------------------------|---------------------------------|
| Indonesia | 6 | 2 | 33.3 | 54.7 |
| South Korea | 9 | 4 | 44.4 | 55.4 |
| Philippines | 10 | 1 | 10.0 | 10.2 |
| Taiwan | 4 | 2 | 50.0 | 69.8 |
| Thailand | 20 | 12 | 60.0 | 69.5 |
| Total | 49 | 21 | 42.8 | 51.9 |

*Note:* a. Leaders with career military backgrounds.

also need to include Police Colonel Thaksin Shinawatra in this category. These six democratic military figures of the twenty-one military leaders surveyed account for only 14.9 percent of the total time of military leaders in office, however.

*Celebrity politicians.* If "militarification" of politics was a hallmark of the Cold War years, "celebritification" seems to be the trend in the current era. This trend flows from political culture to some extent but also reflects electoral system design. Where an electoral system requires nationwide name recall as the major factor in success, this tends to open the door to national celebrities and slam the door on local "favorite sons." The trend to celebritification of politics, to borrow Sheila Coronel's expression, is most evident in the Philippines (see Table 6.4).[26] Former actor Joseph Estrada won the Philippines presidential elections in 1998 and the late Fernando Poe Jr., another action star, missed out in 2004 but would probably have won had other candidates withdrawn to allow a head-to-head race against the incumbent, Gloria Macapagal-Arroyo. Both the vice presidential candidates in the 2004 race were former TV personalities, and regardless who prevailed, their sponsor, the Lopez family, which owns the ABS-CBN network at which they both worked, came out a winner. The Senate race is also based on a national electorate and thus also requires national name recognition for success. The result is a Senate populated by relatives of former presidents, military figures, celebrities, and those married to celebrities. Looking at the senators of this period, there are very few who would clearly fit into the Linz conception of the sort of politicians a quality democracy needs. Lorenzo Tañada, Aquelino Pimentel, Raul Roco, and Kiko Pangilinan come to mind as politicians with policy agendas. Miriam Santiago seemed at first to fit into this category, but she sold out to President Estrada and was instrumental in causing the Senate's paralysis on his impeachment process.

All in all, fifty-two celebrities from showbiz and sports ran for office in

**Table 6.4   Backgrounds of Philippine Senators, 1998–2007**

| Philippines Senate of 24 | 11th Senate (1998–2001) | 12th Senate (2001–2004) | 13th Senate (2004–2007) |
|---|---|---|---|
| Relatives of former presidents | 4 | 5 | 5[a] |
| Showbiz and sports celebrities | 5 | 6 | 5[a] |
| Married to showbiz celebrities | — | 2 | 2 |
| Military or police careers | 4 | 5 | 5 |

*Source:* Based on Sheila S. Coronel and Yvonne T. Chua, "Fame and Family Dominate Senatorial Race," Philippine Center for Investigative Journalism, 19 April 2004, available from www.pcij.org/stories/2004/senate.html.

*Note:* a. Senator Jinggoy Estrada is both an action star and the son of a former president.

the 2004 Philippine national elections.[27] In India, the situation is so well recognized that one website keeps tabs on the political involvement of celebrities under the heading "Star Wars."[28] It lists twenty-eight stars in politics, including eight candidates. Thailand also has shown an incipient trend toward recruiting showbiz personalities for political office with three recent office holders.[29] The problem with this trend is not the intrinsic incompatibility of the two professions. Ronald Reagan, an actor, is remembered by many in positive terms as both a governor and president. The problem with the trend is the motive for the switch in professions by such a large sample. Both professions trade on popularity, require a photogenic appearance, and follow scripts, but ostensibly the film star is far better paid than the meager salary earned by a politician. Accepting the likelihood that a small number of the celebrities will be born-again vocational politicians, the troubling conclusion is that most celebrity candidates see more profit in politics than in showbiz.

*Reelected politicians.* The degree to which politics can become a vocation will depend to a certain degree on the ability of a politician to hold on to his or her seat. It is difficult to achieve very much in one's first term as there is a steep learning curve to negotiate and the more important parliamentary responsibilities often go with seniority. So the vocational politician needs to have some confidence of being returned. As we have noted, the dynastic politician has a strong chance of remaining in office and, indeed, even when term limits come into effect, a relative can take the baton. Where political parties are strong and the politician remains in good standing, particularly where the election is by way of party list, there is also some confidence of being reelected. But these means of political longevity do not necessarily favor politicians with a vocation to serve in the public interest. In the case of dynasties, it is the clan interests that will prevail, and in party-list systems, it is often the amount of funds one can raise that can be decisive. In Indonesia, this process appears to be formalized in political party rules. Vedi Hadiz relates that PDI-P and Golkar charge candidates around US$45,000 to be placed on the party list for DPR seats.[30] The chances of an independent candidate with modest means winning and holding a seat in Asian elections are slight. The vocational politician being sought may well have to have an additional attribute such as family connections, fame, or money.

Once in office, the chances of reelection vary between countries and between elections. Table 6.5 provides in ascending order the percentage of newly elected MPs in lower house elections between 2003 and 2005 in six Asian democracies. The turnover in Thailand was quite modest, demonstrating the then continuing hold of Prime Minister Thaksin over political opin-

Table 6.5   New Members in Lower House Elections, 2003–2005

| Country | Year | Percentage of New Members |
| --- | --- | --- |
| Thailand | 2005 | 20 |
| Japan | 2005 | 27 |
| Philippines | 2004 | 35 |
| Taiwan | 2003 | 40 |
| South Korea | 2004 | 63 |
| Indonesia | 2004 | 73 |

*Source:* Table devised from IPU statistics, parliamentary websites, and correspondence with various parliamentary secretariats.

ion. In 2005, Japan held an early election called by Prime Minister Koizumi over a question of economic policy, and the higher than usual turnover reflects the greater than usual contestation within the LDP, leading to significant changes in representation. The turnover in the Philippines and Taiwan was quite high, suggesting a certain volatility in the electorate on these occasions, but, as we have seen, some of the Philippine "first-termers" are actually returning "three-termers." The figures for Korea and Indonesia are nothing short of dramatic. The South Korean figure of almost two-thirds of MPs retiring or being voted out of office may reflect a backlash from the electorate over the impeachment issue and the aggressive partisanship behind it. A large portion of the reelected candidates were those who broke from the MDP to form the Uri Party with the promise of changing the nature of politics in South Korea. The even larger figure for new members in Indonesia again points to popular disaffection with politics and politicians. It could even be argued that the 2004 election was the true transition election. Many of the leading parliamentarians emerging from the 1999 elections were members of the legislature during Suharto's time.[31] Voters in 1999 perhaps had insufficient time between the fall of Suharto and the subsequent elections to identify new political figures. If so, they certainly rectified this situation five years later.

### Commitment to Values and Goals Relevant to the Collective

Linz's question concerning commitment is largely related to the first question about vocational politicians, in that the converse of goals relevant to the collective is goals relevant to the individual. This question also arises in the discussion on programmatic political parties, because in modern mass society, the individual must usually work through a political party to achieve goals relevant to the community. In the Asian context, however, an intermediate question arises: What is the collective?

The collective Linz conceived in his discussion on improving the quality of democracy concerned that electorate for which the politician was putting him or herself forward as a candidate. In Anderson's terminology, therefore, the collective is an imagined community of people enclosed in electoral borders and bound together by a political process, but generally not known personally to each other. In the Asian context, this concept of the collective can be problematic. A traditional politician in the Philippines or Thailand will think of the collective as that person's extended family, support base, and political dependents. The politician's primary loyalty will be to this often quite large group, which will amount to the collective in whose service that politician is acting. Pork-barreling, nepotism, and favoring family interests, together with a process of doling out small amounts of money to the members of the support base, will be seen as the core work of the office. And though this method might be of some trickle-down benefit to the local constituency, it is certainly not what Linz had in mind. Linz is looking for politicians with a vision for the imagined collective as a whole, regardless of any connection to the politician beyond shared membership of that imagined community.

*A new crop of leaders?*  While the traditional pork-barrel politician continues to be very well represented in Asian leadership elites, I believe we can now argue that the top leadership of countries in Pacific Asia is far more likely to go to politicians whose primary goal is to advance the collective good. South Korea has shown the way with three outsiders in a row, Kim Young Sam, Kim Dae Jung, and Roh Moo Hyun, winning the presidency and reforming the nation's social and political systems, though running into personal and political problems along the way. Japan's Koizumi broke decades of political practice by coming to power outside the LDP factional process, then changing Japan's political style by appealing directly to the electorate through mass media and e-mailed newsletters, and finally calling an early election to gain the electoral authority to push through with necessary economic reforms. Electoral changes and a more assertive Japanese media make it unlikely that there will be a return to the closed-door money politics of the past.

Thailand's Chuan Leekpai, recognizing the new demands of the urban middle class, attempted to woo this group through programs and policies while continuing to rely on traditional coalition-building through pork-barreling in the Democrats' southern fiefdom. Ramos in the Philippines appeared to put the country back on track through competent and reformist governance, but those gains were squandered in the disaster of the Estrada presidency. Chen has played David to the KMT Goliath and in so doing has given native-born Taiwanese a policy voice they did not previously have. Macapagal-Arroyo has the pedigree of a traditional politician, but with the prospect of almost ten continuous years in office, she has an opportunity to strengthen the Philippines with a policy-based approach. Such vocational politicians are providing new role models for Pacific Asia's political class. They are setting the bar higher, and in so doing, educating the electorate to ask more of their representatives. The current batch of vocational politicians may one day be seen as heralding the tipping point away from the traditional clientalistic Asian politician.

*Mahathir and Thaksin.* It would be pleasing to conclude, therefore, that the era of authoritarian and self-serving politicians in Pacific Asia has passed and that we can now look forward to reformist democrats coming to power, but the reality is that there is a hybrid model testing this proposition. That hybrid was personified in the leadership of Thailand's Thaksin, who took as his model the former prime minister of Malaysia, Mahathir. Neither could be described as committed democrats. Mahathir championed the idea of Asian Values, which conveniently underpinned his authoritarian leadership, and viewed democracy as a "Western" form of government installed by colonial powers.[32] Thaksin was more careful in his comments, but he nevertheless said "democracy is just a tool, not our goal,"[33] thus perhaps indicating a lack of commitment to that tool. Neither was particularly tolerant of critics. Mahathir had more means at his disposal to imprison, expel, or bankrupt his critics. Thaksin had fewer legislative weapons, but had the power of wealth and business influence to punish media critics by starving them of advertising revenue, and the power of incumbency to sic tax auditors on them.[34] Mahathir always had a solid majority in parliament behind him, as the electoral process and Malaysia's induced consociationalism heavily favored the incumbent. Thaksin broke the normal shackles of Thai politics by building massive parliamentary majorities in successive elections and finding ways to largely neutralize the Senate. Mahathir was in power for twenty-two years, and Thaksin wished to emulate this feat.

For all the criticisms one can level at Mahathir and Thaksin, one cannot portray them as merely traditional politicians looking out for their kith and kin. They shared a vision of their societies as confident, successful, and respected members of the international community. They shared a talent for conveying their vision to their electorates. They shared a capacity to tackle difficult issues head-on and to defend their actions in the public conversation. These are important attributes of a leader who holds commitments and values relevant to the collective. In retrospect, perhaps Mahathir's greatest contribution was finding an acceptable balance between secular governance and religious values by shaping a public conversation respectful of Islam but not subservient to it. He submitted to the temptation of racial bias in favoring the Malay community, but he stopped short of submitting to the demands of religious bias, though there were steps in that direction in his later years in office. Mahathir performed one other great service to his nation; he eventually stepped aside voluntarily and, forsaking the Lee Kuan Yew model, he did not seek the role of éminence grise, though he did take a few potshots at his successor. While it does not come easily for me to praise him given his repeated baiting of Australia and his anti-Semitism, I believe Mahathir has constructed the platform on which Malaysia may be able in future to overcome its racial obsessions, maintain a separation of mosque and state, and build a quality liberal democracy.

Thaksin's period in power is harder to judge at this early stage after his political demise. What we can say at this point is that Thaksin changed the informal rules of Thai politics. He stumbled on to a form of populism that delivered handsome electoral returns. He even attempted to copy Berlusconi in marrying football support to political support by making an $80 million bid for Liverpool Football Club.[35] For a time he seemed to have forged a support base north of Bangkok that looked likely to dominate national politics. He bypassed the urban middle class in his appeal to the more populous rural and provincial voter. He left traditional politicians who have built their support bases on clientalism with little option but to deal with him and be seen to join him. He had a significant advantage over predecessors in that he could spend his own money in campaigning and vote buying, confident in the knowledge that incumbency would favor a regulatory environment to replenish his coffers.[36] Perhaps this is the path to political modernity in Thailand. Chuan and the Democrats had a strong base in the south and tried to forge an alliance with the middle class while playing traditional politics with provincial power brokers. Thaksin reached a far broader political collective with his appeal of direct populism supported by his CEO rhetoric and his personal example of generating wealth. While Mahathir picked his own time for retirement, Thaksin was forced from office, not by constitutional means, but by an alliance outraged at his personal domination of the political system. This alliance included the Bangkok opinion leaders, the NGO community, and, critically, the king with the military as willing conscripts in the coup.

The dynamism and energy displayed by Mahathir and Thaksin are the qualities required for their dynamic societies. The Mahathir and Thaksin hybrid model of electoral success, however obtained, supporting governance largely based on their personal authority, may well have some appeal in the region and may also generate aspirant imitators. It is a model that may even look familiar to people in the one-party states. On my departure from Vientiane in 1997, I paid a farewell call on then prime minister Khamtai Siphandon. He was 73 and I made a point of commenting how in Australia, our prime ministers seemed to be leaving office at a relatively young age and then pursuing the rewarding life of business or international statesmanship. He sighed deeply and responded that he would very much like to follow this example, "but there is nobody to take my place." Khamtai took on the presidency of Laos the following year, a post he will no doubt hold well into his octogenarian years, as did his predecessor, Nouhak Phoumsavanh.

## The Amount of Political Corruption

Asian political systems are corrupt, and it follows that those participating in the system are caught up in that corruption. The evidence of corruption is ample. We can see it from the perspective of the voters, from the perspective of the politicians, and from the macroeconomic perspective.

*Money politics.* According to Transparency International's 2004 World Corruption Report,

> in the Philippines, an estimated 3 million people nationwide were offered some form of payment in the 2002 *barangay* (community-level) elections—about 7 per cent of all voting-aged adults. In Thailand, 30 per cent of household heads surveyed in a national sample said that they were offered money during the 1996 general election. In Taiwan's third-largest city, Taichung, and its surrounding county, 27 per cent of a random sample of eligible voters reported in 1999 that they had accepted cash during previous electoral campaigns.[37]

Vote buying is a habit that is going to be particularly hard to break.

The cost of winning an election is becoming prohibitive. Thaksin declared a donation of $6 million of his personal wealth to win the 2001 campaign,[38] though it is likely he spent many times that amount. The cost of a presidential election campaign in the Philippines has been estimated at over $50 million,[39] though the law places a limit of around $10 million on presidential campaign spending.[40] In the early 1990s, a campaign for a Philippine congressional seat cost $160,000, while in Taiwan the cost could go as high as $3 million.[41] In northern Thailand in 1995, a campaign for a parliamentary seat cost around $1 million.[42] Those who are not able to finance their own campaigns seek funds from business backers. It stands to reason that the politicians and their backers are looking for a return on their investment. The deal to sell his Shin company tax free to Singaporean interests would no doubt have recouped all of Thaksin's political investments, had it not been the trigger for the coup.

Even respected politicians like Kim Young Sam and Kim Dae Jung have fallen foul of corruption scandals involving their children. Thaksin and Mahathir may be politicians of vision interested in the welfare of the collective, but that does not preclude them from also being interested in their own financial welfare and that of their families. Thaksin understands well the importance of government support, as he made his fortune through a government concession to introduce mobile telephony to Thailand.[43] Thaksin's family company continued to launch new ventures during his incumbency with "significant help from state bodies [and] government favors [that] also benefited several other Thai Rak Thai–connected firms and business families."[44] Mahathir's family is not in the nepotism league of the avaricious Suharto clan, but when his son Mirzan got into financial difficulty after the 1998 crisis, it was the pension fund partly owned by the government and the government oil company under the supervision of the Prime Minister's Department that bailed him out.[45]

Money politics can be traced at the level of macroeconomics. Prior to the enforcement of effective campaign finance laws, South Korean elections were staggeringly expensive. One estimate for total campaign spending in 1992, when presidential, parliamentary, and local elections were held, put the total figure at $3 billion or about 16 percent of South Korea's total annual government budget at that time.[46] The Thai Farmers Bank estimated that the political parties spent 20 billion baht (about US$800 million) in the 1996 elections, an enormous sum when one considers GDP per capita at the time was around $3,000.[47]

*Social tax obligation.* Money politics can thus be seen at the national level in macro terms, but it is also reflected at the level of the individual elected representative. In one reported case in Thailand, the "social tax" of payments, gifts, and contributions required of a lower house member equaled the parliamentary salary, and in another it was claimed to be two and a half times that salary.[48] When I discuss the social tax obligations of a constituency politician with Philippine or Thai parliamentarians, they say similar things: this is part of their political culture and they have no choice but to live by the informal rules. They minimize the ethical issues and seem to have developed their own sense of acceptable conduct based on these informal rules of the game. The rules require many small outgoings and these have to be covered by major incomings. Accordingly, accepting money from business interests in return for policy outcomes sought by those businesses is generally acceptable, but accepting money from gangsters to protect gambling or prostitution interests is generally unacceptable. Using one's public position to direct public money to support development in one's home district is certainly acceptable even when this is clearly seen to bring direct benefits to the politician or his relatives. Helping family members gain government positions is no more than what is expected of a politician. Accumulating wealth while in office is acceptable as long as one distributes some of this back to the politician's supporters. They understand that they may be breaking some laws in this conduct but they don't believe they are corrupt, as the informal understanding in the system is not to enforce the laws strictly.

Could one argue that these social tax obligations are part of the early years of the post-transition democracies and are not necessarily an enduring aspect of consolidated Asian democracy? This would be a comforting conclusion, and there may be some basis for it in the general observation that vote buying and social tax practices are more common in rural areas and tend to weaken in the urban political culture where the more sophisticated middle-class voters stop expecting direct payments from their politicians. But a brief glance at Japan casts doubt on this possible impact of modernization. The social tax practice in Japan remains strong even though the country is wealthy. In a 1987 study, a group of younger LDP Diet members calculated that the costs of wedding gifts, condolence contributions, plus New Year and mid-year gifts for supporters' families surpassed their parliamentary salaries.[49]

It stands to reason that the social tax funds have to be generated regularly from sources other than parliamentary salaries and private income. Much of it comes from official sources disguised as allowances and local development funds. In the Philippines, the allowances and reimbursements to members of Congress increased the salary payments tenfold.[50] But there are many other informal devices to milk money out of the system, including sums obtained for supporting the initiatives of certain leading politicians, and even being paid to attend parliamentary sittings to make up the necessary quorum when a bill of importance to the funder is being debated—estimated in the Philippines at around $1,000 per sitting.[51] Income generation through accepting money to allow passage of legislation is practiced even in Japan's consolidated democracy.[52] The pattern of formal and informal means of generating the funds to meet social tax obligations is mirrored throughout most multiparty Asian parliaments. Because it is not subject to any process of auditing other than victory at the next elections, it is difficult to know how much personal gain results from the system. The conclusion that a considerable percentage of these funds remain at the personal disposal of the lawmaker is inescapable, and the social tax obligation is both a convenient cover and rationalization for what must be recognized as a corrupt practice. This is not a subject readily discussed by the politicians, but perhaps there is an informal code operating in this field establishing a formula for the division of spoils. Those politicians meeting the distribution objective probably consider themselves to be honest.

All this poses something of a dilemma in assessing Linz's criterion concerning corruption. The amount of corruption is vast, but within the informal ethical code among the politicians, there is a different fault line delineating political conduct from corrupt conduct, and most politicians probably believe they have not crossed that line. That belief is, of course, self-serving, but until political culture catches up with the law, politicians will continue to delude themselves about their behavior.

*The Use or Tolerance of Illegal Violence*

In Chapter 3, I discussed violence in politics as one of the twin factors diminishing the prospects for systematization. The other factor is corruption. The discussion of violence and corruption in relation to systematization focused at the macro level on their negative impact on society. But they also have an impact in other related ways, including on the character and behavior of politicians. Linz includes both aspects in his methodology of assessment of politicians. In relation to violence, the criterion can be divided into two categories. The first concerns the use of violence against political opponents, usually in the course of election campaigns. The second is the recourse to violence when in office to achieve policy outcomes. In the second case, there may well be public sympathy with this conduct.

"Guns, goons, and gold" has long been the means to fight elections in the Philippines. Hundreds die in the course of each election campaign; usually the victims are goons at the hands of other goons, but occasionally a popular candidate may be assassinated at the hands of one of his worried opponents. The trend in Philippine politics has been toward diminishing levels of violence. John Linantud plots the trend through body counts: in the 1971 polls, the last before the imposition of martial law, over 900 died in the lead-up to the elections, while in 2004 the count was down to 117, including 29 candidates vying for the 17,500 positions at stake.[53] In the three most recent elections, 1998, 2001, and 2004, the total number of casualties was 962,[54] demonstrating that the problem remains serious but also showing a decreasing trend line. Election violence is a fact of life in Cambodia, may yet become a problem in Indonesia, while it is not unknown in Thailand. It is far less of a problem in Japan, South Korea, and Taiwan. It may be the case that this form of violence is tied to political culture and diminishes as the democratic system matures and the economy grows.

What Linz had primarily in mind is probably more about the second category of violence, given his rider concerning "a majority of citizens are ready to condone it." Extrajudicial executions of critics and opponents was a feature of the Marcos dictatorship in the Philippines, and habits die hard as the State Department reported in 2004:

> Some elements of the security services were responsible for arbitrary, unlawful, and, in some cases, extrajudicial killings; disappearances; torture; and arbitrary arrest and detention . . . police and local government leaders at times appeared to sanction extrajudicial killings and vigilantism as expedient means of fighting crime and terrorism.[55]

In Indonesia, Suharto admitted to instituting a campaign of informal executions of some five thousand criminals in the 1980s.[56] It is particularly disturbing that such practices should continue in Thailand where the National

Human Rights Commission found that the government's campaign against drug pushers had led to thousands of deaths.[57] Human Rights Watch put the number of deaths in Thailand between February and June 2003 at 2,275.[58] The pattern of sectarian violence in Gujarat, India, in 2002, and the subsequent impunity from which its perpetrators have benefited, have led commentators to accuse the state government of complicity.[59]

This is clearly a blight on the development of democracy in these countries. The state has a monopoly on the legitimate use of violence, and in exercising this monopoly, the state must act within the bounds of national, and I would assert, international law. A political system not bounded by the rule of law in its treatment of its citizens, even if its actions are seen positively by a majority of citizens, cannot be accepted as a liberal and consolidated democracy, regardless of the electoral success its governments may achieve. One of the critical tests of future Asian politicians is that they not succumb to the temptation of adopting violence as a short-cut intended to resolve deep problems, even when that action has the tacit support of a large section of the electorate.

### The Willingness to Use Extremist Elements Against Other Democratic Forces

The manifestation of this problem often occurs where the regime or its leader foresees a threat to its power. We have seen the ruthless use of force in Rangoon and Tiananmen Square when regime maintenance was seen to be at risk. Democrats by contrast are required to accept their constitutional removal from office and not attempt to use violence or threats thereof to remain in power. So it is disconcerting to note that in two recent cases, leaders about to lose their positions looked to the armed forces to maintain them in power.

In January 2001, with the Philippine Senate failing in its task of properly investigating President Estrada's corruption, demonstrators filled the streets and Estrada was isolated in Malacañang Presidential Palace. There is an intimate account of what transpired from Executive Secretary Edgardo Angara's diary, which was published in the *Philippine Daily Inquirer*.[60] On 19 January, Estrada looked at his options and spoke to Armed Forces Chief Angelo Reyes before confiding to Angara that Reyes's support could not be counted on. On 20 January, Reyes and Defense Secretary Orlando Mercado addressed the crowd at Epifanio de los Santos Avenue (EDSA), announcing that they had withdrawn their support from Estrada. On 21 January, Estrada left Malacañang and Chief Justice Hilarion Davide swore in Vice President Gloria Macapagal-Arroyo as the new president. The Supreme Court subsequently held that Estrada had in effect resigned and drew on the Angara diary as evidence of Estrada's state of mind at the time.[61] It seems clear that had the military been at his disposal, Estrada would have used it to defeat his opponents, regardless of the views of the chief justice or the crowds in the street.

Gus Dur was elected to the Indonesian presidency after the 1999 elections through a process of haggling within the People's Consultative Assembly, even though his political party, the PKB, only held a handful of seats in the DPR. Gus Dur had a talent for open and inclusive rhetoric that augured well for Indonesian society, but this talent was matched by a propensity to frustrate his partners and confuse his friends. By April 2001, with the DPR threatening to impeach him and his support base extending not much farther than elements of Nahdatul Ulama, the Islamic organization he once led, Gus Dur developed a plan to declare a national emergency and suspend parliament.[62] The army's refusal to follow this plan was Gus Dur's political death knell.

Thailand's military, long accustomed to intervention in Thai politics, had not staged a coup since February 1991 when General Suchinda's group ousted Prime Minister Chatichai, himself a former general, and then violently suppressed the resulting demonstrations in May 1992. The military resisted being drawn into politics at the next critical juncture when the government of another former general, that of Prime Minister Chavalit, whose dismissal as the then defense minister had sparked the 1991 coup, was losing popularity following the 1997 financial crisis. Chavalit asked the military to step in but it refused, and his government fell.[63] The 2006 coup reopens the debate about the Thai military's intervention in politics. Having learned a bitter lesson in 1991 and having acted correctly in 1997, there was a widely held view that the days of Thai coups were over.[64] How readily the military lets go the reins of power following the latest coup will be an important test of its motives.

South Korea's military has long been used to playing a major role in politics. Coups have been more influential than elections in changing the nation's leadership over the Cold War years, but the political changes in 1987 were supposed to put an end to this practice. In 1992, however, with dissident Kim Dae Jung running for the presidency, army generals openly warned that they would stage a coup rather than allow him to win office.[65] As it turned out, Kim Young Sam's victory precluded the generals from making good on their threat. Five years later, when Kim Dae Jung won the elections, the generals quietly went along with the constitutional and electoral processes.

No doubt we will again witness desperate politicians, seeing the end of their tenure approaching and perhaps fearing that corruption prosecutions are imminent, consider resorting to extraconstitutional means of holding on to power. The recent history of Indonesia, South Korea, the Philippines, and Thailand suggests that this is now less likely to occur than in previous periods. Yet the phenomenon of military intervention in politics in Pacific Asia has not as yet been permanently consigned to the history books, and this issue will require continuing vigilance.


## Conclusion

There are no black-and-white answers to the questions posed in assessing politicians in Pacific Asia. The problems of both engineering the political system and reshaping political culture to put in office the sort of vocational politicians that democracy requires if it is to thrive are deep in Pacific Asia. Up to the present democratization period of Pacific Asia's modern history, it was possible to generalize that the less democratic a country, the smaller the decisionmaking audience that needs to be won over, bought, or cowed by that country's politicians. But even as the authoritarian period passes and politicians need to appeal to wider audiences, problems persist. Money politics, narrow loyalties, recourse to violence, and lack of policy objectives are all still prominent problems in the systems in place. The best that can be confidently stated is that the problems are recognized, that a recrafting and reengineering process is taking place, and that some positive results are beginning to emerge. I believe Pacific Asia's politicians are changing and are beginning to reinvent themselves in various ways. They are reflecting the demands of increasingly sophisticated electorates and responding to the requirement for leaders who can decide between increasingly complex policy options. They have both admirable and problematic role models to follow, and accordingly, there can be well-founded hope, but no certainty, that this trend will culminate in most future mainstream politicians behaving in the Linz vocational mold.

One of the factors being sought throughout this book has been the impact of developments and practices in one nation in Pacific Asia on another, to determine whether there is an imagined Pacific Asian democratic and policy community that has some coherence and is thus able to be described and analyzed in a useful way. A policy community is composed of the people who participate in it, and a major category of those people is its leaders, its politicians. Do they imagine this community to exist, and do they feel some responsibility for their neighbors? I believe a shared commitment to democracy is forging this embryonic community. We are beginning to discern a certain empathy developing among the vocational politicians of the region for their like-minded colleagues in other Pacific Asian democracies. There is a closeness that can be achieved between such elected leaders that cannot be shared by their communist, authoritarian, or militarist counterparts. The very precariousness of the métier of the elected politician creates a bond that excludes the politburo or junta member. When democratically elected politicians get together with their glasses of scotch and soda or their sand wedges, it is more often than not to comparisons of opinion polls, policy options, and election prognostication that their conversations will turn. The vocational politician will be more at ease with a similar politician than with an unelected counterpart or with a *trapo* (traditional politician) or *jao pho* (local godfather) politician. There are no opinion polls that attempt to demonstrate this trend, but the obvious embarrassment of those democratically elected leaders of ASEAN to be in the company of the Burmese generals is an important indication of this regional trend. It was only under pressure from ASEAN leaders that the Burmese generals reluctantly agreed to forgo Myanmar's turn at hosting ASEAN meetings in 2006. Perhaps the age of the vocational politician is dawning in Pacific Asia.

## Notes

1. Kenneth P. Ruscio, *The Leadership Dilemma in Modern Democracies* (Northampton, MA: Edward Elgar Publishing, 2004), p. ix.
2. Jürgen Rüland et al., *Parliaments and Political Change in Asia* (Singapore: Institute of Southeast Asian Studies, 2005), p. 196.
3. Ibid., chapter 7, looking at India, Indonesia, South Korea, the Philippines, and Thailand.
4. Juan J. Linz, "Some Thoughts on the Victory and Future of Democracy," Axel Hadenius (ed.), *Democracy's Victory and Crisis, Nobel Symposium No. 93* (Cambridge: Cambridge University Press, 1997), p. 421.
5. Larry Diamond, *Developing Democracy: Toward Consolidation* (Baltimore: Johns Hopkins University Press, 1999), p. 163.
6. William Case, *Politics in Southeast Asia—Democracy or Less* (Richmond, UK: Curzon Press, 2002).
7. Sheila S. Coronel, "Houses of Privilege," Sheila S. Coronel et al., *The Rulemakers—How the Wealthy and Well-Born Dominate Congress* (Manila: Philippine Center for Investigative Journalism, 2004), p. 15.
8. Adam Schwarz, *A Nation in Waiting: Indonesia in the 1990s* (Boulder: Westview Press, 1994), p. 272.
9. Ibid.
10. Ibid., p. 274.
11. Section 107(3) in relation to the House of Representatives, Section 125(3) in relation to the Senate.
12. Pasuk Phongpaichit and Chris Baker, "'Business Populism' in Thailand," *Journal of Democracy* 16, no. 2 (April 2005): 61.
13. Rüland et al., *Parliaments and Political Change*, p. 174.
14. Section 126(1).
15. Michael H. Nelson, "Thai Politics Monitor," Michael H. Nelson (ed.), *Thailand's New Politics—KPI Yearbook 2001* (Bangkok: King Prajadhipok's Institute and White Lotus), p. 390.
16. Section 126(3).
17. Article IV, Section 3(2).
18. J. A. A. Stockwin, "Reforming Japanese Politics: Highway to Change or Road to Nowhere?" Takashi Inoguchi and Purnendra C. Jain (eds.), *Japanese Politics Today: Beyond Karaoke Democracy?* (Melbourne: MacMillan, 1997), p. 84.
19. Soohyun Chon, "The Election Process and Informal Politics in South

Korea," Lowell Dittmer, Haruhiro Fukui, and Peter N. S. Lee (eds.), *Informal Politics in East Asia* (Cambridge: Cambridge University Press, 2000), p. 78.

20. Article II, Section 26.
21. Sheila S. Coronel, "Born to Rule," Coronel et al., *The Rulemakers*, p. 47.
22. Rüland et al., *Parliaments and Political Change*, p. 186.
23. Haruhiro Fukui and Shigeko N. Fukai, "The Informal Politics of Japanese Diet Elections: Cases and Interpretations," Dittmer, Fukui, and Lee, *Informal Politics in East Asia*, p. 34.
24. Eric Johnson, "Family-Bred Politicians Fan Out," *The Japan Times*, 10 September 2005.
25. Azza Karam (ed.), *Women in Parliament: Beyond the Numbers* (Stockholm: International Institute for Democracy and Electoral Assistance, 1998), pp. 74–82.
26. Sheila S. Coronel and Yvonne T. Chua, "Fame and Family Dominate Senatorial Race," Philippine Center for Investigative Journalism, 19 April 2004, available from www.pcij.org/stories/2004/senate.html.
27. Research provided by Armando Doronila.
28. Indian Elections, "Star Wars," www.indian-elections.com/star-wars.html.
29. Former TV personality Janista Liewchalermwong of Chart Thai Party, Bangkok constituency MP; Yuranan Phamornmontree, former movie/TV star, TRTP Bangkok constituency MP; Ekkapoj Panyaem, popular singer, TRTP Pathum Thani constituency MP.
30. Vedi R. Hadiz, "Indonesian Local Party Politics: A Site of Resistance to Neo-Liberal Reform," City University of Hong Kong Working Paper Series No. 61, March 2004, p. 11.
31. Stephen Sherlock, "Struggling to Change: The Indonesian Parliament in an Era of Reformasi," Centre for Democratic Institutions, Australian National University, p. 4, available from www.cdi.anu.edu.au/CDIwebsite_1998-2004/indonesia/indonesia_downloads/DPRResearchReport_S.Sherlock.pdf.
32. Khoo Boo Teik, "Nationalism, Capitalism, and 'Asian Values,'" Francis Loh Kok Wah and Khoo Boo Teik (eds.), *Democracy in Malaysia: Discourses and Practices* (Richmond, Surrey: Curzon Press, 2002), p. 56.
33. Quoted in Phongpaichit and Baker, "'Business Populism' in Thailand," p. 58.
34. Ibid., p. 66.
35. Shawn W. Crispin, "Moving the Goalposts," *Far Eastern Economic Review*, 10 June 2004.
36. Khunying Pojamarn Shinawatra, Thaksin's wife, donated 300 million baht to his Thai Rak Thai Party for the 2001 campaign. Bowornsak Uwanno, "Political Finance in Thailand," unpublished paper presented at a conference on political finance in Seoul, South Korea, 28–30 June 2001, p. 16.
37. Transparency International, *Global Corruption Report 2004*, p. 83, available from www.globalcorruptionreport.org/gcr2004.html.
38. Nelson, "Thai Politics Monitor," p. 411.
39. Francis Fukuyama, Björn Dressel, and Boo-Seung Chang, "Facing the Perils of Presidentialism?" *Journal of Democracy* 16, no. 2 (April 2005): 105.
40. Joel Rocamora, "Campaign Finance and the Future of Philippine Political Parties," unpublished paper presented at a conference on political finance in Seoul, South Korea, 28–30 June 2001.
41. Transparency International, *Global Corruption Report 2004*, p. 84.
42. Marco Bünte, "Consolidating Thai Democracy," Nelson (ed.), *Thailand's New Politics—KPI Yearbook 2001*, p. 194.

43. Duncan McCargo, "Democracy Under Stress in Thaksin's Thailand," *Journal of Democracy* 13, no. 4 (October 2002): 115.

44. Phongpaichit and Baker, "'Business Populism' in Thailand," p. 69.

45. "Nepotism Claims Lead PM's Son to Sell Interests," *South China Morning Post*, 28 April 2001, available from www.freeanwar.net/news012001/scmp280401.htm.

46. Soohyun Chon, "The Election Process," p. 69.

47. Anusorn Limmanee, "Thailand," Wolfgang Sachsenröder and Ulrike Frings (eds.), *Political Party Systems and Democratic Development in East and Southeast Asia—Volume I: Southeast Asia* (Aldershot, UK: Ashgate Publishing, 1998), p. 438.

48. Uwanno, "Political Finance in Thailand."

49. Peter Ferdinand, "Party Funding and Political Corruption in East Asia: The Cases of Japan, South Korea, and Taiwan," Reginald Austin and Maja Tjernström (eds.), *Funding of Political Parties and Election Campaigns* (Stockholm: International Institute for Democracy and Electoral Assistance, 2003), pp. 55–56.

50. Sheila Coronel, "The Perks of Lawmaking," Coronel et al., *The Rulemakers*, p. 142.

51. Ibid., p. 168.

52. Ferdinand, "Party Funding and Political Corruption," p. 64.

53. John L. Linantud, "The 2004 Philippine Elections," *Contemporary Southeast Asia—A Journal of International and Strategic Affairs* 27, no. 1 (April 2005): 83.

54. Ibid., p. 84.

55. US Department of State, *Philippines—Country Reports on Human Rights Practices 2004*, available from www.state.gov/g/drl/rls/hrrpt/2004/41657.htm.

56. Adam Schwarz, *A Nation in Waiting*, p. 249.

57. National Human Rights Commission of Thailand, "The Government's War on Drugs in Right(s) Perspective," *Right Angle* 2, no. 2 (April–June 2003): 1–3, available from www.nhrc.or.th/en/publications/Eng%20Right%20Angle%20V2N2.pdf.

58. Human Rights Watch, "Thailand: Anti-Drug Campaign Reaches New Low," *Human Rights News*, 6 October 2004, available from http://hrw.org/english/docs/2004/10/05/thaila9445.htm.

59. Rakesh Kalshian, "India: Scam Plagued," *The Corruption Notebooks* (Washington, DC: The Center for Public Integrity, Public Integrity Books, 2004), p. 91.

60. *Philippine Daily Inquirer*, 4–6 February 2001.

61. *Estrada v Desierto et al.*, 3 April 2001, available from www.supremecourt.gov.ph/jurisprudence/2001/apr2001/146710_15_r.htm.

62. Fukuyama, Dresell, and Chang, "Facing the Perils of Presidentialism?" p. 107.

63. Neil A Englehart, "Democracy and the Thai Middle Class—Globalization, Modernization, and Constitutional Change," *Asia Survey* 43, no. 2 (2003): 274.

64. Former prime minister Anand Panyarachun argued thus when answering a question during his CDI Annual Address at Parliament House, Canberra, 24 November 1999.

65. Doh C. Shin, *Mass Politics and Culture in Democratizing Korea* (Cambridge: Cambridge University Press 1999), p. 11.

# 7

# Conducting the Public Conversation

"The public voice is made up of many competing voices: a never-ending, turbulent, competitive, euphonious cacophony of debating perspectives contributing to some semblance of a marketplace of ideas."
—Michael Salvador, "Practicing Democracy"[1]

The preceding chapters have focused on the formal institutions of democracy: constitutions, parliaments, courts, elections, and so forth. These institutions make up the structure of the society, its backbone and skeleton. To continue the anatomical analogy, the skeleton structures the democratic body politic to hold in place the flesh and blood of society. The flesh and blood is analogous to the people who form society's political culture. And to pursue the analogy for one last step, the skeleton is a simpler structure to understand and interpret than the other parts of the body. Institutions are more accessible for assessment because they are ostensibly required to follow formal rules that can be studied for their impact and effectiveness. In the study of institutions, the question of political actors' behavior and social groups' attitudes remain relevant in so far as they impact on these structures. But when the study turns to the more general behavior and attitudes of elites and electorates in relation to the public sphere, we drift away from the refuge of institutional compliance with formal rules and enter a vast space where rules may define its boundaries but do not much assist in understanding its substance.

Yet even within the cacophony of the public space, there are institutions that play critically important roles. They are not government institutions even though some of their costs may be borne directly or indirectly by tax dollars. They can be divided in various ways. One dichotomy is between for-profit and not-for-profit institutions, though there might nevertheless be a link, as between Microsoft and the Bill and Melinda Gates Foundation.

Another distinction might be made between political and nonpolitical bodies within a nation's social capital. The distinction between Amnesty International and the Des Moines Choral Society demonstrates this political divide, though the boundary can at times become quite murky. The next chapter will examine the social capital aspects of political culture.

This chapter will look at the conversation taking place in the public sphere. The public conversation is the oxygen of democracy. Its character and complexity will shape the outcomes achieved by democratic polities. When Amartya Sen discusses his three virtues of democracy, they each involve an appreciation of the public conversation.[2] Participation in the political life of a nation is seen as having intrinsic value as part of human freedom in general. Expressing and supporting claims to political outcomes has an instrumental value in society by, amongst other benefits, drawing attention to economic and social needs. The public discussion and exchange of information, views, and analyses has a constructive value by allowing citizens to learn from each other. Each of these values flows from the public conversation, and it follows that each of these values will be enhanced the higher its quality is. The question being asked in this chapter concerns the quality of the public conversations taking place in Pacific Asia's democracies. Has it reached the level of deliberation that is a hallmark of consolidated high-quality democracies? And how should we assess the quality of the mass media, the instrument through which that conversation is shaped and disseminated?

## Attending Village Meetings

The public space can be on the floor of parliament or in the village square. Unlike parliament, the villagers represent themselves and their families and thus offer a more direct and accessible example of the public conversation. One way to enter this public space is with some reminiscences of village debates. I have sat in village houses, public squares, and the precincts of places of worship in Burma, Indonesia, Laos, Thailand, and the Philippines, listening to and observing village meetings. Of course, I was a guest at these meetings and the proceedings were often being translated for my benefit, but I don't believe these factors detract from the authenticity of the processes I observed. If I were to summarize these village meetings in three words, they would be *hierarchy, ceremony,* and *politics.*

The most readily observable fact is that of hierarchy. The village meeting is not a spontaneous event flowing anarchically to an unknown conclusion. It is called for a specific purpose by someone in authority to achieve an accepted end. One is welcomed by the village chief who is flanked by the village notables and supported by cooks, ushers, and other helpers. The villagers take up their positions in appropriate status order. The children snuggle up in a lap, or perch on a branch or simply squat around on the margins. Hierarchy is also the key to unlocking ceremony. The chief begins the welcoming ceremony and others blend in as per the dictates of custom, making speeches or pouring fiery spirits or serving spicy food. The visitor must follow protocol, responding to the welcoming words with expressions of delight at being amongst these fine villagers; gulping down their fiery spirits, even though the sun may still be high; and relishing their delicious food, even though breakfast is an all too recent memory. But before long, politics intrudes.

The villagers have a stake in the meeting. One way or another they are financing it by contributing to the food or simply taking time away from their productive activities. They may also be affected by its outcome, either through the decisions reached or the status achieved. When the meetings are to decide something tangible like contributions to the building of a new primary school, the positioning of a run-of-river electricity generator, or the resolution of a dispute concerning distribution of the proceeds of aid funds, villagers' direct interests are at play and soon hierarchy and ceremony give way to politics and personality. Views will be expressed, oratory wielded, and humor deployed in support of one's interests. The cranky fellow with an axe to grind will point fingers and open old wounds. The aspiring village leader will use a toast to introduce arguments surreptitiously. The women who began the event busying themselves with plates of food will now speak their minds. In other words, the village will conduct a conversation in public about a matter of importance to it. The conversation will be punctuated by laughter, expressions of approval, or grunts of disapproval. The conversation will be moderated by the chief in accordance with established custom, and this will inevitably include a closing speech, which may even attempt to bring the discussion to a conclusion, though this might take place after the esteemed visitor has been dispatched on an obligatory tour of the village's unique features and original handicraft accomplishments.

This public conversation is a necessary part of democracy. The simpler the polity, the less elaborate the means required to conduct the conversation. The needs of the village are relatively modest in these terms. The level of involvement of individual members of the village will be quite high and direct. The result of the conversation may be a clear-cut decision assented to through ceremonial means, or by the silence of any dissenters. Rarely will anything be written down. Village culture is oral culture and this can lead to a new set of confusions. The result may be pretty murky and require subsequent arm twisting or buying off of dissenters in private deals. The village processes will be unique to its ethnopolitical circumstance. In the Philippines, the village priest may play a role. In Burma, the government-appointed representative will need to be given due deference. In Thailand, those well connected to the local political heavyweight may have a disproportionate influence. In Laos, the formality of Communist Party office hold-ers will be followed. These distinctions will influence the style and may have a decisive influence on the substance of the meeting, but they will at least be discernible and, importantly, readable to the participants, though at times confusing to an outsider.

This method of conducting a public conversation makes sense in a small group. After all, a village may have only a few hundred inhabitants. Where we have a large group making decisions on far more complex issues, the village conversation will not achieve the desired result. How does a polity of one billion inhabitants conduct a public conversation?

## Deliberation, Decisionmaking, and Democracy

At this point we need to leave the village and skip through the academic literature to grapple with a problem that has confronted democracy theo-rists since ancient times. One of my purposes in this book is to subject the concept of democracy to persistent unpacking and then to examine the var-ious parts against Pacific Asian practice. Democracy may mean power to the people but this is an insufficient goal in itself. The purpose of democra-cy is to achieve the best possible, or perhaps least worst, form of gover-nance for the people in question. Good governance should entail high-qual-ity decisions that are directly or indirectly taken by the people. So the question the theorists face is how to achieve these high-quality decisions in governance.

### Deliberation

The word *deliberative* has been in vogue for the last quarter of a century to describe the sort of democracy that delivers quality decisions.[3] James Fishkin includes deliberation as one of the three necessary democratic con-ditions alongside political equality and nontyranny.[4] He describes Alexander Hamilton's concern in *Federalist No. 71* that the public in a modern democracy should have an "opportunity for more cool and sedate reflections" as opposed to a "transient impulse" or a mere "inclination" as "an essential part of any adequate theory of democracy."[5] For John Dryzek, deliberation goes to the heart of the authenticity of democracy, which requires "reflective preferences (to) influence collective outcomes."[6]

Having accepted the centrality of deliberation in a democracy does not, however, in itself solve the problem of achieving quality decisions. Large questions remain about the sort of issues requiring deliberation, how the deliberative process is undertaken, and how long does one need to set aside for the process to be complete. Compromises are required between the ideal and the practical. Designs are required to build a form of deliberation into the process of public decisionmaking. Scholars have grappled with the question of whether deliberation should be seen as limited to the formal institutions of democracy, and in particular, the right to vote, or whether it should be seen as part of a far broader phenomenon of public discourse. The inclusiveness of the discourse is another conundrum that has worried academics. How can everybody be included that wishes to participate? How can the system ensure that underprivileged groups have been heard? Can persistent objectors maintain some sort of veto on decision-taking? The answers to these difficult questions must be found in a mix of institutional designs and social practice. Different polities need to find varying combinations of design and practice to satisfy the democratic need for deliberation that will work best in their particular circumstances. And indeed this search for the best fit is an ongoing project, as "a democratic society is in important respects one that is continually striving to make democracy better."[7]

### The "Marketplace of Ideas"

For me, the concept that best encapsulates these notions is the "marketplace of ideas." Oliver Wendell Holmes, drawing on the traditions of Milton, Locke, and the US founding fathers, wrote this evocative and enduring metaphor in his judgment in *Abrams v. United States* (1919). Justice Holmes was elaborating the concept of freedom of speech and the necessity for ideas to compete against each other for the truth to emerge. The metaphor has since found a place in the democracy literature.[8] Free speech may be an end in itself but it is also a building block of democracy. The marketplace metaphor is useful because it suggests a result, a deal. The marketplace is there to facilitate a deal, and in a democracy, that deal is a public decision. The marketplace metaphor is also useful because the marketplace needs structure based on such features as regulation, order, and common knowledge. I like using the term for another reason. Asians love nothing better than a marketplace. The whole continent seems to thrive on the multiplier effects of markets.

The other half of the metaphor concerns ideas—formulated thoughts and opinions. I prefer this construct to the narrower concept of interests. The voter-citizen-consumer-deliberator will often, indeed perhaps mainly, reflect personal material interests in his or her involvement in the public discourse, but there will surely be times when the motivating factor is the power of an idea. Erik Åsard and Lance Bennett, who adopted the metaphor in their book title, quote John Maynard Keynes as follows: "The ideas of economists and political philosophers, both when they are right and when they are wrong, are more powerful than is commonly understood. . . . I am sure that the power of vested interests is vastly exaggerated compared with the gradual encroachment of ideas."[9] Asians are undoubtedly mercantilist, yet a powerful idea like democracy will bring them out into the streets, often risking their most basic interest, their lives.

Part of the power of the Holmes metaphor is how readily it can be conjured up. I can picture crowds in Rizal Park in Manila, or the Sanam Luang in Bangkok, or even Speakers' Corner in Hong Lim Park in Singapore (though here, no doubt, under the watchful eyes of the police) exchanging and debating ideas. Envisioning the resultant "deal" becomes a bit more difficult but is still within the realms of the imagination. But once we scale up to a polity of a million people or one hundred million people or one billion people, we lose the ability to visualize the metaphor, and we are left with the challenge of conceptualizing it.

The problem of scaling up to modern size has been a challenge to democratic theorists as well. Dahl begins his discussion of the question by recalling Aristotle's famous admonition that if citizens are to make wise choices, then they must be few enough in number so that they can know one another's characters.[10] He goes on to point out that in the century from Montesquieu to John Stuart Mill, the entire conception of democracy shifted from the scale of city-state to that of nation-state.[11] I would add that in the modern world we also need to think about democracy in Asia's continent-sized states because, as Dahl reminds us, changes in quantity bring with them challenges to quality.[12] Pressure builds on the institution designers to find means of maintaining as high a quality of democratic decision-making as possible. The marketplace of ideas risks being so big that nobody can make him or herself heard. This is especially true in Asia, where we have three polities of continental dimensions in China, India, and Indonesia, and adding Bangladesh, Japan, and Pakistan, six huge polities with populations of over one hundred million.

Remarkably, we have found a means of allowing a billion people to hold a public conversation. It is through the mass media. And it is to the discussion of how this is accomplished and to a review of the problematic state of the mass media in Asia in shaping and disseminating the public conversation required in a quality democracy, that I now turn.

## Mass Media and Democracy

### Identifying the Ideal

How should we envisage the mass media in a democracy? The ideal situation may be postulated as follows. Ownership of the media is in diverse hands. Some might be owned by large entertainment corporations; others by venerable, civic-minded, and wealthy people like the late Katharine Graham, who steered the *Washington Post* through the excitement and agonies of Watergate; others by numerous shareholders where the journalists then elect their editor, as is the case of *Le Monde*[13] in Paris and *Han-kyoreh Shinmun*[14] in Seoul; and others still by the public and allowed to broadcast and editorialize without interference from the government of the day. Continuing our ideal, newspapers and electronic media cover stories fairly and allow all significant voices to be heard. Journalists are professional and competent with a strong fourth-estate ethic. The market rewards and penalizes the media outlets by reference to their quality, competence, and innovativeness. And finally, the literate and engaged public subscribes to and participates in the process. Of course, nowhere in Asia or elsewhere does this ideal exist. In every society, each of the ideals of diversity, fairness, profitability, and engagement is compromised to a lesser or greater degree. As in all institutions of society, we have to accept something falling well short of the ideal, criticize it, and work to improve it.

The printed and the electronic forms of public communications are the media through which large societies conduct their public conversations. These conduits allow the flow to go in both directions, information is disseminated and feedback is gained. As a mere conduit, the mass media cannot be expected to resolve problems of achieving deliberative democracy, but it can be expected to contribute to that aim. Yet the media is far more than a conduit, a simple mechanistic device. It is a speaker in its own right in the public conversation and must be viewed, as are other political players, in terms of interests, motives, and biases. So when we examine the various roles of the media in a democracy, we need to temper our conclusions with the realization that the discharge of these roles will be affected by the character of the media practitioners and their organizations.

### The Role of the Media in Political Transitions
In relation to the process of democratic transition and consolidation, McCargo assigns three possible roles to the media.[15] The media can be seen as an agent of stability by helping to shore up the established order, an agent of restraint through monitoring and investigative journalism, and an agent of change by helping to shape political developments in times of crisis. These roles are not mutually exclusive nor are their boundaries always distinct. The various media in a nation may act in all three agency roles simultaneously, and indeed, this may even occur within the pages of a single edition of a newspaper. I am less convinced by McCargo's description of the agencies for stability, restraint, and change as analogous, respectively, to the political concepts of conservative, progressive, and transformative,[16] as this gives the impression of the media as necessarily and deeply politically aligned, when the reality is that the chaotic, instinctive, and haphazard may be as influential as political alignment in determining the role it plays.

Asia is teeming with examples of these three different roles of the media in the spectrum of politics, and the first conclusion we can comfortably reach is that there is an important relationship between media and democracy. In analyzing that relationship, a distinction must be drawn between the media's role in democratic transition and its role in democratic consolidation. Bennett is surely correct when he concludes that the media "are much better at bringing down authoritarian regimes than they are at later sustaining stable, participatory democracies."[17] This observation simply reflects human nature and reminds us of the people behind the printing presses, screens, and microphones. To write a story under the headline *"J'Accuse"* is far more fulfilling than to report "Budget Adopted." There is something of a shark's feeding frenzy when journalists get the first sniff of autocrat blood. Here is a story to get your teeth into. The journalist is now not just a bit player in the political game but has been elevated to a key position. This could be the high point of the journalist's career and he or she knows it. Patrick O'Neil describes two sets of conditions for the dissemination, by a normally passive and controlled media, of information undermining an authoritarian regime: either by accident, or in a time of regime crisis where strictures of censorship weaken and there is less fear of state reprisal.[18] I can think of examples of both.

The accident occurred to Romanian dictator Nicolae Ceauşescu, and I remember it well because at the time of the fall of the Berlin Wall I was in charge of the section dealing with East Europe in the Department of Foreign Affairs and Trade. I can still picture the dictator's face the instant it happened. To counter the demonstrations in favor of the dissident pastor Laszlo Tokes from Timisoara, Ceauşescu called for a mass rally in Bucharest on 21 December 1989. His fatal mistake was to order that it be televised live.[19] The entire nation was therefore witness to the unthinkable—anti-Ceauşescu chants coming from one section of the crowd and soon picked up by others. The camera stayed on the dictator's face, but the angry chants could clearly be heard. Ceauşescu stared at the scene with an expression of shock and rapt attention, like a person watching a gory traffic accident unfolding. In that instant, the effectiveness of the entire edifice of repression, along with the carefully crafted impression of the dictator's invincibility, crumbled. Live television had allowed Romania to conduct a telling conversation in an instant.

The example of media assertiveness in the face of regime crisis could be seen in Indonesia as the Suharto New Order regime arrived at its endgame. Suharto had achieved legitimacy both through power and results. The power was evident in the bloody means of his ascension, his wielding of the territorial army to do his bidding, and the punishments awaiting dissidents. The results were also impressive. While we can certainly direct criticisms at the quality of development in the Suharto years, the impressive fact remains that in his first two decades in power, the size of the population living in poverty dropped from 60 to 15 percent.[20] The formula was legitimacy through development, and every institution was directed to contribute to that development. This included the media, whose role was described as "developmental journalism." Former Indonesian information minister Harmoko, speaking at an ASEAN media conference in 1990, explained it as follows:

> The conference recognises the strategic importance of the press and its vital role in the process of national development. Considering the interdependence of ASEAN nations the conference encourages the ASEAN press to promote the paramount goal, including the preservation of political stability, rapid economic growth, social justice, greater regional cohesion and the development of human resources to their full potential.[21]

Developmental journalism was sustained by a sophisticated system of censorship, self-censorship, and social expectations. Truth had, at best, a subsidiary place. There had been some latitude for mildly critical voices in the New Order that were tolerated as long as they were perceived as marginal, though the banning of three mainstream magazines in 1994 showed how narrow the level of toleration could become.[22] When the 1997 currency crisis hit Indonesia and the student demonstrations began, some Suharto allies abandoned ship, and the media took this as its cue, with even the government-owned television station, TVRI, eulogizing the dead students, galvanizing public attention to the crisis, and indicating that the dictator was losing control.[23] Suharto's successor had no option but to bow to the inevitable and dismantle the formal systems of censorship.[24]

Yet even in this example of belated journalistic courage in the face of regime crisis, there may well have been a pivotal accidental moment. Powerless to halt the free fall of the rupiah, Suharto had to turn to the international community for rescue. The picture on every front page of every newspaper in Indonesia showed Suharto signing the "economic surrender" agreement under the watchful eye of International Monetary Fund (IMF) chief Michel Camdessus standing menacingly behind him with his arms folded. The nation was being told that their president was no longer invulnerable.[25]

## Scripted or Unscripted?

In the next section we will be looking at the ills besetting the media in Asia. The list is long: censorship, self-censorship, intimidation, manipulation, corruption, partisanship, problems of profitability, sensationalism . . . This is the day-to-day reality of the media in the democratic consolidation process. All these problems detract from the ideal. But the distinction I wish to explore is not between the often elusive concepts of what is right and what is wrong, or even between the more practical question of what is functioning well and what is not: it is the ascertainable issue of what is scripted and what isn't. I believe this is the distinction at the heart of what a democracy needs from the public conversation conducted in its mass media.

From the outset, we need to acknowledge the enormity of that part of the media that is scripted. Beginning in North Korea, at the extreme of reclusive totalitarianism, everything is scripted.[26] The public conversation is a monologue of lies from Dear Leader where *plenty* means *famine, peaceful* means *warlike,* and *democracy,* a word in the formal title of the country, is denuded of all meaning. Arriving at the socialist journalism of Vietnam, the public conversation is largely one way and, while it has some relativity with reality, it is almost fully scripted to serve the interests of the state and the party. As Peter Mares notes, propaganda is not a dirty word in Vietnam.[27] Yet even in this overridingly information-controlled environment, some unscripted exchanges may take place. In attempting to enhance the prestige of its National Assembly, a very poor cousin of the party and the executive in Vietnam, it was decided to televise live the interpellation sessions. During a visit to Hanoi in 2004, people were enthusiastically telling me about the way the health minister had recently come under such incessant questioning from National Assembly members that she burst into tears. Here was an unscripted moment that said something about a possible shift in the institutional balance of power. Without television coverage, the incident would have had no resonance and thus little significance.

Swinging over to the other end of the spectrum takes us to the Philippines, a country often described as having a free press. Coronel makes the point that the Philippine press may be "rowdy and vibrant" but that it belongs to a media industry that verges from pluralistic to anarchic.[28] A large slice of the content of this free press remains carefully scripted. It's not called propaganda in a country like the Philippines, but the government tries its best to engineer a good press through press releases, selective leaking, favoritism for pliant journalists, and other less benign means. The business community is also in the business of scripting the media; as John Lent points out, "it is no secret that many of the approximately two dozen Manila dailies are kept solely as weapons for their business houses."[29] While not having the clout of the business community, the NGOs and the opposition groups will also try to get their messages across. A degree of pluralism in participation in the public conversation is thus achieved, but this is surely insufficient to qualify as deliberation.

Deliberation requires the public conversation to abandon the script and engage in a genuine confrontation of ideas and interests. The media must play a crucial role in this deliberative process. It needs to not simply give a platform to critics and be prepared to allow the politically incorrect to be aired, though both these requirements are important, it must also mediate the public conversation. In the Philippines this is achieved in part by respected opinion writers who will comment on the script and lead public opinion in assessing it. Writers like Amando Doronila, Belinda Olivares-Cunanan, or even the painfully prolix Max Soliven perform this necessary task. An organization like Coronel's Philippine Center for Investigative Journalism is not constrained by political or business scripts, and so it was able to begin the investigations that snowballed into the exposure of President Estrada's unbridled corruption. Democracy needs an open public conversation, not a recitation of press releases.

## Beset with Problems

In 2000, together with Louise Williams, a foreign correspondent for the *Sydney Morning Herald*, I published a book surveying the state of media freedom in the seventeen polities of Pacific Asia.[30] Our methodology was to put together a team of experts, mainly local journalists, to provide an honest account of the state of media freedom in the region. One of the benefits of this approach was that from conception to publication, the book took only one year to emerge, because journalists, unlike academics, know the meaning of the word *deadline*. The trigger for the book was the fall of Suharto and the discrediting of developmental journalism. We were hopeful that the survey would elaborate on the relationship between media and democracy and demonstrate the critical importance of mass media to the construction of democracy, as well as the essentiality of a democratic system to allow a free mass media to bloom. Our hopes were to a large extent fulfilled, but what the survey also demonstrated was how the media industry in democratizing Pacific Asia was beset with problems.

### Ownership Issues

On the surface, a very positive aspect of mass media in the region is its great diversity. Most major cities have numerous daily newspapers competing for readers. At one point in the 1990s, Malaysia had thirty-nine dailies and the Philippines, twenty-five,[31] while Japan had seven morning dailies each with circulation figures of over one million.[32] When it comes to television and radio, the figures for the number of stations available become astronomical, given the free-to-air, satellite, and cable options available to well-heeled Asians. But when we begin to investigate ownership and aggregate the different channels and papers owned by various groups, the picture becomes less reassuring. The Katherine Graham phenomenon is very much the exception in Asia. In her place, one can find governments, government cronies, businessmen heading conglomerates, and global media moguls.

In Singapore and Malaysia, government patronage is the key. Manufacturing tycoon T. Ananda Krishnan, who effectively owns Malaysia's satellite communications, was described by a newspaper as "a businessman who enjoys the confidence of Prime Minister Mahathir."[33] In the Philippines, Indonesia, and Thailand, it tends to be business interests that dominate, often requiring reporting to bend to the business demands of the day. When the *Manila Times* became particularly active in criticizing President Estrada, his solution was simple. He had his millionaire friend Mark Jimenez buy the newspaper. The criticism stopped and other owners also got the message.[34] In Thailand, the various TV stations are in the hands of private companies, but five of these are still owned by the government and operated under government concessions.[35] The only independent television station, iTV, was bought in 2000 by Shin Corporation, the business vehicle of then prime minister Thaksin.[36] Japan, South Korea, and Taiwan also fit the business mold, but there seems to be less influence from owners. Most Japanese media are owned by large corporations or well-established family companies, which is why Matsutaro Shoriki, who bought the ailing *Yomiuri Shinbun* in the 1920s and turned it into the world's highest-circulation newspaper, stands out so clearly.[37] Though purged by the Occupation powers after the war, he bounced back and is today remembered not only for his newspaper triumph but also for founding the Yomiuri Giants baseball team and launching Japanese TV. McCargo reminds us that ownership can be a problematic concept.[38] Not only must one sort out the various shareholdings to determine who in effect has influence, but the level of "ownership" may cascade down to various pages and columns in the newspapers. As Suharto's information minister, Harmoko was presented with shares in some thirty-one media outlets as insurance against government attack,[39] yet he did not attempt to control every aspect of the day-to-day operations of the media: he relied on various other tools, most prominently self-censorship. The same would be true of the Thai military officers given shares in the leading Bangkok daily *Matichon*.[40]

Ownership is therefore only a partial analytical tool in understanding content. Part of the problem is that the motivation for owning newspapers in particular may not be profit. A Manila tycoon will want to be a newspaper proprietor to protect business interests, influence government, and stoke vanity. These motives, even at a financial loss, can amply satisfy owners. An apparently attractive alternative is to have the journalists own shares in their own newspapers. Several Japanese and South Korean newspapers have taken this path, and there are examples in other Asian countries as well. This is the *Le Monde* model, which is intended not only to protect journalists from owners' influence but also to instill professional pride. I knew several of the leading journalists at *Le Monde* when I lived in Paris in the late 1970s, and they certainly had pride in their newspaper and pursued an abrasive independence and intellectualism. But even so venerable a daily as *Le Monde* has its critics, and the most recent attack on it accuses the senior management of partisanship in support of various politicians of both the left and the right.[41] Once again, we are resigned to falling short of the ideals we set.

### Journalistic Ethics

That is also very much the case in relation to journalistic ethics. I saw firsthand the environment in which Asian journalists are required to operate when, as head of the Centre for Democratic Institutions, I hosted a workshop for parliamentarians in Bangkok in 2001. The workshop brought together parliamentarians from Australia, Indonesia, the Philippines, and Thailand, ostensibly to study "leadership" but also in the hope of generating some networking opportunities and, subliminally, to give the newly elected and inexperienced Indonesian parliamentarians some role models among their more experienced regional peers. I invited two highly placed Thai politicians to address the gathering and opened these talks to the local media. Bhichai Rattakul, the then deputy prime minister from the Democrat Party, gave a most thoughtful presentation on the challenge facing Thailand in putting into practice the high ideals set in the 1997 Constitution. Not a single member of the local press attended the occasion. The following day, Thaksin, a former deputy prime minister but at the time an opposition politician who had recently formed the new Thai Rak Thai political party addressed the group and talked about the need to bring a CEO mentality to governing Thailand. On this occasion, the room was packed with TV cameras and pushy journalists. Thaksin reveled in the attention. When it came to question time, a Philippine parliamentarian expressed appreciation for Thaksin's presentation but asked for examples of how the CEO process could be brought into politics. Thaksin responded that the questioner should speak to Thaksin's principal adviser after the session. I was bemused by the attention lavished on Thaksin and disappointed by the way Bhichai was ignored, and so I asked a Thai journalist for the reason. The reason turned out to be very simple. Thaksin paid all the journalists a handsome allowance for attendance while all Bhichai did was spend half the night carefully preparing his own speech so that printed copies would be available to the press.

Having dealt with developmental journalism, we now come to the "envelopmental" kind. The practice of stuffing banknotes in envelopes and handing them to journalists is sadly widespread in Asia. In discussing this with journalists from Indonesia, the Philippines, and Thailand, their responses are very similar—"we don't get paid enough and we have to accept allowances to supplement our meager income." Of course the word *allowance* is often a misnomer. Envelopes are handed over not simply to compensate the journalist for the cost of covering the beat but also to ensure press releases are given prominence and even to have entire stories, written by the payer, published under the journalist's name. It is always difficult to quote exact figures on issues of corruption because its practice is rarely admitted, but Kyu Ho Youm quotes a 1989 Korea Press Institute survey of 700 journalists in which 93 percent said they had received money from their news source, a practice that he describes as a "deep-rooted cultural and social norm of accepting cash gifts as a way of journalistic life."[42] The practice is so well established in Indonesia that Jakarta City Hall actually published a budget in late 2004 with over $330,000 set aside for facilitation payments to journalists.[43] Financial dependency on the source of information is clearly antithetical to the most basic concept of journalistic ethics.

### Censorship and Self-censorship

One of the more hopeful signs Williams and I were able to point to in our 2000 publication was the diminishing role of formal state censorship in the region. As a formal governmental action, censorship is no longer practiced in democratizing Pacific Asia, but it remains in vogue in authoritarian Pacific Asia. In Burma, China, Laos, North Korea, and Vietnam, censors continue to do their job in the interests of the *Tatmadaw* (the Burmese army), or one-party socialism, or *Juche* autarky. In these countries, the media are either owned or controlled by the executive, or there are means of censoring private publications. In 2004, I had a taste of what this means for an individual journalist when, with Graeme Dobell, a journalist who hosted a weekly TV program reporting on proceedings in the Australian Parliament, I conducted a workshop by satellite for Vietnamese journalists on the ins and outs of broadcasting parliament.[44] There was lively participation by the Vietnamese media and parliamentary officials present, one of whom asked about relevant broadcasting restrictions in Australia. Graeme gave a detailed response outlining the Speaker's rules for maintaining the decorum of the Parliament and the accepted journalistic practices of not gratuitously portraying parliamentarians in an undignified way. The Vietnamese journalist nodded thoughtfully and replied that Vietnam also has rules on this subject, but they came under the headings of treason, sedition, and revealing state secrets.

But the absence of formal censorship in democratizing Pacific Asia should not be given a Manichaean interpretation that there is therefore press freedom. As Asian journalists know full well, there is a massive gray area in between these ends of the spectrum. In Malaysia[45] and Singapore[46] there is an array of weapons to wield against the press, beginning with annual media licensing laws. Other weapons in this arsenal include security laws, official secrets acts, visa restrictions, and limitations on the number of copies of printed material that can be sold. When the ammunition runs dry, vindictive governments can always find innovative new ways to muzzle the mass media. Murray Hiebert of the *Far Eastern Economic Review* was convicted in Malaysia of the archaic offense of "scandalizing the court" in 1997 because of criticism he reported of that country's legal system.[47] Geoffrey Robertson described the charge against Hiebert as an anachronism from the eighteenth century.[48] The Singapore leaders have found a most effective and profitable way to deal with their opponents through the laws of libel. In the section on newspapers I wrote for an encyclopedia of Southeast Asian history, I described former prime minister Lee Kuan Yew as "a notoriously successful libel litigant."[49] Journalists have provided a lucrative source of libel awards. In 1994, Lee, together with his son Lee Hsien Loong, the current prime minister, and Goh Chok Tong, the prime minister in the intervening period, successfully sued the *International Herald Tribune* because an article implied that Lee junior's rise was due to nepotism.[50] Lee Kuan Yew sued the *Tribune* again a couple of months later because of an article that implied Singapore had a compliant judiciary. This brought Lee a further windfall. The problem of allowing courts of dubious worth to determine the libel actions against journalists has again been demonstrated in the case of Bambang Harymurti in Jakarta. I am proud to call Bambang a friend, and he demonstrated his commitment to press freedom in the dangerous Suharto years when he was an editor of *Tempo*. Back at the helm of *Tempo* in the now democratizing Indonesia, Bambang ran afoul of powerful businessman Tomy Winata, who brought suit and convinced the prosecution to lay criminal charges. In September 2004, the Central Jakarta District Court found Bambang guilty of criminal libel and sentenced him to one year in prison. In South Korea, it is not the courts but the tax officers who are used as the government's weapon of choice against critical newspapers. *JoongAng Ilbo* appears to have paid the price of criticism of the Kim Dae Jung administration by being closely audited by the tax authorities.[51]

The government's power to revoke publishing or broadcasting licenses, arrest journalists, expel foreign journalists, sue journalists, and even imprison them has a particularly bracing effect on any editor deciding the fate of a story critical of the government. By occasionally using the coercive powers available to the state to punish critical journalists, the state triggers a weapon far more subtle and insidious than censorship: self-censorship. Closures, expulsions, convictions, bankruptcies, and imprisonments need not be common features of the repressive machinery if, having seen them occasionally applied, the media industry and the general population believe that the government is willing to use these measures. The main form of control then becomes self-censorship. Self-censorship is principally applied by the media industry, but it can go well beyond. James Gomez has investigated the phenomenon in relation to Singapore and describes the way

the entire population seems to apply a government muzzle to itself: colleagues refuse to fraternize with a government critic, printers refuse to
accept jobs from opposition figures, hotels cancel reservations when they
find out they are required by an opposition politician, advertisers withdraw
their business from magazines carrying critical voices, libraries do not stock
critical books, distributors refuse to sell them or alternatively price such
books prohibitively, and, needless to say, these books are not reviewed in
the mainstream media.[52] An entire polity thus abandons its democratic right
and duty to deliberate.

Another form of self-censorship is practiced in Japan and South Korea,
where most of the mainstream news emerges from *kisha* clubs—"a *kisha*
club is a room attached to a government ministry or commercial organization where reporters from the big media outlets spend their day attending
briefings, processing news releases and cultivating official contacts."[53]
Walter Hamilton estimates the number of press clubs in Japan at 400–500 to
which half of Japan's 25,000 journalists are assigned.[54] He further argues
that 80 percent of the information picked up in these press clubs, often
through fraternization with news sources at the latter's expense, is off-the-
record and not for publication.[55] Clearly, this is not a system conducive to
critical assessment on the part of the watchers: it does not promote the concept of deliberation, and it detracts significantly from the public conversation. It is true that all "beat" journalists will develop a familiarity with their
main sources and try not to jeopardize it. But the relationship must remain
at arm's length, it must not be fully dependent, and it may have to be sacrificed if circumstances so dictate.

### Partisanship

The final problem I wish to mention is the difficult issue of partisanship.
Partisanship presents itself differently in different countries. In the contemporary United States, one selects one's news source the same way as selecting one's music station, according to tastes for country music or heavy
metal or whatever. Conservatives love Fox and liberals watch CNN. The
ideal of objectivity is unobtainable and may even be implausible. Instead of
professing objectivity, I prefer journalists simply to report events as they
see them. I prefer to consume news and commentary from journalists who
are not aligned to political forces even if they make known their own political views. There is a very fine line thus dividing reporting and disguised
propaganda, unscripted and scripted, partisan and nonpartisan. In Indonesia,
in 1965, the concept of partisanship was considered perfectly normal and
the Information Ministry instructed all newspapers to affiliate formally with
a political party or mass organization.[56] This, of course became moot as
Suharto, Golkar, and the military became the dominant political forces. The

choice for the Indonesian media, as in any one-party state, was not between various political forces, but simply between support for the authorities or silence.

The Asian country where press partisanship is most stark is Cambodia. Cambodia is not a one-party state, but the dominant party at times behaves as if it were. It is a fascinating place where the leadership must bend its authoritarian instincts to demonstrate a façade of acceptance of the processes of multiparty democracy implanted under the UN period. The result is the continuation of an authoritarian system where the leadership is above the law, but, unlike the one-party states, Prime Minister Hun Sen must suffer the existence of a small but noisy NGO sector and two opposition parties. Hun Sen's party, the Cambodian People's Party, controls all the television stations and all but one radio station.[57] The newspapers, however, entered the political scene in the post–Khmer Rouge period as mouthpieces for their various political groups and this continues to characterize the print media, with the honorable exception of the *Phnom Penh Post*, the English-language paper.[58] The mass media in Cambodia therefore does not allow the people to conduct a public conversation. The news circulated is all scripted in service mainly of the government with a small segment favoring the interests of the opposition groups. Individuals have sufficient freedom of speech to allow the courageous critic to speak out, but he or she will not be heard widely in the vernacular media.

## Part of a Global Conversation

### Huay Xai

Thomas Friedman has made an art form of describing unlikely encounters on the globalization superhighway,[59] and so I feel emboldened to mention one such event. It occurred in the mid-1990s in Huay Xai, Laos. There is not much to occupy one's time after dark in Huay Xai. This sleepy town on the Mekong glories under the title of capital of Bokeo Province, which itself trades on the fact of being part of the Golden Triangle. Even so, things get pretty quiet after dark, unless of course the annual fair happens to be in full swing. Everybody is then drawn to the bright lights and the chirpy music painfully distorted through the overworked amplifiers. The exhibits are not particularly scintillating, with their earnest display of generators and pumps, their stalls of handicrafts and garishly colored Chinese plastic toys, and their official tourist promotion posters, but the crowd doesn't seem to mind. The food counters are far more interesting for the culinary courageous. The sweet sticky rice served in banana leaves is everybody's favorite. The more adventurous have a nibble at the roasted grasshoppers, and I came to appreciate the fat wasp maggot, which tasted a bit like ricotta cheese with a dash of honey. The gambling games had a wonderful innocence about them compared to our ugly addiction to wretched rows of joyless slot machines sucking money out of the pockets of people who invariably can't afford to lose it. In Bokeo, it is the guinea pig that decides where the smart money will ride. A huge horizontal roulette wheel is surrounded by the happy throng clutching their tickets. Each ticket number corresponds to one of thirty little huts on the edge of the wheel. The carnie spins the wheel and the crowd gives a collective cheer. In the middle of the wheel is an unnumbered hut and in this hut is a little guinea pig. The poor creature emerges from its now wildly spinning home dizzy and confused. It takes its bearings and sniffs the wind, it stumbles around and tries to blink itself to its senses and, finally, it scampers into one of the thirty numbered huts to the raucous acclaim of the winning ticket holders.

The main attraction, however, is not an exhibit, but the fairgoer. People-watching is the main game in Huay Xai as it is everywhere else in the world. There are children everywhere thrilled at a night out in the flood of lights. Many Hmong villagers in their traditional black clothes with colorful red trim have come to town for the fair. The town people are out in force, as are a smattering of tourists. Some Isai folk from Thailand have come over the river as well, their pockets full of baht. The Mekong is still high enough to allow a large riverboat from Jinghong in China's Yunnan province to be moored at its river berth, bringing Chinese tourists also, surprisingly, clutching wads of Thai baht. We all saunter from one stand to another with eyes wide and smiles fixed.

One of the stands has a more robust look, with a uniformed, unsmiling guard perched outside. This is the exhibit of the joint venture sapphire miners displaying their enticing little stones. Bokeo has been known for its precious stones for centuries, but before the foreign miner came along, it was an artisanal activity conducted with crude digging tools. Now it is being undertaken with excavators, conveyor belts, and sifters, and Bokeo Province, which stands to gain 10 percent of the profits, is already beginning to show signs of a nascent rentier mentality. Yet it is not the sapphires, but the next exhibit, that is attracting the big crowd.

People seem to be hurrying to the next large tent, children running at pace, adults converging in a determined walk. The excitement is clearly evident, and I am in that not uncommon position of being the foreigner who is the last to know. The human gravity is having its effect on me too as I edge toward the large tent. The ubiquitous generator is purring away noisily. The inevitable chords and wires are scattered in apparent careless randomness. The giveaway clue is behind the tent—a large satellite dish ready to capture that dangerous creature, the outside world. With the realization of what is about to be offered, I feel a disturbing nervousness. All of a sudden it seems that it is me and my culture that are to be put before the critical gaze of these viewers, many of whom have never seen a TV before. I start to calculate the situation. It is one of the very large dishes, suggesting a capacity to tune in on a variety of satellite footsteps. Being in the center of Southeast Asia, this opens up the possibility of literally hundreds of stations. Perhaps it would tune into the official Lao TV program, but who would pay good money for that? More likely it would be one of the Thai soap operas, but it was surely too late in the day for these and anyway most town folks already get Thai TV through antennae on stilts. What about a Bollywood musical extravaganza with dozens of dancers doing silly steps in unison? Political correctness would suggest Vietnamese TV and some propaganda program about the marvelous achievements of the Hanoi government, but people pay money for entertainment, not propaganda. Then an ugly realization dawns on me: media mogul Rupert Murdoch's STAR TV (Satellite Television for the Asian Region). I begin immediately to calculate the damage. Perhaps it would only be some ridiculously out-of-date police drama like *Starsky and Hutch*. "Out-of-date" is a relative concept, I console myself, and to Hmong villagers even *Starsky and Hutch* would be from the next century. Or perhaps it would be something uplifting and accessible like a nature program from National Geographic. I convince myself that this is the most likely outcome, and I pay my few hundred kip, about 25 cents, to enter.

The tent is packed, every seat is taken and people are lined up along the walls. The kids have camped on the floor directly in front of the set. There is an expectant air with plenty of chat going on. I maneuver my way to very near the front where one can barely see the screen, but I enjoy a wonderful view of the viewers. The entrepreneur is fiddling with the set, the decoder box and the wires giving an air of purposeful competence. The minutes tick by, but the audience is patient. I try to engage my neighbor in conversation about what is to be shown, but my limited Lao and his limited English do not span the incomprehension gap. When I ask "STAR TV?" he nods vigorously. But when I test this exchange by asking "BBC TV?" his affirmation is equally enthusiastic. I think he only understood the word TV.

The fiddling seems to take an eternity when suddenly the screen flickers to life, silencing the crowd. False alarm. The power is getting through, but the satellite has not locked onto its target yet. The chatter resumes happily, Asian patience working its magic. The sound suddenly precedes the picture, and I can immediately tell that we are tuned into promos for STAR TV. But STAR TV carries Discovery Channel, I remember, and I hold onto this thought with grim optimism. The promos and ads are a delight to the kids. Looking at their reaction, I conclude that most of them have only ever heard of TV but have never watched it. Many of the adults are clearly also fascinated with the mere fact that the screen is alive. So the moment has come when Western culture will be presented to these good-natured, unspoiled people for the first time. The ads are winding down and the final promo is on—show time is here.

When the program credits begin I give a loud involuntary gasp that has to be covered with some forced coughing to divert attention from myself. The term "worst-case scenario" won't leave my stubbornly analytical thoughts. I accept that TV is fantasy, and I realize that the human mind can deal with absurdity, but this program is so over the top that no virgin viewer could possibly comprehend it. The audience is listening intently to the presenter's incomprehensible heroic announcements unaware of the action that is soon to begin. I have a strong urge to hit the pause button and launch into a couple of hours of explanation to put the program in context, but instead I watch silently, horrified into paralysis.

The protagonists swagger onto the screen—the McMahon World Wrestling circus has come to Huay Xai. As it turns out, I need not have worried. The Bokeo folk love the show. What is not to like about behemoths in choreographed battle? They don't bother intellectualizing about what the show depicts of Western society; they simply gasp at the falls and giggle at the facial expressions. The entrepreneur knows his audience, which eventually leaves with the satisfaction of money well spent.

### Technology as Tool for Transformation

The reach of technology is impressive. Even Pyongyang, the most totalitarian regime in the region, cannot completely block out the outside world. The coverage of Chinese cell phones reaches over the border into North Korea.[60] Now North Koreans can obtain a prepaid Chinese cell phone and call relatives in South Korea. They usually keep the phone buried, as the authorities have placed a ban on all cell phone services. Separated relatives in Korea can, with difficulty and courage, talk to each other, and news of the outside world can seep into North Korea. But let's face the facts; this is not in itself going to bring down Dear Leader and his military.

Mass communications technology has the power to change the world, but it will have most impact on those societies that embrace it. Open societies with open skies and open airwaves will become information societies and gain the most from the information economy. The working world is now neatly divided between people who check their e-mails first thing in the morning and those who do not. In closed or tightly controlled societies, the impact of the new technologies requires more nuanced assessment.

Upon first glimpse of the possible transformative impact of mass communications technology, a certain hyperbole was inevitable. Murdoch gave his famous "dissidents" speech in 1993:

> Advances in the technology of telecommunications have proved an unam-
> biguous threat to totalitarian regimes everywhere. Fax machines enable
> dissidents to bypass state-controlled print media; direct dial telephone
> makes it difficult for a state to control interpersonal voice communica-
> tions; and satellite broadcasting makes it possible for information-hungry
> societies to by-pass state-controlled television stations.[61]

Murdoch was not alone in talking up technology's transformative
potential. Speaking about transnational media technology, Peter Eng argued
that these "have transformed much of Southeast Asia from a region where
the people silently kowtowed to the authorities to one where all groups,
government and private, agree that public opinion matters."[62] Tedjabayu
Basuki, referring to the Indonesian situation, was of the view that the
Internet "would be too powerful to control."[63] Krishna Sen and David Hill
also saw the possibilities inherent in the way Indonesian "public-access
Internet put the latest information technology in the hands of the people."[64]
Williams took an upbeat view of the power of technology, but added an
important caveat:

> The spectacular advances in communications and information technology,
> the advent of satellite TV and the globalization of the media made the old-
> time censors, with their quaint armoury of scissors and thick black pens,
> obsolete. New battle lines are being drawn for control of the Internet and
> the airwaves, but the speed of transmission and the volume of information
> flashing its way around the world mean this is a much more difficult line
> to hold.[65]

Advanced technology makes the job of controlling the mass media, and thus
the public conversation, more complex, but that has not changed deep-seat-
ed authoritarian instincts. Governments, like those in Pyongyang and
Rangoon, with crude tools at their disposal have to ban or control the hardware—banning cell phones in North Korea or licensing fax machines in
Burma. The effect of such crude controls is that these countries cannot enter
the information superhighway, and as the world economy turns increasingly
into an information economy, the autarkic approach of the leadership of
these countries is reinforced. Sadly for the Burmese and North Korean people, autarky means penury.

Penury is not what other states in the region are after. China, Malaysia,
Singapore, and Vietnam want wealth and so they want to travel down the
information superhighway, but they do not want to forsake all controls over
traffic. The complexity and cost of attempting to control the new technology does not deter them. Leader of the pack is Singapore, whose ambitions in
this field are heightened by the possibilities inherent in controlling such a
compact geographic area. Singapore banned satellite dishes and is able to
enforce the ban and, in place of the global providers, cabled up the city-

state for programming from government-owned Singapore CableVision (acquired by StarHub in 2002).[66] The Internet is a more difficult medium to control, but that has not deterred the Singapore authorities. Singapore has one of the highest rates of Internet use, but all three Internet service providers are run by government-controlled companies.[67] In 1994, the government put 80,000 accounts under surveillance in an ostensible swoop against pornography, and in 1999 it scanned almost half of all accounts, this time supposedly to check for viruses.[68] Singaporean Internet users know that there is no privacy online and that they are required to continue to practice the ingrained habit of self-censorship in cyberspace. China and Vietnam have borrowed from Singapore's example. Alarmed at the way independent groups like the Falun Gong could communicate so effectively through the Internet, China passed legislation prohibiting Internet activities that undermine the interests of the state and spends huge sums of money on monitoring the Internet, importing Internet "nanny" techniques, requiring registration of Chinese websites, and installing filtration systems to block offensive websites.[69]

The most interesting of these countries with authoritarian instincts is Malaysia. Mahathir had always shown commendable determination to raise Malaysian living standards and drag the country into the technological first world. His vision of Malaysia in 2020 was one of economic success and technological savvy. One of his plans was to create the Malaysian Multimedia Super Corridor, and for this he needed investment from the global telecommunications corporations. So the one thing he could not do was to attack the Internet, and the tactics employed by Singapore have therefore been eschewed in Malaysia.[70] The result is that "the Internet has become a popular medium where the latest information, intellectual exchange, criticisms of the government and even gossip can be publicly obtained" and many politically independent and pro-*reformasi* websites mushroomed.[71] Malaysia tolerated the hardware and instead focused its attack on the messenger. The most-popular independent source of news in Malaysia is *Malaysiakini.com* under the stewardship of Steven Gan. Gan told me that advertisers have been warned off by officials and that the operation has had to move to a subscription basis to be sustainable. Mahathir had said *Malaysiakini.com* was funded by George Soros, which left the website editor in the difficult position of proving a negative.[72] The latest attack on the messengers in Malaysia has been through police questioning of bloggers.[73]

In the same way that the Internet is no panacea for freedom of expression, satellite TV does not resolve the problem of facilitating a public conversation in a society that is otherwise closed to the free flow of news. There is much pressing to be done on the remote control under the many satellite footprints over Asia, but ultimately little choice in terms of independent news. The global news providers are the most reliable conveyers of breaking news and occasionally interesting commentary. Of the global public broadcasters, BBC World has the language and brand name advantages over the French and German stations. To protect that brand, "the BBC has been unyielding in its insistence that the news must be run in its entirety or not at all."[74] Because of its unyielding stance, BBC World displeased the Chinese authorities, and when Murdoch wished to cement his STAR TV coverage in China, commercial expediency dictated that he accede to the demand that the BBC be dropped from the STAR line-up.[75] When it comes to commercial networks, CNN is the leading brand and provides a credible, if drearily repetitive, news service. But William Atkins suggests that at least in relation to the service covering Malaysia, CNN edited its materials so as not to fall afoul of the prickly former prime minister.[76] Short-wave radio has lower start-up costs and is of less interest to the commercial sector, and so it has remained an invaluable source of information in closed societies, so long as its sponsoring governments are prepared to pay for it. In the Suharto years, the best way Indonesians could guess at what was happening in East Timor was to listen to Radio Australia. Today, BBC Radio remains the preferred source of information for news-starved Burmese.

The global conversation made possible by modern technology has a number of impacts, some obvious and others more subtle. Clearly it can allow news of events to infiltrate societies otherwise closed to bad news. It can contextualize the situation in a country. Consumers of, and participants in, the global conversation can thus work out where their country stands in relation to the third wave of democratization and be motivated by the example of events in other countries. It can provide a platform for critical voices that would otherwise be silenced at home. That voice might be a simple film of events, as was the case in 1992 when the Suchinda government blocked coverage of the violent suppression of demonstrators in Bangkok, but viewers recorded the CNN satellite coverage of the event and distributed the tapes widely.[77] The global conversation can overtly or implicitly sustain universal norms, even if only by employing its terminology and referring to concepts like human rights, transparency, and accountability. In doing so, it may introduce discussion on otherwise taboo subjects like empowerment of women. And finally, the global conversation can set quality standards for local media to aspire to emulate.

A powerful example of that influence was provided by Ramindar Singh, editor of the *Sunday Times* in India, at an International Workshop on Freedom of Information for Good Governance, organized in New Delhi in August 2001 by the Asian Centre for Democratic Governance. He related the decision to set up a website for the leading Delhi newspaper, *Times of India*. Working on the premise that all serious newspapers these days have their own Web editions, the *Times of India* decided to follow suit. It did so

with minimal resources and simply reused existing copy from the print edition. The Web edition of the paper was popular, especially among the Indian
diaspora; the hits multiplied, feedback flowed freely; and advertisers
became interested. It soon became apparent to Singh and his colleagues that
the *Times of India* had inadvertently stumbled into competition with the
great papers of the world, and its readers were comparing the product with
*The Times* of London, the *New York Times,* and other great newspapers. The
result, according to Singh, is that the Web edition of the *Times of India* now
leads the print edition. The quality of the Web edition had to be improved to
such an extent, in the face of serious competition, that additional care and
resources had to be poured in with the effect of raising the quality of the
print edition as well.

## Positive Developments

### Local Journalists and Foreign Correspondents

There is something about journalists. They are a cynical lot, always looking
for hidden motives and tactics. They are irreverent, verging at times on the
iconoclastic. They tend to be curious and questioning, suspicious of authority, and skeptical of press releases. This description crosses civilizational
divides. It certainly applies to many Asian journalists I know. The profession attracts these sorts of people wherever it is practiced relatively honestly. The doyen of Asian journalists is Amando Doronila, a veteran in the
fight for freedom of speech in the Philippines, who faced up to Marcos and
then was a thorn in the side of his successors. I knew him from my Manila
days in the time of Cory Aquino's presidency and asked him to write the
preface to the 2000 book I edited with Williams. In his spare and elegant
prose, he made a number of important points: "Journalists everywhere have
a universal bond—they are all the same. . . . Press freedom is a language
journalists know by instinct. It is not a western construct . . . as soon as the
windows opened to the new wind of change, journalists jumped into the
stream of press freedom like fish swimming in water."[78]

The most important thing going right in the public conversation occur-
ring in democratizing Pacific Asia is that many of the right people are being
attracted to the profession of journalism. Asia is breeding ever more vocational journalists. I have had the privilege of meeting many of them—the
established names and the idealistic men and women who have gravitated to
the profession in the bloom of the transition to democracy. One of the sec-
tors in which the CDI was active was skills training for journalists from
Southeast Asia and the Pacific Islands. In selecting the journalists for these
courses, we adopted an innovative shortcut because we simply did not have

the time or skills to sift through the hundreds of applications that would be generated by public advertising. We asked some of the well-established journalists in the field to make the CDI course known to promising young journalists, who would then apply directly to us. So, for example, in Indonesia we asked Aristides Katoppo, chief editor, *Sinar Harapan;* Andreas Harsono, chief editor, *Pantau Magazine;* Goenawan Mohamad, senior editor, *Koran Tempo* and *Tempo Magazine;* Bambang Harymurti, chief editor, *Koran Tempo* and *Tempo Magazine;* Lukas Luwarso, executive director, *Dewan Pers;* and Atmakusumah Astraatmadja, director, *Dewan Pers* to spread the word, and as a result, we had an excellent cohort for the course on investigative journalism delivered by Murdoch University in Perth (named after Sir Walter, an Australian academic, not Rupert, the media mogul). In discussions with Asian journalists, one point became clear. There was no criticism of their systems or profession that I could make that they had not already made, often more vociferously and always more expertly.

The fourth-estate mentality is alive and strong in the profession. The journalists remember well the system under authoritarian rule where they were seen as part of the establishment. In Suharto's Indonesia, journalists who were not members of the Indonesian Journalists' Union were not employable, and when disaffected journalists established an independent journalists' union in 1994, its leaders ended up in prison for "spreading hatred" against the Indonesian government.[79] In Marcos's Philippines, critical journalists had the options of fleeing the country, risking imprisonment, or, at the very least, being banished from the profession. In Mahathir's Malaysia, Rashid, a Malaysian journalist, speaking about his colleagues said:

> I began to see the Malaysian journalist as one of the saddest creatures in the nation. Our readers dismissed us as lapdogs of the government; the government considered us instruments of policy. But the truth was that Malaysian journalism was replete with people of intelligence and integrity, good and honourable Malaysians, who were finding their careers demanded enormous efforts of conscience.[80]

Journalists who have known the days of repression will revel in the days of press freedom. The pendulum of problems then swings over toward the anarchy side. Sensationalism, plagiarism, inaccuracy, and lax ethics have now become the issues. Yet even here, it is the journalists themselves who are in the front line of tackling these problems through training programs, independent journalists' associations, regional solidarity groupings like the South East Asia Press Alliance, and industry press councils. Once again, they are the experts on their own problems. I recall discussing with some journalists from the Philippines a disgraceful episode from Australian commercial radio where prime-time journalists had criticized certain corporations, then gone on those corporations' payrolls, after which they began praising the very same corporations. In a bewilderingly disconnected reply, the Filipinos all began referring to the well-known Australian heavy-metal band AC/DC. When I asked what on earth rock music had to do with it, they roared in laughter at my confusion. ACDC turns out to be shorthand for a known form of journalistic shakedown in the Philippines. It stands for Attack Collect, Defend Collect.

Having praised local journalism, it may sound inconsistent to list as the next category of things going right in the public conversation being conducted in Pacific Asia the English-language press in the region. The English-language press, in countries dominated by the vernacular press, brings with it the traditions and values of Western journalism. Foreigners and locals will work together in these newspapers and learn from each other. Even though the English-language newspapers do not have high circulation figures, they are read by the elites and often perform an invaluable role of setting the agenda and opening up difficult subjects. Even in as difficult a media environment as exists in Cambodia, the *Phnom Penh Post* attempts to uphold high standards of journalism. The *Jakarta Post* is the most reputable newspaper in Indonesia. *The Nation* in Bangkok beats the *Bangkok Post* in terms of investigative journalism, though the latter probably wins out in relation to the professionalism of the presentation. The *Korea Herald,* the *Korea Times,* the *Taipei Times,* and the *Japan Times* are other leading examples in Pacific Asia.

Perhaps the most influential English-language voice in the region over many decades was the weekly *Far Eastern Economic Review*. Like so many who are interested in Asia, I was an avid reader and occasional contributor to its Travelers' Tales. To have all the *FEER* editions is to have a comprehensive modern history of Pacific Asia. *FEER* found the right concoction of inside reporting, critical analysis, and fond irreverence that made it compelling reading. Over the years, it had its skirmishes with authorities in various countries, but such was its reputation that it managed to weather all the political storms. *FEER* was clearly an opinion leader in the region and often set the tone for reporting in national dailies. It brought the best of Western journalism to the East. That is what makes its demotion so poignant and bitterly ironic. It was brought down in 2004 by that pillar of the West, its owner Dow Jones, which turned it into a far less influential monthly.[81] With the death of *Asiaweek* in 2001, the dilution of *FEER* has left a significant void in the Asian journalism scene that must now be filled by Asian journalists themselves.

Another significant role is played by the foreign correspondents in the region. Writing for prestigious Western newspapers that can afford to place journalists in the field, they again carry with them high standards of professionalism and probity, and most of them live up to these. Being transient members of the societies they are observing limits them in terms of the depth of their knowledge about how things work locally, but it also frees them from the constraints of having to abide by unwritten strictures of self-censorship. Foreign correspondents can deal with the tough stories that local journalists may find hard to tackle. The breakthrough exposé of money politics under Japanese prime minister Tanaka in 1974 would not have gained the legs it did under the prevailing *kisha* club mentality. The break came from persistent questioning during his appearance at the Foreign Correspondents' Club.[82]

## The Internet and the Blogosphere

Having debunked the notion of the Internet as panacea, it is nevertheless important to acknowledge the critically important role it is playing in allowing Asian societies to conduct their necessary public conversations. Indonesian students experienced the liberating power of the Internet in 1990 when John McDougall, an American who ran an information dissemination company in Jakarta, launched the *Apakabar* website and soon attracted thousands of "Netizens" consuming and constructing the public conversation that was forbidden to them beneath the ether.[83] Basuki describes *Apakabar* as "a site for extremely open and democratic debates on Indonesia . . . an important factor in accelerating Indonesian society's awareness of the need to re-evaluate its values."[84] This set a general pattern for societies closed to free information flow. Willy Wo-Lap Lam confirms that in China, "with the growth of the Internet, civic associations can air their own views on websites."[85]

Even in Asian societies where information is not formally controlled, the Internet can play a role that traditional media forms find uncomfortable, as has happened in the United States with the *Drudge Report* phenomenon, or Australia's *Crikey.com,* which claims that it "goes where the other media won't go." This was well demonstrated by the brash new Web-based news provider in India called *Tehelka.com.* In March 2001, *Tehelka* broke a huge story about corruption in the defense procurement sector that went all the way to the top of the defense establishment. The story had tremendous public impact because it was a sting operation filmed by the journalists and replayed incessantly on mainstream TV.[86] When I met *Tehelka*'s CEO, Tarjun Tejpal, the following year, I was full of praise for his investigative journalism, but he was in a rather morose mood. He feared reprisals from the military, and his offices were protected by sandbags while he had no option but to take protective security measures. He complained that the only one being punished was *Tehelka* itself. It was being investigated, sued, and harassed. He also had another complaint, echoed by Gan from *Malaysiakini,* about the impermanence of Web journalism as opposed to print journalism, even if newspapers are tomorrow's fish-and-chips wrapping.

Web-based electronic news mimics print news forms in that it adopts a storytelling form with storytellers (Web journalists) and listeners (Web surfers). The blogosphere, on the other hand, dispenses with the hierarchy of storytelling and launches a far more democratic medium in terms of the public conversation, because the product takes the actual form of conversation among voluntary participants. A Web log, or blog, is merely a website with individual comments in the form of postings appearing in reverse chronological order. The technology is simple enough, but the challenge is having one's voice heard in the etherized cacophony. The estimate of the Perseus Corporation is that in 2004 there were 10 million blogs.[87] The formula for generating blogs is basically Internet penetration plus youth, and Pacific Asia has plenty of both. The blogosphere serves as a useful counterbalance to the press in liberal democracies, thus generating the sobriquet of the "fifth estate."[88] It is also a useful medium in which censorship is difficult to apply because its vastness makes it so difficult to police. China is said to have 600,000 bloggers among its 100 million Web surfers.[89] Because political controls have such a high priority in China, resources are devoted to controlling even blog content through filtering devices, regulation of cybercafes, and harassment of bloggers.[90] But the message is still getting across, with the censors often one step behind the bloggers. I was delighted to read recently that a senior Chinese government official doesn't bother reading the turgid official press, but would never miss a scathing essay by my fellow Reagan-Fascell Democracy Fellow Jiao Guobiao, who is blacklisted in China, whenever they are posted on the blogs.[91]

### Talk Radio and TV

Writing in 1996 in *FEER*, Simon Elegant argued: "the prevalence or otherwise of talk radio serves as a crude barometer of the degree of political freedom countries enjoy."[92] In fact, far from being crude, this measure strikes me as an elegant means of gauging the degree of freedom in Pacific Asia. Traveling around the region, one can quickly confirm that in one-party states there is no room for the risky, unpredictable voices emerging from talk radio, whereas in open societies, talk radio and talk TV are growing in audience size, audience involvement, and political influence. The best example in the region may be in Taiwan where talk show hosts like Sisy Chen and Hu Chung-hsin command huge audiences and are acknowledged as political forces.[93] To employ a well-known political science test and ask what taxi drivers are listening to, I would estimate that over half of the hundreds of times I have sat in cabs in Asia, the radio has been tuned to talk programs.

The place where the talk show is most contested is where the single-party system and the open-society system overlap, in Hong Kong. Radio talk show hosts are hugely popular in the former British colony, and their level of popularity appears to grow with their courage in criticizing Chinese policies, Chinese politicians, and Chinese cronies. The result is that the host's courage is then severely tested. In 2004, the two most popular talk show hosts, Wong Tuk-man and Albert Cheng King-hon, who have been described as "benchmarks for freedom of the press in Hong Kong,"[94] were both forced off their shows because of threats. Cheng went on to win a seat in the Legislative Council, while Wong returned to radio several months later but had his exposure reduced from a daily broadcast to a weekly slot. Without freedom of speech and a legal system that confidently enforces it, talk show hosts lead a very tenuous existence if they engage in or entertain criticisms of the authorities. Talk radio and TV provide a critically important platform for the unscripted voice to be heard.

Politicians in democratic countries listen carefully to that unscripted public voice. In Australia, one of the most important agenda setters is talk-back radio, with politicians taking careful note of the subjects raised and the opinions expressed. Electronic media allowing an unscripted public voice to ordinary citizens provide a means of influencing opinion quite broadly. The voice being heard by the audience is the voice of a peer, and it is possible that it can therefore attract affirmation more readily than the less-immediate voice heard through editorials or from experts. There seems to be a bandwagon effect in the repetition of similar views from many peer voices that politicians take very seriously. The influence of the host on the public voice can be significant. That is why the most popular talk show hosts are either feted by politicians or threatened by those who dislike the resulting messages.

The pollsters, focus group facilitators, public pulse takers, and social surveyors will argue that their services provide the means to gauge the public mood. They do provide a valuable service in reflecting public opinion at that moment, but it is a service that they, not the members of the public they are surveying, have initiated. In modern societies, the most democratic and effective way for individual public voices to be heard daily is through the electronic media by means of talk radio and blogging. Talk radio and blogging have the essential qualities of being unscripted, uncontrolled, and often unpredictable. Of course, these forms of the public conversation may also be uninformed, unsophisticated, and, yes, unimpressive. Never mind. It is not the contention of democrats that the public must always be wise, but simply that its voice must always be heard.

## Conclusion

The most important thing going right in the region, therefore, is the growing engagement of the public voice in politics through the mass media. Media proprietors, media practitioners, and even blog hosts may have their own motives and their own personal and political axes to grind, but they must still discharge their duty as a conduit between the rulers and the ruled in a democratic society. Where the content is fully scripted, it is not a conversation but a series of soliloquies. Deliberative democracy needs an unscripted conversation, and this requires the public to have a voice. Just as parliamentarians act on the public's behalf in our representative democracies, so we often have journalists asking our questions and speaking our thoughts. But this form of agency has validity only if there is the alternative of having one's voice heard more directly. Occasionally, the public must act directly in politics through elections, policy submissions, demonstrations, boycotts, and civil society activism. In the public conversation, also, members of the public must have the ability, which they must occasionally exercise, to speak directly. The traditional means—and it remains a high-quality way for an individual to speak his or her mind—is by writing a letter to the editor or submitting an op-ed piece. But very few voices will be heard this way in our mass societies. Electronic means of talk radio and blogs allow the conversation to be multiplied many times in keeping with the needs of our mass societies.

Many other things are going right in the public conversations being conducted in Pacific Asia. The activism of local journalists, the contribution of foreign correspondence, and the standards set by the global providers are all raising the quality of that public conversation. The quality increases with the degree of openness of the society in which the public conversation is being held. So the rather long list of problems encountered in the conduct of the public conversation should not be seen as disabling factors. These problems show that the emerging democracies of Pacific Asia, like all other democracies, are falling short of the ideals of diversity, fairness, profitability, and public engagement that quality democracies aspire to in their public conversations, but a general conclusion can nevertheless be hazarded that there is sufficient quality in these conversations to qualify them as a telling part of that process of deliberation required in democracies.

## Notes

1. Michael Salvador, "Practicing Democracy," Michael Salvador and Patricia M. Sias (eds.), *The Public Voice in a Democracy at Risk* (Westport: Praeger, 1998), p. 4.

2. Amartya Sen, "Democracy as a Universal Value," *Journal of Democracy* 10, no. 3 (1999): 10.

3. Joseph M. Bessette, "Deliberative Democracy: The Majoritarian Principle in Republican Government," Robert A. Goldwin and William A. Shambra (eds.), *How Democratic Is the Constitution?* (Washington, DC: American Enterprise Institute, 1980), pp. 102–116.

4. James S. Fishkin, *Democracy and Deliberation: New Directions for Democratic Reform* (New Haven: Yale University Press, 1991), pp. 35–41.

5. Ibid., pp. 35–36.

6. John S. Dryzek, *Deliberative Democracy and Beyond—Liberals, Critics, Contestations* (Oxford: Oxford University Press, 2000), p. 2.

7. Ibid., p. 86.

8. For example, Erik Åsard and W. Lance Bennett, *Democracy and the Marketplace of Ideas—Communication and Government in Sweden and the United States* (Cambridge: Cambridge University Press, 1997).

9. Ibid., p. 28.

10. Robert A. Dahl, *Toward Democracy: A Journey—Reflections: 1940–1997, Volume 1* (Berkeley: Institute of Governmental Studies Press, 1997), p. 377.

11. Ibid., pp. 385–386.

12. Ibid., p. 378.

13. "Key Dates in the History of Le Monde," *Le Monde* in English, 30 November 2006, available from www.lemondeinenglish.com/keydates.php.

14. Kyu Ho Youm, "Democratization and the Press: South Korea," Patrick H. O'Neil (ed.), *Communicating Democracy—The Media & Political Transitions* (Boulder: Lynne Rienner Publishers, 1988), p. 181.

15. Duncan McCargo, *Media and Politics in Pacific Asia* (London: Routledge Curzon, 2003), pp. 3–4.

16. Ibid., p. 4.

17. W. Lance Bennett, "The Media and Democratic Development: The Social Basis of Political Communication," O'Neil (ed.), *Communicating Democracy—The Media & Political Transitions*, p. 195.

18. Patrick H. O'Neil, "Democratization and Mass Communication: What Is the Link?" O'Neil (ed.), *Communicating Democracy—The Media & Political Transitions*, p. 8.

19. Richard A. Hall and Patrick H. O'Neil, "The Media: A Comparison of Hungary and Romania," O'Neil (ed.), *Communicating Democracy—The Media & Political Transitions*, p. 133.

20. Adam Schwarz, *A Nation in Waiting—Indonesia in the 1990s* (Boulder: Westview Press, 1994), p. 58.

21. Australian Broadcasting Corporation, *Development Journalism*, 17 March 2001, www.abc.net.au/ra/media/radio/s257121.htm.

22. Andreas Harsono, "Indonesia—Dancing in the Dark," Louise Williams and Roland Rich (eds.), *Losing Control—Freedom of the Press in Asia* (Canberra: Asia-Pacific Press, 2000), pp. 82–83.

23. Ibid., pp. 85–86.

24. Ibid., pp. 87–90.

25. McCargo, *Media and Politics*, p. 95.

26. Krzysztof Darewicz, "North Korea—A Black Chapter," Williams and Rich (eds.), *Losing Control*, pp. 138–146.

27. Peter Mares, "Vietnam—Propaganda Is Not a Dirty Word," Williams and Rich (eds.), *Losing Control*, pp. 239–257.

28. Sheila S. Coronel, "Philippines—Free as a Mocking Bird," Williams and Rich (eds.), *Losing Control*, p. 148.

29. John A. Lent, "The Mass Media in Asia," O'Neil (ed.), *Communicating Democracy—The Media & Political Transitions*, p. 156.

30. Williams and Rich (eds.), *Losing Control*.

31. Zaharom Nain, "The Structure of the Media Industry—Implications for

Democracy," Francis Loh Kok Wah and Khoo Boo Teik (eds.), *Democracy in Malaysia—Discourses and Practices* (Richmond, Surrey: Curzon Press, 2002), p. 112.

32. Walter Hamilton, "Japan—The Warmth of the Herd," Williams and Rich (eds.), *Losing Control,* p. 96.

33. Quoted in Nain, "The Structure of the Media Industry," p. 120.

34. Sheila Coronel, "Investigating the President," 2001, available from www.pcij.org/investigate.html.

35. Lent, "The Mass Media in Asia," p. 153.

36. Julian Gearing, "Taming the Media," *Asiaweek* 27, no. 6 (16 February 2001).

37. Hamilton, "Japan," p. 97.

38. McCargo, *Media and Politics*, pp. 7–9.

39. Ibid., p. 7.

40. Ibid.

41. Pierre Péan and Philippe Cohen, *La Face Cachée du Monde* (Paris: Mille et une Nuit, 2003).

42. Kyu Ho Youm, "Democratization and the Press," p. 187.

43. Bambang Nurbianto and Damar Harsanto, "Indonesia: Council, Journalists Question Budget for Media," *Jakarta Post*, 22 December 2004.

44. Available at www.cdi.anu.edu.au/CDIwebsite_1998-2004/vietnam/Vietnam_GDLN_Mar04.htm.

45. Kean Wong, "Malaysia, in the Grip of the Government," Williams and Rich (eds.), *Losing Control,* pp. 118–119.

46. Garry Rodan, "Singapore—Information Lockdown, Business as Usual," Williams and Rich (eds.), *Losing Control,* p. 173.

47. Kean Wong, "Malaysia," pp. 122–123.

48. Speech to the 12th Commonwealth Law Conference, 13–16 September 1999.

49. Roland Rich, "Newspapers and Mass Media in Southeast Asia," Ooi Keat Gin (ed.), *Southeast Asia—A Historical Encyclopedia from Angkor Wat to East Timor* (Santa Barbara: ABC-CLIO, 2004), pp. 963–966.

50. Rodan, "Singapore," pp. 177–178.

51. Roger du Mars, "South Korea—Fear Is a Hard Habit to Break," Williams and Rich (eds.), *Losing Control,* p. 205.

52. James Gomez, *Self-Censorship: Singapore's Shame* (Singapore: Think Centre, 2000).

53. Hamilton, "Japan," p. 99.

54. Ibid.

55. Ibid., p. 100.

56. Krishna Sen and David T. Hill, *Media, Culture, and Politics in Indonesia* (Oxford: Oxford University Press, 2000), p. 52.

57. John Marston, "Cambodian News Media," Damien Kingsbury, Eric Loo, and Patricia Payne (eds.), *Foreign Devils and Other Journalists* (Melbourne: Monash Asia Institute, 2000), p. 190.

58. Ibid., p. 201.

59. Thomas L. Friedman, *The Lexus and the Olive Tree* (New York: Farrar, Straus and Giroux, 1999). Thomas L. Friedman, *The World Is Flat: A Brief History of the Twenty-First Century* (New York: Farrar, Straus and Giroux, 2005).

60. "Cell Phones Spark 'Communications Revolution' in North Korea," *Chosun Ilbo,* 2 December 2004.

61. Quoted in William Atkins, "Obstacles to Openness: International Television Services and Authoritarian States in East Asia," Kingsbury, Loo, and Payne (eds.), *Foreign Devils,* p. 263.

62. Peter Eng, "The Democracy Boom," Cecile C. A. Balgos (ed.), *News in Distress—The Southeast Asian Media in a Time of Crisis* (Quezon City: Philippine Centre for Investigative Journalism and the Dag Hammarskjöld Foundation, 1999), p. 16.

63. Tedjabayu Basuki, "Indonesia: The Web as a Weapon," Balgos (ed.), *News in Distress,* p. 102.

64. Sen and Hill, *Media, Culture, and Politics,* p. 197.

65. Louise Williams, "Censors at Work, Censors out of Work," Williams and Rich (eds.), *Losing Control,* pp. 4–5.

66. Atkins, "Obstacles to Openness," p. 269.

67. Rodan, "Singapore," p. 183.

68. Ibid., pp. 183–184.

69. Willy Wo-Lap Lam, "China—State Power Versus the Internet," Williams and Rich (eds.), *Losing Control,* p. 54.

70. Nain, "The Structure of the Media Industry," p. 137.

71. Mustafa K. Anuar, "Defining Democratic Discourses—The Mainstream Press," Francis Loh Kok Wah and Khoo Boo Teik (eds.), *Democracy in Malaysia,* p. 163.

72. Burnama, "Malaysiakini Seeking Opposition Support to Clear Name, Says Zainuddin," *Southeast Asia Press Alliance,* 13 February 2001, available from www.seapabkk.org.

73. SEAPA, "A New Malaysian Blogger Targeted for Policing," 22 March 2005, available from www.seapabkk.org.

74. Atkins, "Obstacles to Openness," p. 270.

75. Ibid., p. 265.

76. Ibid., p. 270.

77. Kavi Chongkittavorn, "Thailand—A Troubled Path to a Hopeful Future," Williams and Rich (eds.), *Losing Control,* p. 220.

78. Amando Doronila, "Preface—Press Freedom in Asia: An Uneven Terrain," Williams and Rich (eds.), *Losing Control,* pp. xiv–xv.

79. Damien Kingsbury, "Constraints on Reporting Australia's Near Neighbours," Kingsbury, Loo, and Payne (eds.), *Foreign Devils,* p. 28.

80. Quoted in Wong, "Malaysia," p. 115.

81. See Lin Neumann, "No FEER, No Favour," *The Standard* (Hong Kong), 31 October 2004.

82. Hamilton, "Japan," p. 101.

83. Basuki, "Indonesia," p. 103.

84. Ibid.

85. Lam, "China," p. 41.

86. See Naunidhi Kaur, "Tehelka Trials," *Frontline* 19, no. 14 (6–19 July 2002), available from www.flonnet.com/fl1914/19141200.htm.

87. Rebecca MacKinnon, "The World-Wide Conversation: Online Participatory Media and International News," *Working Papers Series* (Cambridge: The Joan Shorenstein Center, Harvard, 2004), available from www.ksg.harvard.edu/presspol/Research_Publications/Papers/Working_Papers/2004_2.pdf.

88. Daniel W. Drezner and Henry Farell, "Web of Influence," *Foreign Policy,* November/December 2004, p. 37.

89. OpenNet Initiative, "Internet Filtering in China in 2004–5: A Country Study," p. 46, available from www.opennetinitiative.net/modules.php?op=mod-load&name=Archive&file=index&req=viewarticle&artid=1.

90. Ibid.

91. Nicholas D. Kristof, "Death by a Thousand Blogs," *New York Times*, 24 May 2005.

92. Quoted in John Lent, "The Mass Media in Asia," p. 166.

93. Larry Teo, "Taiwan: Talk Show Hosts Help Make or Break Campaign," *Straights Times*, 11 March 2004, reproduced in www.asiamedia.ucla.edu/print.asp?parentid=8784.

94. Ambrose Leung, Benjamin Wong, and Gary Cheung, "Hong Kong: A Second Popular Radio Host Goes off the Air," *South China Morning Post,* 14 May 2004, reproduced in www.asiamedia.ucla.edu/print.asp?parentid=11126.

# 8

# Changing Political Culture

"Asian values also were increasingly summoned in aid in recent years
as a sort of all-purpose justification for whatever Asian governments
were doing or wishing to do. Old men who wanted to stay in power,
old networks of corruption intent on survival, old regimes that feared the
verdict of the ballot box could pull down the curtain between East and
West and claim whatever they were doing was blessed by an ancient
culture and legitimized by the inscrutable riddles of the East."
—Christopher Patten, *East and West*[1]

In previous chapters, a common explanatory variable emerging as a key factor
influencing the consolidation of democracy has been political culture. In relation to institutional crafting, I noted that an engaged electorate will probably
make even poorly designed systems work, while an apathetic electorate will
not make the most ingenious design achieve its intended results. In relation to
establishing the rule of law, the sad reality is that so many Asians see the law
as an instrument of taxation, conscription, and exploitation, not as a protector,
a fair means to resolve disputes, and a guarantor of rights. In relation to politicians and their political parties, the style and substance of political actors are
shaped by the popular environment in which they practice their craft. In conducting the public conversation, the fundamental requirement is broad and
unscripted participation. More generally, in relation to the concept of democratic consolidation itself, we need to look for conduct that is "reliably known,
regularly practiced, and voluntarily accepted by . . . politicians and citizens."[2]

This brings the discussion to the difficult question of political culture,
which, in the Asian context, requires an examination of issues such as political behavior, Confucianism, and "Asian Values." The key question being
addressed in this chapter is whether the political cultures of the emerging
democracies of Pacific Asia lend themselves to the consolidation of democracy. And if some aspects of that culture are antithetical to democratic practice, can they be changed? Before coming to these questions, we must tackle a preliminary question—How can we gauge political culture?

Returning to Diamond's definition of political culture as "a people's predominant beliefs, attitudes, values, ideals, sentiments, and evaluations about the political system of the country and the role of the self in that system,"[3] it becomes clear that this is not a topic that can be tackled, as in previous chapters, by describing institutions and assessing their effectiveness. Sentiments may be hard to isolate, values may be difficult to articulate, and attitudes may shift and change. It can be difficult to formulate generalities, but it is unhelpful to produce endless lists of particularities. There will be no rule without its exceptions, yet those exceptions may be so broad as to throw doubt on the rule rather than to prove it. There are certain tests we might be able to apply. One is to fall back on the helpful question of who benefits from a particular social construct or characterization. We need to be particularly wary of self-serving theories. Another danger we face in this field is falling to the temptations of orientalism and ascribing to Asian peoples irrational behavioral patterns simply because they are "not like us." There is a related danger of seeing Asians as "just like us" and thus forgetting centuries of distinctive socialization.

### Opinion Polling

A tempting methodology to employ is the opinion poll, particularly in view of the large-scale polling being conducted around the world, including in recent years in Asia. The increasing depth and breadth of polling, and the growing sophistication of the questioning process, allow for a result that may be useful to analysts. Polling has particular merit where the question is toward the specific and the factual rather than about general sentiments. Polling results are most useful when they are taken in societies that have become accustomed to opinion polling through decades of use. And opinion poll results can be helpful to track change when they are part of a longitudinal series of polls taken in the same societies over many years. But where specificity is blurred, where societies are not familiar with polling practices, and where there are insufficient previous results with which to track changes, doubts arise about the value one can derive from a poll. The most recent polling of Asian countries to appear on my desk is the AsiaBarometer Survey of 2003.[4] It contains the results of surveys of city dwellers conducted in ten Asian countries. Examining its results on trust in institutions leads to some curious conclusions (see Table 8.1).

The survey tells us a number of quite interesting things about attitudes at the time of polling:

- Chinese urbanites trust their legal system less than their other major institutions.
- Indian city dwellers are more wary of their parliament than of their army.

**Table 8.1    AsiaBarometer 2003 Survey on Trust in Institutions**

| Country | Trust in Institution (%) | | | |
| --- | --- | --- | --- | --- |
|  | Central Government | The Army | Legal System | Parliament |
| China | 91 | 91 | 76 | 85 |
| India | 78 | 97 | 75 | 70 |
| Japan | 18 | 36 | 36 | 12 |
| South Korea | 22 | 43 | 43 | 11 |
| Malaysia | 91 | 84 | 84 | 89 |
| Thailand | 86 | 67 | 67 | 70 |

*Source:* Takashi Inoguchi et al., *Values and Life Styles in Urban Asia—A Cross-Cultural Analysis and Sourcebook Based on the AsiaBarometer Survey of 2003* (Tokyo: The University of Tokyo and Mexico: Institute of Oriental Culture, 2005), pp. 359–361.

- Malaysians in the urban centers are a very trusting group.
- Thai city dwellers have doubts about their army, their legal system, and their parliament.
- Japanese and Koreans are a skeptical lot with great doubts about their parliaments.

From a comparativist perspective, the figures tell us very little. One certainly could not make any value judgments about the worth of parliaments in the region based on this trust survey, for to do so would lead us to the absurd conclusion that the pliant parliament of Malaysia is eight times more trustworthy than its counterpart in Seoul with all its contestation and oversight of government. By the same token, Beijing's representative body would be seen as a ridiculous seven times more trustworthy than Tokyo's. Turning to the results on trust in governments, there seems to be a reverse correlation based on the degree of authoritarianism whereby the more democratic the government, the less it is trusted by the people. So perhaps the survey tells us something about the difficulty of gauging opinions in authoritarian settings and something about the skepticism that seems to have become the default setting in democracies. Aside from these rather modest conclusions, I don't believe opinion polling is at this stage a particularly useful instrument in a comparative understanding of Asian nations' political cultures.

## Expert Analysis

Having turned away from this numerical analysis, we are left to grapple with the pronouncements of experts and practitioners, and while these cannot be reduced to numbers, I believe they may nevertheless prove to be more enlightening. There can be no better place to begin than with the acute observations in Lucian Pye's *Asian Power and Politics*.[5] Pye dissects the countries of Pacific Asia anthropologically, linguistically, and socially, demonstrating vast erudition in breadth of knowledge and understanding. He looks at power flows and status relationships in both the Confucian and the Theravada Buddhist worlds. His focus shifts from kings and nobility to the practices of commoners in everyday life. He takes into account such formative elements as child-rearing, education of girls and boys, and the place of the father in the family. He looks at spiritual practices, perspectives on ancestor worship, and the organization of religious life. He examines the public space and the conduct practiced therein, including the factors that make the various societies rank such conduct from the laudable to the reprehensible. By reading Pye, a visitor to Pacific Asia will be better able to discern the underlying reasons for locals' approval or otherwise of foreign conduct that will be seen as either "refined" or "coarse." The visitor will start understanding where the locals "are coming from" and get a glimpse of how they see the world. Pye was one of the pioneers in placing Asian culture on the political map and thus providing us with a key to an understanding of Asian politics.

Pye's authority is such that when he concludes that the prospects for democracy in Pacific Asia are "not good," we need to sit up and take notice.[6] He builds his conclusion on a number of solid arguments. Politics in this part of the world mimics family relationships, and the key aspect of that relationship is the dominance of the father figure, who has vast power and authority and who dispenses these for the benefit of his family. The family analogy puts Asian peoples in an infantile or at best a juvenile category. It also establishes the dominant leadership style as one of paternalism, a term that does not have the same stigma in the East as in the West. Flowing from their various cultures and histories, countries of Pacific Asia have imbued leadership with spiritual and moral qualities that have elevated these leaders, dynastic or otherwise, above the realm of public criticism. Public criticism itself is seen as unseemly and coarse. Finally, leadership is not seen in terms of determining public policy, but rather, the main purpose of that leadership is maintaining society in its current balance. This results, according to Pye, in the leaders' devotion to ritual far more than to the affairs of state. An echo of this can even be seen today in the labyrinthine complexity of ritualized life of the Japanese Imperial Household.

Another significant figure in the study of Southeast Asia, Niels Mulder, comes to a not dissimilar conclusion.[7] He argues that Southeast Asians tend to see society in dichotomous terms. Ordinary individuals belong to the realm of family and village life, while the leaders living in the center form part of a different world. Kings, generals, and bureaucrats live in the public world, which is seen as a stage on which they perform their power plays and intrigues. Ordinary people understand their role as inconspicuous viewers peeping through the foliage at the distant stage. No involvement from the audience is permitted unless required from the stage. One of the consequences, according to Mulder, is that the bulk of the population, and even the majority of the middle class, is "without a tradition of critical thinking about and participation in the public world."[8] Mulder depressingly concludes that the conjunction of this traditional role with modern consumer lifestyle creates "a culture of cynicism and indifference regarding the 'public' world of politics."[9]

According to Pye and Mulder, Asian societies are not well-suited to the practice of democracy, which requires an underlying presumption of broad egalitarianism, expressed through equal voting rights and a certain openness and participation in the practices of public life, such as contributing to the public conversation. But expert opinion is divided on this point. Some authors see a Pacific Asian model of democracy emerging. For Francis Fukuyama, the success of democracy in Pacific Asia is a justification of the theory of the impact of modernization on societies transcending the hold of those societies' cultures.[10] Peter Preston argues that an elite-led version of representative democracy is developing in Pacific Asia, based on indigenous traditions blended with introduced ideas and delivered through fairly standardized democratic institutional architecture.[11] Steve Chan sees the democratic transition in East Asia as a form of politics "catching up" with the economic reforms that have taken root in these countries.[12] Cal Clark takes note of Pye's cultural dimensions of authority, but concludes his essay with the observation that "many Asian countries have found a way to reconcile active democratic politics with their own social and political institutions."[13]

Expert opinion is inevitably divided and therefore provides no more certainty than opinion polling, but it does open some interesting lines of inquiry. Weight needs to be given to the impact of Asian cultural norms, which self-evidently continue to shape their societies in distinct ways. At the same time, the objective reality of the growing democratization of Pacific Asian societies cannot be ignored. How can these apparently conflicting processes be reconciled?

## Path Dependence or Self-Determination?

A good definition of this concept is, "path-dependence exists when the outcome of a process depends on its past history, on the entire sequence of decisions made by agents and resulting outcomes, and not just on contemporary conditions." Countries cannot change their histories, which have put them on a specific and unique path. It is because of this path dependency that the factors raised by observers like Pye and Mulder become so important. When applied to technology, path dependency can be demonstrated in the way certain inventions lock in future technologies. I am typing on a QWERTY keyboard because this was the layout suitable for manual type-writers a century ago. The layout was initially alphabetic but the inventor, Christopher Scholes, decided to introduce variations, including placing commonly used pairs of letters, such as *sh, ck, th,* and *pr,* on alternating sides of the keyboard to reduce jamming of the manual typewriter's swing-arms. By the time the more-efficient Dvorak keyboard design came along, typists had learned to touch type on QWERTY, and the costs and effort of retraining and coordination made it impossible in practice to switch away from the inefficient existing keyboard. Path dependence had locked key-board technology on a path that becomes harder to leave with the initiation of each additional user into QWERTY's mysteries.

### Negotiability of Political Culture

Does path dependency work the same way in relation to social organiza-tion? Is Pacific Asia so bounded by its paternalism and its public/private bifurcation that it is locked on a path that cannot lead to democracy? To begin to answer this question, we need to recall, as does Pye, that all politi-cal cultures are mixed.[14] Aat Vervoorn reminds us that in searching for the differences between various cultures, there is a tendency to minimize the reality that there is a broad pattern of variations *within* a particular culture.[15] Different facets of a culture may either facilitate or impede the adoption of a certain course of action. The hold of village traditions may impede certain aspects of modernization, while traditional respect for scholarship may facilitate change. What the tradition is, how it is interpreted, and what weight to give to competing traditions are subject to human intervention. That intervention may privilege one aspect of political culture and down-play another. The intervention itself, in the form of argument, debate, and deliberation, is also shaped by the political culture, and so one should not expect that the deliberative processes of one society will mirror those of another.

A society's political culture therefore has an important element of nego-tiability. Pye is careful not to overstate the imprint that political culture will have on a society's future choices when he notes that "culture is unquestion-ably significant, in some undetermined degree, in shaping the aspirations and fears, the preferences and prejudices, the priorities and expectations of a people as they confront the challenges of political and social change."[16] The degree of influence of political culture is undetermined because of the element of negotiability. Negotiability is available because of a second fea-ture of political culture: its capacity for change. One of the disservices, amidst the bringing of much enlightenment, which early anthropology per-formed, was to instill in its students a notion of timeless traditional societies. Unlike the growing and evolving societies from which they came, the societies under study by the anthropologists were seen as static and unchanging. This was put in a positive light in that they were described as in balance with their environment and in keeping with their social forces. But it was nevertheless wrong. The anthropologists simply did not stay long enough to witness the inevitable changes that all societies must undergo. More recent anthropology has begun to see culture less in terms of bounded traditions and more as an ongoing practice in a dynamic process.[17] Jared Diamond points out that the motor driving change is primarily the natural environment.[18] Changing environments have tended to push peoples from nomadic to sedentary lives, from village to urban existence, from pastoral to industrial modes of production, and from local to global ways of thinking. Changes impact on all groups in all civilizations, though the degree and speed of change will differ, as will the responses to various change stimuli. Political culture will therefore change along with the lifestyle changes and the changes in social outlook.

Pye argues that people cling to their cultural ways and that "cultural change therefore involves true trauma."[19] I agree that this can often be the case, but I believe that the converse proposition, that trauma usually brings about cultural change, tells us something more fundamental about the process of social and political change. The trauma may be environmentally induced or it may be the result of human intervention. In relation to the changing political culture of Pacific Asia in modern history, one might list the major traumatic events as colonialism, World War II, the Cold War, and the 1997 financial crisis. Each traumatic event brought forward myriad responses that led to changes in behavior and attitude in a process of accretion leading to the crystallization of new elements in political culture. The new elements may blend in syncretically with the old elements of political culture, supplant them, or modify them. Thinking about the individual as a member of a nation may be a new element of political culture, but it need not supplant traditional self-identification as a member of a family. Thinking of oneself as an equal member of that nation regardless of gender, religion, or caste, on the other hand, may well supplant traditional patriarchal, theocratic, or hierarchical modes of thinking.

### On the Road to Mandalay

The new ways of thinking may emerge from traumatic situations or simply from contact with foreign ideas. The vector for foreign ideas may be the merchant, the soldier, or the diplomat. I had occasion to see the process at work. Diplomats stand between two nations and often between two cultures. They represent their home nations in their countries of accreditation, and more often than not, they also informally act on behalf of their hosts. The diplomat is in the privileged position of understanding both sides of any discussion including some of the unarticulated premises on which arguments are based. The diplomat also knows how to get a message across, at times having to transcend cultural reticence and national ideas of politesse. Representing your own nation is what you are paid to do, but when you take on the responsibility of helping out your hosts, difficulties and dilemmas can arise. I faced such a difficulty when acting for the Australian aid program in Burma in the early 1980s.

The story begins with the Vietnamese invasion of Cambodia in 1978. Regardless of what actually motivated Hanoi's actions, perhaps the correct reaction should have been to cheer heartily that the Vietnamese army had done what so many people around the world were calling for—overthrowing the genocidal Khmer Rouge regime. But the reaction from the ASEAN countries in a very frosty period of the Cold War was to punish Vietnam. Australia went along with its ASEAN partners and suspended its aid program to Vietnam. One of the projects that had been planned was the construction of a milk plant in Vietnam, for which a great deal of equipment had already been purchased. This equipment was now lying in a warehouse in Australia and the auditor-general was complaining about the waste of taxpayers' money. So the Australian aid agency decided to look for a new recipient, and it turned out to be Burma. Turning this decision into reality was the job of the Australian embassy in Rangoon, and the ambassador passed the file to me, his deputy.

Dealing with the Australian end of things was pretty straightforward. There were forms, timetables, and milestones to be filled, followed, and passed. There were bureaucrats who needed to put ticks in the correct boxes, commercial advisers who needed to be shepherded through the Burmese maze, and the occasional politician who wished to make a self-congratulatory speech. Dealing with the Burmese side was more difficult. There were three sets of people to deal with. At the level of the central government were the people from the Foreign Ministry and the Foreign Economic Relations Department of the Finance Ministry. Because this was grant aid rather than a soft loan and because Australia and Burma were currently sharing a period of friendly relations, these dealings were arduous but not particularly problematic.

One level down was the Ministry for Cooperatives that would be the implementing agency for the project. Under the Ne Win regime, as under current practice, most of the ministers were former military officers, and this ministry was no exception. The minister was a former artillery officer, and he liked nothing better than to take a screwdriver to machines and see just how they worked. UNICEF would eventually learn about the colonel's inclination very much to their cost. In those days, the early 1980s, computers did not sit on laps or in the palm of one's hand; they each filled a room.

They were called mainframes and the colonel wanted one. He was a great believer in the power of machinery to deliver economic development, and a computer was the latest word in machinery. So UNICEF devised a project that would deliver a mainframe to a specially designed air-conditioned room that the colonel had built next to his office. The mainframe was eventually delivered, installed, and tested to everybody's satisfaction, and the Rangoon UNICEF office gave a collective sigh of satisfaction. What they didn't know was that on the very evening of its installation, the colonel stayed late and when everyone else had left the floor, he went into the air-conditioned room next to his office . . . with his screwdriver. He wanted to know how the pistons and coils worked this new machine. I guess at a certain point in the evening the colonel must have realized the enormity of the damage he had caused and so he simply stuffed all the wires and little bits he had been tinkering with back in the mainframe and screwed the panel back in place. The upshot of this episode was total silence. No one ever reported the machine broken, ministry staff went off to Singapore for their training on its use, and the UNICEF staff were somehow kept at bay. Ne Win had probably never heard of a computer, but the colonel did not want to risk the "old man's" wrath if he learned that a machine then worth $100,000 had been sabotaged by aggressive curiosity.

Casting my mind back to my first call on the colonel, I recall the dusty entrance, the garish red betel nut expectoration stains on the wall, the dark corridors, the steps in brutal concrete, and a gleaming white air-conditioned office housing a shiny mainframe standing proudly to attention. The colonel ushered me in, waved away my congratulatory comments on having such state-of-the-art technology, and started asking me questions about what sort of equipment we wished to bring to the project. What I remember best from this initial conversation was the colonel's categorization of milk drinkers into three types: those who drink milk cold, those who drink milk hot, and those who do not drink milk at all. "The Burmese fit into the last category," he explained. This was the first, but by no means the last, wrinkle in the project that the embassy would be expected to iron out. This particular problem was partially resolved by the colonel's promise that he would ensure that the army would buy sweetened condensed milk from the plant for soldiers' rations. Later, I would be more reassured by the fact that Burma had many Indian tea houses that served gallons of milky sweet tea a natural market for the project.

The final group of people involved on the Burmese side consisted of the members of the Mandalay Cooperatives organization. These ranged from the head of the office and his staff, to all the villagers who owned or wanted to own dairy cows and who would be looking to the milk plant to buy their produce. The project was really about them. Mandalay Province could sustain many dairy cows and here was a new source of income for the villagers and nutrition for their children. I came to know some of the Mandalay people well, and it was my respect and affection for them that pushed me ever harder to make the project work.

I will not expose all my scars from this ill-fated project but concentrate my recollections on the site chosen for the milk plant. The local leaders had designated a field 10 kilometers from Mandalay as the site, and when I visited it I was struck by its beauty. The field rolled down gently from the road with wildflowers peeking through the grass and giant water buffalo wandering by, dutifully obeying the instructions of the little boys accompanying them. Near the road were two enormous trees with expansive branches and pendulous red fruit hanging down. Under the trees, villagers sheltered from the sun while taking a break from their toils. Placing a huge metal "box" in the middle of this bucolic idyll seemed a bit incongruous, but progress is progress. The Australian engineers went to work, and a couple of months later they arrived in Burma with a plan of the plant on the chosen site. I don't think the exchange that occurred in our subsequent meeting could be described as a blazing row, but I made it clear that chopping down the two trees to make way for the plant was unacceptable. On our visit to Mandalay, I continued the campaign to save the trees. The Mandalay people were surprised to witness the Australians squabbling this way, and they were reluctant to "take sides," even though it was about their land. But I did manage to elicit from them the fact that these *let-pan bin* trees were much liked by the local people for the shelter they offered and for the sour curry made from the fruit. Emboldened, I accused the engineers of lazily wanting to clear the site for their convenience, but they argued that they were simply following normal practice in taking the highest ground on the site. To their credit, the engineers agreed to undertake further research. They found records going back to colonial times of rainfall and flooding in the area and they concluded that only the highest land on the site, where the two trees now stood, could withstand a "once in a century" flood.

I was beaten. The two trees had stood for hundreds of years. They are called red silk-cotton trees in English, and their botanical name is *Bombax heptaphyllum*. They must have seen a lot of Mandalay's history unfold below them. They must have sustained generations of Burmese villagers. But now they came down and made way for the Australian milk plant. I left the post long before the milk plant was finished, but I subsequently heard that it never met its economic projections and that it never reached anything like peak capacity. I also heard that it was later privatized and purchased by Nestlé Thailand, which proceeded to mothball the plant to ensure it would not compete with its Thai operations. So on that road to Mandalay, in place of the two ancient and revered trees, there is an ugly and useless monument to modernity.

Three years in Burma flew by and the day came when the posting was finished. This is a frantic time of hand-over briefing, packing, and farewell partying. However well one plans the process, the final day is inevitably one of chaos and confusion. It was already clear that we had neglected a critical law of travel—the smaller the baby, the more hand luggage will be needed! We were already well beyond the most generous airline baggage limits. In the midst of this chaos came a rap on the door. With an airplane to catch that afternoon and already catastrophically over the weight limits, a Burmese well-wisher had decided to send us a farewell gift. The problem was that the gift came in a crate the size of a desk and it was almost as heavy. When we pried open the crate, I felt the tears welling in my eyes. It was a large oil painting in heavy teak frame. The subject—the two magnificent *let-pan bin* trees from the field in Mandalay. Upon learning of the final decision that they would be cut down, the Mandalay Cooperatives people commissioned an artist to sit down and paint the scene as a farewell gift to me.

The story has an epilogue. I had some contact with a couple of the Australian contractors working on this project in subsequent years. They had much enjoyed their stints in Mandalay and had formed close relations of friendship and collegiality with the local cooperatives leaders. One point they noticed was that unlike many Asian rural people they had been in contact with, after having witnessed the ugly debate over the site of the milk plant, the Burmese interlocutors had become far more assertive in asking questions and seeking answers on all aspects of the project. So perhaps the two trees are gone, but a slight change in the political culture of a small group of people in Mandalay remains.

### Change Is the Norm, Stasis Is Not

A people cannot change the path on which they have traveled, but they can decide on the path they will take in future, even though the process of change can be a slow one and hindered by the static rituals to which some societies cling. They are path dependent only insofar as they have built up a set of common experiences and mores on which to base future decisions. Path dependence is therefore not deterministic, but it is influential in shaping political culture. Ultimately, all peoples retain a right of self-determination. This is true in terms of strict human rights law as articulated in common Article 1 of the two major human rights covenants.[20] It is also true in the practical sense that decisions are taken by choosing between options. The choice may be constrained by social attitudes and societal mores, but it remains a choice. The peoples of Pacific Asia may be familiar and even comfortable with systems based on paternalism and patriarchy but it remains open for them to choose to embark on a new course such as the difficult path of building their democracies.

A final point about the process of change is that its source need not be indigenous. The seed needs to take root in local soil, but the seed may well be from outside the locality. This can readily be seen in the spread of grains, spices, and intoxicants around the world. It can be seen in the borrowing of appropriate technology by one society from another. It is true also of concepts in science, mathematics, and writing scripts. If not for the spread of such ideas between countries, cultures, and civilizations, Italians would still be using Roman numerals, would not be smoking, and would have never tasted spaghetti. Instead they have Arabic numerals, the zero from India, tobacco from the Americas, and noodles from China. If this is true of food, technology, and science, why should it not be true of concepts in governance? The test is whether it is a good idea, not whether it is indigenous.

## The Emergence of Asian Civil Society

### Volcanic Explosions

Pye's book was published in 1985 and is based on research conducted over the preceding decade. He studied an Asia that had emerged from colonialism but remained caught in the rigidities of the Cold War. He studied an Asia that was in the early stage of embarking on its "economic miracle." He studied an Asia in transformation from the rural norm to the era of megacities. Pye would have been well aware of the Kwangju uprising in 1980 that saw student protest against the imposition of martial law in South Korea turn into a mass uprising calling for democracy, but it is understandable that he might have discounted the significance of that event as a harbinger of popular assertiveness stirring in the whole of Pacific Asia. After all, the incident occurred in Kim Dae Jung's home region and may have been seen as a local reaction to the discriminatory policies of the central authorities. And, of course, the uprising was brutally repressed, thus maintaining the impression of invincible authoritarianism in Asia. But no sooner was his book published than the next explosion of popular sentiment took place in Manila in 1986 in the form of the EDSA "people power" demonstration that chased away President Marcos. Next came the June Uprising in Seoul in 1987 demonstrating civil society could challenge the state.[21] The incidents of popular demand for democracy continued in Tiananmen Square in Beijing (1989), on the streets of Rangoon (1990), in Sanam Luang in the heart of old Bangkok (1992), at Trisakti University in Jakarta under the banner of *reformasi* (1998), and in Dataran Merdeka in Kuala Lumpur in support of Anwar Ibrahim (1998). Some of these protest movements found immediate success, some did not. But just as the demands of the Kwangju uprising were eventually and spectacularly realized almost two decades later in the election of Kim Dae Jung, so may the other "unsuccessful" movements eventually bear fruit.

If Asians are pliant people accepting of paternalistic authority, what are they doing in the streets demanding change? If they see leaders as inhabiting a theater world in which ordinary people are mere spectators, then why are they clambering onto the stage and trying to replace the actors? Kwangju, Manila, Seoul, Beijing, Rangoon, Bangkok, Jakarta, and Kuala Lumpur seem to be telling a powerful story about popular demand for democracy. But we need to take care in generalizing conclusions based on such events. After all, these are the explosions in society, not the mundane realities. Perhaps these explosions are only indicative of people having reached their limits of tolerance of authoritarianism and are therefore insufficient pieces of evidence in favor of a popular will for democracy. We need evidence of Asian peoples working for democracy, not just protesting against tyrants. We need to look beyond the volcanic explosions to determine the extent of the bubbling lava hidden within. We need to search for Pacific Asian civil society.

### Bubbling Lava

Civil society is essential to democracy in many ways. In discussion of civil society, I will adopt Larry Diamond's definition: "Civil society is the realm of organized social life that is open, voluntary, self-generating, at least partially self-supporting, autonomous from the state, and bound by a legal order or a set of shared values."[22] Robert Post and Nancy Rosenblum identify three overarching roles played by civil society in a democracy.[23] It serves as a center for collective resistance against authoritarian or unconstitutional government, and, as Hannah Arendt argued, the absence of associational activity prepares the ground for totalitarianism.[24] It also serves as a means of recruiting individuals into the practice of democracy through the process of advocacy for various causes and social movements. Finally, civil society performs an important function in socialization of the political values at the heart of democracy by building social capital based on relationships of trust and by inculcating civility in the pursuit of social goals. Civil society is a Western construct, and the symbiotic relationship between democracy and civil society is deep and long-standing. At a certain point in their evolution, they began to act as mutually reinforcing mechanisms. The concept of civil society traced its origins to the associations of merchants in towns in medieval Europe outside the bounds of feudal and ecclesiastic structures.[25] The interplay between the two processes was subtle and steeped in the intricacies of Europe's old world history, perhaps explaining why the relationship was most boldly asserted by an old world visitor to the new world. Robert Putnam reminds us that Alexis de Tocqueville, when he visited the

United States in the 1830s, was most impressed with the vibrancy of the country's associational life, which Tocqueville saw as a key reason for the strength of US democracy.[26]

Asian societies are supposed to be family focused, ascriptively organized according to status groups, and dominated by the center. This is infertile soil for the growth of the foreign seed of associational enthusiasm, which is based on voluntarism, not ascription; equality, not fixed hierarchy; and most often requires the pursuit of new social or policy goals, not existing state goals. It should follow from the alien historical roots of civil society in European political culture that Asian societies would not take to the NGO phenomenon with much enthusiasm. In fact, the reality is quite the opposite. Where the people of Asian societies are free to associate on a voluntary and consensual basis, they have done so with great energy. Table 8.2 provides a broad guide to the size of the not-for-profit sector in seven countries of Pacific Asia, all of which have a population of over 20 million.

The growth of this realm of organized social life is recent. From uncertain beginnings in the period when the development state was venerated for having achieved high growth rates, NGOs quite suddenly became the darlings of the international donor community, who saw in them a means of bypassing corrupt bureaucrats and reaching disadvantaged people by investing in the dedication and efficiency of the membership of the NGO movement. Barnett Baron of the Asia Foundation traces the change in emphasis among donors toward NGOs as dating only from the late 1980s.[27] It gained impetus after the 1997 financial crisis with the further loss of confidence in Pacific Asian states' capacity to continue central control over the direction of economic and social activity. NGOs are now an established part of the

**Table 8.2    Size of the Third Sector in Pacific Asia, 2000**

| Country | Number of Nongovernmental Organizations (NGOs) | Comment |
|---|---|---|
| Indonesia | 190,000 | Includes NGOs, cooperative groups, and farmer groups |
| Japan | 70,000 | 1997 figure, does not include 180,000 religious groups |
| South Korea | 60,000 | 1998 figure, of which 11,000 are registered |
| Malaysia | 30,000 | 1999 figure, half of which are religious societies |
| Philippines | 96,000 | Upper estimate, does not include 35,000 cooperatives |
| Taiwan | 13,000 | 1997 figure |
| Thailand | 18,000 | Estimate |

*Source:* Derived from data in Asia Pacific Philanthropy Information Network, *Philanthropy and the Third Sector in Asia and the Pacific,* available from www.asianphilanthropy.org/index. html, which is based on the International Classification of Non-profit Organisation (ICNPO), developed by the Comparative Nonprofit Sector Project, and coordinated with the Centre for Civil Society Studies, Johns Hopkins University, Baltimore.

Official Development Assistance (ODA) process in both donor and recipient countries as generators of funds, deliverers of aid, and participants in the decisionmaking and oversight process. The extent of donor country NGO involvement can be appreciated when one considers that in 2003 the amount of grant aid spent by NGOs in developing countries outside the ODA process came to over $10 billion.[28] The main role therefore earmarked for NGOs in this process was that of aid deliverer. But it did not take long before the deliverers were also engaging in advocacy in support of aid effectiveness. This mirrors both a distinction and a convergence in the civil society sector, where NGOs may undertake charitable and development work, or advocacy and cause-oriented work, and often a combination of both. It did not take long for Asian NGOs to follow the example of their Western counterparts and involve themselves in the public life of their nations and participate in its public conversation in the field of development assistance and well beyond, going to the very heart of democratic politics.

## Country Case Studies

*South Korea.* Perhaps the country in Pacific Asia where NGOs have developed the most political punch is in South Korea. Because the emergence of civil society had its roots in the antiauthoritarian activism of the 1960s and 1970s and in the democracy movement of the 1980s,[29] leading South Korean NGOs quickly gravitated to the political debate, with the Citizens' Coalition for Economic Justice (CCEJ) and the People's Solidarity for Participatory Democracy (PSPD) particularly prominent among them. Before long, the issue of corruption became the driving force behind their activism, and it manifested itself in a remarkable manner in 2000 when a coalition of 450 NGOs formed the Citizens' Alliance for the 2000 General Elections (CAGE).[30] The method employed by CAGE was to blacklist candidates it considered unfit for office, invariably because of issues of probity. The list included candidates from all the major political parties and covered sitting members, including some quite prominent figures. The CAGE blacklist began to have its effects even before the elections as, of the 113 on the original list, 11 did not seek nomination and 48 failed to gain the endorsement of their party.[31] CAGE then blacklisted 86 candidates, including 22 "most problematic" cases, of which 59, including 15 on the list of 22, were not elected.[32] CAGE repeated the exercise for the 2004 legislative elections, with 1,053 NGOs participating, and saw 59 of the 87 blacklisted candidates fail to gain election.[33] The figures appear quite striking but some caveats need to be added. Analysis of the results demonstrated that regionalism remained the major issue shaping the election results, as has traditionally been the case in South Korea. Furthermore, the blacklist campaign also did not translate into greater voter participation.[34] But the CAGE initiative did demonstrate the ability of civil society to coordinate positions and gain a voice on the political stage. Surely a politician would rather not be on this list. When I visited the head office of PSPD, the leading NGO in CAGE, in 2002, I was not surprised to see a parliamentarian paying a courtesy call on the organization and working the room. This, I was told, was now common practice among those wishing to stay off the dreaded blacklist.

*Japan.* The evolution of civil society in Japan followed a different course from that in South Korea. Keiko Hirata explains that the emergence of civil society in Japan is also a recent phenomenon and that it has found the greatest expression through the Japanese development assistance program.[35] According to this analysis, a combination of the stranglehold over all aspects of social policy by the bureaucracy in Japan's postwar development state and the Confucian social mores to seek consensus meant that NGOs were few in number and were in effect excluded from Japan's decisionmaking "iron triangle" of bureaucracy, business, and the LDP. The loss of credibility of the Japanese development state through globalization, corruption scandals, and weak economic performance opened the way for new forces to emerge on the policy stage. These initially concentrated their efforts on local environment issues and the anti–Vietnam War cause. Hirata argues that the Indochina refugee crisis of the 1970s sensitized community groups to involve themselves in relief efforts, which in turn led to involvement in development efforts in Southeast Asia.[36] There followed a slow eclipse in ODA priorities away from infrastructure projects toward more "soft aid" projects, which NGOs were in a better position to deliver than large corporations. Given the fact that the size of Japan's aid program is matched only by that of the United States, there was considerable scope for NGO activism. The twist in the process is that this level of NGO activism is now having an effect on Japanese democracy by bringing the citizenry into the political process to seek policy outcomes. I was able to witness this process when I was invited to participate in a conference in 2002 at the Japanese Diet to look at ways in which Japan might involve itself in democracy promotion efforts. The striking aspect of the conference was the prominence of the NGO voice either directly or through sympathetic members of the Diet. Having arrived on the Japanese policy scene, it is clear that the Japanese NGO community has no intention of letting go.

*The Philippines.* Mulder believes that "the Philippines may easily count the most NGOs per head of population in the world, and they are spread out all over the country."[37] The associational spirit is alive and strong in the Philippines, and wherever one goes in the archipelago there are welfare groups, church groups, business groups, Rotary Clubs, cause-oriented groups, and village associations to be found. The Philippine Constitution expressly recognizes the role of NGOs in the community.[38]

As is so often the case, the Philippines provides examples of both best and worst practice in this field. Worst practice is in the tendency to fissiparousness. Each of these organizations tends to follow legalistic patterns, including general assemblies and election of officers. There is invariably an electoral contest for these positions, often fought hard and passionately with rhetoric and campaign promises wielded by the contestants. So far so good. The problems begin when one of the candidates is declared as winner. What next happens all too often is a refusal to accept the outcome by the defeated candidate. Appeals and calls for a revote will often tie the organization in knots, and when the appellant fails, a common step is to gather one's supporters and form a new organization. This may be one reason why there are so many NGOs.

Best practice is to be found in the national legal regime for not-for-profit civil society organizations in the Philippines. They enjoy both tax exemption and donation tax deductibility. Most important, the sector has achieved a status within the government of self-regulation to certify those that may benefit from this tax advantage. To achieve this result in 1999, six of the country's largest national NGO networks[39] organized the Philippine Council for NGO Certification, or PCNC.[40] PCNC draws its legal authority from its agreement with the Department of Finance to undertake the certification role, and it has now expanded its goal to promoting professionalism, accountability, and transparency within the NGO movement.

*Indonesia.* I saw the evolution of Indonesian civil society over the course of a tumultuous decade. In the Suharto years it was difficult and dangerous to be a member of an NGO. Nongovernmental organizations were seen as antigovernment organizations and treated accordingly. The relationship was epitomized in the 1993 torture and murder of Marsinah, a dedicated young woman organizing labor unions in East Java. The military authorities were clearly responsible, but the system decided to charge her employers with the crime. It took another dedicated NGO, Lembaga Bantuan Hukum (LBH, Legal Aid Institute), to take up the case and produce evidence of the local military's role for the truth to emerge.[41] NGOs like LBH operated under considerable threat. One of their tactics was to associate themselves with foreign NGOs as a means to mitigate that threat by leaving open the possibility that an attack on LBH or its members could involve foreigners and thus lead to international repercussions and criticism of Indonesia. As one NGO advocate put it, "turning to the developed countries is like borrowing their democracy in order to enable [local] people to air their aspirations."[42] In those days, local NGOs therefore saw considerable value in international collaboration.

With the fall of Suharto came an explosion of civil society activism. The number of new actors was both encouraging and bewildering. I could not keep up with all the new acronyms being generated, and I joked with my Indonesian friends that the only factor limiting this growth of NGOs was that there were only twenty-six letters in the alphabet. There was no need any longer for foreign NGOs to be active on the ground in order to provide "cover" for their Indonesian counterparts; what was now required was a program to pass on the skills needed for the successful operation of Indonesian civil society. CDI developed such a program in partnership with the peak body of Australian developmental NGOs, the Australian Council for International Development (ACFID), and we set about training Indonesian NGO leaders on issues of advocacy, organization, and management. The training was conducted in Australia over several weeks, with one week being devoted to assigning the Indonesians to individual Australian counterpart NGOs. As with all training programs, some of it worked well and other parts less well, but the feedback from all involved was positive and we were confident that the skills imparted would be spread to many more Indonesian activists through the multiplier effect that Indonesians like to call "socializing an idea."

A few years after this program had been initiated I popped into Jakarta to discuss its continuation. I met with various civil society interlocutors to discuss their needs and, especially in reading the body language and interpreting the polite but faint praise for the CDI/ACFID program, it slowly dawned on me that a wonderful thing had happened—we had become obsolete! The Indonesians didn't need us anymore. They had begun by "borrowing our democracy" in the difficult days of the New Order, then by learning from our experiences in the transition days they often called the "democrazy period," and finally, now that they were so busy playing their part in Indonesia's often chaotic deliberative debate, they had no time for us and no need for us, though cash contributions were always welcome.

## Challenges Facing Civil Society

There are therefore good grounds for optimism when considering the future of civil society in Pacific Asia. NGOs have established themselves deeply in each of the region's democracies and have thus formed a body of opinion and activism that will stand as a bulwark against any authoritarian temptations. But optimism should not mask criticism because deep problems remain. They remain in terms of the regulatory environment in which NGOs must operate, they remain in relation to funding and sustainability, and they remain with regard to the degree to which activist NGOs are representative of these societies' mass base.

*Regulatory Environment*

The Philippine system of self-regulation is not common practice in the region. Throughout the region, governments look for ways of exercising controls over the sector through registration and supervision of members and money. The instinct on the part of governments in the region is for civil society to require the state's permission. Baron concludes that "the net result is that throughout the region, the registration and supervision of NGOs and foundations is characterized by enormous scope for bureaucratic discretion."[43] This provides governments with a means of controlling their possible critics. And if we employ Robert Klitgaard's famous formula, C = M + D − A (Corruption equals Monopoly plus Discretion minus Accountability), it is clear that this situation also leaves open the strong possibility of corrupt abuses against NGOs.[44]

But the problems go beyond the formal regulatory environment and the relationship of civil society with the bureaucracy: they also encompass the vulnerability of civil society activists to reprisals from the other subjects of their criticisms. As Mulder puts it, "civil society activists need to be courageous people, because landowners, port authorities, industrial polluters, 'developers,' and illegal loggers often unleash rather uncivil means when they see their interests infringed upon."[45] This brings us back to the centrality of the rule of law to the functioning of a democratic society. The deliberative public conversation requires a system to protect free speech. Democratic societies must therefore develop the courage to confront their most powerful members. The means of doing so is primarily through journalists and NGO activists, and they in turn need to be protected by society and its laws if they are to perform their vital function.

*Funding and Sustainability*

The second major problem is money. Japanese NGOs can find an indirect form of subsidy through their involvement with the aid sector, but this is not open to the other countries of the region. Many NGOs require a direct form of subsidy from ODA funds. In Cambodia, US legislation precludes the aid program from direct cooperation with the government and so the program focuses largely on NGOs.[46] The program sustains a number of NGOs active in political advocacy and accountability. This small and courageous group of NGO leaders is a major source of policy contestability, deliberation, and oversight in a country where the leader's instinct is to rule by decree. Without foreign support, I doubt that the various Cambodian advocacy NGOs would survive. Cambodia may be an extreme example of the phenomenon of NGO aid dependence, but the problem exists to varying degrees among many of the developing countries of the region.

Ultimately, civil society must form a coherent part of the society as a whole and this requires that it be sustained by that society. A survey of philanthropy practices in the region found that charity is widely practiced throughout the region, but that NGOs received only about 25 percent of the charitable flow.[47] Until the flow of local funds to NGOs deepens, ODA will remain a major source of civil society funding. One problem that arises with foreign funding of civil society is its selectivity. Put simply, the Western donors tend to fund organizations with which they are comfortable and which stand above reproach or criticism in the lowest common denominator logic of closely watched public money. Accordingly, the civil society organizations that attract money look pretty much like civil society organizations in the West. They tend to have similar goals and attract similar people. They are either secular or perhaps Christian. Their politics tends to be liberal and humanitarian. None of this poses a problem. If there is a problem, it is in the exclusion of other parts of civil society from the bounty of the ODA table.

### Representativeness

This leads us to the third and most vexing problem in our survey of civil society in Pacific Asia—To what degree is civil society representative of the people as a whole? The concern is that the civil society organizations that foreign interlocutors speak to are merely a reflection of the views and interests of those foreigners. One view is that these organizations are elitist creatures with a tenuous relationship to the undereducated masses that have little comprehension of the programmatic goals of the civic action supposedly taken on their behalf.[48] This view situates the NGO leaders among the educated, often foreign educated, members of the middle class cut off from the rural masses and urban poor. There is clearly some truth in this characterization of Asian NGO leaders. I recall my meeting with the head of a women's organization in Jakarta established to assist poor and abused women. The president was a matronly woman who would probably have been offended at being described as middle class. She was dripping with gold jewelry and the diamond in her ring was so big that I feared it would burst out of its fragile golden claws. I wondered at the time whether "poor, abused women" would find it comfortable to confide in such a patrician figure. But when I looked around the office, I was reassured to see other women of various ages and ethnicities with whom clients might be more at ease. We therefore need to be careful not to turn characterizations into caricatures.

The records show many successful assemblies of the poor and peasants' rights organizations participating in the public debate, and at times obtaining some redress for their complaints. A strong example can be seen in the activism and success of Thailand's Assembly of the Poor, which was able to gain the ear of the then prime minister and tackle problems concerning water usage from the Pak Moon dam.[49] NGOs have been active on the issue of agrarian reform in the Philippines for many years, with mixed results.[50] The radical decentralization program in Indonesia "has provided the impetus for the growth of a public sphere at the local level."[51] An example cited in the literature concerns the Forum for a Prosperous Majalaya, a town near Bandung.[52] Its members represented the major town stakeholders, including workers, teachers, religious leaders, as well as hawkers and pedicab drivers, working together to address issues ranging from poor roads to community tensions. Civil society therefore defies facile descriptions as elitist or a middle-class phenomenon. As positive results are obtained from citizen participation in the deliberative process, so will the number of participants grow and their base broaden.

There remains a final difficult issue of taxonomy in working out where to place the largest of the civil society organizations in the region. These are the religious groups that count millions of adherents. They can be found in their Christian, Buddhist, and Islamic colorations. In the Philippines, the Catholic Church is strong and feeds much of local civil society in the form of Basic Christian Communities and similar mainstream groups. But other Christian sectarian groups such as the home-grown Iglesia ni Cristo and the charismatic El Shaddai movement, each with millions of members, also exert a powerful social and political influence. Buddhist groups in Thailand, such as the Santi Asoke sect, attempt to influence politics. Buddhist groups in Japan have given rise to NGOs, such as the Shanti Volunteer Association established by Soto Zen Buddhists,[53] as well as political parties, such as Komeito or Clean Government Party established by Sokagakkai.[54] The significance of sectarian civil society is well illustrated in Indonesia. Civil society has been alive and strong in Indonesia for a lot longer than the current spate of development and advocacy NGOs, in the form of Islamic associational communities. Organizations such as Nahdatul Ulama (NU), the largest association of traditional Muslims, and Muhammadiyah, the largest association of modernist Muslims, have followings in the tens of millions.[55] These Indonesian Muslim groups represent a far larger slice of civil society than does the mainly secular NGO movement. They act as educators, health-care providers, and providers of the major social safety net should the family be unable to care for an individual. Much of their funds come in the form of local donations, though some is derived from the Middle East. It would be odd to conceive of civil society without the inclusion of these religion-based groups. Just because civil society originated in the West does not mean that its form must slavishly follow the Western model. The key test is whether the religious group is committed to working within the existing legal and social bounds of its society. If so, it is important to integrate and cooperate with such organizations in the broader civil society family. If not, democracy faces a point of crisis in deciding how to deal with the group, the broad options being to tolerate it, ignore it, marginalize it, demonize it, or prosecute it.

## Values, Fables, and Fallacies

### Asian Values

I am a little embarrassed to write about Asian Values. It is like resurrecting a long-defeated foe for a final gratuitous swipe. Mark Thompson got the flavor right when he entitled his 2001 article in the *Journal of Democracy* "Whatever Happened to 'Asian Values'?"[56] Nobody is espousing the cause any more and so perhaps we should simply let sleeping dogs lie. The reason I persevere is that I believe the ideas behind the Asian Values debate continue to have some resonance in the region. Furthermore, now that the issue is no longer controversial, we can look more dispassionately, and perhaps more honestly, at the underlying assumptions. One necessary step is to drop the capital letter and thus scale down the self-serving politicians' doctrine of Asian Values back to the scholarly investigation of Asian values.

Neil Englehart does us a great service in tracing the political origins of Asian Values, the doctrine.[57] The story begins in the uncertain days following Singapore's unhappy 1965 divorce from Malaysia in the midst of the Cold War, as Mao's China was asserting itself and Sukarno's Konfrontasi was a very recent memory. Fearing that they would become "hotbeds of communism"[58] and wishing to encourage the use of English as the national language, Singapore's People's Action Party (PAP) in the 1970s closed down traditional Chinese schools, the natural carriers of the Confucian tradition, on the island. With the waning of Cold War rhetoric in the 1980s, the Singapore electorate "turned against" the PAP's parliamentary monopoly and elected a single opposition politician to parliament. The PAP reaction was to attempt deeper social engineering by launching the Confucian Ethics campaign as a "code of personal conduct," according to Minister of Education Goh Keng Swee.[59] But Singapore is a multicultural city, and so the education curriculum offered five courses under the heading Religious Knowledge, though the government's emphasis was clearly on the Confucian Ethics course. Singaporean students, however, voted by enrollment. The most popular course was Buddhist Studies with 44.4 percent of the enrollment, followed by Bible Knowledge with 21.4 percent, and only then came Confucian Ethics with 17.8 percent. By 1990, the Confucian enterprise was abandoned, but the PAP decided to replace it with a new doctrine of state called "Shared Values." The five Shared Values were identified as nation before community and society above self; family as the basic unit of society; community support and respect for the individual; consensus not conflict; and racial and religious harmony. John Clammer finds these values curious because of "their vagueness, their culturalist assumptions, their implicit recognition of the lack of any founding myth or charter in a political culture that is symbolically impoverished, their premise that all of the different religions and cultures that make up Singapore do in fact have common values, their exclusion of any discussion of human rights, equality or gender."[60] Clammer concludes that this strategy "attempts not to create change but to preempt it."[61] In other words, the campaign was essentially a political ploy to cement PAP authority and legitimacy.

Singapore's Shared Values, Indonesia's Pancasila,[62] and the various values-laden campaigns in Malaysia, such as the National Culture Policy,[63] the Bangsa Malaysia push,[64] and the "Look East" campaign,[65] all spoke of a political need to articulate something distinctive and valuable in the Malay zone of Pacific Asia. It would all come together in the Asian Values doctrine, with Singapore's Lee Kuan Yew and Malaysia's Mahathir Mohammed as its principal patrons. Clammer's accusation of vagueness in relation to Shared Values can as easily be directed at its successor, Asian Values. The following list of words and phrases have at various times been attributed to the doctrine: order, duty, obedience, stability, hard work, frugality, discipline, teamwork, reverence for education, consensual approach, social harmony, respect for elders, strong leadership, collective good over individual rights, and acceptance of broad state intervention. Quite a list! But just as impressive a list can be elaborated for all the advantages of the Asian Values doctrine to its patrons: to respond to Western criticism over human rights and democracy; to legitimize the regime in power; to justify draconian internal security laws; to protect "traditional practices" against Western influence; to maintain broad state intervention and all the personal benefits it brings to the leadership; and to stifle criticism. One need look no further than these substantial benefits to understand the self-interested nature of the doctrine for incumbents. Asian Values were about the politics of staying in power and maintaining the largely unfettered nature of that power.

I heard the death knell of Asian Values at a conference in Kuala Lumpur in September 1998. Kuala Lumpur remains an attractive city, even though Malaysia's booming economy has at times transformed it into a giant building site, so a visit to Kuala Lumpur is always an occasion to look forward to. There was a special reason to look forward to this trip, given my love of sports. The Sixteenth Commonwealth Games were being held in Kuala Lumpur that very month. So in the evenings after our conference deliberations were completed, I would sneak off to stadiums where Australian athletes competed. The games were brilliantly organized and easy to attend, but the stands were hardly full and yet tickets were not for sale. I learned that this was because of the government's insistence that large Malaysian companies buy thousands of tickets to ensure the games' financial success. The companies clearly saw this simply as an ad hoc tax and most of these tickets remained unused. I managed to attend a few good events nevertheless. One night I saw Australian swimmers win every gold medal on offer. Another time it was our field hockey team thrashing India. At the velodrome, it was again all Australia, although on the night I attended we magnanimously allowed a Kiwi cyclist to win one of the events. Of the 214 gold medals in competition, Australia won 80, thus demonstrating that our national sport is . . . winning. The Malaysians had gone to a lot of trouble to ensure a successful Commonwealth Games, and there was an undercurrent that Australia was ruining the party by being impolite and hogging all the gold. The local tabloid finally snapped, and its front-page headline screamed: "WHERE ARE WE? KOALA LUMPUR?"

The conference was also fascinating. It was the annual meeting of Transparency International (TI) and the debates were lively. The meeting welcomed into its midst a prominent member, Olusegun Obasanjo, the former president of Nigeria, who had recently been released from unjust imprisonment and who, unbeknownst to us at the time, would soon reclaim Nigeria's presidency in an electoral triumph. Little did we know that as one political prisoner was being released, another, Deputy Prime Minister Anwar Ibrahim, would be arrested at his home a few miles away only days after the meeting ended. The speech I remember best was delivered by the head of the Malaysian chapter of TI, Tunku Abdul Aziz, and dealt with Asian Values. The attack on Asian Values was so devastating that it could only have credibility by being led by a member of the Malaysian establishment. The Tunku described Asian Values as

> a morally indefensible and decadent heritage, one grounded in complete and utter disdain for transparency and accountability in the management of those matters that have "public interest" implications. In retrospect, Asian Values were used to justify excesses in both human and economic terms. They became part of a political culture that demanded complete acquiescence and conformity, regardless of the damage to the human spirit and enterprise.[66]

The patrons of Asian Values have passed from the scene, and with them have gone the defenders of the thesis. Ultimately, the doctrine was simply too convenient and self-serving and was clearly seen as such both inside these societies and out. It was a political instrument whose time came, and went. The Chinese government was happy to join in on any tactic to attack what they saw as Western smugness over human rights and democracy, but the other countries of Northeast Asia were rather leery of being dragged into the Mahathir side of the argument. Kim Dae Jung[67] and Lee Teng-hui[68] took particular pains to argue for the universal applicability of human rights and democracy. So the doctrine never really escaped its origins in the Malay region of Southeast Asia. In Northeast Asia, the term employed has been *Confucianism*.

*Confucianism*

The debate on Confucianism and its relationship to human rights and democracy has been slightly less polemical and slightly more academic.[69] Those arguing in favor of cultural relativism see in Confucianism similar results as proposed by the proponents of Asian Values, in the form of communal adherence to wise leadership.[70] These arguments suffer from similar fallacies as befall the arguments supporting Asian Values. Critics tend to split into two camps. One camp adopts an ecumenical approach seeking to find in the local cultural tradition, in this case Confucianism, the same principles in different words.[71] This entails a hermeneutic search through ancient texts, which are then subjected to modern reinterpretation. The other camp argues the universal application of human rights and democracy.[72] There is merit in both these approaches, but there is also an element of fable in the reconstruction of these ancient "truths." In the ecumenical case, the search for local roots of democracy strikes me as too ambitious. All we need to seek in a society's cultural heritage are a moral basis of society and an ambition for society to be improved. The interplay of societal morality and ambition can open the path to growth, reform, and experimentation, which in turn can lead to liberal democracy. I am not suggesting that liberal democracy is an inevitable result of the interplay of these forces. Choices still need to be made, new paths chosen. Those choices will be based on myriad factors, including emulation, competition, and inertia. Those making the choices will need to wrestle with problems of vested interests, the costs of transformation, and the need to forge a social consensus on the vision of the future. But the underlying question to be asked should be whether a society is open to liberal democracy, not the far more problematic question of whether there are seeds of liberal democracy in every culture.

My sympathies lie with the universalist interpretation. The diversity of humanity should not obscure its underlying unity. Its unity can be seen in genetics, in the common ancestry of its evolutionary history, and even in the discipline dedicated to human diversity, anthropology, where Claude Lévi-Strauss pointed to certain universal social practices.[73] So it should not be surprising to find universally held self-perceptions about human worth and dignity. Where the universalists tend to be drawn toward their own fables is in the occasional hint that the concepts of human rights and democracy were there all along and we simply needed to recognize and embrace them. This at times flows from an overly wide reading of the concept of the *inherent* nature of human rights. A better interpretation of the universalist argument is that in our efforts to improve our societies, we have devised the liberal democratic form of governance. This includes a menu of institutional designs for representative democracy, and a legally enforceable set of rights allowing individuals to interact with those institutions. We should not deny the novelty of this system. The ancient Greeks gave us the word but not the modern practice of democracy. If we use 1948 as the birth of liberal democracy in that it saw the triumph of the Churchillian second wave of democracy, as discussed in Chapter 1, and was the year of the adoption of the Universal Declaration of Human Rights, then modern liberal democracy has only been practiced for two generations. Western civilization is clearly open to liberal democracy, but its component parts are continually struggling to make it a reality. It is a difficult and at times inefficient form of governance, posing many questions of interpretation and requiring many compromises in response to those questions. Liberal democracy will forever remain an ideal toward which societies can only hope to approach, rather than reach.

## Conclusion

Leaving the ancient Greeks and returning to Pacific Asia, the issue that has been discussed in this chapter is whether the political cultures of the emerging democracies of Pacific Asia are in some way antithetical to the consolidation of democracy, or put in positive terms, Are these societies open to liberal democracy? I certainly believe they are. Neither their histories nor their values preclude them from striving for the best form of governance. Indeed, one of the most remarkable features demonstrated by Pacific Asia over the course of one generation has been its capacity to reinvent itself from village to city, from agriculture to commerce, from the local to the global. It certainly has the capacity to reinvent itself from authoritarianism to liberal democracy.

Does it follow that values in Pacific Asia are identical to values in the Western world? Clearly not! One of the reasons that Asian Values, the doctrine, had some currency in Asia is that it was based on a kernel of truth in respect to Asian values, the practice. That kernel of truth must be measured in degrees and not absolutes. Frugality is understood in many cultures, but Pacific Asia has demonstrated a great capacity for it, exemplified in record national economic saving practices. Education is highly prized virtually everywhere, but Pacific Asia seems to have taken to tertiary education with particular vigor. Teamwork is praised throughout the world, but groups in Pacific Asia have shown a capacity to work together in particularly difficult and demanding situations. These factors may be measured in small degrees of differences, but it may be these small degrees that can provide that small but decisive comparative advantage in an increasingly competitive world.

The key argument from the cultural relativists is that Asians will put the group before the individual. Taken to its authoritarian conclusions, this allows the leader the right to interpret the will of the group and reject dissenting views from individuals as culturally inappropriate. A number of things need to be said in rebuttal. First and obviously, the importance of family and community is not a feature unique to Asia. No society would have survived without the strength of the family as its basic unit. Second, the "atomization" of society into a collection of individuals appears to be a process that transcends civilizational divides and accompanies lifestyle changes. It is as true in the cities of Asia and Africa as it is in the West. Societies wealthy enough to provide state-supported social safety nets take some pressure off families that otherwise must discharge this responsibility. As social welfare regimes develop in Pacific Asia, so might the impression be gained that families are not as tightly knit as previously. Third, we need to be alive to the strong possibility that the different level of individual assertiveness in different societies is simply a matter of style, not substance. Asian individuals may be politely insistent, while Western counterparts may concede in a flurry of bluster. Finally, even if Asian individuals often prefer to subsume their views to the will of the group, as of course often do individuals of all other civilizations, they are fully entitled to do so as a matter of choice. The problem only arises when their leaders make that choice on their behalf.

I began this chapter expressing some doubts about opinion survey–based findings concerning political culture, so it may sound inconsistent to conclude it with a rhetorical appeal to that method. But I believe I know the results of the questionnaire without even undertaking the survey. I think we all know what the results would be in response to the following questions asked anywhere in the areas where it is said Asian and Confucian values predominate:

- Do you wish to have a legally enforceable right not to be tortured?
- Do you wish to have a legally enforceable right to speak your mind?
- Do you wish to have a say in the government of your country?
- Do you wish to participate in a decision on the retention of your leaders?

## Notes

1. Christopher Patten, *East and West—China, Power, and the Future of Asia* (New York: Times Books, 1998), p. 134.

2. Philippe C. Schmitter, "Parties Are Not What They Once Were," Larry Diamond and Richard Gunther (eds.), *Political Parties and Democracy* (Baltimore: Johns Hopkins University Press, 2001), p. 68.

3. Larry Diamond, *Developing Democracy—Toward Consolidation* (Baltimore: Johns Hopkins University Press, 1999), p. 163.

4. Takashi Inoguchi et al., *Values and Life Styles in Urban Asia—A Cross-Cultural Analysis and Sourcebook Based on the AsiaBarometer Survey of 2003* (Tokyo: The University of Tokyo and Mexico: Institute of Oriental Culture, 2005).

5. Lucian W. Pye with Mary W. Pye, *Asian Power and Politics—The Cultural*

*Dimensions of Authority* (Cambridge, MA, and London: The Belknap Press of Harvard University Press, 1985).

6. Ibid., p. 339.

7. Niels Mulder, *Inside Southeast Asia—Religion, Everyday Life, Cultural Change* (Amsterdam: The Pepein Press, 1996).

8. Ibid., p. 225.

9. Ibid.

10. Francis Fukuyama, "Confucianism and Democracy," *Journal of Democracy* 6, no. 2 (April 1995): 20–33.

11. P. W. Preston, *Pacific Asia in the Global System: An Introduction* (Oxford: Blackwell Publishers, 1998), pp. 245–246.

12. Steve Chan, "Democratic Inauguration and Transition in East Asia," James F. Hollifield and Calvin Jillson (eds.), *Pathways to Democracy—The Political Economy of Democratic Transitions* (New York and London: Routledge, 2000), pp. 178–191.

13. Cal Clark, "Modernization, Democracy, and the Developmental State in Asia," Hollifield and Jillson (eds.), *Pathways to Democracy—The Political Economy of Democratic Transitions,* p. 177.

14. Pye, *Asian Power and Politics,* p. 12.

15. Aat Vervoorn, *Reorient—Change in Asian Societies,* 2nd ed. (Oxford: Oxford University Press 2002), p. 41.

16. Pye, *Asian Power and Politics,* p. 20.

17. Ann-Belinda S. Preis, "Human Rights as Cultural Practice: An Anthropological Critique," *Human Rights Quarterly* 18, no. 2 (1996): 286–315.

18. Jared Diamond, *Guns, Germs, and Steel: The Fates of Human Societies* (New York: W. W. Norton & Company, 1999).

19. Ibid.

20. Both the International Covenant on Civil and Political Rights and the International Covenant on Economic, Social and Cultural Rights begin with Article 1 (1): "All peoples have the right of self-determination. By virtue of that right they freely determine their political status and freely pursue their economic, social and cultural development."

21. Sunhyuk Kim, "Civil Society and Democratization in South Korea," *Korea Journal* 38, no. 2 (Summer 1998): 223.

22. Diamond, *Developing Democracy,* p. 221.

23. Robert C. Post and Nancy L. Rosenblum, "Introduction," Nancy L. Rosenblum and Robert C. Post (eds.), *Civil Society and Government* (Princeton, NJ: Princeton University Press, 2002), pp. 17–19.

24. Hannah Arendt, *The Origins of Totalitarianism* (New York: Shocken Books, 2004), p. 414.

25. Tom G. Palmer, "Definitions, History, Relations," Rosenblum and Post (eds.), *Civil Society and Government,* pp. 50–56.

26. Robert D. Putnam, "Bowling Alone: America's Declining Social Capital," Larry Diamond and Marc F. Plattner (eds.), *The Global Resurgence of Democracy,* 2nd ed. (Baltimore: Johns Hopkins University Press, 1996), pp. 290–291.

27. Barnett F. Baron, "The Legal Framework for Civil Society in East and Southeast Asia," *The International Journal of Not-for-Profit Law* 4, no. 4 (July 2002): 2.

28. OECD, "Table 2—Total Net Flows by DAC Countries by Type of Flows," *Statistical Annex of the 2004 Development Co-operation Report,* available from www.oecd.org/dac/stats/dac/.

29. Kim, "Civil Society and Democratization," p. 233.

30. Eui Hang Shin, "The Role of NGOs in Political Elections in South Korea—The Case of the Citizen's Alliance for the 2000 General Elections," *Asian Survey* 43, no. 4 (July/August 2003): 703.

31. Ibid., p. 708.

32. Ibid., p. 710.

33. Eunyong Kim, PSPD, comments to Asia Regional Training Workshop, Thailand, 5–11 August 2005, available from www.newtactics.org/file.php?ID=814#257,1.

34. Shin, "The Role of NGOs," p. 713.

35. Keiko Hirata, *Civil Society in Japan—The Growing Role of NGOs in Tokyo's Aid Development Policy* (New York: Palgrave Macmillan, 2002).

36. Ibid., p. 30.

37. Mulder, *Inside Southeast Asia*, p. 209.

38. Section 23 states: "The State shall encourage non-governmental, community-based, or sectoral organizations that promote the welfare of the nation."

39. The Association of Foundations, the League of Corporate Foundations, the Philippine Business for Social Progress, the Bishops-Businessmen's Conference for Human Development, the Caucus of Development NGO Networks, and the National Council for Social Development Foundations.

40. Fely I. Soledad, "The Philippine Council for NGO Certification," *The International Journal of Not-for-Profit Law* 3, no. 2 (December 2001).

41. R. William Liddle, "Regime: The New Order," Donald K. Emmerson (ed.), *Indonesia Beyond Suharto—Polity, Economy, Society, Transition* (New York: M. E. Sharpe, 1999), p. 47.

42. Augustinus Rumansara, "INFID's Experience," Rustam Ibrahim (ed.), *The Indonesian NGO Agenda—Toward the Year 2000* (Jakarta: CESDA-LP3ES, 1996), p. 267.

43. Baron, "The Legal Framework for Civil Society," p. 3.

44. Robert Klitgaard, "International Cooperation Against Corruption," *Finance & Development* 35, no. 1 (March 1998): 3–6, available from www.imf.org/external/pubs/ft/fandd/1998/03/pdf/klitgaar.pdf.

45. Niels Mulder, *Southeast Asian Images—Towards Civil Society* (Chiang Mai, Thailand: Silkworm Books, 2003), p. 232.

46. USAID/Cambodia, *Interim Strategic Plan 2002–2005*, available from www.dec.org/pdf_docs/PDABW893.pdf.

47. Baron, "The Legal Framework for Civil Society," p. 4.

48. Mulder, *Southeast Asian Images*, p. 228.

49. Duncan McCargo, "Democracy Under Stress in Thaksin's Thailand," *Journal of Democracy* 13, no. 4 (October 2002): 120.

50. Walden Bello, *The Anti-Development State—The Political Economy of the Permanent Crisis of the Philippines* (Quezon City: University of the Philippines, 2004), pp. 33–35.

51. Syarif Hidayat and Hans Antlöv, "Decentralisation and Regional Autonomy in Indonesia," Philip Oxhorn, Joseph S. Tulchin, and Andrew D. Selee (eds.), *Decentralization, Democratic Governance, and Civil Society in Comparative Perspective—Africa, Asia, and Latin America* (Baltimore: Johns Hopkins University Press, 2004), p. 281.

52. Hans Antlöv, "Not Enough Politics! Power, Participation, and the Democratic Polity," Edward Aspinal and Greg Fealy (eds.), *Local Power and Politics in Indonesia—Decentralisation and Democratisation* (Singapore: Institute for Southeast Asian Studies, 2003), pp. 78–79.

53. Hirata, *Civil Society in Japan*, p. 39.

54. Tomohito Shinoda, "Japan," Wolfgang Sachsenröder and Ulrike Frings (eds.), *Political Party Systems and Democratic Development in East and Southeast Asia—Volume II: East Asia* (Aldershot: Ashgate Publishing, 1998), pp. 104–106.

55. Liddle, "Regime: The New Order," p. 43.

56. Mark R. Thompson, "Whatever Happened to 'Asian Values'?" *Journal of Democracy* 12, no. 4 (2001): 154–165.

57. Neil A. Englehart, "Rights and Culture in the Asian Values Argument: The Rise and Fall of Confucian Ethics in Singapore," *Human Rights Quarterly* 22, no. 2 (2000): 548–568.

58. Ibid., p. 555.

59. Ibid., p. 556.

60. John Clammer, *Values and Development in Southeast Asia* (Selangor Darul Ehsan, Malaysia: Pelanduk Publications, 1996), p. 41.

61. Ibid.

62. Pancasila is the state philosophy of Indonesia summarized in five principles: (1) belief in the one and only God; (2) just and civilized humanity; (3) the unity of Indonesia; (4) democracy guided by inner wisdom in unanimity arising out of deliberation among representatives; and (5) social justice for all the people of Indonesia.

63. Which emphasized Islam and Malay culture as the essential bases of "national culture." Francis Loh Kok Wah, "Developmentalism and the Limits of Democratic Discourse," Francis Loh Kok Wah and Khoo Boo Teik (eds.), *Democracy in Malaysia: Discourses and Practices* (Richmond, Surrey: Curzon Press, 2002), p. 25.

64 Translated as "Nation State" and meaning "people who identify themselves with the country, speak Bahasa Malaysia and accept the Constitution." Ibid., p. 33.

65 Calling for emulation of Japan's economic and social success. Khoo Boo Teik, "Nationalism, Capitalism, and 'Asian Values,'" Wah and Teik (eds.), *Democracy in Malaysia*, p. 53.

66 Tunku Abdul Aziz made a similar statement at the 113th International Training Course conducted by the Asia and Far East Institute for Prevention of Crime and Treatment of Offenders in 1999, from which this quote is drawn. See "Strengthening Integrity: The Importance of Transparency and Accountability in Economic Sustainability," p. 390, available from www.unafei.or.jp/english/pdf/PDF_rms/no56/56-28.pdf.

67. Kim Dae Jung, "Is Culture Destiny? The Myth of Asia's Anti-Democratic Values," *Foreign Affairs* 73, no. 6 (1994): 189–194.

68. For example, Lee Teng-hui, Speech for 31st Annual Meeting Southwest Conference on Asian Studies via Videoconference Between Taipei and Sam Houston State University, available from www.roc-taiwan.org/houston/event/20021119/2002111901.html.

69. For example, Michael C. Davis (ed.), *Human Rights and Chinese Values—Legal, Philosophical, and Political Perspectives* (Hong Kong: Oxford University Press, 1995).

70. Without supporting them, Joseph Chan elaborates some of the arguments in "An Alternative View," *Journal of Democracy* 8, no. 2 (1997): 35–48.

71. For example, Du Gangjian and Song Gang, "Relating Human Rights to Chinese Culture: The Four Paths of the Confucian Analects and the Four Principles of a New Theory of Benevolence," Davis (ed.), *Human Rights and Chinese Values*, pp. 35–56.

72. For example, Jack Donnelly, "Human Rights and Asian Values: A Defense

of Western Universalism," Joanne R. Bauer and Daniel A. Bell (eds.), *The East Asian Challenge for Human Rights* (Cambridge: Cambridge University Press, 1999), pp. 60–87.

73. Claude Lévi-Strauss, *Mythologyques* I–IV (trans. John Weightman and Doreen Weightman) (Chicago: University of Chicago Press, 1973, 1983, 1990, 1990).

# 9

# Comparing Democracies

> ""Our assumption is that the quality of democracy
> can contribute positively or negatively to the quality
> of society, but the two should not be confused.""
> —Alfred Stepan and Juan J. Linz, "Toward Consolidated Democracies"[1]

Our survey has taken us skipping across a continent from the robust debates of India to the placid mask of Japan, with stops along the way in Indonesia, South Korea, the Philippines, Taiwan, and Thailand, while also glancing at some of their neighbors. I have seen fit to apply the description of "democracy" to the various protagonists (though Thailand's membership in the group may now be in doubt), yet the most casual of visitors will see the distinctions among these societies more readily than their supposed similarity. The unifying term *Asia* has been seen to be an impostor, superimposed upon a huge landmass without the knowledge of its inhabitants by an ignorant outsider in need of facile labels. Is the unifying term *democracy* any more appropriate to compartmentalize this group of countries in contradistinction to its neighbors? In casting the net of democracy over the seven countries, we run into the problem that not only do they look so different to the casual observer, but they also appear very different from each other in terms of governance.

## Why Don't Democracies Look Alike?

### A Menu of Institutional Options
The most obvious response to this question is that all democracies have a menu of institutional options from which to choose in crafting their governance infrastructure. How many tiers of government should there be? How strong should the center be in its relations with the periphery? What powers should be delegated, decentralized, or devolved? Should the head of state be

251

an executive or ceremonial figure? Should the system be parliamentary or presidential? Should the parliament be unicameral or bicameral? What electoral system to adopt for each of the chambers at each of the tiers of government? Should the legal system have civil law or common law features? Is international law directly applicable or must it be transformed into national law? These broad choices already open the way to dozens of different configurations of governance infrastructure. Beneath the broad choices is a wide array of detailed choices about terms of office and term limits, appointment and dismissal processes, as well as the structure of oversight and accountability mechanisms. We all know that the devil is in the details, and any number of these second-level choices can impart a significant imprint on the system as a whole.

Simply on the basis of governance infrastructure, we can begin to explain why these seven democracies look so different from each other. There are three parliamentary types (if Thailand continues to be listed under its 1997 Constitution) and four presidential systems, though South Korea might be better termed as semi-presidential. Among two of the three parliamentary systems, the head of state is an inherited office (Japan, Thailand), while the third is appointed (India). All four presidents are directly elected, but one is elected by the two-round method (Indonesia). All four presidents are subject to term limits; two are restricted to a single term (South Korea, the Philippines), and two may seek two terms (Indonesia, Taiwan). Five of the countries have based their legal system on civil law, while the two others have common-law features (India, the Philippines); however, all seven are strongly influenced toward legal convergence by the rules of globalization. Four have bicameral systems (India, Japan, the Philippines, Thailand), two are unicameral (South Korea, Taiwan), while Indonesia, as argued in a previous chapter, can be placed in the unicameral, bicameral, tricameral, or one-and-a-half chamber categories, depending on one's perspective. I have argued that the seven countries have electoral systems affording between three and five dimensions of representation. India is the only country with a federal system, but it would not be an exaggeration to argue that Korea's informal, but stubborn, regionalism is in practice also influential in terms of its impact on governance. While not formally federal, Indonesia and the Philippines have directly elected subnational units of governance. Indonesia is grappling with a radical form of decentralization, while Thailand observes the results very closely as it considers a form of budgetary decentralization.[2]

## Various Vocabularies of Governance

On the formal level, the variations manifest themselves in distinctive vocabularies of governance. Emperors, kings, presidents, and prime ministers all find their place in one or more of the systems under review. In terms of territorial units, there are federal states, provinces, and regencies. In describing electoral systems, we have a smorgasbord of options, including first past the post, proportional representation, and block votes, for single-member districts, multimember districts, and the national constituency. There are open party lists and closed party lists, mixed systems and uniform systems, and quotas for women or constructed privileges for underprivileged tribes or castes. The variation in vocabulary could continue in relation to electoral commissions, ombudsmen, and auditors, each working under a specific set or rules and practices.

I could rest my case at this point, relying on the reality of structural, terminological, and numerical differentiations. In describing and measuring such structures, however, there is a nagging suspicion of simply dealing with a façade. Are we appreciating the infrastructure of governance or glancing lazily at its superstructure? The differences between these seven democracies go far deeper than the differences in their governance establishments. They go to the quality and depth of their democracies, their capacities to tackle the most pressing social issues, and their ability to obtain results that find broad favor and avoid minority rejection. In discussing these qualitative differences we transcend the numerical and are condemned to grapple with the conceptual.

Robert Dahl's seven conditions for polyarchy referred to in the first chapter have inspired the discussion in the balance of this book.[3] We have looked at institutional design choices, building the rule of law, politicians and their parties, the public conversation, and aspects of political culture. Dahl's seven conditions are the minimal requirements for a democracy. It is only when these conditions are met in their most basic form that a polity passes the threshold that distinguishes democratic from nondemocratic forms of government. Yet it would be a poor-quality democracy that merely reached the threshold of each of the requirements. The quality of a democracy increases the further a polity progresses in each of the requirements. The variations in democracy can therefore also be measured in terms of the extent to which a polity demonstrates strengths or weaknesses in these basic requirements. Democracy is a system with different mixes of strengths and weaknesses, and describing these provides us with a more satisfying means of assessing the variations in the seven democracies in question. There is clearly an element of subjective judgment in determining this democracy mix. The method does not have the compelling simplicity of a numerical score. But we should not be taken in by the apparent numerical certainties, because when we analyze the construction of such numerical scores, we find unarticulated subjective judgments in their supporting premises. The key to the plausibility of both methods lies in the solidity of the evidence marshaled to back the judgment. My evidence is in the preceding chapters and, based on that evidence, the following commentary on the countries under review attempts to draw together the individual character and quality of their democratic systems.


## Five Different Democracies

### The Philippines

The country with the strongest democratic rhetoric nevertheless remains at risk of jeopardizing its democracy. US political rhetoric took deep root in the Philippines. Talk about democracy, elections, and office holders is ubiquitous throughout the archipelago. Election Day is a popular festival of democracy. I was an observer of the May 2001 congressional elections in Manila, and traveling around the city, one could not see a square inch of wall, fence, or tree without candidates' posters stuck on it. The actual voting process is laborious. Voters must fight their way through a mob milling around the school doubling as a voting place to find their names on the roll, locate the classroom where their precinct is voting, produce identification, place two thumbprints on the ballot and on the confirmation slip, receive a drop of indelible ink on the cuticle on the index finger of the right hand, hand write as many as thirty names on the ballot paper while squeezed into a primary school bench, tear off the confirmation slip, and finally place it and the completed ballot in separate slots in the ballot box. At Pinaglaban Elementary School in San Juan, Metro Manila, I put the stopwatch on a couple from the time they had reached the head of the queue to begin the voting process. It took them a full 12 minutes to complete the marathon. Multiply this by 35 million voters and you get an idea how large an undertaking it is to conduct an election. Sensibly, Election Day is declared a public holiday. In each tiny classroom, there are four officials manning the electoral gauntlet through which voters pass under the bored gaze of up to a dozen observers and other hangers-on representing the various candidates and NGOs. There are 220,000 precincts, giving you an idea of how labor intensive the process is. Just about every teacher in the country is enlisted to run the system, and one week after the 2001 election, they had still not been paid their 900 pesos ($16) for several days of work overseeing the balloting and counting, while occasionally being required to lay down their lives to protect ballot boxes from the goons of disappointed candidates.

Lots of things went wrong with the 2001 elections. The voter lists prepared by COMELEC, the Electoral Commission, were a mess, and thousands of voters were unable to find their names and were thus effectively disenfranchised. The counting process is so cumbersome and time-consuming that it is almost an invitation to attempt fraud; look away for a moment and someone will add a zero to a column and steal the result, a process so well known in the Philippines that it has a commonly used name—*dagdag-bawas* or add-subtract. Even the poll watchers had a hard time of it. NAMFREL's vaunted Quick Count was in disarray because it ultimately relied on a dubious piece of technology—the fifth carbon paper producing a sixth copy of the official canvassers' return. The sixth copy was, needless to say, often illegible. For all the mobs, the mess, and the mayhem, there was nevertheless something inspirational about the participation of the people of the Philippines in the elections. The teachers of the Philippines showed their customary diligence and courage. As most teachers and most election observers are women, the role of the women of the Philippines in making even this flawed process work must be highlighted. The other heroes were the voters themselves. Enthusiastically and conscientiously, the voters participated in huge numbers, still convinced, even after so many disappointments, that democratic multiparty elections will deliver better government.

In spite of such problems, the regular holding of elections, along with their decisiveness in determining the individuals winning office, is one of the better aspects of Philippine democracy. The participatory nature of Philippine public life is another admirable feature. Filipinos have tremendous associational energy, even though they may at times lack the stamina to see things through to their conclusion. The public conversation is frenetic, conducted through the media, the Internet, and even text messages. There is a freedom of expression that is unconstrained by such qualities as truth, consistency, or even coherence. Even the libel laws have very little impact, as could be seen when President Aquino failed in her 1989 libel suit against *Manila Star* columnist Max Soliven, who falsely accused her of hiding under her bed during one of the many coup attempts against her presidency.

This brings us to the weaknesses in Philippine democracy. The democracy rhetoric is matched by a legal rhetoric also borrowed from the United States. There is always talk of having one's day in court, taking a matter to the highest court in the land, or prosecuting to the fullest extent of the law. Sadly, it is mainly talk. There are well over 10,000 statutes on the books, few of which are effectively enforced. Justice is both delayed and denied in too many cases. Various traits of the Philippine character ranging from lack of follow-through, inattention to detail, and a national propensity for forgiveness combine to make the law a most uncertain institution. When I left the Philippines in 1989 at the conclusion of my posting, Colonel Gringo Honasan had just escaped from custody after being arrested for his leadership of a failed coup d'état against President Aquino in which dozens of people had lost their lives. When I returned a few years later, he was a senator, having negotiated his way from prisoner-on-the-run to leading politician. Clearly, there is something wrong with this picture. The Philippines may at times have rule of lawyers, but it is a long way from having built a system of rule of law. Indeed, the country is generally weak on systematization, and this limits the policy effectiveness of whichever government is in power and compromises the ability of democratic governments to deliver results.

The participatory energy of the people of the Philippines is a strength, as was shown in the overthrow of the Marcos regime, but it is now turning into a weakness as "people power" begins to trump electoral power. To put a mob on the streets is a relatively straightforward operation requiring money and a few connections. People power has unseated two presidents. Has it set in motion a cycle in which each president in turn becomes a target of his or her enemies? President Macapagal-Arroyo is clearly in the cross-hairs of her political enemies. The only institution to benefit from this situation is the armed forces. They remain the arbiters of nonconstitutional leadership changes simply through the decision whether or not to protect the incumbent. Either way, the safeguarded incumbent or the incoming leader is indebted to the armed forces. It is therefore of little surprise that the phone conversation between President Macapagal-Arroyo and the COMELEC official that was the cause of such upheaval in Philippine politics in 2005 was intercepted and released by military intelligence sources.

### Thailand

Thailand strikes me as a far more systematized country. Its traditions of royal and bureaucratic rule have allowed it to develop more-effective policy reach than is the case in the Philippines. In the drafting, adoption, and defense of the 1997 Constitution, Thailand has shown a capacity for self-analysis and a talent for public deliberation that augured well for the construction of its democracy. While the constitution was open to the criticism of being overengineered and attempting to achieve too much by the method of institutional crafting, it appeared, until the 2006 coup, to be establishing a status of permanence that its predecessor documents were unable to achieve. Constitutionalism in and of itself as a pillar of rule of law is, therefore, half the battle. The coup has jeopardized this progress and has disappointed those who believed Thailand had broken with its past history of military coups and self-serving constitutions.

Thailand has also had more success than the Philippines in terms of economic development, allowing for the growth of a substantial middle class and a greater ability to assure high levels of education, which is the fuel that accelerates changes in political culture. Its associational energy is perhaps not as high octane as in the Philippines, but Thai NGOs, including those representing the poorest segments of society, can nevertheless point to some important impacts on the policy debate. All in all, Thailand can boast some impressive achievements.

Inevitably, more ink will be spilled on problems than on achievements. The first question in this regard is whether Thai politics is even more deeply in the thrall of the military than is the Philippines. Thailand's modern political history is replete with military rule and, as shown in Table 6.3, almost 70 percent of its post–World War II governance has been in military hands. Oddly, this contrasts with the Philippines, where the only general to turn president gained office through ballots, not bullets. At the time of writing, Thailand was again indirectly ruled by the military and directly ruled by a military appointee who happens to be a former general. One reason the Thai military has not been weaned from politics is the need to protect its business interests. By the time a future civilian government inevitably moves against the military's business holdings, constitutionalism and commitment to democracy will need to be so well established as to provide no space for the military to maneuver its way back into politics.

The second problem is equally troubling because it is so difficult to determine its extent. How corrupt is the Thai system of governance? Is it a superficial social malaise that finds expression in petty bribery and vote buying, or are these merely manifestations of a deeper problem? Vote buying has been the focus of much of the attention, perhaps because it has been so well organized in some constituencies, and so effective in delivering the purchased votes. Even this malaise has a silver lining. A Thai academic told me of the paper he delivered at a conference in Africa, where he lamented the practice of vote buying in his country. Many of his African listeners were confused by his talk and sought him out afterward to discuss the issue. Their interpretation was that the practice of vote buying proved that a vote was negotiable and therefore valuable. It showed that voting was an act of choice because it was subject to being influenced by money. It showed that voting would determine the result of the election, and that votes had to be solicited one way or another by those seeking office. From their perspective, vote buying demonstrated Thai citizens' freedom to vote in an election that determines who is in government, and this struck them as an enviable aspect of the Thai political system that few African countries could match.

On balance, I agree with William Callaghan that the emphasis on vote buying in the diagnosis of political ills is misplaced.[4] While the evidentiary link is always difficult to substantiate, the reality is that political incumbency is a means to gaining or protecting wealth in Thailand. Historically, incumbency has been achieved through membership of, first royalty, and then the bureaucracy and the military, or through hotly contested elections. The rewards of incumbency justify the enormous outlay required to win those elections. The problem therefore does not lie with the rural folk who happily accept a bribe to secure their vote; the problem lies in the system that allows such financial rewards to be available to those in office. There are many vocational politicians in Thailand who enter the game for reasons of public service, policy delivery, and constituency responsibilities. If and when this group achieves critical mass in politics, Thailand will take important strides in returning to democracy.

The third problem that Thailand needs to face is the use of violence by the state. The state has a monopoly on the legitimate use of violence and, if for no other reason, this means it must be particularly sparing in employing it. Ultimately, a liberal democracy must aim for a situation where only negligible levels of legitimate violence are ever employed. The first test is whether the violence used by the state is lawful. The recent campaign against drug traffickers was outside the law. It should have generated public indignation and it should have led to resignations, but it did not. The death in custody of dozens of Muslim detainees in the south is another case of the illegitimate use of state violence, even if those deaths were not caused intentionally by the military but resulted from reckless disregard for the lives of the detainees. The key test distinguishing nonauthoritarian from authoritarian rule is the former's willingness to be bound by the rule of law. Thailand's leaders need to demonstrate their adherence to the rule of law even when a useful shortcut is identified and even when the specific use of violence is fleetingly popular. In this regard, the lack of widespread protest over the 2006 coup does not legitimize it.

### Indonesia

I remain upbeat about democracy in Indonesia, but I find it difficult to justify my optimism. The realistic examination of Indonesia's situation produces a lengthy list of pitfalls and problems. As with the other Southeast Asian nations, the discussion needs to begin with the military. The military no longer has dedicated seats in parliament and no longer formally subscribes to the doctrine of *dwifungsi,* or dual military and socioeconomic functions, but that should not be taken as conclusive evidence that its role in politics has ended. Tentara Nasional Indonesia (TNI) remains a territorial army, spread throughout the archipelago and exercising influence in political decisions big and small. Its ranks produced the current president, and it may well produce some of his successors. Behind most *bupatis* running the government of a regency, there is usually a colonel staring over his shoulder. And in view of the fact that less than one-third of TNI's budget comes from the state budget,[5] it is unlikely to withdraw from the nation's economic life in the near future. Professionalization of the armed forces, concentration on national defense, and acceptance of civilian oversight are all substantial hurdles facing TNI and Indonesian democracy.

Next on the list of problems comes the issue of Indonesian nationhood, or put bluntly, Is Indonesia a nation or a Javanese empire? Only the former can transform itself into a democracy. A choice to employ the military approach in dealing with the separatist movements in Aceh and Papua would lead to a conclusion that we are looking at an empire rather than a nation. Negotiating settlements in the rebellious provinces would point to the sort of accommodations reached in democratic nations. The uncertain impact of decentralization places another question mark over Indonesia's political coherence, as does the fact that the geographic divides are in part reinforced by religious divides. It is not the territorial army that holds Indonesia together nor the common language, but a certain sentiment of unity within diversity in an uncertain world. One of the most important contributors to this sentiment is the common act of voting in meaningful elections. As free, fair, and meaningful elections multiply in Indonesia, so will the sense of shared national destiny grow and concerns about Javanese domination recede. It is democracy, not the armed forces, that can forge an Indonesian nation.

After the military and nationhood, the next issue that needs to be tackled would appear to be Islam. Almost 90 percent of Indonesia's 250 million people list Islam as their religion, making it the world's most populous Islamic nation. A perception has developed in some quarters that Islam is incompatible with democracy, fed by such commentators as Bernard Lewis, who describes the democratization record of Islamic countries as "one of almost unrelieved failure."[6] But for this perception, and the accompanying global breast beating about the woes of Islam, Islam would not be given high priority as a problematic issue in Indonesian politics. Indeed even a mere decade ago, Islam in Indonesia would have been seen as a side issue of relatively narrow scholarly interest. Unlike neighboring Malaysia, where the banner of Islam is used as a contested symbol of ethnic Malay advancement in a multicultural society, Indonesians did not see Islam as a significant issue politically, and Indonesian society was comfortable with the practice of Islam within a state ideology of Pancasila that legitimized all monotheistic religions.[7] Indonesian Islam has demonstrated a "culture of tolerance, equality and civility"[8] and an associational energy and stamina that should be the envy of other civil society groups. Indonesia has the capacity to build a democracy while maintaining its faith in religion, including Islam. If Islam is to become a problem in Indonesia, it will be an imported problem imposed on the nation through the teachings of an inappropriate Wahhabism or the demands of a misconceived global war against terrorism.

I can foresee Indonesia taming its military, building its nationhood, and skirting the global debate on Islam, thus sustaining my optimism for its democracy. The main doubt, I believe, lies in the vexed issue of systematization. There is an undercurrent of violence running through Indonesian society, usually hidden behind a pleasing façade of smiles, manners, and jokes. This is the society where the word *amok* originated, which is a fitting description of what happened to that society in the anticommunist and anti-Chinese riots of 1965, and what nearly happened again after 1998 when various forces stirred up interreligious and anti-Chinese violence. It is kept alive by military and police practice and by the numerous militias that follow suit. It is part of the armory of many provincial politicians and interest group leaders. Indonesia is a long way from achieving a state monopoly on the legitimate use of violence exercised sparingly under rule of law. Indonesia is also a long way from taming systematization's other nemesis, corruption. Violence and corruption are more threatening to Indonesia's democracy than military machismo, ethnic separatism, and religious intolerance, because the twin evils will eat away at the community's confidence in their system of government. Without this respect for the legitimacy of their institutions, it will become difficult for people to behave with the self-denying civility required by democracy. I remain hopeful, however, that Indonesia will find a path to that goal.

*    *    *

It comes as little surprise that these three countries of Southeast Asia should look so different from each other despite their peoples' many similarities. These countries have quite distinct colonial histories, religious beliefs, and political cultures. Their political distinctiveness goes well beyond their differing institutional choices. Philippine democracy leans heavily on the participatory and associational energy of its people. Thai democracy has been more deliberatively crafted and bureaucratically administered but remains in the thrall of the military and the king. Indonesian democracy displays the more ad hoc nature of its construction and the Islamic and nationalist characteristics of its electorate. All three systems are unified mainly in their need for greater systematization that can only be achieved by taming both corruption and violence.

Having achieved Organisation for Economic Cooperation and Development (OECD) levels of development in wealth, health, and education, South Korea and Taiwan are in a strong position to further build and consolidate their democracies. Both countries display a restless energy for reform and renovation deliberated within contexts of polarization and cleavage unique to each of them. Both countries appear to have formed a societal consensus in favor of democracy and are requiring their elites to bend to this societal will. Both countries are building their democracies on the basis of their individual histories and traditions but are sufficiently confident in their own national abilities to borrow ideas where necessary. Both countries also share the difficult negative attribute that their democracies are, to a certain extent, hostage to outside forces.

### Taiwan
Taiwanese are proud to point out that the election of President Chen Shuibian in 2000 marked the first time in thousands of years of Chinese history

that power has been peacefully transferred subsequent to an election victory. With so meager a political culture of practicing democracy, Taiwan's progress down that path is nothing short of remarkable. It regularly holds free, fair, and meaningful elections and abides by the results. It has virtually reengineered its system of governance, drawing on Chinese political history and adding binding rules for the protection of human rights. It has shown a capacity for institutional innovation and is leading the region on issues such as equity in gender representation. Taiwanese civil society is vibrant and its public conversation is lively. Taiwan therefore has many features of a very positive story.

There are nevertheless some major uncertainties hanging over Taiwanese democracy. The first concerns the KMT. As noted in Chapter 4, the KMT behaved as a Leninist party during its period in power, only loosening its grip on society with the end of the Cold War. Under native-born Lee Teng-hui, the party hoped to transform itself from an authoritarian party into the permanently dominant party in a system of minimal political contestation. But the KMT now finds itself out of office and facing a surprisingly resilient DPP. The current situation sees aggressive politics being played by both parties. A major test of Taiwanese democracy will occur when the DPP eventually loses power, thus satisfying Huntington's two alternations test. To what degree will this change in power be seen as a normal part of the political process and be accepted with equanimity by the DPP? And to what degree will the KMT seize upon its eventual restored incumbency as a means of recreating a situation of permanent dominance? It is not yet certain that the behavior of Taiwan's political class during the next change in government will, in Schmitter's phrase, conform to democratic conduct that is "reliably known, regularly practiced, and voluntarily accepted by . . . politicians and citizens."[9] The eve of the 2004 presidential elections saw the bizarre shooting incident that seemed to sway an undecided electorate toward Chen's reelection. This certainly did not conform to the Schmitter formula, but it may simply have been a regrettable but haphazard incident. The next change in government will require close attention.

The other dark cloud hanging over Taiwanese democracy is the mainland. The issue of independence or reunification, and if the latter, whether it will be one country/two systems or simply one country, or whether the issue is in fact to be resolved or to continue indefinitely on its present uncertain course, are the dominant questions facing Taiwan. The China issue dominates Taiwan's relations with the rest of the international community, where it remains stuck in a Cold War posture. It is the dividing line for the dominant cleavage in Taiwanese society between native born and mainland born. It dominates the domestic political agenda, where the DPP has ridden to power on the back of appeals to nativist sentiment by hinting at moves toward regularizing Taiwan's international status without ever explicitly promising a declaration of independence. China has said such a declaration would be a casus belli, a threat of war that no government in Taipei, or indeed in Washington, can take lightly. The KMT is wedded to the one-China argument, but it realizes that native Taiwanese far outnumber former mainlanders in Taiwan and that the one-China argument only sits comfortably with the latter group. The problem with this level of national uncertainty is that it does not allow Taiwan to slip into a state of normality insofar as its political discourse is concerned. Normal politics in Taiwan is constantly crisis-prone, with the crisis not measured in terms of job numbers, interest rates, or inflation figures, but rather in terms of possible blockade, invasion, and war. So for all its achievements in building the institutions of democracy and moving toward a political culture of policy contestability, Taiwanese people cannot be confident that their democracy is consolidated while their polity exists in virtually a permanent state of crisis.

### South Korea

Of the five democratizing countries of Pacific Asia, South Korea's democratic achievements are probably the most impressive. The list reads like a manual for democratic transition. South Korea has banished the military from politics through the force of popular will, twice defied the military-industrial establishment to elect opposition presidential candidates, survived an impeachment process with all protagonists following the rule of law, mobilized civil society as a force for reform and integrity in politics, and begun the difficult process of structural economic reform. All this has been accomplished since the end of the Cold War and maintained despite, and perhaps even strengthened by, the 1997 financial crisis.

There are encouraging signs that further important steps will be taken in the coming years in the construction of South Korea's democracy. The Internet generation seems finally to be freeing itself of the stultifying constraints of regionalism, if this generation's strong vote for the Uri Party throughout the country can be taken as a foretaste of future politics. The power of the *chaebols* is being challenged both by political figures and the demands of globalization. Of particular interest, Koreans appear to be insisting that corruption be banished from politics. This seems to be driven less by theoretical idealism and far more because people are simply fed up with the inequality and unfairness caused by high-level money politics. The battle against corruption is taking place in the public conversation, in the design and construction of the institutions of accountability, and in the prosecution of *chaebol* CEOs, high-level officials, and their kin. If Koreans can educate themselves out of the hold of regionalism, and if they can bring political corruption down to tolerable limits, they will take giant steps toward the consolidation of their democracy.

The greatest threat to South Korean democracy comes from yet another Cold War remnant traced along the 38th parallel. The problem manifests itself in various ways. The first and obvious way is the direct threat of military conflict with a neighboring army numbering one million soldiers within marching distance of Seoul. The threat is compounded by North Korea's development of nuclear and missile technology. The threat is made more acute by the abject failure of North Korea's brand of totalitarianism to satisfy the most basic needs of its people. The only way the North can now compete with the South is militarily. This therefore presents itself as a problem of enormous magnitude.

Ironically, however, it is not the direct threat from the North but the South's response to it that poses an even greater threat to South Korean democracy. The issue dominates the political agenda, often to the exclusion of the pressing reform issues that require political and public attention. The issue distorts South Korea's relations with the world and with the United States by holding the security relationship above all else. The issue holds South Korean politics hostage to the idiosyncrasies and adventurism of Kim Jong Il. The issue creates a deep policy cleavage in South Korean society that overpowers the social, economic, and environmental policy divides. The question that constantly insists on a response is unchanging—What to do about North Korea? Should South Korean society militarize itself to match the threat from the North? In which case, should issues of democracy and human rights take a subsidiary place? Should South Korean society placate the North and thus indirectly help maintain its totalitarian system? Should relatively wealthy South Korean society bail out the North from its self-imposed penury? Should South Korean leaders play the devious games devised by Kim Jong Il, using family reunions or visits as the playing pieces? Can South Koreans ignore the terrible plight of their countrymen in the North's gulag system? Can South Korea afford the cost of assuring the welfare of twenty million impoverished people upon reunification? Until these and similar questions are answered, Korean democracy cannot contemplate the normality of comfortable consolidation.

\* \* \*

Five democratizing countries, five hopeful electorates, five sets of difficult problems. Each country is unique in its situation and its search to find the best solutions to its various problems, but even though none of these countries' democracies look alike, it is possible to categorize the key issue so as to draw an important distinction between Southeast Asia and Northeast Asia. In Indonesia, Thailand, and the Philippines, the problems come under the heading of the struggle for systematization. In South Korea and Taiwan, the major heading must be security.

## Role Models and Recruits

The principal focus of this study has been the five post–Cold War democratizing countries of Pacific Asia. A comment is also required on the two established democracies in Asia, India, and Japan. They stand as testimony to the possible. They provide evidence that democracy is not inimical to Asian societies. They act as role models for their neighbors. A comment is also required on two illiberal electoral democracies in Pacific Asia, Malaysia and Singapore, for surely they are the next candidates for liberal democracy.

### India

India defies all theories of democratization. Its income per capita, human development index, and the various health and education levels fall below those of Indonesia and the Philippines, the poorest of Pacific Asia's democracies. At the same time, it has a middle class numbering in the hundreds of millions. It is the size of a small continent and has commensurate diversity in terms of ethnicity, linguistic groups, castes, and religions. Its institutional infrastructure was designed before the term *consociationalism* was even coined, yet it seems to have fully mastered the concept, thus holding together and effectively representing its vast electorate. Defying the arguments of those who see in federalism the seeds of separatism, India's federal divisions have been stable and the system has demonstrated its ability to sustain occasional crises of instability in its states without affecting the balance of the nation. India has shown its talent for inheriting colonial institutions, such as parliament and common law, and transforming them into well-known and accepted local institutions. But for the short period of Indira Gandhi's Emergency, India would compete with Japan for the title of the oldest continuously functioning democracy in the non-Western world. For all its faults, which Indians would be the first to acknowledge, Indian democracy is a phenomenon of first-order importance in any study of democratization.

Various theories have been proposed to explain India's passion for democracy. The explanations range broadly over historical bases, societal characteristics, and political dynamics. Steve Muhlberger argues that there are examples of governance in ancient India that are analogous to democracy.[10] Amartya Sen makes clear that Indians are the masters of the public conversation and that democracy allows them to give full voice to this societal inclination.[11] The political science literature is replete with scholarly analysis of why democracy works in India.[12] What can be said in summary is that there are both aspects unique to India about the functioning of its democracy as well as lessons for others to be drawn from the success of Indian democracy. It is difficult to imagine what other system of governance might work in India. Authoritarianism would require such a vast apparatus of repression and discipline that it is almost unimaginable to conceive of it working in the natural chaos that is India. Charismatic rule is a more promising option, but in a country that worships so many gods in so many different ways, it is even beyond the reach of a Gandhi to have the entire nation obediently follow the single authority of one leader. It may be that India is condemned to practice democracy. Its very diversity can be accommodated by no other system of government. As has been pointed out, this diversity does not only create multiple crosscutting layers of cleavage and ascription, but it establishes individuals with multiple identities.[13] These identities cascade from nationality to language group to religion to caste to class to locality and eventually to political opinion with such complexity as to preclude ready political classification. There is no option but for these multifaceted individuals to support a system in which they consider they are managing themselves. Only democracy offers such a system. Perhaps some of the component parts of India could forsake democracy were they to stand as nations in their own right. But as a single polity, India has embraced democracy as the only system that will somehow placate all the nation's cleavage groups and keep everybody on talking terms.

There is an understandable temptation to put Indian democracy to one side as unique and so different from any other national system that there are no lessons to be drawn from its example. It is certainly unique, but there are nevertheless important points about Indian democracy that can be instructive. The first is to reject some of the proposed preconditions for the adoption of democracy. According to some ideas about democratic preconditions, material conditions such as income levels, literacy standards, and rates of economic development would have precluded India from becoming a democracy half a century ago and would still raise doubts about it today. India has defied those doubts. Societal conditions such as homogeneity and elite cohesion also fall foul of the Indian example. India's strength lies in diversity, not homogeneity, and the possible early cohesion by the postcolonial elites has long given way to deep fractiousness and contestation. If India can defy all the mooted preconditions for democracy, so can others.

Another lesson can be drawn from the way Indian democracy values each individual even if other aspects of its social heritage may devalue certain castes, classes, or tribes. This was brought home to me when I visited the Indian Electoral Commission in New Delhi in 1999 and was shown how half a billion voters had been listed on electronic electoral rolls. This is a feat that has defeated their Philippine counterparts and that even the United States has difficulty matching. I was a little skeptical at first. I said there must be one million Patels on the rolls, so how can one be distinguished from another? My host scrolled down to a Patel who was identified by way of full name, address, and similar details of a close relative. He argued that this method of triangulation is sufficient to identify every individual voter. I was impressed but unconvinced. I noted that India must have tens of millions of homeless people. Were they also triangulated or simply ignored? I asked smugly. My host scrolled further down the endless list of Patels until he found one who lived under the third lamppost south on Boundary Road and had a brother who lived in the railroad station. Now I was convinced. India's homeless can vote and therefore have a political voice, and so they cannot be ignored.

The Indian example is also instructive because of India's size. How far can democracy scale up? India shows that it can be practiced, in spite of enormous difficulties, on a very large scale indeed. Federalism helps to break the problems down into slightly more manageable parts, though Uttar Pradesh itself has a population of 176 million. To manage such a large democracy requires appropriate institutional design features like India's practice of holding national elections over several days. It also requires an acceptance that the system will at times be cumbersome and unresponsive. Democracy's efficiencies can only be measured in the long term. A country in Pacific Asia that can take heart from the Indian example is Indonesia. Its vast size, scattered islands, population cleavages, and wealth inequalities don't look quite so daunting when compared to India. If Indians have the talent to make democracy work, then surely Indonesians can aspire to replicate the feat. Another giant nation that shares a border with India and is often compared with it may also one day look to Indian democracy as a precedent. We will discuss China in the final chapter.

### Japan

In characterizing Indian democracy, one would put more weight on its deliberative and participatory qualities than on the disciplined functioning of its institutions. In characterizing Japanese democracy, the reverse is probably closer to the mark. Japan also defies an important aspect of democratic theory in that its current democratic structure was imposed by the United States after Japan's unconditional surrender in war. Therefore concepts such as evolving democracy or even adopting democracy do not gain support from Japan's example, though one interpretation has Japan "embracing" the system imposed on it.[14]

Japan's democracy has a strong institutional basis. It has been built on a rigid rule of law, a disciplined and dominant political party, a powerful bureaucracy, and a strong economy that rose phoenix-like from the ashes of World War II. In the Cold War years, the qualities upon which Japan's democracy were built allowed it to thrive. Concerned about security, the Japanese electorate was happy to delegate policy decisions to the iron triangle of the LDP supported by the bureaucracy and facilitating the prosperity of the corporate sector. In return, the voters were rewarded with jobs, a relatively egalitarian distribution of the national income, and a US security umbrella. It is of little surprise that a new generation of Japanese, who see

World War II in more of a historical than a personal context, should question some of the underlying assumptions of the Japanese democracy formula once the security issue began to lose its hold after the end of the Cold War. The Japan we see today is reconstructing its political system, less constrained by the perceptions of a previous generation and more open to new ideas and experiments. The constant in this reconstruction process is a commitment to constitutional democracy.

Some of the elements of the new construction are beginning to emerge. The 1955 system is no longer appropriate, but it has many stakeholders who have a strong interest in seeing some of its features retained. Neither the LDP, nor the bureaucracy, nor corporate Japan is simply going to give up its privileges without an attempt to incorporate at least some of them into the post-1955 system now under construction. To counter these forces for the status quo, the Japanese electorate and its media are demonstrating far more assertiveness in demanding change. What we are seeing is the end of LDP hegemony over the political system and its redesign into a fairer basis for the contestation for power. We are seeing a committed opposition taking advantage of that redesign in attempting to wrest power from the LDP. We are seeing more personality politics and less factional influence, as demonstrated by former prime minister Koizumi's relative political longevity. We are seeing more participation in politics by cause-oriented civil society groups outside the traditional channels of interest and industry groups. We are witnessing some cracks in the *kisha* club system that has dominated Japanese news reporting. We are even seeing the much-vaunted legal system come under review, with debate over amendments to the constitution and the introduction of a jury system in criminal trials. Throughout the process of reconstruction, the institutions of democracy have continued to function effectively, though the economy has not yet found its previous spark.

The Japanese system of governance is as unique to its circumstances as are those of the other countries being examined. It cannot be taken from the shelf and applied elsewhere. What is able to be borrowed is the process of democratic renewal that is taking place. Ultimately, institutions alone cannot sustain a democracy: people must involve themselves to trigger, and then encourage, democratic renewal. In hindsight, the 1995 Kobe earthquake may have been the event that brought the public back to center stage of Japanese democracy. The Japanese government mishandled the relief effort with the slack being taken up by over one million individual citizens.[15] This event both stripped the bureaucracy of its aura of prowess in governance and gave civil society groups the confidence to organize and involve themselves in public life. The Japanese public was thus able to seize the initiative from the politicians and demand basic reforms that would allow for greater public participation in policymaking. The delegative democracy of the 1955 system was deemed no longer acceptable, and a new system is now being designed and implemented. As noted, some institutional structures of the new system, such as the electoral design, are already in place. Other aspects, such as a two-party system, are only emerging. The final features, including constitutional amendment, may take a few more years to crystallize.

South Korea and Taiwan, in particular, follow developments in Japan closely and will be encouraged by the reform process they are witnessing as it parallels their own. If there is a general lesson to be drawn, it is that societies must remain open to reform and to adapt their institutions to the needs of the times. There is a wide range of options in the pursuit of the ideal of democracy. Each society must look for the right mix and, though trial and error is the most common method, there will be times when a society can also learn from the successes and errors of neighbors.

## Malaysia and Singapore

Casting our eyes over Pacific Asia, there are two countries that are in a strong position soon to join the ranks of the liberal democracies of the region. If one were to ask the governments of Malaysia and Singapore, they would insist that they are already practicing fully fledged democracy, and indeed the US State Department would appear to be endorsing this view in respect to Malaysia in inviting it to the Third Ministerial Meeting of the Community of Democracies in 2005.[16] Perhaps in a Malaysia under Abdullah Badawi there is more substance to this proposition than there was when the country was ruled by Mahathir Mohammed. But until government control of the media ends, human rights are respected, and the threat to dissenting political activists is lifted, doubts must remain over Malaysian democracy. Singapore's argument is based on the effectiveness of its governance.[17] The economic and social results obtained by the industrious city-state provide strong support for that argument. The problem is that this is the same argument used over the years by the Marcoses, Suhartos, and Park Chung Hees of Pacific Asia. Authoritarian states like to describe themselves as democracies but usually consider it necessary to add an adjective to the description. Democracy was thus limited and modified by such adjectives as "guided" or "disciplined." In Singapore's case, the adjectives in use are "trustee democracy" and "pragmatic democracy."[18] In all the previous cases, the argument had a "use by" date and the adjective was eventually stripped away. Singapore is suggesting that it is the exception to the rule.

In Chapter 5, I posited the formula under which the ruling parties of these two countries have successfully remained in power to date. The formula requires a permanent state of crisis threatening the future of the nation. In Malaysia, the crisis is based on the country's multiethnic composition and the position of disadvantage in which the Malay majority sees itself. In Singapore, the crisis is constructed from the island's geographic vulnerabilities. In response to the permanent state of crisis, the ruling parties present themselves as incomparably competent and indispensable managers, implicitly threatening *après moi le déluge*. However, the key to the success of the formula lies in its third component: the two parties must control the information received by the public about the nation-threatening crisis and the government's level of competence in its management. Without manipulating these messages to their rulers' benefit, the formula would not work for long. It seems doubtful that an increasingly sophisticated public, with access to information through the Internet and foreign news sources, will continue indefinitely to be constrained by the crisis/competence messages being served up by their governments. In Malaysia, the issues of corruption and nepotism may be the means of breaking free of the government's imposed discourse, and it is to Prime Minister Badawi's credit that he has had the sound political instincts to embrace the battle against corruption as his own. In Singapore, it may be exasperation with the "nanny" state and the regimentation it imposes that could be the issue that awakens the public. Singapore may be industrious, but it is rare to hear it described as innovative. Yet it is the latter quality that will bring success in this century, whereas it was the former that brought wealth in the last.

When the electorates of these two countries snap out of the political trance into which they have been induced, when their civil societies find their voice, when the media defies the constraints and allows that voice to be heard, when a true choice of leadership is available, and when the currently dominant political parties learn to lose and thereafter to participate in a party system offering true contestability, Malaysia and Singapore will become leading democracies in Pacific Asia. They will then discover that, rather than being a permanent crisis, the intercommunal discourse will become a subsidiary and ultimately manageable element in Malaysian politics. They will then understand that Singapore's geography is as much advantage as it is vulnerability. Most of all, they will come to appreciate that the strength of their nations rests on the talents of its people and does not need to place all its reliance on the projected competence of its ruling parties.

## Conclusion

Democracies may contain similar structures and features, but they will nevertheless look as different from each other as do individual human bodies. The difference in appearance between a Masai warrior and a Kalahari bushman may be stark, but they are still composed of the same structures and organs. Democracies may appear as very different, but they still require common structures, like free, fair, and meaningful elections.

Nor should we expect that democracies are constructed in the same order sequence. Our study of the various democracies of Pacific Asia demonstrates that there is no teleological sequence imposed upon the process of democratization. As shown in Table 5.1, some of the countries had long-established and strong political parties, but the party systems in which they operated were immature and are only now evolving into essentially two-party formats. All these countries began postcolonial life with a representative assembly; whereas the Indian parliament fulfilled its legislative and oversight duties from an early stage, most of the other parliaments took decades to finally assert themselves. The establishment of the rule of law has taken different courses in different countries. Judicial oversight appears strong in countries like Japan, India, and, more recently, South Korea but has not yet fully matured in the Southeast Asian democracies. Even the sequence seen by many as most persuasive,[19] economic growth leading to a growing middle class, which then demands political reform, has not been followed in India where democracy took hold in the years of economic stagnation before the more recent market liberalization process. Sequencing is therefore open to individual national negotiation. Perhaps what can be said is that there may be sequencing patterns that are propitious though not essential for democratic consolidation. Several of Pacific Asia's democracies have seen similar patterns of market freedom under soft-authoritarian regimes ostensibly regulated by façades of institutions that, upon popular demand, were able to be transformed into substantive institutions performing the roles required of them in a liberal democracy.

Different histories, different geographies, different political cultures, different qualities and quantities of institutional ingredients, and different sequencing of political development will cause different polities to look . . . different. But they may yet be able to fall under the unifying description of "democracy." There may also be a factor for convergence and for consolidation in their common membership of a civilization, and this is the subject of the final chapter.

## Notes

1. Alfred Stepan and Juan J. Linz, "Toward Consolidated Democracies," *Journal of Democracy* 7, no. 2 (1996): 31.

2. Douglas Webster, "Implementing Decentralization in Thailand: The Road Forward," Michael H. Nelson (ed.), *Thai Politics: Global and Local Perspectives— KPI Yearbook No. 2 (2002/2003)* (Bangkok: King Prajadhipok's Institute, 2004), pp. 473–500.

3. Robert A. Dahl, "Polyarchy," *Toward Democracy: A Journey—Reflections: 1940–1997, Volume 1* (Berkeley: Institute of Government Studies Press, 1997), pp. 94–95. The seven conditions are: (1) constitutionally invested elected officials implement government policy; (2) elected officials are chosen in free, fair, and frequent elections; (3) elections are run on the basis of universal adult suffrage; (4) vir-

tually all adults have the right to run for elective office; (5) citizens have freedom of expression; (6) citizens have a right to seek alternative sources of information; and (7) citizens have a right to form political parties and NGOs.

4. William Callaghan, "The Discourse of Vote Buying and Political Reform in Thailand," *Pacific Affairs* 78, no. 1: 95–113.

5. Angel Rabasa and John Haseman, *The Military and Democracy in Indonesia: Challenges, Politics, and Power* (Santa Monica: Rand Corporation, 2002), p. 70.

6. Bernard Lewis, *The Crisis of Islam—Holy War and Unholy Terror* (New York: Modern Library, 2003), p. 118.

7. The distinction between Islam in Indonesian and Malaysian politics is well brought out by Greg Fealy, "Islamisation and Politics in Southeast Asia: The Contrasting Cases of Malaysia and Indonesia," Nelly Lahoud and Anthony H. Johns (eds.), *Islam in World Politics* (London and New York: Routledge, 2005), pp. 152–169.

8. Robert W. Hefner, *Muslims and Democratization in Indonesia* (Princeton, NJ: Princeton University Press, 2000), p. 218.

9. Philippe C. Schmitter, "Parties Are Not What They Once Were," Larry Diamond and Richard Gunther (eds.), *Political Parties and Democracy* (Baltimore: Johns Hopkins University Press, 2001), p. 68.

10. Steve Muhlberger, "Democracy in Ancient India," available from www.nipissingu.ca/department/history/muhlberger/histdem/indiadem.htm.

11. Amartya Sen, "Argument and History," *The New Republic*, 8 August 2005, pp. 25–32.

12. For example, Niraja Gopal Jayal (ed.), *Democracy in India* (New Delhi: Oxford University Press, 2001).

13. Madhu Purnima Kishwar, *Deepening Democracy—Challenges of Governance and Globalization in India* (New Delhi: Oxford University Press, 2005), pp. 230–231.

14. John W. Dower, *Embracing Defeat: Japan in the Wake of World War II* (New York: W. W. Norton and Company, 1999).

15. Keiko Hirata, *Civil Society in Japan—The Growing Role of NGOs in Tokyo's Aid Development Policy* (New York: Palgrave Macmillan, 2002), pp. 33–34.

16. US Department of State, *Countries Invited to the Third Ministerial Meeting of the Community of Democracies*, available from www.state.gov/g/drl/44739.htm.

17. Bilahari Kausikan, "Government That Works," *Journal of Democracy* 8, no. 2 (1997): 24–34.

18. Prime Minister Goh Chok Tong quoted by Kausikan, "Government That Works," pp. 26–27.

19. Francis Fukuyama, *State Building—Governance and World Order in the Twenty-First Century* (London: Profile Books, 2004), pp. 19–27.

# 10

# Crystal Ball Gazing

"In the distant future, when people look back at
what happened in [the twentieth] century, they will find
it difficult not to accord primacy to the emergence of
democracy as the preeminently acceptable form of governance."
—Amartya Sen, "Democracy as a Universal Value"[1]

Pacific Asia's quest for democracy is of critical importance to its individual countries and their peoples. By embracing democracy, these countries will probably claim an advantage in governance and development.[2] They may eventually also benefit from a democratic peace dividend.[3] They are far more likely to enjoy the benefits of human rights protected and promoted by the state.[4] There is little need to look further than these substantial advantages to justify the pursuit of democracy in these countries or the study of this process. But it seems to me that the democratization of Pacific Asia will point to implications going well beyond the countries of Pacific Asia and beyond the region itself. It will have global implications.

Returning to the waves of democratization described in Chapter 1, it is clear that the first two waves overwhelmingly concerned Western civilization. The Jeffersonian wave flowed from the dawning of secular rationalism. Its democratic implications would slowly capture the support of large numbers of people of Europe, as well as the settler societies of large parts of the Americas and Oceania. The Churchillian wave was dominated by the painful victory of democracy over fascism in Europe that was completed with the Iberian transitions to democracy and the subsequent Latin American transitions they influenced. The Gorbachevian wave of democratization, however, has a more global reach. In the course of this third wave, many countries on several continents decided in favor of transitions away from authoritarianism. Did these transitions consistently lead to the consolidated practice of high-quality democracy? The reality is that very few of these transition countries outside the confines of Western civilization have consolidated their democracies. Which leads to the next question—Will the

273

practice of quality democracy remain largely confined to the West? A convincing negative response to this question must be based on empirical reality. Indian democracy provides the first clue that democracy is not simply a Western phenomenon. After India, the most significant body of large countries outside the Western group attempting to consolidate their democracies is to be found in Pacific Asia. The total population of the six democratizing countries of Pacific Asia comes to over 600 million people, while the population of the Western countries is a little over 1 billion. The size of these countries, together with their economic clout, make their process of democratization a phenomenon of global interest.

The significance of the group of countries under review is therefore undoubted. Yet they are significant for a reason going beyond their size and strength. Their significance turns on their civilizational distinctiveness. Pacific Asia's quest for democracy will help answer a fundamental question about democracy itself. Is democracy ultimately the appropriate form of government for all people in all nations among all civilizations? To begin to answer this question in the positive, we need to examine the way in which non-Western countries are practicing democracy and in particular pose the question: Can democracy be consolidated in the nations of a non-Western civilization? If consolidated democracy can span two civilizations then it is not limited simply to the West, and this logically opens the possibility that it can span three or four or all six civilizations. India already provides a promising initial response. Japan contributes further to this answer. Many more consolidated democracies in Pacific Asia will help complete that response. The next question we need to answer is whether there are any particular reasons why the countries of Pacific Asia should be incapable of consolidating their democracies.

## Pacific Asia Has Run Out of Excuses

### The "Cruel Dilemma," "Unfit for Democracy," and Other Excuses

A new opinion always seems to carry more authority when it comes from the then champion of the prevailing contradistinctive view. It attracts attention because it carries with it both the titillation of confession and the aura of revelation. And so it is with Jagdish Bhagwati, who wrote an influential book in 1966 in which he argued that developing countries faced a "cruel dilemma"—they had to choose between democracy and development, because democratically elected governments would not be able to demonstrate the discipline and resolve required to demand from their electorates the sacrifices so necessary for economic development.[5] Bhagwati has had a change of heart and now believes that "the quality of democracy greatly affects the quality of development."[6]

The "cruel dilemma" is only one of many excuses that have been proffered over the years to explain why democracy is not appropriate for this or that country. Sen explained the process of making such excuses as follows:

> Throughout the nineteenth century, theorists of democracy found it quite natural to discuss whether one country or another was "fit for democracy." This thinking changed only in the twentieth century, with the recognition that the question itself was wrong: A country does not have to be deemed fit *for* democracy; rather, it has to become fit *through* democracy. This is indeed a momentous change, extending the potential reach of democracy to cover billions of people, with their varying histories and cultures and disparate levels of affluence.[7]

Other excuses to join the "unfit for democracy" and "cruel dilemma" arguments have emerged over the years. Poverty, illiteracy, and underdevelopment top the list. A variation on these is the argument that a nation must first of all secure economic rights for its people before "granting" political rights. This is a convenient argument for authoritarian rulers who fall back on stock generalizations that their people are not ready for democracy or that their people prefer to have food in their stomachs than ballots in their hands. Sen's argument strips bare these justifications for authoritarianism. People want food and ballots. And to continue Sen's line of reasoning, ballots lead to food, as he demonstrated in his argument that "no substantial famine has ever occurred in any independent and democratic country with a relatively free press."[8]

What needs to be conceded is that poverty certainly makes the task of building democracy more daunting, and illiteracy makes the establishment of rule of law particularly problematic. By putting the issue in terms of its level of difficulty, developing countries are rescued from their cruel dilemma and put on notice that democratic governance can be achieved, but the level of difficulty increases with poverty. So wealth, literacy, and development should not be seen as preconditions for democracy but rather as enablers of the process.

Development and literacy problems in Pacific Asia have largely been resolved. Table 10.1 compares the six selected countries of Pacific Asia with other regions of the world and demonstrates that all are comparable to the OECD countries in terms of literacy; all but Indonesia are within OECD proportions in gross educational enrollment ratios; and all are nearly at or above 70 years life expectancy at birth. In comparing income levels, three of the countries are in the OECD league; Thailand is on a par with the averages in Latin America and Central/Eastern Europe; and Indonesia and the Philippines are well above the African and South Asian averages. All the

**Table 10.1   Comparing Human Development in Pacific Asian Democracies, 2003**

| | Life Expectancy at Birth (years) | Adult Literacy Rate (% of ages 15+) | Combined Gross Enrollment Ratio (%) | Gross Domestic Product per Capita (PPP US$)[a] | Human Development Index Value |
|---|---|---|---|---|---|
| Indonesia | 67 | 88 | 65 | 3,230 | 0.692 |
| Japan | 82 | 99 | 84 | 26,940 | 0.938 |
| South Korea | 75 | 98 | 92 | 16,950 | 0.888 |
| Philippines | 70 | 93 | 81 | 4,170 | 0.753 |
| Taiwan | 77 | 96 | 93 | 22,808 | 0.895 |
| Thailand | 69 | 93 | 73 | 7,010 | 0.768 |
| African states | 46 | 63 | 44 | 1,790 | 0.465 |
| Arab states | 66 | 63 | 60 | 5,069 | 0.651 |
| Central/East Europe | 70 | 99 | 79 | 7,192 | 0.796 |
| Latin America/Caribbean | 71 | 89 | 81 | 7,223 | 0.777 |
| OECD | 77 | 99 | 87 | 24,904 | 0.911 |
| South Asia | 63 | 58 | 54 | 2,658 | 0.584 |

*Sources:* UNDP 2004 report reflecting the 2003 Human Development Index, http://hdr.undp.org/statistics/data/; Ko Shu-ling, "Taiwan 24th in Development Index Ranking," *Taipei Times,* 2 December 2003, p. 3; World Economic Outlook Database, International Monetary Fund, 2002, www.imf.org/external/pubs/ft/weo/2002/01/data/.

*Note:* a. PPP is purchasing power parity.

democracies of Pacific Asia have a higher Human Development Index score than the average in the African, Arab, and South Asian regions. Development remains a challenge in Indonesia and the Philippines; however, in relation to democratic consolidation, the challenge does not disable these nations from consolidating their democracies, but it does complicate the problem.

## Compelling Excuses

Conflict is a powerful excuse. Whether the conflict has degenerated to war or is simmering and threatening war, democracy cannot be seen as an instant peace panacea. Retaining democratic structures as a country descends into civil war, as in Sri Lanka, is a difficult undertaking. Building democratic structures for the first time in a country wracked by conflict strikes me as a task of Sisyphean proportions.

Another compelling excuse concerns the nature of the polity in which democracy is seeking to be implanted. If there is no community imagined as such by its inhabitants, it is difficult to see how that territory can build the communal institutions of democracy. This was brought home to me by a colleague from the Solomon Islands. He told me that it was only when he left his country for the first time and traveled to New Zealand to attend university that he heard the term *Solomon Islander* and realized, to his surprise, that it was being applied to him. He had only ever thought of himself as a Malaitan, a reference to his home island in the nation archipelago. It is little wonder that the Solomon Islands is finding it difficult to build the national institutions of democracy. As already noted, the road to Westminster passes through Westphalia.

Poverty, war, and nation building are all challenges that have been faced, and largely overcome, in Pacific Asia. The question of nation does not present itself in Pacific Asia in the same way as it does in parts of Africa or Melanesia. Nations such as Japan, Korea, and Thailand have seen themselves as communities akin to Westphalian nations for centuries. The same level of confidence cannot be employed for Indonesia, the Philippines, and Taiwan. The first two are archipelagos that came together as nations via the imaginations of colonial officials. Both adopted national vernacular languages as unifying mechanisms. Both adopted the governmental structures of unitary states upon independence to reinforce that unity. Both championed the archipelagic concept in the UN Law of the Sea Convention to bring a greater spatial coherence to that constructed unity. And both built up their international respectability to give that unity international legitimacy. The strategies have largely succeeded. As an autocracy, Indonesia had the feel of a Javanese empire. As a democracy, it seems less orderly on the surface, but its roots are spreading farther and penetrating more deeply. Aceh and West Papua remain areas of considerable difficulty needing to be resolved by deliberation and negotiation, not by force of arms. Let us hope it does not require a tragedy of tsunami proportions to allow the Papua question to be resolved as the Aceh issue appears to be. The Philippines has made considerable strides in integrating the Muslim south into its midst, but as the example of Thailand has shown, this is an issue that needs continuing attention.

South Korea and Taiwan also face the daunting question of "nation." Both polities were divided or formed through divisions in the course of the Cold War. Unlike Southeast Asia, the Cold War has left unresolved these two intranational issues in Northeast Asia. Both the North Korea/South Korea and the China/Taiwan divides are possible flashpoints for serious conflicts. Given the primordial importance of security in any polity's priorities, it is little wonder that these divides weigh heavily on South Korean and Taiwanese democracy. The influence is particularly evident in Taiwan, where the issue of Taiwan's place vis-à-vis China is the dominant national concern. The Korean divide also weighs heavily on politics in Seoul and contributes to South Korea's deep conservative/progressive polarization.[9]

While there is a necessity for a broadly common imagined community among the people of a polity to hold it together as a nation, the nation prob-

lems in Indonesia, the Philippines, South Korea, and Taiwan, while significant, are not such as to preclude that common imagination from forming.
They add a level of difficulty in these societies' consolidation of their
democracies; they color the deliberative rhetoric of politics; and they put
pressure on politicians to temper populism that might jeopardize security.
But they do not add up to an unfulfilled precondition.

We can conclude that the above six countries of Pacific Asia have no
excuses available for not practicing democracy, and they have accepted this
reality. The task for Indonesia and the Philippines looms as more difficult
than may be the case for the other polities, but even these two countries are
sufficiently coherent, literate, and developed to be able to overcome the difficulties these challenges pose. While this analysis has been directed at the
region's democracies, it could also be applied to nearly all the other nations
of Pacific Asia with very similar conclusions.

## Civilizational Consensus

Chapter 2 elaborated six ways to view Pacific Asia. Three were geographic,
by positive, negative, and oceanic perspectives, and the others were architectural, civilizational, and imagined. Having a variety of perspectives
inevitably raises the question of which is the most influential. The answer
depends on the issue being considered. For trade and security issues, the
geographic perspectives would be dominant because of the importance of
contiguity or at least proximity and of access to trade routes in these fields.
For the purposes of diplomacy, the regional architecture may be the most
important feature, because it readily allows diplomatic initiatives to be pursued. Which perspectives are most influential for consolidating democracy
in Pacific Asia?

It seems to me that for community building the most influential perspective is the common imagination of the members of that community. It is
when a community is generally imagined by its members to exist, that it
takes substance. When that imagined community correlates to a civilizational category, the substance becomes more profound. To understand how
Pacific Asia might imagine itself as a community of democracies, it may be
instructive to compare Pacific Asia to a region of the world comprising
many different nations where democracy is nevertheless well and truly consolidated.

### Democracy in Europe

Aspects of democracy in Europe have been under construction for centuries.
Once forged, some nations of Europe stuck to their democratic system
through thick and thin; others vacillated as they experimented with other

forms of governance. It was not until the mid-1970s that fascism was fully discarded, and not until the late 1980s that communism was superseded. Before the defeat of fascism and communism, liberal democracy as the appropriate form of governance was the norm in most of Western Europe but was contested within European civilization as a whole. Democracy is practiced within a nation-state, but that nation-state exists within geographic and civilizational contexts that have a deep impact on the nation and its practice of democracy. Individual countries practicing liberal democracy can readily be listed, but there is a different quality to this practice if the country is isolated from other democracies. The quality of the practice of democracy is deepened if its practitioners are members of a group of nations determined both to practice democracy internally and to share the benefits of so doing with their like-minded neighbors. In other words, there is an enhanced quality of democracy in a group of democracy practitioners that goes beyond the sum of its parts. In Europe, the first coherent group of like-minded nations practicing democracy was the European Economic Community (EEC) and its associates. The economic performance and social cohesion of the members of this group contributed to the eventual defeat of both fascism and communism by demonstrating the superior qualities of democracy and the market economy.

By 1990, it was possible to describe the group of like-minded democracies not as the EEC but simply as Europe, because in November of that year, in the post–Cold War euphoria that energized the continent, the countries of Europe, in adopting the Charter of Paris, articulated their determination to make democracy their *only* possible form of government. Among the commitments in the Charter of Paris was the determination throughout Europe to "undertake to build, consolidate and strengthen democracy as *the only system of government of our nations*" (emphasis added).[10] This statement marks the end of any contestation over the appropriateness of democracy for Europe, though, of course, it does not mark the attainment of the ideal of democracy. It expresses a civilizational consensus in favor of democracy and a commitment to construct it in accordance with human rights and fundamental freedoms. It is at this point, I believe, that we can confidently describe democracy as consolidated in Europe, employing the sternest interpretation of the "only game in town" test. The civilizational consensus in favor of democracy establishes European democracy's irreversibility because it has eliminated all those forms contesting governance status. This may or may not be the "end of world history" as evocatively argued by Fukuyama,[11] but it is clearly the historical end of Europe's debate over whether or not to embrace democracy unequivocally.

It is possible, and perhaps in some cases, even highly likely, that some nations of Europe would have persevered with the construction of their democracies irrespective of this civilizational consensus. But the absence of the civilizational consensus comes at a cost and perhaps even raises a doubt about democracy's irreversibility. The most apparent cost is the loss of the democratic peace dividend.[12] Established democracies do not go to war against each other, and so consolidated democratic nations surrounded by other consolidated democratic nations can face the future without concerns over border wars or violent irredentism. The peace dividend goes much further. Borders can be opened and restrictions on regional travel lifted. This encourages the people-to-people links that further reinforce the democratic peace. The dividend extends to trade and commerce, where open borders, open highways, and open skies allow for vast markets to be created for the benefit of both producers and consumers. The civilizational consensus also establishes confidence in the political system internally. No plausible alternative is being put forward by any significant group in similar societies. The public conversation may continue to be vociferous in its espousal of various policy options, but there are no significant voices calling for the replacement of democracy as a system of government. This allows democracy successfully to traverse difficult periods of economic downturn and social change. The example of the commitment to democracy of neighbors reinforces the commitment to democracy at home in a continuous virtuous cycle.

Care is needed in understanding the role of a civilizational consensus in that it is probably not a necessary element for the national consolidation of democracy. Botswana and Costa Rica were able to sustain a certain commitment to the practice of democracy in spite of once being surrounded by non-democratic regimes. But their isolation within a broader region where democracy was the exception rather than the rule impacts negatively on the quality of their democracies. The absence of a civilizational consensus also raises a doubt about the sustainability of democracy, and the doubt grows with the level of hostility generated by those neighbors and is compounded by any disadvantageous disparities in power. A civilizational consensus in favor of democracy improves that quality and removes that doubt. It instills confidence that democracy has indeed been consolidated. A civilizational consensus in favor of democracy is therefore the decisive milestone that confirms democracy's irreversibility. Europe has passed that milestone. Has Pacific Asia?

## A Civilizational Consensus in Pacific Asia?

When Thailand returns to the fold and Malaysia and Singapore join Indonesia, Japan, South Korea, the Philippines, and Taiwan as liberal democracies in Pacific Asia, the region will have made an enormous stride in making democracy its normal mode of governance. The battle in these eight countries will not yet have been won, but the correct societal goal will have been set—to build high-quality democracies. The goal is a difficult one with various pathways and differences in the pace of progress. History is not linear and there will be setbacks along the way. It will be up to each of the countries to audit its own progress toward the ideals it has set for itself by monitoring the milestones it has passed. Each country will find that the construction of democracy brings with it certain salutary features. Public criticism of leaders and policies becomes constructive input, not regime-threatening sedition. The public conversation becomes unscripted and unpredictable, not turgid and propagandistic. It seems to be a feature of democratic systems that politicians are not revered, except perhaps posthumously, but they may nevertheless be reelected. Rather than being above the law, leaders in democratic countries are probably even more subject to its strictures because of the relentlessness of the media-driven public gaze under which they must operate. The electorates in democracies learn to live with disappointment and disillusionment. Hopefully, they do not become cynical but, rather, develop the capacity to learn from setbacks. These electorates accept the occasional inefficiencies of democratic life as the norm and thus don't look for leadership from messianic figures offering ultimately impossible utopian solutions. As suggested in the previous chapter, the individual democracies of Pacific Asia are moving in this direction.

## Searching for a Civilizational Consensus

In searching for a civilizational consensus, it is helpful for it to be solemnly articulated in a document. The Treaties of Westphalia in 1648 set down the newly formed consensus on the organization of Europe through nation-states, and the 1990 Charter of Paris articulated Europe's commitment to democracy. Neither the Sinic nor the Indic civilizations has comparable documentation. The consensus therefore needs to be found in an analysis of civilizational practice. In analyzing the practice of members of these civilizations, one is immediately confronted with their diversity in political organization. It is important to view this diversity in its proper context. A preliminary question is whether a glaring exception is sufficient to nullify a general consensus. North Korea is a totalitarian state. Does that in itself mean Sinic civilization as a whole cannot form a consensus in favor of democracy? Returning to Europe for a comparison, Moldova is having great difficulty living up to its constitutional status as a parliamentary democracy, but this clearly does not invalidate the European consensus for democracy. A single recalcitrant state therefore need not of itself invalidate a civilizational consensus. A consensus does not necessarily require uniform practice of all its members.

Pacific Asia, however, has not one but several recalcitrant states. Burma is a military dictatorship; Brunei is ruled by inherited power; while

China, Vietnam, and Laos maintain one-party political systems. The next step in this argument is to make sense of this diversity by assigning weight to the influence of individual countries in the formation of a civilizational consensus. Thus, for example, Brunei carries little weight in view of its small population, regardless of its vast wealth. Burma has a large population but finds itself on the periphery of Pacific Asia both geographically and politically. North Korea maintains so abhorrent a system of government as to be shunned by all and a model for none. Brunei, Burma, and North Korea can therefore comfortably be set aside as exceptional in their various ways. Our search is for the mainstream, not the side streams.

The search for the mainstream in Pacific Asian political ideology, however, immediately confronts the reality that there are two strong streams of thought. The market-based democracies number eight, though the liberal democracies among them only have five candidates. The market-based autocracies run by communist parties have three countries in China, Vietnam, and Laos, with a fourth, Cambodia, probably currently fitting better in this camp than on the democracies list. Commitment to the market is a unifying feature of Pacific Asia, but the political chasm dividing the two streams of thought is deep. Communism in Pacific Asia has not gone the way of its fraternal ally in Europe. Chinese and Vietnamese communist parties have sought renewed legitimacy not through revolutionary rhetoric, nor through exploiting supposed class divisions, but through the more rigorous test of economic performance. Of their Marxist-Leninist political heritage, Marxism has been largely discarded but Leninism remains strong. The symbols have been stripped back to the memory of Mao Zedong and Ho Chi Minh, though even these icons of communist legitimacy will ultimately have difficulty resisting the inevitable process of historical reinterpretation that will soon replace the official hagiographies. The key remaining element of their political heritage is the monopoly of the party on making all decisions of importance. Anathema of alternation of power holders is the ultimate distinction between the communist stream and its democratic competitor.

I caught some of the flavor of this in 2000 when, during a visit to Hanoi, I called on the Vietnamese Central Council for Theoretical Research that advises the party on matters related to the social sciences. The learned gentlemen of the council were most hospitable and seemed to be enjoying our discussion of various controversies in the social sciences. We spoke about gender relations, about social safety nets, and about the plight of indigenous people. The level of frankness on their part came as a surprise to me. They said Vietnam had achieved a great deal in raising the status of women, but there was a long way to go. They lamented the poor social welfare services provided by the state and argued the need for a radical improvement. They listened to my description of the aboriginal struggle for land rights in Australia and saw some parallels in the plight of some

Montagnard people in Vietnam. Encouraged by this degree of openness, I steered the conversation to the issue of democracy, which, after all, they would have understood from my business card, it was my function to promote. Again they listened politely to my presentation on the benefits of policy contestation and the need for the electorate to make regular and periodic choices between competing points of view represented by organized groups such as political parties. At this point, however, the good-natured conversational to-and-fro ended, and the Vietnamese side turned to the head of their delegation, who proceeded to deliver a set speech about the wisdom of the Communist Party and the complete faith the Vietnamese people have in it. A multiparty system was a foreign idea, he said, that the Vietnamese people would never accept. Vietnam would follow its own path and would not be swayed by foreign ideologies. The discussion had clearly come to an end, and my only response, as my Vietnamese counterpart railed against foreign ideologies, was to give a long and hard look at the portraits of Karl Marx and Friedrich Engels that had pride of place on the wall to my left.

### The Core State Is China

The problem of two major political currents running through the region is more serious than might be suggested by the simple count of adherents to one group or the other. In his analysis of the dynamics of civilizational politics, Huntington makes a distinction between the core state in a civilization and those states in the concentric circles around that core state.[13] Core states exert a disproportionate influence over their civilizations on issues such as security, social mores, and political ideology. The 1950 pact between France and Germany that led to today's European Union confirmed these two countries as the core influence at the heart of continental Europe.

In Pacific Asia, the core country is China. This is true from historical, cultural, and strategic perspectives, and its truth is only occasionally diminished in the various, often self-imposed, historical periods of Chinese decline. Today, China is certainly not in decline, and its economic vitality reinforces its historical role as the core nation in Pacific Asian civilization and provides confirmation for the way China has traditionally seen itself as that core nation, or in its own parlance, the middle kingdom. It is difficult to see how a civilizational consensus in favor of democracy can emerge without China's concurrence. Japan's commitment to democracy goes some way to counteract China, but Japan, though a country of great influence in the region, has not been able to usurp the position of the region's core country. History and demography weigh too heavily in China's favor.

There is a cruel irony in the attitude toward democracy in Asia's two major civilizations. Sinic civilization in Pacific Asia has half a dozen practicing democracies, but its core state is at present hostile to it. Indic civilization in South Asia has a core state that has resolutely adopted democracy as its form of governance, but it is surrounded by states that are unwilling to make this choice or unable to make it work. The result is that a civilizational consensus for democracy is compromised in both civilizations. In neither civilization is it possible to say that the milestone of civilizational consensus has been passed, and therefore a doubt persists about the irreversibility of democracy among its Asian practitioners.

In the absence of such a civilizational consensus, neither Pacific Asia nor the Indian subcontinent can benefit fully from the democratic peace. Taiwan faces a direct threat from China, as does South Korea from North Korea. The rest of the region—and indeed the world—has to endure the uncertainty of these possible intraregional conflicts. The democratic peace theory would come under a severe test were Pakistan to become a consolidated democracy, as the thesis holds that consolidated democracies do not go to war against each other. Until such time, the theory goes untested in South Asia, and India gains no benefit from it. The theory also goes untested in Pacific Asia for as long as China adheres to its present political orthodoxy.

The democratic peace theory deals with the issue of war, but the democratic peace dividend delivers far more than the absence of war. It allows nations to thrive in cooperation with each other. Europe provides the example, and I would propose a simple test—look at a map of the continent and count the number of international borders through which a private vehicle can cross without obtaining prior permission. Open borders imply open societies and democracy thrives in such societies. Looking at the map of Europe, I lost count after reaching thirty such borders. In all of Asia, I believe the comparable figure is one or perhaps two. A private car may cross the causeway between Malaysia and Singapore after payment of the relevant charges. Until the troubles in southern Thailand, it was also possible to cross fairly freely between Malaysia and Thailand, but security checks make this more difficult today. None of the other scores of borders in Pacific Asia is open to private vehicles. The reasons for these blocked borders go well beyond infrastructure problems. It is mainly because of governance and security problems. Democracy and its fellow traveler, peace, would open up those borders, just as it would open these societies to fulfill their potential.

## Crystal Ball Gazing

China holds the key to the formation of a civilizational consensus for democracy in Pacific Asia. Having arrived at the last subheading of the last chapter, this is not the place to begin an in-depth analysis of the future of China. Some key questions nevertheless need to be posed. There is no denying the progress China has made since accepting the futility of blindly following simplistic ideological notions. Slogans as policy led China to the disaster of the Cultural Revolution. Pragmatism and the market have released the pent-up commercial savvy of the Chinese people and put China on the road to material success. China's Human Development Index score has jumped a commendable 232 points from .523 in 1975 to .755 in 2003.[14] Market reforms have been a success, but governance reforms have been mixed. Chinese people have more associational freedom than in the past, have greater access to information, and have been granted the right to vote freely in local elections. On the negative side, freedom of speech remains limited, rule by law has not been replaced by rule of law, and the party remains dominant in the nation's public life. This mix of partial freedom and growing expectations, met by a determination to maintain the party's hegemony, produced the tragedy of Tiananmen Square in 1989. The question to be posed is whether market reform can succeed without political reform. Can a one-party system successfully manage a capitalist economy?

China's economic success, its growing prestige, and its military capacities require that we take seriously the governance formula of single-party capitalism. Backed by a new ideological brew of nationalism, developmentalism, and Maoist foundation myths, and delivering significant economic results clearly benefiting large segments of Chinese society, the "Beijing formula" is a formidable challenge to the "Washington formula" of market democracy. The reason the Chinese formula has worked to date may, however, be specific to a certain time period. After the famines and poverty under Mao, the Chinese people were very grateful for a period of pragmatism and realism. After watching the Soviet Union's collapse, and the collapse of living standards accompanying it, Chinese reformers understandably gravitated more toward gradual change than "big bang" upheaval. The generation that lived through the Maoist period will be very happy for Deng Xiaoping's cat to catch the mice regardless of its color. But the generation of spoilt "young emperors" living through the period of material opportunity will be far more demanding. Can the single-party system demonstrate the dexterity to keep up with these demands? It is here that the Beijing formula displays its basic weakness. Central planning of the economy failed and economic decisionmaking was in large part allowed to pass to individual consumers and producers. Central planning of politics remains, however, as individuals in the form of deliberators and voters are given a highly constrained role. Will these consumers and producers not wish also to become deliberators and voters?

I must leave to the China experts the task of tackling such large questions, noting that one recent study sees some movement toward democratic processes in China while another considers China's transition to democracy to be trapped.[15] It may be worthwhile looking at some neighboring precedents. A conclusion that flows from the examples of other Asian countries is that the formula of single-party capitalism cannot be relied on indefinitely. It has been attempted by military governments and authoritarian civilian governments in various parts of Pacific Asia. The episodes vary from country to country, but the underlying logic remains. Developmentalism and nationalism cannot sustain governmental legitimacy forever. It might succeed for an entire generation or it might succeed while an impression of permanent crisis persists, but eventually a challenge arises over which it is unable to prevail without recourse to force and repression. Even the use of force may only delay the inevitable demise of the authoritarian system. People with economic freedom eventually insist on having political freedom because one complements the other. It is difficult seeing China as an exception to this process.

If China wishes to learn from an applicable precedent, then it need look no further than Taiwan, where another Leninist party successfully managing a capitalist economy was forced to accede to popular demands for political openness, which soon opened the Pandora's box of democracy. That process led to the electoral defeat of the Leninist party, which, if it returns to power in subsequent elections, will be required to govern without its Leninist methods. Taiwanese people were not satisfied with economic freedom alone. The same lesson can be drawn from South Korea's determined march to democracy, where economic growth alone could not rescue the generals. The limits of authoritarian developmentalism can also be seen in the recent history of Indonesia. Singapore stands for the time being as an exception, but it is hardly a precedent for China, which has a population of well over a billion and over a dozen cities with populations larger than that of the city-state. Asian governments will be judged by their economic results, but they will also be judged on their democratic credentials. Neither Confucian heritage nor Asian Values stood in the way of the demand for democracy in so many Asian countries to date. Thailand will return to the fold. Malaysia and Singapore will be the next democratic dominoes. China, I believe, will follow thereafter.

Amartya Sen shared a deep insight when he proclaimed that in the twentieth century, democracy became a universal value. Democracy may be seen as valuable everywhere, but in many places it is also said to be inapplicable. As we have seen, the arguments for the inapplicability of democracy include poverty, inexperience, and a cultural heritage hostile to its tenets. These arguments are invariably proffered by incumbents, be they generals, general secretaries of communist parties, or benevolent wise men who always know best. The challenge of the twenty-first century is to have democracy accepted, not simply as a universal value, but as the normal form of government for all countries. In the first decade of this century, "democracy as the only system of government for our nations" can only be a description of the situation in Europe and, indeed, the Western world. To be confident that this outcome can apply universally, it is important to see non-Western adherents to the irreversible adoption of democratic governance. That has certainly occurred in various non-Western nations, with India and Japan being the leading examples. Satisfying though these examples are, they do not parallel the Western example of a civilizational consensus for democracy. What is required is for another of the world's civilizations to adopt "democracy as the only system of government for our nations." It is only then that we can be confident that democracy is not a Western practice copied by a few others, nor simply a universal value, but that it is the universally applicable system of government.

The democratic systems of the countries of Pacific Asia have their faults, as this book has shown. There continue to be setbacks and stumbles along the path to democracy. But I still see a commitment in the region to continue to construct higher-quality forms of democracy. The construction process will be shaped through lessons learned by electors and elected alike both from their own mistakes and from the practice of neighboring states. Pacific Asian democracy has critical mass, but it has not yet reached the point of irreversibility that comes with a civilizational consensus for democracy. When the Chinese stream eventually flows into the democratic mainstream, as I believe it will, Pacific Asia will be the next civilization to embrace democracy unequivocally.

## Notes

1. Amartya Sen, "Democracy as a Universal Value," *Journal of Democracy* 10, no. 2 (1999): 4.

2. Morton H. Halperin, Joseph T. Siegle, and Michael M. Weinstein, *The Democracy Advantage: How Democracies Promote Prosperity and Peace* (New York: Routledge, 2004).

3. Bruce Russett, *Grasping the Democratic Peace* (Princeton: Princeton University Press, 1993).

4. Roland Rich, "Bringing Democracy into International Law," *Journal of Democracy* 12, no. 3 (July 2001): 23–25.

5. Jagdish Bhagwati, *Economics of Underdeveloped Countries* (New York: McGraw-Hill, 1966).

6. Jagdish Bhagwati, "New Thinking on Development," *Journal of Democracy* 6, no. 4 (1995): 59.

7. Sen, "Democracy as a Universal Value," p. 3.

8. Ibid., pp. 7–8.

9. Hahm Chaibong, "The Two South Koreas: A House Divided," *Washington Quarterly* 28, no. 3 (Summer 2005): 57–72.

10. Charter of Paris for a New Europe, 19–21 November 1990, available from www.osce.org/documents/mcs/1990/11/4045_en.pdf.

11. Francis Fukuyama, *The End of History and the Last Man* (New York: Avon Books, 1993).

12. Russett, *Grasping the Democratic Peace.*

13. Samuel P. Huntington, *The Clash of Civilizations and the Remaking of World Order* (New York: Simon and Schuster, 1996), chapter 7.

14. UNDP, *HDR 2003*, available from http://hdr.undp.org/reports/global/2005/pdf/HDR05_HDI.pdf.

15. Suzanne Ogden, *Inklings of Democracy in China* (Cambridge, MA, and London: Harvard University Asia Center, 2002). Minxin Pei, *China's Trapped Transition: The Limits of Developmental Autocracy* (Cambridge, MA: Harvard University Press, 2006).

# Abbreviations

| | |
|---|---|
| ABS-CBN | Alto Broadcasting System–Chronicle Broadcasting Network |
| ACFID | Australian Council for International Development |
| APEC | Asia Pacific Economic Cooperation |
| ARF | ASEAN Regional Forum |
| ASEAN | Association of South East Asian Nations |
| BBC | British Broadcasting Corporation |
| BJP | Bharatiya Janata Party (India) |
| BJS | Bharatiya Jana Sangh |
| BN | Barisan Nasional (National Front) (Malaysia) |
| BSPP | Burma Socialist Programme Party |
| CAGE | Citizens' Alliance for the 2000 General Elections (South Korea) |
| CCEJ | Citizens' Coalition for Economic Justice (South Korea) |
| CDC | Constitutional Drafting Commission (Thailand) |
| CDI | Centre for Democratic Institutions (Australia) |
| CNN | Cable News Network |
| COMELEC | Commission on Elections (Philippines) |
| CP | Chart Pattana Party (Thailand) |
| CPP | Cambodian People's Party |
| DPD | Dewan Perwakilan Daerah (Representative Assembly of the Regions) (Indonesia) |
| DPJ | Democratic Party of Japan |
| DPP | Democratic Progressive Party (Taiwan) |
| DPR | Dewan Perwakilan Rakyat (People's Representative Assembly) (Indonesia) |
| DPRD | Dewan Perwakilan Rakyat Daerah (Regional Representative Assemblies) (Indonesia) |
| DPRK | Democratic People's Republic of Korea |
| EDSA | Epifanio de los Santos Avenue (Philippines) |
| EEC | European Economic Community |
| FEER | *Far Eastern Economic Review* |
| FPTP | first past the post |
| FUNCINPEC | United Front for an Independent, Neutral, Peaceful, and Cooperative Cambodia |
| GDP | gross domestic product |

| | |
|---|---|
| GNP | Grand National Party (South Korea) |
| Golkar | Sekretariat Bersama Golongan Karya (Joint Secretariat of Functional Groups) (Indonesia) |
| IMF | International Monetary Fund |
| IPU | International Parliamentary Union |
| iTV | Independent Television Station (Thailand) |
| JSP | Japan Socialist Party |
| KBL | Kilusang Bagong Lipunan (New Society Party) (Philippines) |
| KMT | Kuomintang (Taiwan) |
| LAMMP | Laban ng Makabayang Masang Pilipino (Struggle of the Nationalist Filipino Masses) |
| LBH | Lembaga Bantuan Hukum (Legal Aid Institute) (Indonesia) |
| LD | Laban ng Demokratikong Pilipina (Philippine Democratic Party) |
| LDP | Liberal Democratic Party (Japan) |
| LP | Liberal Party (Philippines) |
| LPP | Lao People's Party |
| LPRP | Lao People's Revolutionary Party |
| MCA | Malaysian Chinese Association |
| MDP | Millennium Democratic Party (South Korea) |
| MIC | Malaysian Indian Congress |
| MP | member of Parliament |
| MPR | Majelis Permusyaratan Rakyat (People's Consultative Assembly) (Indonesia) |
| NAMFREL | National Citizens Movement for Free Elections (Philippines) |
| NAP | New Aspiration Party (Thailand) |
| NGOs | nongovernmental organizations |
| NP | Nacionalista Party (Philippines) |
| NPC | Nepali Congress Party |
| NU | Nahdatul Ulama (Indonesia) |
| ODA | official development assistance |
| OECD | Organisation for Economic Cooperation and Development |
| PAP | People's Action Party (Singapore) |
| PAS | Islamic Party of Malaysia |
| PCIJ | Philippine Center for Investigative Journalism |
| PCNC | Philippine Council for NGO Certification |
| PDI-P | Democratic Party of Indonesia–Struggle |
| PDP | Phalang Dharma Party (Thailand) |
| PDS | Prosperous Peace Party (Indonesia) |
| PFP | People First Party (Taiwan) |
| PKB | Partai Kebangkitan Bangsa (National Awakening Party) (Indonesia) |

| | |
|---|---|
| PKI | Communist Party of Indonesia |
| PKS | Prosperous Justice Party (Indonesia) |
| PMP | Partido ng Masang Pilipino (Party of the Philippine Masses) |
| PNG | Papua New Guinea |
| PNI | Indonesian National Party |
| PPP | Development Unity Party (Indonesia) |
| PR | proportional representation |
| PSPD | People's Solidarity for Participatory Democracy (South Korea) |
| QWERTY | arrangement of typing keyboard |
| SBY | Susilo Bambang Yudhyono (president of Indonesia) |
| SEAPA | Southeast Asia Press Alliance |
| SLFP | Sri Lankan Freedom Party |
| TI | Transparency International |
| TNI | Tentara Nasional Indonesia (Armed Forces of Indonesia) |
| TRTP | Thai Rak Thai Party |
| TVRI | Public Television Indonesia |
| ULD | United Liberal Democratic Party (South Korea) |
| UMNO | United Malays National Organisation (Malaysia) |
| UN | United Nations |
| UNICEF | United Nations Children's Fund |
| UNP | United National Party (Sri Lanka) |

# Bibliography

All websites accessed 30 November 2006.

Anderson, Benedict R. "Elections and Participation," R. H. Taylor (ed.), *The Politics of Elections in Southeast Asia*. Washington, DC: Woodrow Wilson Center Press and Cambridge University Press, 1996.
———. *Imagined Communities*, 2nd ed. London: Verso, 1991.
Antlöv, Hans. "Not Enough Politics! Power, Participation and the Democratic Polity," Edward Aspinal and Greg Fealy (eds.), *Local Power and Politics in Indonesia—Decentralisation and Democratisation*. Singapore: Institute for Southeast Asian Studies, 2003, pp. 72–86.
Anuar, Mustafa K. "Defining Democratic Discourses—The Mainstream Press," Francis Loh Kok Wah and Khoo Boo Teik (eds.), *Democracy in Malaysia—Discourses and Practices*. Richmond, Surrey: Curzon Press, 2002, pp. 138–164.
Arendt, Hannah. *The Origins of Totalitarianism*. New York: Shocken Books, 2004.
Åsard, Erik, and W. Lance Bennett. *Democracy and the Marketplace of Ideas—Communication and Government in Sweden and the United States*. Cambridge: Cambridge University Press, 1997.
ASEAN Secretariat. "Final Report of the East Asia Study Group," 4 November 2002, available from www.aseansec.org/viewpdf.asp?file=/pdf/easg.pdf.
Asia Pacific Philanthropy Information Network. *Philanthropy and the Third Sector in Asia and the Pacific*, available from www.asianphilanthropy.org/index.html.
Atkins, William. "Obstacles to Openness: International Television Services and Authoritarian States in East Asia," Damien Kingsbury, Eric Loo, and Patricia Payne (eds.), *Foreign Devils and Other Journalists*. Melbourne: Monash Asia Institute, 2000, pp. 255–274.
Austin, Reginald, and Maja Tjernström (eds.). *Funding of Political Parties and Election Campaigns*. Stockholm: International Institute for Democracy and Electoral Assistance, 2003. Papers presented at the Democracy Forum for East Asia's seminar "Political Finance and Democracy in East Asia: The Use and Abuse of Money in Campaigns and Elections," Seoul, Korea, 28–30 June 2001, available from www.ned.org/forum/asia/june01/introduction.html.
Australian Broadcasting Corporation. *Development Journalism*, 17 March 2001, available from www.abc.net.au/ra/media/radio/s257121.htm.
Australian Electoral Commission. *Voter Turnout 1901–Present (National Summary)*, available from www.aec.gov.au/_content/what/voting/turnout.htm.
Australian Parliamentary Handbook. "Referendums and Plebiscites," available from www.aph.gov.au/library/handbook/referendums/index.htm.

Aziz, Tunku Abdul. "Strengthening Integrity: The Importance of Transparency and Accountability in Economic Sustainability," 113th International Training Course, Asia and Far East Institute for Prevention of Crime and Treatment of Offenders, 1999, available from www.unafei.or.jp/english/pdf/PDF_rms/no56/ 56-28.pdf.

Baron, Barnett F. "The Legal Framework for Civil Society in East and Southeast Asia," *The International Journal of Not-for-Profit Law* 4, no. 4 (July 2002).

Basuki, Tedjabayu. "Indonesia: The Web as a Weapon," Cecile C. A. Balgos (ed.), *News in Distress—The Southeast Asian Media in a Time of Crisis.* Quezon City: Philippine Center for Investigative Journalism and the Dag Hammarskjöld Foundation, 1999, pp. 101–107.

Bello, Walden. *The Anti-Development State—The Political Economy of the Permanent Crisis of the Philippines.* Quezon City: University of the Philippines, 2004.

Bennett, W. Lance. "The Media and Democratic Development: The Social Basis of Political Communication," Patrick H. O'Neil (ed.), *Communicating Democracy—The Media & Political Transitions.* Boulder: Lynne Rienner Publishers, 1998.

Bessette, Joseph M. "Deliberative Democracy: The Majoritarian Principle in Republican Government," Robert A. Goldwin and William A. Shambra (eds.), *How Democratic Is the Constitution?* Washington, DC: American Enterprise Institute, 1980, pp. 102–116.

Bhagwati, Jagdish. *Economics of Underdeveloped Countries.* New York: McGraw-Hill, 1966.

———. "New Thinking on Development," *Journal of Democracy* 6, no. 4 (1995): 50–64.

Blondel, Jean. "Party Systems and Patterns of Government in Western Democracies," *Canadian Journal of Political Science* 1, no. 2 (1968): 180–203.

Borooah, Vani, and Martin Paldam. "Why Is the World Short of Democracy? A Cross-Country Analysis of Barriers to Representative Government." Paper presented at the European Public Choice Society Annual Conference, University of Durham, 31 March–3 April 2005.

Borthwick, Mark. *Pacific Century: The Emergence of Modern Pacific Asia*, 2nd ed. Boulder: Westview Press, 1998.

Bourchier, David. "Politics of Law in Contemporary Indonesia," Kanishka Jayasuriya (ed.), *Law, Capitalism, and Power—The Rule of Law and Legal Institutions.* London: Routledge, 1999, pp. 233–252.

Bradsher, Keith. "Taiwan Vote Hard to Read, Analysts Say," *New York Times,* 16 May 2005.

Braudel, Fernand. *A History of Civilization* (trans. by Richard Mayne). New York: Allen Lane, The Penguin Press, 1994.

Brown, Adam. "Estrada Arrested on Corruption," Associated Press, 25 April 2001, available from www.globalpolicy.org/nations/corrupt/2001/0425estr.htm.

Buhmann, Karin. *Implementing Human Rights Through Administrative Law Reforms—The Potential in China and Vietnam.* Copenhagen: Djøf Publishing, 2001.

Bünte, Marco. "Consolidating Thai Democracy," Michael H. Nelson (ed.), *Thailand's New Politics—KPI Yearbook 2001.* Bangkok: King Prajadhipok's Institute and White Lotus, 2002, pp. 177–218.

Burnama. "Malaysiakini Seeking Opposition Support to Clear Name, Says Zainuddin," *Southeast Asia Press Alliance*, 13 February 2001, available from www.seapabkk.org.

Busse, Anna Grzymala. *Redeeming the Communist Past: The Regeneration of Communist Successor Parties in East Central Europe.* Cambridge: Cambridge University Press, 2002.

Callaghan, William. "The Discourse of Vote Buying and Political Reform in Thailand," *Pacific Affairs* 78, no. 1 (2005): 95–113.

Case, William. *Politics in Southeast Asia—Democracy or Less.* Richmond, UK: Curzon Press, 2002.

"Cell Phones Spark 'Communications Revolution' in North Korea," *Chosun Ilbo,* 2 December 2004.

Chaibong, Hahm. "The Two South Koreas: A House Divided," *Washington Quarterly* 28, no. 3 (Summer 2005): 57–72.

Chaihark, Hahm, and Sung Ho Kim. "Constitutionalism on Trial in South Korea," *Journal of Democracy* 16, no. 2 (April 2005): 28–42.

Chan, Joseph. "An Alternative View," *Journal of Democracy* 8, no. 2 (April 1997): 35–48.

Chan, Steve. "Democratic Inauguration and Transition in East Asia," James F. Hollifield and Calvin Jillson (eds.), *Pathways to Democracy—The Political Economy of Democratic Transitions.* New York and London: Routledge, 2000, pp. 178–191.

"Charter of Paris for a New Europe," 19–21 November 1990, available from www.osce.org/documents/mcs/1990/11/4045_en.pdf.

Cheng, Tun-Jen. "Democratizing the Quasi-Leninist Regime in Taiwan," *World Politics* 41, no. 4 (1989): 471–499.

Cheong, Yong Mun. "The Political Structures of the Independent States," Nicholas Tarling (ed.), *The Cambridge History of Southeast Asia—Volume Two: The Nineteenth and Twentieth Centuries.* Cambridge: Cambridge University Press, 1992, pp. 387–466.

Chon, Soohyun. "The Election Process and Informal Politics in South Korea," Lowell Dittmer, Haruhiro Fukui, and Peter N. S. Lee (eds.), *Informal Politics in East Asia.* Cambridge: Cambridge University Press, 2000, pp. 66–82.

Chongkittavorn, Kavi. "Thailand, A Troubled Path to a Hopeful Future," Louise Williams and Roland Rich (eds.), *Losing Control—Freedom of the Press in Asia.* Canberra: Asia-Pacific Press, 2000, pp. 219–239.

Chu, Yun-han. "The Legacy of One-Party Hegemony in Taiwan," Larry Diamond and Richard Gunther (eds.), *Political Parties and Democracy.* Baltimore: Johns Hopkins University Press, 2001, pp. 266–298.

———. "Taiwan's Year of Stress," *Journal of Democracy* 16, no. 2 (April 2005): 43–57.

Clammer, John. *Values and Development in Southeast Asia.* Selangor Darul Ehsan, Malaysia: Pelanduk Publications, 1996.

Clark, Cal. "Modernization, Democracy, and the Developmental State in Asia," James F. Hollifield and Calvin Jillson (eds.), *Pathways to Democracy—The Political Economy of Democratic Transitions.* New York and London: Routledge, 2000, pp. 160–177.

Conde, Carlos H. "Philippine Death Squads Extend Their Reach," *International Herald Tribune,* 23 March 2005.

Coronel, Sheila S. "Born to Rule," Sheila S. Coronel et al., *The Rulemakers—How the Wealthy and Well-Born Dominate Congress.* Manila: Philippine Center for Investigative Journalism, 2004, pp. 44–117.

———. "Guns and Goons," Sheila S. Coronel et al., *The Rulemakers—How the Wealthy and Well-Born Dominate Congress.* Manila: Philippine Center for Investigative Journalism, 2004, pp. 78–85.

————. "Houses of Privilege," Sheila S. Coronel et al., *The Rulemakers—How the Wealthy and Well-Born Dominate Congress*. Manila: Philippine Center for Investigative Journalism, 2004, pp. 3–43.

————. "Investigating the President," Philippine Center for Investigative Journalism, 2001, available from www.pcij.org/investigate.html.

————. "The Perks of Lawmaking," Sheila S. Coronel et al., *The Rulemakers—How the Wealthy and Well-Born Dominate Congress*. Manila: Philippine Center for Investigative Journalism, 2004, pp. 118–171.

————. "Philippines—Free as a Mocking Bird," Louise Williams and Roland Rich (eds.), *Losing Control—Freedom of the Press in Asia*. Canberra: Asia-Pacific Press, 2000, pp 147–168.

————. "The Philippines: Robin Hood Politics," *The Corruption Notebooks*. Washington, DC: The Center for Public Integrity, Public Integrity Books, 2004, pp. 251–265.

Coronel, Sheila S., and Yvonne T. Chua. "Fame and Family Dominate Senatorial Race," Philippine Center for Investigative Journalism, 19 April 2004, available from www.pcij.org/stories/2004/senate.html.

Crispin, Shawn W. "Moving the Goalposts," *Far Eastern Economic Review*, 10 June 2004.

Croissant, Aurel. "Electoral Politics in South Korea," Aurel Croissant (ed.), *Electoral Politics in Southeast & East Asia*. Singapore: Friedrich-Ebert-Stiftung, Office for Regional Co-operation in Southeast Asia, 2002, pp. 233–276.

Cruttwell, Peter. *History Out of Control—Confronting Global Anarchy*. Devon, UK: Resurgence Books, 1995.

Dahl, Robert A. "Polyarchy," *Toward Democracy: A Journey—Reflections: 1940–1997, Volume 1*. Berkeley: Institute of Governmental Studies Press, 1997, pp. 93–105.

————. *Polyarchy: Participation and Opposition*. New Haven: Yale University Press, 1971.

Dalton, Russell J. "Decline of Party Identification," Russell J. Dalton and Martin P. Wattenberg (eds.), *Parties Without Partisans*. Oxford: Oxford University Press, 2000, pp. 19–36.

Darewicz, Krzysztof. "North Korea—A Black Chapter," Louise Williams and Roland Rich (eds.), *Losing Control—Freedom of the Press in Asia*. Canberra: Asia-Pacific Press, 2000, pp. 138–146.

Davis, Michael C. (ed.). *Human Rights and Chinese Values—Legal, Philosophical, and Political Perspectives*. Hong Kong: Oxford University Press, 1995.

de Bary, Wm. Theodore. "Confucianism and Human Rights in China," Larry Diamond and Marc F. Plattner (eds.), *Democracy in East Asia*. Baltimore: Johns Hopkins University Press, 1998, pp. 42–54.

Diamond, Jared. *Guns, Germs, and Steel: The Fates of Human Societies*. New York: W. W. Norton & Company, 1999.

Diamond, Larry. *Developing Democracy: Toward Consolidation*. Baltimore: Johns Hopkins University Press, 1999.

Diamond, Larry, and Richard Gunther. "Introduction," Larry Diamond and Richard Gunther (eds.), *Political Parties and Democracy*. Baltimore: Johns Hopkins University Press, 2001, pp. ix–xxxiv.

Diamond, Larry, and Leonardo Morlino. *Assessing the Quality of Democracy*. Baltimore: Johns Hopkins University Press, 2005.

Di Palma, Giuseppe. *To Craft Democracies—An Essay on Democratic Transitions*. Berkeley: The University of California Press, 1990.

Donnelly, Jack. "Human Rights and Asian Values: A Defense of Western Universalism," Joanne R. Bauer and Daniel A. Bell (eds.), *The East Asian*

*Challenge for Human Rights.* Cambridge: Cambridge University Press, 1999, pp. 60–87.

Doorenspleet, Renske. *Democratic Transitions: Exploring the Structural Source of the Fourth Wave.* Boulder: Lynne Rienner Publishers, 2005.

Doronila, Amando. "Preface—Press Freedom in Asia: An Uneven Terrain," Louise Williams and Roland Rich (eds.), *Losing Control—Freedom of the Press in Asia.* Canberra: Asia-Pacific Press, 2000, pp. xi–xvi.

Dower, John W. *Embracing Defeat: Japan in the Wake of World War II.* New York: W. W. Norton and Company, 1999.

Drakakis-Smith, David. *Pacific Asia (Routledge Introductions to Development).* London and New York: Routledge, 1992.

Drezner, Daniel W., and Henry Farell. "Web of Influence," *Foreign Policy* (November/December 2004): 32–40.

Dryzek, John S. *Deliberative Democracy and Beyond—Liberals, Critics, Contestations.* Oxford: Oxford University Press, 2000.

du Mars, Roger. "South Korea—Fear Is a Hard Habit to Break," Louise Williams and Roland Rich (eds.), *Losing Control—Freedom of the Press in Asia.* Canberra: Asia-Pacific Press, 2000, pp. 190–207.

Duverger, Maurice. *Political Parties: Their Organisation and Activity in the Modern State.* London: Methuen, 1954.

Elections New Zealand. "General Elections 1996–2005 –Seats Won by Party," available from www.elections.org.nz/elections/article_126.html.

Embassy of the United States of America, Jakarta. "Wrap-up of MPR Legislative Actions," 1999, available from www.usembassyjakarta.org/econ/wrapup-mpr.html.

Eng, Peter. "The Democracy Boom," Cecile C. A. Balgos (ed.), *News in Distress—The Southeast Asian Media in a Time of Crisis.* Quezon City: Philippine Center for Investigative Journalism and the Dag Hammarskjöld Foundation, 1999, pp. 15–26.

Englehart, Neil A. "Democracy and the Thai Middle Class—Globalization, Modernization, and Constitutional Change," *Asia Survey* 43, no. 2 (2003): 253–279.

———. "Rights and Culture in the Asian Values Argument: The Rise and Fall of Confucian Ethics in Singapore," *Human Rights Quarterly* 22, no. 2 (2000): 548–568.

*Estrada v Desierto et al.,* 3 April 2001, available from www.supremecourt.gov.ph/jurisprudence/2001/apr2001/146710_15_r.htm.

Evans, Grant. *Asia's Cultural Mosaic—An Anthropological Introduction.* Singapore: Prentice Hall, 1993.

———. *Lao Peasants Under Socialism.* New Haven: Yale University Press, 1990.

Fealy, Greg. "Islamisation and Politics in Southeast Asia: The Contrasting Cases of Malaysia and Indonesia," Nelly Lahoud and Anthony H. Johns (eds.), *Islam in World Politics.* London and New York: Routledge, 2005, pp. 152–169.

Ferdinand, Peter. "Party Funding and Political Corruption in East Asia: The Cases of Japan, South Korea, and Taiwan," Reginald Austin and Maja Tjernström (eds.), *Funding of Political Parties and Election Campaigns.* Stockholm: International Institute for Democracy and Electoral Assistance, 2003, pp. 55–69.

Fernando, Christopher. *Skeletal Submission,* available from www.freeanwar.net/news/SkeletalSubmission.html (accessed 21 March 2005).

Fishkin, James S. *Democracy and Deliberation: New Directions for Democratic Reform.* New Haven: Yale University Press, 1991.

Freedom House. *Democracy's Century—A Survey of Global Political Change in the*

*Twentieth Century*, 1999, available from www.freedomhouse.org/reports/century.html.

Friedman, Thomas L. *The Lexus and the Olive Tree.* New York: Farrar, Straus and Giroux, 1999.

———. *The World Is Flat: A Brief History of the Twenty-First Century.* New York: Farrar, Straus and Giroux, 2005.

Fukui, Haruhiro, and Shigeko N. Fukai. "The Informal Politics of Japanese Diet Elections: Cases and Interpretations," Lowell Dittmer, Haruhiro Fukui, and Peter N. S. Lee, *Informal Politics in East Asia.* Cambridge: Cambridge University Press, 2000, pp. 23–41.

Fukuyama, Francis. "Confucianism and Democracy," *Journal of Democracy* 6, no. 2 (April 1995): 20–33.

———. *The End of History and the Last Man.* New York: Avon Books, 1993.

———. *State Building—Governance and World Order in the Twenty-First Century.* London: Profile Books, 2004.

Fukuyama, Francis, Björn Dressel, and Boo-Seung Chang. "Facing the Perils of Presidentialism?" *Journal of Democracy* 16, no. 2 (April 2005): 102–116.

Gangjian, Du, and Song Gang. "Relating Human Rights to Chinese Culture: The Four Paths of the Confucian Analects and the Four Principles of a New Theory of Benevolence," Michael C. Davis, *Human Rights and Chinese Values—Legal, Philosophical, and Political Perspectives.* Hong Kong: Oxford University Press, 1995, pp. 35–56.

Gearing, Julian. "Taming the Media," *Asiaweek* 27, no. 6 (16 February 2001).

Gershman, Carl. "The Clash Within Civilizations," *Journal of Democracy* 8, no. 4 (1997): 165–170.

Gillespie, John. "Concept of Law in Vietnam: Transforming Statist Socialism," Randall Peerenboom (ed.), *Asian Discourses of Rule of Law.* London: Routledge Curzon, 2004, pp. 113–145.

Gomez, James. *Self-Censorship: Singapore's Shame.* Singapore: Think Centre, 2000.

Goodman, David, and Gerald Segal. *Towards Recovery in Pacific Asia (ESRC Pacific Asia)*, 1st ed. London and New York: Routledge, 2000.

Government Information Office (Taiwan). *History of Constitutional Revisions in the Republic of China,* 1999, available from www.taiwandocuments.org/constitution07.htm.

———. *The Significance of Taiwan's Constitutional Reforms* (10 June 2005), available from www.gio.gov.tw/taiwan-website/4-oa/20050610/2005061001.html.

———. *Taiwan 2004 Legislative Yuan Election* (2004), available from www.gio.gov.tw/taiwan-website/5-gp/election2004/ele_10.html.

Gunther, Richard, and Larry Diamond. "Species of Political Parties—A New Typology," *Party Politics* 9, no. 2 (2003): 167–199.

———. "Types and Functions of Parties," Larry Diamond and Richard Gunther (eds.), *Political Parties and Democracy.* Baltimore: Johns Hopkins University Press, 2001, pp. 3–39.

The Habibie Centre. "The House Divided: The Conflict Between the National and the People's Coalition in the Parliament," *Postscript* 1, no. 7 (November 2004): 3–6, available from www.habibiecenter.or.id/download/postscript_edisi7.pdf.

Hadiz, Vedi. "Indonesian Local Party Politics: A Site of Resistance to Neo-Liberal Reform," City University of Hong Kong Working Paper Series No. 61, March 2004.

Hall, Richard A., and Patrick H. O'Neil. "The Media: A Comparison of Hungary and

Romania," Patrick H. O'Neil (ed.), *Communicating Democracy—The Media & Political Transitions*. Boulder: Lynne Rienner Publishers, 1998, pp. 125–145.

Halperin, Morton H., Joseph T. Siegle, and Michael M. Weinstein. *The Democracy Advantage: How Democracies Promote Prosperity and Peace*. New York: Routledge, 2004.

Hamilton, Walter. "Japan—The Warmth of the Herd," Louise Williams and Roland Rich (eds.), *Losing Control—Freedom of the Press in Asia*. Canberra: Asia-Pacific Press, 2000, pp. 93–114.

Harsono, Andreas. "Indonesia—Dancing in the Dark," Louise Williams and Roland Rich (eds.), *Losing Control—Freedom of the Press in Asia*. Canberra: Asia-Pacific Press, 2000, pp. 74–92.

Hassall, Graham, and Cheryl Saunders. *Asia-Pacific Constitutional Systems*. Cambridge: Cambridge University Press, 2002.

Hefner, Robert W. *Muslims and Democratization in Indonesia*. Princeton, NJ: Princeton University Press, 2000.

Hidayat, Syarif, and Hans Antlöv. "Decentralisation and Regional Autonomy in Indonesia," Philip Oxhorn, Joseph S. Tulchin, and Andrew D. Selee (eds.), *Decentralization, Democratic Governance, and Civil Society in Comparative Perspective—Africa, Asia, and Latin America*. Baltimore: Johns Hopkins University Press, 2004, pp. 266–294.

Hirata, Keiko. *Civil Society in Japan—The Growing Role of NGOs in Tokyo's Aid Development Policy*. New York: Palgrave Macmillan, 2002.

Hohe, Tanja. "Delivering Feudal Democracy in East Timor," Edward Newman and Roland Rich (eds.), *The UN Role in Promoting Democracy: Between Ideals and Reality*. Tokyo: United Nations University Press, 2004, pp. 302–319.

Hooker, M. B. *Adat Law in Modern Indonesia*. Kuala Lumpur: Oxford University Press, 1978.

———. *A Concise Legal History of South East Asia*. Oxford: Clarendon Press, 1978.

Human Rights Watch. "Thailand: Anti-Drug Campaign Reaches New Low," *Human Rights News*, 6 October 2004, available from http://hrw.org/english/docs/2004/10/05/thaila9445.htm.

Huntington, Samuel P. "After Twenty Years: The Future of the Third Wave," *Journal of Democracy* 8, no. 4 (1997): 3–12.

———. *The Clash of Civilizations and the Remaking of World Order*. New York: Simon and Schuster, 1996.

———. *Political Order in Changing Societies*. New Haven and London: Yale University Press, 1968.

———. *The Third Wave—Democratization in the Late Twentieth Century*. Norman and London: Oklahoma University Press, 1991.

Huxley, Andrew. "Introduction," Andrew Huxley (ed.), *Thai Law: Buddhist Law—Essays on the Legal History of Thailand, Laos, and Burma*. Bangkok: White Orchid Press, 1996, pp. 1–29.

——— "Thai, Mon, and Burmese Dhammathats—Who Influenced Whom?" Andrew Huxley (ed.), *Thai Law: Buddhist Law—Essays on the Legal History of Thailand, Laos, and Burma*. Bangkok: White Orchid Press, 1996, pp. 81–132.

Hwang, Balbina Y. "The Elections in South Korea: A Victory for the Electoral Process." The Heritage Foundation Issues (19 April 2004), available from www.heritage.org/Research/AsiaandthePacific/wm484.cfm.

IFES Election Guide. Election results for Thailand, 2005, available from www.electionguide.org/resultsum/thai_parl05.htm.

Indian Elections. "Election FAQ's: Delimitation of Constituencies," 30 November

2006, available from www.indian-elections.com/electionfaqs/delimitation-of-constituencies.html.

Inoguchi, Takashi, et al. *Values and Life Styles in Urban Asia—A Cross-Cultural Analysis and Sourcebook Based on the AsiaBarometer Survey of 2003*. Tokyo: The University of Tokyo and Mexico: Institute of Oriental Culture, 2005.

International Institute for Democracy and Electoral Assistance. "Voter Turnout Thailand" (May 2006), available from www.idea.int/vt/country_view.cfm?CountryCode=TH.

International Monetary Fund. "World Economic Outlook Database," 2002, available from www.imf.org/external/pubs/ft/weo/2002/01/data/.

Inter-Parliamentary Union. "PARLINE Database," available from www.ipu.org/parline-e/parlinesearch.asp.

Jacobson, David. "Media Change Tone on Constitutional Revision," *Japan Media Review*, 9 May 2005, available from www.japanmediareview.com/japan/blog/Events/519/index.cfm.

Jain, Purnendra C. "Party Politics at the Crossroads," Takashi Inoguchi and Purnendra C. Jain (eds.), *Japanese Politics Today: Beyond Karaoke Democracy?* Melbourne: MacMillan, 1997, pp. 11–29.

Japan Democratic Party. Website available from www.dpj.or.jp/english/about_us/dpj_profile.html.

Japan Parliament. Website available from www.shugiin.go.jp/index.nsf/html/index_e_strength.htm.

Jayal, Niraja Gopal (ed.). *Democracy in India*. New Delhi: Oxford University Press, 2001.

Jesudason, James. "The Resilience of the Dominant Parties of Malaysia and Singapore," H. Giliomee and C. Simkins (eds.), *The Awkward Embrace: The Dominant Party and Democracy in Mexico, South Africa, Malaysia, and Taiwan*. Amsterdam: Harwood Academic Publishers, 1999, pp. 127–172.

Jones, David Martin. *Political Development in Pacific Asia*. Cambridge: Polity Press, 1997.

"Judgement of 2 September 2004," Dalam Mahkamah Persekutuan Malaysia (bidang kuasa rayuan), rayuan jenayah no. 05-6-2003 (w), *Malaysia Today,* 2 September 2004, available from www.malaysia-today.net/english/Judgement_DSAI_1.htm.

Kalshian, Rakesh. "India: Scam Plagued," *The Corruption Notebooks*. Washington, DC: The Center for Public Integrity, Public Integrity Books, 2004, pp. 90–107.

Kang, C. S. Eliot. "The Development State and Democratic Consolidation in South Korea," Samuel S. King (ed.), *Korea's Democratization*. Cambridge: Cambridge University Press, 2003, pp. 220–244.

Karam, Azza (ed.). *Women in Parliament: Beyond the Numbers*. Stockholm: International Institute for Democracy and Electoral Assistance, 1998.

Kaur, Naunidhi. "Tehelka Trials," *Frontline* 19, no. 14 (6–19 July 2002), available from www.flonnet.com/fl1914/19141200.htm.

Kausikan, Bilahari. "Government That Works," *Journal of Democracy* 8, no. 2 (April 1997): 24–34.

Kerkvliet, Benedict J. Tria. "Contested Meanings of Elections in the Philippines," R. H. Taylor (ed.), *The Politics of Elections in Southeast Asia*. Washington, DC: Woodrow Wilson Center Press and Cambridge: Cambridge University Press, 1996, pp. 136–163.

"Key Dates in the History of Le Monde," *Le Monde* (in English), available from www.lemondeinenglish.com/keydates.php.

Khilnani, Sunil. *The Idea of India.* New York: Farrar, Straus and Giroux, 2001.

Kim, Eunyong. "Building Credible Documentation," comments to Asia Regional Training Workshop, Thailand, 5–11 August 2005, www.newtactics.org/file. php?ID=814#257,1.

Kim, Sunhyuk. "Civil Society and Democratization in South Korea," *Korea Journal* 38, no. 2 (Summer 1998): 214–236.

Kim Dae Jung. "Is Culture Destiny? The Myth of Asia's Anti-Democratic Values," *Foreign Affairs* 73, no. 6 (1994): 189–194.

King, Dwight Y. *Half-Hearted Reform: Electoral Institutions and the Struggle for Reform in Indonesia.* Westport: Praeger, 2003.

King, Phil. "Putting the (Para) Military Back into Politics—The Taskforces of the Political Parties," *Inside Indonesia*, January–March 2003, available from www.insideindonesia.org/edit73/king%20satgas.htm.

Kingsbury, Damien. "Constraints on Reporting Australia's Near Neighbours," Damien Kingsbury, Eric Loo, and Patricia Payne (eds.), *Foreign Devils and Other Journalists.* Melbourne: Monash Asia Institute, 2000, pp. 17–37.

Kishwar, Madhu Purnima. *Deepening Democracy—Challenges of Governance and Globalization in India.* New Delhi: Oxford University Press, 2005.

Klein, James R. *The Battle for Rule of Law in Thailand: The Constitutional Court of Thailand.* Canberra: Centre for Democratic Institutions, available from www.cdi.anu.edu.au/CDIwebsite 1998-2004/thailand/ThaiUpdate2003_Klein. htm.

Klitgaard, Robert. "International Cooperation Against Corruption," *Finance & Development* 35, no. 1 (March 1998): 3–6, available from www.imf.org/external/pubs/ft/fandd/1998/03/pdf/klitgaard.pdf.

Kokpol, Orathai. "Electoral Politics in Thailand," Aurel Croissant (ed.), *Electoral Politics in Southeast & East Asia.* Singapore: Friedrich-Ebert-Stiftung, Office for Regional Co-operation in Southeast Asia, 2002, pp. 277–297.

Kovick, David. "Taiwan," Peter M. Manikas and Laura L. Thornton (eds.), *Political Parties in Asia—Promoting Reform and Combating Corruption in Eight Countries.* Washington, DC: National Democratic Institute for International Affairs, 2003, pp. 317–370.

Kovick, David, and Laura L. Thornton. "Cambodia," Peter M. Manikas and Laura L. Thornton (eds.), *Political Parties in Asia—Promoting Reform and Combating Corruption in Eight Countries.* Washington, DC: National Democratic Institute for International Affairs, 2003, pp. 41–74.

Kratoska, Paul, and Ben Batson. "Nationalism and Modernist Reform," Nicholas Tarling (ed.), *The Cambridge History of Southeast Asia—Volume Two: The Nineteenth and Twentieth Centuries.* Cambridge: Cambridge University Press, 1992, pp. 249–324.

Kristof, Nicholas D. "Death by a Thousand Blogs," *New York Times*, 24 May 2005.

Krygier, Martin. "Transitional Questions About the Rule of Law: Why, What, and How?" *East Central Europe L'Europe du Centre Est Eine wissenschaftliche Zeitschrift* 1 (2001): 1–34.

Kubota, Akira. "Big Business and Politics in Japan—1993–95," Takashi Inoguchi and Purnendra C. Jain (eds.), *Japanese Politics Today: Beyond Karaoke Democracy?* Melbourne: MacMillan, 1997, pp. 124–143.

Lam, Willy Wo-Lap. "China—State Power Versus the Internet," Louise Williams and Roland Rich (eds.), *Losing Control—Freedom of the Press in Asia.* Canberra: Asia-Pacific Press, 2000, pp. 37–57.

Lee, H. P. "Competing Conceptions of Rule of Law in Malaysia," Randall Peerenboom (ed.), *Asian Discourses of Rule of Law*. London: Routledge Curzon, 2004, pp. 225–249.

Lent, John A. "The Mass Media in Asia," Patrick H. O'Neil (ed.), *Communicating Democracy—The Media & Political Transitions*. Boulder: Lynne Rienner Publishers, 1998, pp. 147–170.

Leones, Errol B., and Miel Loraleda. "Philippines," Wolfgang Sachsenröder and Ulrike Frings (eds.), *Political Party Systems and Democratic Development in East and Southeast Asia—Volume I: Southeast Asia*. Aldershot, UK: Ashgate Publishing, 1998, pp. 289–342.

Leung, Ambrose, Benjamin Wong, and Gary Cheung. "Hong Kong: A Second Popular Radio Host Goes off the Air," *South China Morning Post*, 14 May 2004, reproduced in www.asiamedia.ucla.edu/print.asp?parentid=11126.

Lévi-Strauss, Claude. *Mythologyques* I–IV (trans. John Weightman and Doreen Weightman). Chicago: University of Chicago Press, 1973, 1983, 1990, 1990.

Lewis, Bernard. *The Crisis of Islam—Holy War and Unholy Terror*. New York: Modern Library, 2003.

Liddle, R. William. "Regime: The New Order," Donald K. Emmerson (ed.), *Indonesia Beyond Suharto—Polity, Economy, Society, Transition*. New York: M. E. Sharpe, 1999, pp. 39–70.

———. "A Useful Fiction: Democratic Legitimation in New Order Indonesia," R. H. Taylor (ed.), *The Politics of Elections in Southeast Asia*. Washington, DC: Woodrow Wilson Center Press and Cambridge: Cambridge University Press, 1996, pp. 34–60.

Limmanee, Anusorn. "Thailand," Wolfgang Sachsenröder and Ulrike Frings (eds.), *Political Party Systems and Democratic Development in East and Southeast Asia—Volume I: Southeast Asia*. Aldershot, UK: Ashgate Publishing, 1998, pp. 403–408.

Linantud, John L. "The 2004 Philippine Elections," *Contemporary Southeast Asia—A Journal of International and Strategic Affairs* 27, no. 1 (April 2005): 80–101.

Lindsey, Tim, and Simon Butt. "Indonesian Judiciary in Constitutional Crisis," *Jakarta Post*, 6–7 August 2004, reproduced in www.law.unimelb.edu.au/alc/indonesia/.

Linz, Juan J. "The Perils of Presidentialism," *Journal of Democracy* 1, no. 1 (Winter 1990): 51–69.

———. "Some Thoughts on the Victory and Future of Democracy," Axel Hadenius (ed.), *Democracy's Victory and Crisis, Nobel Symposium No. 93*. Cambridge: Cambridge University Press, 1997, pp. 404–426.

———. "The Virtues of Parliamentarism," Larry Diamond and Marc F. Plattner (eds.), *The Global Resurgence of Democracy*, 2nd ed. Baltimore and London: Johns Hopkins University Press, 1996, pp. 154–161.

Linz, Juan, and Alfred Stepan. *Problems of Democratic Transition and Consolidation: Southern Europe, South America, and Post-communist Europe* (Baltimore: Johns Hopkins University Press, 1996).

———. "Toward Consolidated Democracies," *Journal of Democracy* 7, no. 2 (April 1996): 14–33.

Lipset, Seymour Martin, and Stein Rokkan (eds.). *Party Systems and Voter Alignments*. New York: Free Press, 1967.

Lo, Fu-chen, and Yue-man Yeung (eds.). *Emerging World Cities in Pacific Asia*. Tokyo: United Nations University Press, 1993.

Lowry, Robert. *The Armed Forces of Indonesia*. Sydney: Allen and Unwin, 1996.

MacKinnon, Rebecca. "The World-Wide Conversation: Online Participatory Media and International News," *Working Papers Series*. Cambridge: The Joan Shorenstein Center, Harvard, 2004, available from www.ksg.harvard.edu/presspol/Research_Publications/Papers/Working_Papers/2004_2.pdf.

Manikas, Peter M., and Dawn Emling. "Indonesia," Peter M. Manikas and Laura L. Thornton (eds.), *Political Parties in Asia—Promoting Reform and Combating Corruption in Eight Countries*. Washington, DC: National Democratic Institute for International Affairs, 2003, pp. 75–138.

Mares, Peter. "Vietnam—Propaganda Is Not a Dirty Word," Louise Williams and Roland Rich (eds.), *Losing Control—Freedom of the Press in Asia*. Canberra: Asia-Pacific Press, 2000, pp. 239–257.

Marston, John. "Cambodian News Media," Damien Kingsbury, Eric Loo, and Patricia Payne (eds.), *Foreign Devils and Other Journalists*. Melbourne: Monash Asia Institute, 2000, pp. 171–208.

Masters, Edward. *Indonesia's 1999 Elections: A Second Chance for Democracy.* New York: Asia Society, 1999, available from www.asiasociety.org/publications/indonesia/#The%20Party%20System.

McCargo, Duncan. "Democracy Under Stress in Thaksin's Thailand," *Journal of Democracy* 13, no. 4 (October 2002): 112–126.

———. *Media and Politics in Pacific Asia.* London: Routledge Curzon, 2003.

McCargo, Duncan, and Ukrist Pathmanand. *The Thaksinization of Thailand.* Copenhagen: Nordic Institute of Asian Studies, 2005.

McFaul, Michael. "The Fourth Wave of Democracy and Dictatorship—Noncooperative Transitions in the Postcommunist World," *World Politics* 54, no. 2 (2002): 212–244.

McKean, Margaret, and Scheiner, Ethan. "Japan's New Electoral System: la plus ca change . . . ," *Electoral Studies* 19, no. 4 (2000): 447–477.

Muhlberger, Steve. "Democracy in Ancient India," 1998, available from www.nipissingu.ca/department/history/muhlberger/histdem/indiadem.htm.

Mulder, Niels. *Inside Southeast Asia—Religion, Everyday Life, Cultural Change.* Amsterdam: The Pepein Press, 1996.

———. *Southeast Asian Images—Towards Civil Society.* Chiang Mai, Thailand: Silkworm Books, 2003.

Muntarbhorn, Vitit. "Rule of Law and Aspects of Human Rights in Thailand: From Conceptualization to Implementation?" Randall Peerenboom (ed.), *Asian Discourses of Rule of Law.* London: Routledge Curzon, 2004, pp. 346–370.

Mutalid, Hussin. *Parties and Politics: A Study of Opposition Parties and the PAP in Singapore.* Singapore: Times Media Private Limited, 2003.

Nain, Zaharom. "The Structure of the Media Industry—Implications for Democracy," Francis Loh Kok Wah and Khoo Boo Teik (eds.), *Democracy in Malaysia—Discourses and Practices.* Richmond, Surrey: Curzon Press, 2002, pp. 111–137.

National Democratic Institute for International Affairs. "Advancing Democracy in Indonesia: The Second Democratic Legislative Elections Since the Transition," June 2004, available from www.accessdemocracy.org/library/1728_id_legelections_063004.pdf.

———. "The Fundamental Change That Nobody Noticed—The MPR Annual Session, November 2001," January 2002, available from www.accessdemocracy.org/library/1378_id_gov_112002.pdf.

———. "Indonesia's Change of President and Prospects for Constitutional Reform," October 2001, available from www.accessdemocracy.org/library/1319_id_presconstref102001.pdf.

――――. "Indonesia's Road to Constitutional Reform: The 2000 MPR Annual Session," October 2000, available from www.accessdemocracy.org/library/1077_id_constireform.pdf.

――――. "Political Party Strategies to Combat Corruption, A Joint Project of NDI and the Council of Asian Liberals and Democrats (CALD)," January 2002, available from www.ndi.org/worldwide/asia/combatcorruption/executivesummary.asp.

National Human Rights Commission of Thailand. "The Government's War on Drugs in Right(s) Perspective," *Right Angle* 2, no. 2 (April–June 2003): 1–3, available from www.nhrc.or.th/en/publications/Eng%20Right%20Angle%20V2N2.pdf.

Neary, Ian. *The State and Politics in Japan.* Cambridge: Polity Press, 2002.

Nelson, Michael H. "Political Turmoil in Thailand: Thaksin, Protests, Elections, and the King," *eastasia.at* 5, no. 1 (September 2006).

――――. "Thai Politics Monitor," Michael H. Nelson (ed.), *Thailand's New Politics—KPI Yearbook 2001.* Bangkok: King Prajadhipok's Institute and White Lotus, 2002, pp. 283–442.

"Nepotism Claims Lead PM's Son to Sell Interests," *South China Morning Post,* 28 April 2001, available from www.freeanwar.net/news012001/scmp280401.htm.

Neumann, Lin. "No FEER, No Favour," *The Standard* (Hong Kong), 31 October 2004.

Noi, Chang. "The Numbers of the 2005 Election," *The Nation,* 28 February 2005.

Norris, Pippa. *Electoral Engineering—Voting Rules and Political Behavior.* Cambridge: Cambridge University Press, 2004.

Nurbianto, Bambang, and Damar Harsanto. "Indonesia: Council, Journalists Question Budget for Media," *Jakarta Post,* 22 December 2004.

Oberdorfer, Don. *The Two Koreas: A Contemporary History.* New York: Basic Books, 1997.

O'Donnell, Guillermo. "Illusions About Consolidation," Larry Diamond et al. (eds.), *Consolidating the Third Wave Democracies—Themes and Perspectives.* Baltimore: Johns Hopkins University Press, 1997, pp. 40–57.

OECD (Organisation for Economic Cooperation and Development). "Table 2—Total Net Flows by DAC Countries by Type of Flows," *Statistical Annex of the 2004 Development Co-operation Report,* available from www.oecd.org/dac/stats/dac/.

Ogden, Suzanne. *Inklings of Democracy in China.* Cambridge, MA, and London: Harvard University Asia Center, 2002.

O'Neil, Patrick H. "Democratization and Mass Communication: What Is the Link?" Patrick H. O'Neil (ed.), *Communicating Democracy—The Media & Political Transitions.* Boulder: Lynne Rienner Publishers, 1998, pp. 1–20.

OpenNet Initiative. "Internet Filtering in China in 2004–5: A Country Study," available from www.opennetinitiative.net/modules.php?op=modload&name=Archive&file=index&req=viewarticle&artid=1.

O'Sullivan, Patrick. "Dominoes or Dice: Geography and the Diffusion of Political Violence," *The Journal of Conflict Studies* 16, no. 2 (Fall 1997): 97–108.

Palmer, Tom G. "Definitions, History, Relations," Nancy L. Rosenblum and Robert C. Post (eds.), *Civil Society and Government.* Princeton, NJ: Princeton University Press, 2002, pp. 48–78.

Pangilinan, Francis. "Philippine Politics Post Estrada," available from www.cdi.anu.edu.au/CDIwebsite_1998-2004/philippines/Pangilinan_Address_Jul03.htm.

Patten, Christopher. *East and West—China, Power, and the Future of Asia.* New York: Times Books, 1998.

Péan, Pierre, and Philippe Cohen. *La Face Cachée du Monde*. Paris: Mille et une Nuit, 2003.

Peerenboom, Randall. *China's March Toward Rule of Law*. Cambridge: Cambridge University Press, 2002.

———. "Competing Conceptions of Rule of Law in China," Randall Peerenboom (ed.), *Asian Discourses of Rule of Law*. London: Routledge Curzon, 2004, pp. 113–145.

Pei, Minxin. *China's Trapped Transition: The Limits of Developmental Autocracy*. Cambridge: Harvard University Press, 2006.

Peou, Sorpong. "The UN's Modest Impact on Cambodian Democracy," Edward Newman and Roland Rich (eds.), *The UN Role in Promoting Democracy: Between Ideals and Reality*. Tokyo: United Nations University Press, 2004, pp. 258–281.

*Philippine Daily Inquirer,* 4–6 February 2001.

Philippines Liberal Party. *Platform and Policies*, available from www.cald.org/website/lpp.htm.

Phongpaichit, Pasuk, and Chris Baker. "'Business Populism' in Thailand," *Journal of Democracy* 16, no. 2 (April 2005): 58–72.

Phongpaichit, Pasuk, and Singsidh Piriyarangsan. *Corruption and Democracy in Thailand*. Bangkok: Chulalongkorn University, 1994.

Plattner, Marc. "The Democratic Moment," Larry Diamond and Marc Plattner (eds.), *The Global Resurgence of Democracy*, 2nd ed. Baltimore: Johns Hopkins University Press, 1996, pp. 36–48.

Post, Robert C., and Nancy L. Rosenblum. "Introduction," Nancy L. Rosenblum and Robert C. Post (eds.), *Civil Society and Government*. Princeton, NJ: Princeton University Press, 2002, pp. 1–25.

Preis, Ann-Belinda S. "Human Rights as Cultural Practice: An Anthropological Critique," *Human Rights Quarterly* 18, no. 2 (1996): 286–315.

Preston, P. W. *Pacific Asia in the Global System: An Introduction*. Oxford: Blackwell Publishers, 1998.

Putnam, Robert D. "Bowling Alone: America's Declining Social Capital," Larry Diamond and Marc F. Plattner (eds.), *The Global Resurgence of Democracy*, 2nd ed. Baltimore: Johns Hopkins University Press, 1996, pp. 290–306.

Pye, Lucian W., with Mary W. Pye. *Asian Power and Politics—The Cultural Dimensions of Authority*. Cambridge, MA, and London: The Belknap Press of Harvard University Press, 1985.

Qing, Wu. "The Rule of Law in Service to the People," *Enhancing Democratic Governance in East Asia—Empowering People and Institutions for Building Sustainable Society*. Report of the international workshop on Asian democratic governance held on 26–27 March 2004, United Nations University, Tokyo, pp. 92–110, available from www4.ocn.ne.jp/~adp/ADG.pdf.

Rabasa, Angel, and John Haseman. *The Military and Democracy in Indonesia: Challenges, Politics, and Power*. Santa Monica: Rand Corporation, 2002.

Ramseyer, J. Mark, and Eric Rasmusen. "Why Is the Japanese Conviction Rate So High?" *Journal of Legal Studies* 30, no. 1 (2001): 53–88.

Rangarajan, Mahesh, and Vijay Patidar. *India—First Past the Post on a Grand Scale*. Administration and Cost of Elections Project, available from www.aceproject.org/main/english/es/esy_in.htm.

Reed, Steven R. "A Story of Three Booms: From the New Liberal Club to the Hosokawa Coalition Government," Takashi Inoguchi and Purnendra C. Jain (eds.), *Japanese Politics Today: Beyond Karaoke Democracy?* Melbourne: MacMillan, 1997, pp. 108–123.

Reilly, Benjamin. *Democracy and Diversity: Political Engineering in the Asia-Pacific*. Oxford: Oxford University Press, 2006.

Reynolds, Andrew, Ben Reilly, and Andrew Ellis. *Electoral System Design: The New International IDEA Handbook*. Stockholm: International Institute for Democracy and Electoral Assistance, 2005.

Rich, Roland. "Analysing and Categorising Political Parties in the Pacific Islands," Roland Rich with Luke Hambly and Michael Morgan (eds.), *Political Parties in the Pacific Islands*. Canberra: Pandanus Books, 2006, pp. 1–26.

———. "Bringing Democracy into International Law," *Journal of Democracy* 12, no. 3 (July 2001): 20–34.

———. "Brunei, Burma, Cambodia, Laos, Mongolia—A Few Rays of Light," Louise Williams and Roland Rich (eds.), *Losing Control—Freedom of the Press in Asia*. Canberra: Asia-Pacific Press, 2000, pp. 16–36.

———. "Democracy in the Balance," Julian Weiss (ed.), *Tigers' Roar: Asia's Recovery and Its Impact*. New York: M. E. Sharpe, 2001, pp. 149–156.

———. "Designing Democracy Along the Pacific Rim," *Democracy at Large* 2, no. 1 (December 2005).

———. "Newspapers and Mass Media in Southeast Asia," Ooi Keat Gin (ed.), *Southeast Asia—A Historical Encyclopedia from Angkor Wat to East Timor*. Santa Barbara: ABC-CLIO, 2004, pp. 963–966.

———. "Recognition of States: The Collapse of Yugoslavia and the Soviet Union," *European Journal of International Law* 4, no. 1 (1993): 36–65.

Rocamora, Joel. "Campaign Finance and the Future of Philippine Political Parties." Unpublished paper presented at a conference on political finance in Seoul, South Korea, 28–30 June 2001.

Rodan, Garry. "Singapore—Information Lockdown, Business as Usual," Louise Williams and Roland Rich (eds.), *Losing Control—Freedom of the Press in Asia*. Canberra: Asia-Pacific Press, 2000, pp. 169–189.

Roh, Jeong-ho. "Crafting and Consolidating Constitutional Democracy in Korea," Samuel S. King (ed.), *Korea's Democratization*. Cambridge: Cambridge University Press, 2003, pp. 181–200.

Rokkan, Stein. *Citizen, Elections, Parties: Approaches to the Comparative Study of the Process of Development*. Oslo: Universitetsforlaget, 1970.

Rüland, Jürgen, et al. *Parliaments and Political Change in Asia*. Singapore: Institute of Southeast Asian Studies, 2005.

Rumansara, Augustinus. "INFID's Experience," Rustam Ibrahim (ed.), *The Indonesian NGO Agenda—Toward the Year 2000*. Jakarta: CESDA-LP3ES, 1996, pp. 263–276.

Ruscio, Kenneth P. *The Leadership Dilemma in Modern Democracies*. Northampton, MA: Edward Elgar Publishing, 2004.

Russett, Bruce. *Grasping the Democratic Peace*. Princeton: Princeton University Press, 1993.

Sachsenröder, Wolfgang. "Party Politics and Democratic Development in East and Southeast Asia—A Comparative View," Wolfgang Sachsenröder and Ulrike Frings (eds.), *Political Party Systems and Democratic Development in East and Southeast Asia—Volume I: Southeast Asia*. Aldershot: Ashgate Publishing, 1998, pp. 1–35.

Said, Edward. *Orientalism*. London: Peregrine Books, 1985.

Salvador, Michael. "Practicing Democracy," Michael Salvador and Patricia M. Sias (eds.), *The Public Voice in a Democracy at Risk*. Westport: Praeger, 1998, pp. 3–21.

Sartori, Giovanni. *Parties and Party Systems—A Framework for Analysis*, Vol. 1. Cambridge: Cambridge University Press, 1976.

————. "The Party Effects of Electoral Systems," Larry Diamond and Richard Gunther (eds.), *Political Parties and Democracy*. Baltimore: Johns Hopkins University Press, 2001, pp. 90–105.

Schmitter, Philippe C. "Parties Are Not What They Once Were," Larry Diamond and Richard Gunther (eds.), *Political Parties and Democracy*. Baltimore: Johns Hopkins University Press, 2001, pp. 67–89.

Schwartz, Stephen. "Introduction," Stephen Schwartz (ed.), *The Transition from Authoritarianism to Democracy in the Hispanic World*. San Francisco: Institute for Contemporary Studies, 1986, pp. xvii–xxv.

Schwarz, Adam. *A Nation in Waiting: Indonesia in the 1990s*. Boulder: Westview Press, 1994.

SEAPA (Southeast Asian Press Alliance). "A New Malaysian Blogger Targeted for Policing," 22 March 2005, available from www.seapabkk.org/.

Sen, Amartya. "Argument and History," *The New Republic*, 8 August 2005, pp. 25–32.

————. "Democracy as a Universal Value," *Journal of Democracy* 10, no. 3 (1999): 3–17.

Sen, Krishna, and David T. Hill. *Media, Culture, and Politics in Indonesia*. Oxford: Oxford University Press, 2000.

Sesser, Stan. *The Lands of Charm and Cruelty—Travels in Southeast Asia*. London: Picador, 1994.

Sherlock, Stephen. "Consolidation and Change: The Indonesian Parliament After the 2004 Elections," Centre for Democratic Institutions, Australian National University, 2004, available from www.cdi.anu.edu.au/CDIwebsite_1998-2004/research_publications/research_Consolidation&Change_Indoelections_2004.htm.

————. "Struggling to Change: The Indonesian Parliament in an Era of Reformasi," Centre for Democratic Institutions, Australian National University, 2002, available from www.cdi.anu.edu.au/CDIwebsite_1998-2004/indonesia/indonesia_downloads/DPRResearchReport_S.Sherlock.pdf.

Shin, Doh C. *Mass Politics and Culture in Democratizing Korea*. Cambridge: Cambridge University Press, 1999.

————. "Mass Politics, Public Opinion, and Democracy in Korea," Samuel S. King (ed.), *Korea's Democratization*. Cambridge: Cambridge University Press, 2003, pp. 47–78.

Shin, Eui Hang. "The Role of NGOs in Political Elections in South Korea—The Case of the Citizen's Alliance for the 2000 General Elections," *Asian Survey* 43, no. 4 (July/August 2003): 697–715.

Shinoda, Tomohito. "Japan," Wolfgang Sachsenröder and Ulrike Frings (eds.), *Political Party Systems and Democratic Development in East and Southeast Asia—Volume I: Southeast Asia*. Aldershot: Ashgate Publishing, 1998, pp. 88–131.

Shu-ling, Ko. "Taiwan 24th in Development Index Ranking," *Taipei Times*, 2 December 2003.

Soares, Mário. "The Democratic Invention," Marc F. Plattner and João Carlos Espada (eds.), *The Democratic Invention*. Baltimore: Johns Hopkins University Press, 2000, pp. 34–41.

Soledad, Fely I. "The Philippine Council for NGO Certification," *The International Journal of Not-for-Profit Law* 3, no. 2 (December 2001), available from www.icnl.org/JOURNAL/vol3iss2/cr_apacific.htm#PHILIPPINES.

South Korean National Assembly. Website, available from http://korea.assembly.go.kr/mem/mem_04.jsp.

Sridharan, E., and Ashutosh Varshney. "Toward Moderate Pluralism: Political Parties in India," Larry Diamond and Richard Gunther (eds.), *Political Parties and Democracy.* Baltimore: Johns Hopkins University Press, 2001, pp. 206–237.

Statoids. "Regencies of Indonesia," Gwillim Law, available from www.statoids.com/yid.html.

Stepan, Alfred, and Juan J. Linz. "Toward Consolidated Democracies," *Journal of Democracy* 7, no. 2 (1996): 14–33.

Stockwin, J. A. A. "Reforming Japanese Politics: Highway to Change or Road to Nowhere?" Takashi Inoguchi and Purnendra C. Jain (eds.), *Japanese Politics Today: Beyond Karaoke Democracy?* Melbourne: MacMillan, 1997, pp. 75–91.

Suryadinata, Leo. *Elections and Politics in Indonesia.* Singapore: Institute of Southeast Asian Studies, 2002.

Tapp, Nicholas et al. (eds.). *Hmong/Miao in Asia.* Chiang Mai: Silkworm Press, 2004.

Tarling, Nicholas. *The Cambridge History of Southeast Asia,* Vol. 2. Cambridge: Cambridge University Press, 1998.

Taylor, R. H. "Introduction," R. H. Taylor (ed.), *The Politics of Elections in Southeast Asia.* Washington, DC: Woodrow Wilson Center Press and Cambridge: Cambridge University Press, 1996, pp. 1–11.

Teik, Khoo Boo. "Nationalism, Capitalism and 'Asian Values,'" Francis Loh Kok Wah and Khoo Boo Teik (eds.), *Democracy in Malaysia: Discourses and Practices.* Richmond, Surrey: Curzon Press, 2002, pp. 51–73.

Teng-hui, Lee. Speech for 31st Annual Meeting Southwest Conference on Asian Studies via Videoconference Between Taipei and Sam Houston State University, 2002, available from www.roc-taiwan.org/houston/event/20021119/2002111901.html.

Teo, Larry. "Taiwan: Talk Show Hosts Help Make or Break Campaign," *Straits Times,* 11 March 2004, reproduced in www.asiamedia.ucla.edu/print.asp?parentid=8784.

Thompson, Mark R. "Whatever Happened to 'Asian Values'?" *Journal of Democracy* 12, no. 4 (2001): 154–165.

Thornton, Laura L. "Thailand," Peter M. Manikas and Laura L. Thornton (eds.), *Political Parties in Asia—Promoting Reform and Combating Corruption in Eight Countries.* Washington, DC: National Democratic Institute for International Affairs, 2003, pp. 371–426.

Thornton, Laura L., and David Kovick. "South Korea," Peter M. Manikas and Laura L. Thornton (eds.), *Political Parties in Asia—Promoting Reform and Combating Corruption in Eight Countries.* Washington, DC: National Democratic Institute for International Affairs, 2003, pp. 263–316.

Transparency International. *Corruption Surveys and Indices,* available from www.transparency.org/surveys/index.html#cpi.

———. *Global Corruption Report 2004,* available from www.globalcorruptionreport.org/gcr2004.html.

Turner, Mark, and Owen Podger. "Decentralization in Indonesia—Lessons for Policy Makers and Practitioners," Asian Development Bank, 2003, www.decentralization.ws/icd2/papers/decent_indonesia.htm.

UN. *Report of the International Commission of Inquiry on East Timor to the Secretary-General,* A/54/726, S/2000/59, 31 January 2000.

UN Development Programme. *Human Development Report 2002—Deepening Democracy in a Fragmented World,* available from http://hdr.undp.org/reports/global/2002/en/.

———. *Human Development Report 2004*, available from http://hdr.undp.org/statistics/data/.

———. *Human Development Report 2005,* available from http://hdr.undp.org/reports/global/2005/pdf/HDR05_HDI.pdf.

University of Richmond. *Constitution Finder*, available from http://confinder.richmond.edu/.

USAID/Cambodia. *Interim Strategic Plan 2002–2005*, available from www.dec.org/pdf_docs/PDABW893.pdf.

US Department of State. *Countries Invited to the Third Ministerial Meeting of the Community of Democracies*, available from www.state.gov/g/drl/44739.htm.

———. *Philippines—Country Reports on Human Rights Practices 2004*, available from www.state.gov/g/drl/rls/hrrpt/2004/41657.htm.

———. *Democracy,* available from www.state.gov/g/drl/democ/.

Uwanno, Borwornsak. "Political Finance in Thailand." Unpublished paper presented at a conference on political finance in Seoul, South Korea, 28 30 June 2001.

Uwanno, Borwornsak, and Wayne D. Burns. "The Thai Constitution of 1997: Sources and Process," *University of British Columbia Law Review* 32, no. 2 (1998): 227–247.

Vervoorn, Aat. *Reorient—Change in Asian Societies,* 2nd ed. Oxford: Oxford University Press, 2002.

Wah, Francis Loh Kok. "Developmentalism and the Limits of Democratic Discourse," Francis Loh Kok Wah and Khoo Boo Teik (eds.), *Democracy in Malaysia: Discourses and Practices*. Richmond, Surrey: Curzon Press, 2002, pp. 19–50.

Webster, Douglas. "Implementing Decentralization in Thailand: The Road Forward," Michael H. Nelson (ed.), *Thai Politics: Global and Local Perspectives—KPI Yearbook No. 2 (2002/2003)*. Bangkok: King Prajadhipok's Institute, 2004, pp. 473–500.

Williams, Louise. "Censors at Work, Censors out of Work," Louise Williams and Roland Rich (eds.), *Losing Control—Freedom of the Press in Asia*. Canberra: Asia-Pacific Press, 2000, pp. 1–15.

Williams, Louise, and Roland Rich (eds.). *Losing Control—Freedom of the Press in Asia.* Canberra: Asia-Pacific Press, 2000.

Wilson, Ian Douglas. "The Changing Contours of Organised Violence in Post New Order Indonesia," Asia Research Centre Working Paper No. 118, April 2005, available from www.arc.murdoch.edu.au/wp/wp118.pdf.

Wong, Kean. "Malaysia, in the Grip of the Government," Louise Williams and Roland Rich (eds.), *Losing Control—Freedom of the Press in Asia*. Canberra: Asia-Pacific Press, 2000, pp. 115–137.

Wood, Alan T. *Asian Democracy in World History*. New York: Routledge, 2004.

WuDunn, Sheryl. "Reinventing Lives," Nicholas D. Kristof and Sheryl WuDunn, *Thunder from the East—Portrait of a Rising Asia*. New York: Alfred A. Knopf, 2000, pp. 143–161.

Youm, Kyu Ho. "Democratization and the Press: South Korea," Patrick H. O'Neil (ed.), *Communicating Democracy—The Media & Political Transitions*. Boulder: Lynne Rienner Publishers, 1998, pp. 171–194.

Zhang, Yumei. *Pacific Asia (The Making of the Contemporary World)*. London and New York: Routledge, 2002.

# Index

Camdessus, Michel, 193
Case, William: on Southeast Asian elites, 160
Ceauşescu, Nicolae, 192
Celebritification of politics, 18, 169
Celebrity politicians, 169–170
Cell phones, 204, 205
Censorship of media, 198
Centre for Democratic Institutions (Australian National University): and broadcasting parliament, 198; and cross-fertilization in relation to judiciary, 115; and leadership, 197; and parliamentarism, 48–49; and skills training for journalists, 208–209; and skills training for people in NGOs, 236
Ceremony, 187
*Chaebols* (Korean business conglomerates), 35, 164, 262
Chamlong Srimuang, 75; and Phalang Dharma Party, 137
Chan, Steve: on political culture and democracy in Pacific Asia, 223
Change, 229–230; foreign ideas and, 225–226, 229; and political culture, 225. *See also* Path dependence
Chang Myon, 35
Charismatic parties. *See* Personalistic parties
Charity funding: and NGOs in Asia, 238
Charter of Paris, 281; and democracy, 279
Chart Pattana Party (CP), 137
Chart Thai Party, 137, 138, 147
Chatichai Choonhavan, 168, 180; and Chart Pattana Party, 137; and Chart Thai Party, 137
Chavalit Yongchaiyudh, 168, 180; and New Aspiration Party (NAP), 137
Chen, Sisy, 212
Cheng, Albert King-hon, 213
Chen Shui-bian, 36, 68, 172; attempted assassination of, 46, 261; and corruption, 144; and DPP, 144; impeachment proceedings against, 53
Chiang Ching-kuo, 36
Chiang Kai-shek, 35, 36, 52, 109
Chile: and third wave of democratization, 10
China, 30; in 1975, 2; and "Asian Values," 242; and blogs, 212; and censorship of media, 198; and central planning of economy, 285; civil society organizations in, 124; as core state of Pacific Asia, 283; and democracy in Pacific Asia, xi–xii; and economic development, 285; and formation of civilizational consensus for democracy in Pacific Asia, 284–285; governance reforms in, 285; Internet in, 206, 211; and Japan, 283; as market-based autocracy, 282, 285; and pragmatism, 285; and precedent of other authoritarian states' move to democracy, 286; procuracy in, 100, 101; and Taiwan, 35, 36, 37, 42, 144, 261–262, 277, 284; and rule by law, 99, 100; and self-censorship of satellite TV news, 207; Tiananmen Square protests (Beijing), 179, 230; and transition to democracy, 285–286, 287; undemocratic state, 281; use of violence to retain power, 179
Chinese law, 87
Chuan Leekpai, 172, 174
Chun Doo Hwan, 35, 73, 97
Churchillian wave of democratization. *See* Second wave of democratization (Churchillian)
Citizens' Coalition for Economic Justice (CCEJ), 233
Citizens' Alliance for the 2000 General Elections (CAGE), 233–234
Civilizational breakdown of democracies, 10–11
Civilizational component of democracy, 19
Civilizational consensus in favor of democracy: absence of, 280; China and formation of, 284–285; documentation of, 281; in Europe, 279–280, 281; in Indic civilization, 284; in Pacific Asia, 280–284; in Sinic civilization, 284
Civilizational core states, 283
Civilizational divides, 25–27
Civilizational perspective of Pacific Asia, 25–27
Civil law, 101, 252
Civil society and NGOs, 15, 19; in Asia, 232–233; and bureaucracy, 237; in

cian, 169; impeachment proceedings against for corruption, 53–54, 114, 179; mass media and investigation of corruption of, 195

Europe: and civilizational consensus in favor of democracy, 279–280, 281; civil society and NGOs in, 122, 231; democracy in, 278–280; development of political parties in, 122, 140; and open borders, 284. *See also* Charter of Paris; European Economic Community (EEC); European Union

European Economic Community (EEC), 279

European Union, 283

Evans, Gareth: and end of Cold War, 9

Evans, Grant: on Asia as East of Europe, 24

Executive: and international law, 86; judiciary and power of, 101, 110, 115; parliaments and power of, 52–56. *See also* Impeachments of presidents; Rule of law

Expert analysis: and political culture, 221–223

Extrajudicial means of dealing with criminality and political opponents, 103–104, 178–179; public passivity in face of, 103–104

*Far Eastern Economic Review (FEER)*, 210

Fascism, 4, 279; and reverse and second waves of democratization, 4, 6, 273; and third wave of democratization, 5–6

Federalism: India and, 68, 70, 252, 264, 266; Indonesia and, 60, 68

Fernando, Christopher, 95

Financial crisis (1997): and Kim Young Sam, 145; and South Korea, 262; and Suharto's New Order, 32, 193; and Thailand's 1997 Constitution, 56; and Thailand's and Indonesia's reform process, 74

First past the post (FPTP) electoral system: India, 62, 63, 149; presidential elections, 146, 148

First wave of democratization (Jeffersonian), 4, 7, 273; and democratic institutions, 41

Fishkin, James: on deliberation, 188

Foreign correspondents, 210–211; of prestigious Western newspapers, 210–211; and public conversation, 210, 214

Foreign ideas: and changes in political culture, 225–226, 229. *See also* Ideas

Forum for a Prosperous Majalaya, 239

France, 283

Franco, Francisco, 5

Freedom House: *Democracy's Century* and third wave democracies, 10, 11; and measures of freedom, 5, 7

Free speech, 189; mass media and, 195; the Philippines and, 255; talk radio and TV and, 212, 213

French law: and law in Asia, 88

Friedman, Thomas: on unlikely encounters on globalization superhighway, 201

Frings, Ulrike: on Asian political parties, 125

Fukuyama, Francis: on end of history, 279; on political culture and democracy in Pacific Asia, 223

FUNCINPEC Party. *See* United Front for an Independent, Neutral, Peaceful, and Cooperative Cambodia (FUNCINPEC Party)

GABRIELA, 167

The Gambia: and second wave of democratization, 5

Gan, Steven, 206, 211

Gandhi, Indira, 49, 52, 115, 134; emergency, 3, 49, 52, 134, 264

Gandhi, Sonia, 134

Gangsterization of politics, 18, 163; and political violence, 45, 46

German law: and law in Asia, 88

Germany, 283

Global commercial legal system, 104–105

Global conversation, 207–208

Globalization and law, 104–105, 115–116, 252

Goenawan Mohamad, 209

Goh Chok Tong, 132, 199

Goh Keng Swee, 240

"Goldilocks typology" of political parties, 128–146; "just right," 140–146;

# About the Book

What does democracy look like in Pacific Asia? Can democratic governance in the region survive the challenges of corruption, violence, and soft authoritarianism? What impact are economic pressures likely to have? These are among the broad questions tackled in *Pacific Asia in Quest of Democracy,* a comparative study of democratic structures and practices in Indonesia, the Philippines, South Korea, Taiwan, and Thailand.

Roland Rich offers an original approach to a series of traditional topics: the institutions and legal underpinnings of democracy, the roles of political parties and politicians, the significance of a changing political culture. He also draws on his long experience living and working in the region to explore the public conversations taking place and the media that facilitate them.

His elegantly written work suggests that, although the countries of Pacific Asia lack a long democratic tradition, much more significant are the innovative democratic designs and the enthusiasm for democratic participation exhibited there.

**Roland Rich** is the executive director of the United Nations Democracy Fund. He previously served in the Australian Department of Foreign Affairs and Trade and in 1998–2005 was executive director of the Centre for Democratic Institutions at the Australian National University. His many publications include *The UN Role in Promoting Democracy, Losing Control: Freedom of the Press in Asia,* and *Political Parties in the Pacific Islands.*